The Jury in America

The Jury in

America

John Guinther

and

The Civil Juror:

A Research Project
Sponsored by the
Roscoe Pound Foundation

Bettyruth Walter, PhD
Research Director

Facts On File Publications
New York, New York ● Oxford, England

The Jury in America

Copyright © 1988 by The Roscoe Pound Foundation

Library of Congress Cataloging-in-Publication Data

Guinther, John.
    The jury in America.

    Includes index.
    1. Jury—United States.   I. Title.
KF8972.G85   1988   347.73'752   87-30498
ISBN 0-8160-1772-7   347.307752

Interior design by Ron Monteleone

Printed in the United States of America
10 9 8 7 6 5 4 3 2 1

To the memory of twelve good men and true: John Baily, John Brightman, Edward Bushel, James Damask, John Hammond, Henry Henley, Wil. Lever, Henry Michel, Charles Milson, Wil. Plumstead, Thomas Veer, Gregory Walket.

Contents

Acknowledgments

The research and writing of *The Jury in America* was funded by the Roscoe Pound American Trial Lawyers Foundation, and included a generous grant by James H. Ackerman, a Trustee of the Foundation. However, the content of the book, and the opinions expressed, are entirely the author's own and are not intended to reflect the views of either the Pound Foundation or any of its members.

The author is grateful to many people whose cooperation made the writing of the book possible. It was David S. Shrager, president of the Pound Foundation, who first saw the need for a book that would objectively study the civil jury system in America. His unfailing help and support eased the writing and research task, and his professional expertise gave guidance to the content of the Pound jury surveys. The Foundation's immediate past president, Michael F. Colley, helped shepherd the project through to approval and continued to play a major role in its development. Trustee Theodore Koskoff also lent his support when needed, as did Trustees Robert Begam and Eugene Pavalon. Throughout, Judith Barnett, then the Foundation's executive director, handled with indefatigable competence all the requests which the author made. An especial thanks also goes to Richard S. Jacobson, consultant to the Pound Foundation.

Both the author's and the Foundation's gratitude is expressed to the judges who believed that the Foundation's juror survey could make a contribution to a better understanding of how the justice system works and who extended their unstinting cooperation to the project. They are: Hon. Clarence C. Newcomer, of the Eastern District of Pennsylvania Federal Court; from the Philadelphia Common Pleas Court, the Hon. Abraham J. Gafni, Hon. Bernard J. Goodheart, Hon. Richard B. Klein, Hon. William M. Marutani; from the Montgomery County Common Pleas Court, the Hon. Anita B. Brody and the Hon. Samuel W. Salus, III. For the Columbus survey, Judges Dale Crawford, William T. Gillie, T.V. Martin, Clifford A. Rader, Frank A. Reda, and Lewis E. Williams lent their support and cooperation.

Bettyruth Walter, the research director of the jury survey, and the author of two earlier studies that incorporated surveys of jurors, provided important help in the formulation of the survey's questions; she also arranged for and supervised the accumulation of the data on which she reports at the book's conclusion. Dr. Walter was also of great help to the author in providing him with source materials that he might otherwise have missed, and giving generously of editorial advice whenever called upon.

Over the years, the writer of this book has frequently turned to the jurist-author Lois G. Forer for her penetrating insights concerning the workings of the American courts, and he did so for *The Jury in America*. Once again, she helped him see what he might otherwise not have seen, and also provided him with a fascinating study of civil juries (see Chapter Four) over which she had presided. The Hon. Edward R. Becker, judge of the Third Circuit Court of Appeals, provided both help and encouragement in the writing of Chapter Eight. Judge Emil Goldhaber of the United States Bankruptcy Court for the Eastern District of Pennsylvania provided help at a point when it was sorely needed.

The author's gratitude is also extended to Harold Kohn who provided a valuable analysis of the jury's role in complex antitrust litigation, and whose knowledge of the early history of the development of the plaintiff's bar is reflected in several of the chapters that ensue. Three other attorneys, expert in criminal law, were of especial assistance in evaluating the criminal case that was the subject of the Hastie mock jury study experiment. They are Dennis J. Cogan, Moira Dunworth, and Donald J. Goldberg; Ms. Dunworth, throughout the entire history of the project, also listened and gave excellent advice. Richard Abel provided two articles that helped meaningfully in formulating the analysis of alternative dispute resolution devices. The jury authority and legal scholar David Kairys not only provided material that was especially helpful in the writing of the first section of Chapter Three but also aided the author with his recollections of the pivotal Camden 28 trial in which he served as lead counsel for the defendants.

Additional thanks are extended to Tom Goddard of the Association of Trial Lawyers; to Tom Bendorf for his help at several junctures; to Barbara Bryant of Market Opinion Research in Detroit for her help in formulating the jury survey and for her role in developing the Phoenix phone survey; to Donald Light whose encyclopedic knowledge of the American health care system helped develop a section of Chapter Seven; to Monte Preiser whose knowledge of the whooping cough vaccine cases helped inform that section of the same chapter; to Mark Peterson of the Rand Institute for Civil Justice; to J. Robert Hunter of the National Insurance Consumers Organization; and to Professor Claude Lilly of Florida State University. Amiram Elwork generously shared his understandings of the problems of communication in judicial instructions. Tom Munsterman of the National Center for State Courts was equally helpful in his area of expertise.

A very special thanks is extended to Victor Eugene Flango of the National Center for State Courts. His interest in the project, his cooperation, and his explanations of the strengths and weaknesses of state court statistics discussed in Chapter Six made it possible for the author to navigate safely through many a difficult shoal. If errors remain, they are the author's.

The author's daughter, Carol Guinther, listened to his complaints and worries, as no one else could have, and shared his excitement when things went well. The author's agent, Elizabeth Knappman, participated with enthusiasm in this project as she has on previous ones. Dolores Walker, secretary to David Shrager, was unfailingly patient and helpful. Finally—but so importantly—the author's gratitude is extended to Karen Maschmeyer and Roberta Sawyer whose splendid skills with a word processor and whose equally splendid cooperation and good humor saw the manuscript through more versions than they would probably like to remember.

Introduction

I

There is nothing else quite like them in our society: A group of strangers brought together and required to sit in silence and listen to different versions of a story in which they have no personal interest, and who are then locked inside a room where they must stay while they try to sort out what they believe to be the truth from all they have heard.

They are the members of the jury. There may be as few as six of them, as many as 12. They may be required to reach a unanimous decision, or they may not. They have no purpose, no continuing function, beyond their verdict. Once they have made it, they fade back into their community with no further responsibilities toward the events which for a brief period (sometimes no more than a few hours) or a long one (sometimes for a year or more) have held them captive. Yet, because of the conclusions they reach, some who have come before them have forfeited their lives and others have been required to pay out millions of dollars to pay for the harm they were found to have done. Jury decisions, at times, have changed the course of history, have caused laws to be discarded or rewritten, have wrought guarantees of our freedoms. In accomplishing all this, the jurors give no reasons for their actions, and—unlike any other group imaginable—seek nothing for themselves; they are, as Supreme Court Justice William O. Douglas once said, the only agency of our government that has no ambition.[1]

They have been described as the conscience of the community, bringing the peoples' values of right and wrong to bear upon the cold and narrow proscriptions of the law.[2] Thomas Jefferson and others have seen them as the public's line of defense against the state when it acts oppressively, and Jefferson, for that reason, once declared that the right to trial by jury was more precious to the maintenance of a democracy than even the vote.

However, for each advocate of the jury throughout its long history in America, there seems to have been a matching opponent. For Jefferson, it was Alexander Hamilton, who declared that jurors could understand only the most simple and obvious points, and any case that moved beyond that should be removed from their ken. Nearly 200 years after Hamilton, Erwin Griswold, then Dean of the Harvard Law School, argued against the jury even more broadly when he asked: "Why should anyone think that twelve persons brought in from the street, selected in various ways, for their lack of general ability, should have any special capacity for deciding controversies between persons?"[3]

Former Chief Justice of the United States Supreme Court Warren Burger long entertained doubts about the capabilities of juries,[4] yet one of his most influential colleagues, Byron White, has written eloquently in defense of them.[5] Sometimes, the message is a mixed one. The great federal court judge Learned Hand often spoke warmly of the jury system,[6] yet, when presiding over the trial of Communist Party members in 1950, stated that criminal cases involving such momentous issues as the subversion of the American government might be too serious to be trusted to jurors.[7] One of Hand's colleagues, Judge Jerome Frank, went much further; describing juries as the premier example of irrationality in the law,[8] he could see reasons for doing away with them in criminal cases entirely.[9] By and large, however, most of the attacks on the jury, from Hamilton's day onward, have been leveled against its employment in civil cases.[10] Justice Burger's concerns were largely in that direction, as were most of Frank's and those of Lord Devlin[11] and other notable American[12] and British legal scholars.

The attacks on the civil jury became more frequent during the 1970s, when, we have been told, the nation's courts were suddenly engulfed by lawsuits encouraged, in part, by the improperly high awards that juries allegedly make. The defendants increasingly were doctors and hospitals charged with malpractice, along with pharmaceutical manufacturers and other businesses said to have marketed injurious products. As a supposed consequence of the litigation and the so-called "blockbuster" jury awards, insurance companies raised the prices of their policies and when they did so, the new costs were generally passed on to the public.

During the 1970s, also, the sharp rise in the nation's crime rate brought an ever-burgeoning number of felony and misdemeanor cases into the nation's courtrooms, creating lengthy delays during which the accused might be out on the street, on bail, to commit other crimes. The backlog problems were worsened by the supposed onerous weight of a bulging civil case docket. In this festering situation, the jury trial could be seen as the culprit, by its length tying up courtrooms and thereby adding to the glut of untried matters, both civil and criminal. (The typical criminal case, for example, can be decided by a judge in about 45 minutes; the same case heard by a jury averages three days.) As Justice Burger has seen it, stringent limitations in access to our courts—and to juries, particularly in civil cases—are required to prevent a complete collapse of the effective and timely dispensation of justice.

In the chapters ahead, we will investigate in some detail the various aspects of the debate surrounding the jury system, and will focus principally on the employment of juries in civil cases, since it is at the heart of the controversy. When possible, we will separate fact from fiction, and see where the truth lies in that sense. However, since the justice system consists of different people with different duties engaged in handling highly varied matters in many areas, we hardly have the makings of a scientific laboratory situation in which we can experiment with the hope of getting absolute proofs. Therefore, at times we are going to have to be content with developing probabilities, based on the best evidence available. At still other times, we are going to find we have no facts and no sound way to discover them.

The issue of supposed jury generosity provides one example. As will be observed in Chapter Seven, we have virtually no reliable research on the subject and perhaps we never can, since the question raised is so subjective, i.e., when is the money awarded too much money? The lack of data on that score, however, has not stood in the way of proposals to limit the access not only to trial by jury but also to the courts themselves and to our common law right to be made financially whole from the losses others have wrongfully caused us. Such proposals may or may not have merit on their own, but it is useful in evaluating them to know when they have no apparent basis in fact.

As this example and some of the preceding discussion suggests, in evaluating the role of the jury, we have to resolve, as nearly as we can, two separate but related problems.

The first problem is that of purpose and performance. Why do we have juries? What is their role intended to be within our courts? How do they go about their duties and how well or poorly, on the whole, do they perform them?

In thinking about that problem, we have to be aware that juries have a function even when they aren't functioning. That is, decisions are regularly made about the course a case will take based on the participants' beliefs of what would *likely* happen if the case were tried by a jury. It is probably no exaggeration to say that, directly or indirectly, the large majority of civil cases are settled without trial for this reason. Similarly, in criminal cases, defense lawyers particularly agonize over whether theirs is a ''good'' or ''poor'' jury case.

The second problem to be resolved about juries concerns their impact on society. For instance, if the relatively slow-moving jury trial, during a time of crowded court dockets, significantly delays the rendering of justice, that is a matter of public concern. Or, to return to our previous example, if, for whatever reasons, jury verdicts are higher now than they have ever been, then we have to consider whether these verdicts, in fact, do or do not cause the escalations in insurance rates that lead to higher prices for goods and services. Finding out the truth in this issue is also a matter of public interest.

There is another, broader question. Let us suppose our best information suggests that judges are somewhat more likely to reach proper verdicts than are juries. Would that finding mean that juries should, therefore, be abandoned? Or is it possible juries perform other functions that have a significance for us as citizens that goes beyond comparisons of competence?

The Jury in America, therefore, is about how juries function and also about the role they play in our society as an instrument of justice. Part One, though not exclusively so, attempts to find answers to the function issues. Thus, Chapter One provides a history of the jury system, how and why it came into being, and the ways in which its duties have changed over the years. Chapter Two examines the structure of the present-day American justice system and the jury as a performer within it. Chapters Three and Four describe what we know about the jury as a fact-finding body, ranging from methods of selecting jurors through the secret deliberations by which they render their verdicts.

Part Two is principally concerned with the societal questions. A more detailed description of its contents is given in the section beginning on page 105.

II

Throughout the text, but most notably in Chapters Three and Four, references are made to studies of the jury system, including one undertaken by the Roscoe Pound Foundation as part of the research for this book. Assessments of the strengths and weaknesses of the various studies are provided as guideposts.

Although the comments and conclusions are designed to stand on their own, some readers may be interested in learning more about the methodologies employed in jury studies and the problems confronting researchers. The remaining pages of this Introduction offer such an overview.

We have two main sources of knowledge about how juries function, one academic and the other non-academic. The latter category consists primarily of what we might call folklore wisdom. Prominent under this heading are the many books and magazine articles in which lawyers attempt to explain to their peers, primarily based on their own experience, how to go about selecting a jury and trying a case before one. Although the advice, from author to author, is frequently contradictory and little or none of it is based on approved research techniques, it is, nevertheless, the product of considerable experience in the day-to-day battles of the courtroom and can be quite insightful. Because of it, important assumptions may be made by the lawyer-readers about the handling of cases, so that what might be unprovable in theory becomes "true" in practice. (For instance, in Chapter Three the extraordinary variety of advice given on whom to choose and whom to exclude from a jury: lawyers following one expert's advice will create juries—and thereby a "truth" of the trial to follow—different from those who follow the prescriptions of another expert.)

Former jurors add to the harvest of folklore information. Their service has been an unusual event in their lives, and it would be surprising if they were not interested in describing it; one study[13] suggests that more than 80% do so, which helps explain why, even though only 6% of Americans have served on a jury, 55% know someone who has.[14] Juror anecdotage, therefore, has become a significant source of knowledge for many Americans about the jury system, helps formulate their opinions of it, and makes them more or less willing to serve if called. (Perhaps a more fecund source of information, and misinformation, about the jury are television shows[15] and movies—such as *Twelve Angry Men*—along with media interviews of jurors after the close of a sensational case.)

Occasionally, jurors publish articles about their experiences.[16] Such reminiscences usually have no trouble finding a publisher since editors recognize that the public—as well as scholars and lawyers—are curious about what goes on behind those locked doors. Each article, however, by its nature can deal only with one jury or, in jurisdictions where jurors can serve on more than one panel, at most a handful of juries, which suggests that this form of reportage has too narrow a base from which to draw meaningful inferences.

Academic researchers seem to think so. In the literature consulted for this book, almost no references[17] have been found to firsthand jury accounts. Nevertheless, for the researcher, such accounts can have value. For example, suppose that the juror-author reveals that during deliberations it became clear that the panel members did not understand the judge's explanation of the term "preponderance of the evidence." This is a crucial definition in civil cases; a misunderstanding of it could lead to a plaintiff winning or (most likely) losing wrongly. That the one jury didn't understand doesn't imply that all or even most juries won't; but it does alert the researcher to a subject that warrants further investigation. Moreover, since the firsthand account is the only access an investigator can have to non-controlled recountal of what actually goes on in the jury room, it has value for that reason alone. (As we shall see, there are controlled methods of questioning jurors; since they are geared exclusively to the information the researcher wants to learn, they arrive absent the nuances that a juror's own independent restructuring of the event offers.)

At their considerable worst, folklore tales of juries can be distorting and mischievous. Consider, for example, the following passage from *Courts on Trial* (1949) by Judge Jerome Frank: "Again and again," he writes, "it has been disclosed that juries have arrived at their verdicts by one of the following methods: (1) Each juror . . . writes down the amount he wants to award; the total is added and the average taken as a verdict. (2) The jurors, by agreement decide for one side or the other by a flip of a coin. (3) A related method [came in a case which] 'it was . . . agreed . . . to prepare 24 ballots—12 for manslaughter and 12 for murder . . . place them all in a hat, and each juror draw one ballot therefrom, and render a verdict . . . as the majority should appear . . .'"[18] Note how Frank employs the "what-everybody-knows" approach, replete with non-attributed quotes and secondhand stories—exactly the kind of "evidence" he would never have allowed in his courtroom—to "prove" through anecdotage that the jury system doesn't work.

Academic jury studies, from the modest to the wide-ranging, are also abundant. During the 1970s, according to one survey,[19] 160 studies of this kind were published, many by law professors, but also by psychologists, sociologists, and other students of the behavioral sciences who are often fascinated by the jury as an exercise in group dynamics.[20] That interest was nothing new. An earlier reporter had unearthed more than 300 studies printed prior to 1955,[21] and that was before the University of Chicago Jury Project which, starting in the second half of that decade,[22] began to churn out articles by the dozen (its major contribution, though not its final one, coming with the publication of *The American Jury* in 1966[23]).

The fundamental limitation, which applies to all studies seeking to evaluate the jury, rises from the researcher's lack of access to the participants while the process is in progress. The only opportunity that a researcher ordinarily has to hear a juror express an opinion of any kind, prior to the verdict, is during *voir dire*, the "to speak the truth" questioning that occurs *before* trial and is designed to eliminate prospective jurors who show bias; although indications of individual personality traits might be discerned at that point, nothing of the group dynamic can be seen, since the group doesn't yet exist. During the trial, a trained observer often will be able to pick up body-language signals from the silent panel, but evaluating such signals with certainty is impossible, since there is no way of knowing if they are responses to testimony or to the novel situation in which the jurors find themselves. Most importantly, and most frustratingly for the researcher, he or she has no access to the key event, the decision-making itself.[24] Although, as we shall see, researchers have attempted to solve the access dilemma in a number of ingenious ways, their problem defines our threshold question: How reliable can any information be about an action when the actors act only when they are offstage?

We can learn some things. At the end of each trial, we know *what* the jury did even if we don't know *why*, so that, hypothetically, if we take enough *whats*, from enough trials, we should be able to develop our inferences into fairly reliable predictions.

From the *what*, it should be also possible, at least occasionally, to discover *whys*. For instance, during Prohibition, juries regularly refused to convict on bootlegging and other liquor law cases; from the consistency of this *what* we know the *why*: They disapproved of the Volstead Amendment.

Recognizing the significance of the *what* issues, many jury studies focus on it; they are, in that sense, product-oriented. Still others, however, see the *what* flowing from the *why*; they are process-oriented. A few try to combine both approaches.

Expert Opinion Analysis. The monumental work of this kind, *The American Jury* (1966) by Harry Kalven, Jr. and Hans Zeisel, has probably been quoted more frequently—by, among others, the United States Supreme Court[25]—than any other contribution to the subject. The book, based on research conducted by the University of Chicago Jury Study Project in the late 1950s, consists primarily of an elegant and wide-ranging statistical analysis of 3,576 criminal jury cases, as reported upon by 555 cooperating judges.[26] (At the time of publication, the study also had on hand reports on 4,000 civil trials but only a cursory analysis of them was offered.[27]) Although only one of every seven judges asked to participate did so, the size of the case sample is still far larger than that of any other jury study of its kind before or since.

Despite its sample size, *The American Jury* has limitations as a credible research source. They are considered here in some detail not only because of the book's undoubted influence—advocates of the jury system are especially fond of citing it—but also because of the manner in which the book illuminates many of the problems that confront both the authors and the readers of jury studies.

One problem with *The American Jury* is aging of material—a problem authors have no control over but of which readers must be aware. In the case of the Kalven and Zeisel effort, in the years since the judges first sent them their reports, public interest movements, most notably those relating to civil rights, have had a major impact on American life and predictably on the ways juries may view certain types of cases, certain litigants, certain defendants in criminal cases. (The feminist movement, for example, may have made juries more prone to convict in rape cases than Kalven and Zeisel found them to be.) Moreover, crime generally has become a much graver problem than it was in the late 1950s, so that the Kalven and Zeisel conclusion that juries are more lenient than judges in criminal cases is open to question. (Indeed, one much more recent study than theirs, as we shall see in Chapter Two, indicates—if not entirely convincingly—that the opposite is now true.) Also, in the years following the book's publication there was a widespread adoption of non-unanimous verdict juries and juries of fewer than 12 members, which may have brought about configurations in juror decision-making different from those of the late 1950s, when the 12-person unanimous jury was still in near-universal usage. (See Chapter Four.)

Although it is often possible to make allowances for the effect of aging on some of a study's findings, the study's inherent credibility depends on the research method employed by the authors. *The American Jury* relied exclusively on judges as assessors of jury abilities. In defense of their method, Kalven and Zeisel refer to the "undeniable . . . expertise of judges," describing them as a source of the "greatest professional competence."[28] However, we know from other sources that the "expertise of judges" is not always that "undeniable."

Some judges are incompetent or biased or mentally unbalanced, and it is, in part, to protect the people from them—according to the Supreme Court of the United States[29]—that we have juries in the first place. The number of "bad" judges is a matter of conjecture, but—considering all the efforts that have taken place to reform the judicial selection process—it seems to be widely recognized that there is a problem with judicial quality. A journalistic study of the common pleas bench in a major American city (1978),[30] based on interviews with experienced and highly-regarded attorneys in both civil and criminal practice, found that of 81 judges, only one was considered fully competent to hear all kinds of cases by more than 75% of the interviewees and only three others were considered fully competent by two-thirds of the respondents. A much higher level of ability—using many of the same lawyers and the same research method—was discovered for the federal bench in the same city, although, even there, 10% of the judges were assessed as below the competency level.[31]

Adopting the more favorable federal figure, let us assume that only 10% of the judges responding to the University of Chicago study were not competent, and that (again based on the federal study) 20% were outstanding, with the remainder falling somewhere in between. If Kalven and Zeisel had had the means—which they didn't—to ascertain who the 20% outstanding judges were or, minimally, to eliminate the worst 10% (who might not know a correct jury verdict when they heard one), their study would have had a higher degree of reliability. It might be argued that since 555 responded, the possible impact of the bottom 10%, or 55, judges would be negligible, and that, consequently, we can assume that the "jury-correct" verdict rate that was discovered—better than 75%[32]—is valid. However, when we learn[33] that just 17 judges out of 555 accounted for 21% of the reports, that 73 accounted for half the total, and that one percent of the judges provided 10% of the cases, the draw becomes a much more narrow one, raising the possibility that infection by incompetent judges could be severe, perhaps to the extent of as many as three-quarters (55 of 73) of those who provided half the statistics.

But even were we to assume the judge sample was sufficiently ample to conquer the competency problem, we are still faced with a definitional problem, i.e., what is a correct verdict? Kalven and Zeisel tried to deal with this issue,[34] arriving at a number of perceptive insights, but, as they recognized, correctness remains an elusive concept.

For example, in order to avoid what they see as an unjust result for a party, juries sometimes refuse to apply the law as given them by the judge. When that happens, the juries are self-evidently incorrect on the law, yet may be correct in providing justice. The correctness definition problem also has a second dimension which rises from the multilayered duties which many juries are expected to discharge. A rarity, indeed, is the case in which the jury has only a single decision to make. To use the civil sphere for one typical example, let us suppose we have a case involving a single plaintiff and three defendants. The jury finds for the plaintiff, correctly as the judge sees it, but also finds all three defendants liable whereas the judge would have held only two of them to account. Alternatively, we have a case in which the jury correctly finds for the plaintiff, correctly apportions liability among the various defendants, but then awards the plaintiff either too much or too little money, or awards the appropriate amount but assesses one defendant an unduly high portion of it. Did these juries reach correct or incorrect verdicts? Similar examples can be found in the criminal sphere, not only in multiple-defendant cases but also in those in which the jury correctly finds the defendant guilty but then incorrectly, according to the judge, assesses the degree of guilt. Based on these commonplace situations, it becomes apparent that employing ''correctness'' or ''incorrectness'' to describe jury abilities is—even if we accept the premise, as we shouldn't, that every judge is capable of making such an evaluation—fraught with such definitional variations that it becomes virtually meaningless as a criterion.

However, as long as we assume that ''correctness'' only refers to how often judges thought their juries reached an approximately *reasonable* conclusion on the evidence and the law, then perhaps we can say—very gingerly—that judges generally think their juries are ''correct'' the 75% of the time that *The American Jury* discovered. Yet once we have said this, what have we said? Is it a mark of strength for the jury system that it produces ''correct'' verdicts three times out of four, or should we take that as a reason for abolishing it? In other words, if we knew that judges in bench trials were correct in their verdicts 90% of the time, or 60% of the time, then we would have learned something significant about jury abilities with their 75% ratio. But *The American Jury* provides no illumination on this point because its authors were faced with this problem: They had no practical way of learning how often judges are ''correct.''

The one seemingly feasible way of finding an answer is learn to how often judge verdicts are reversed on appeal—25% of the time according to a 1960 study[35]—but this approach turns out, on analysis, to be of virtually no help. Appeals are frequently based on novel or technical points of the law and are decided primarily for precedential purposes by the upper courts. Or, to put it another way, an appeals court may agree with the judge that the defendant was liable on the evidence, but the legal issue that has been raised and now resolved, perhaps for the first time, is such that it demands a new trial. (Appeals courts, for that matter, are rarely in the business of directly reevaluating the evidence in a case, save to the extent it might apply to the legal issue raised.) Consequently, though we may make some inferences about a judge's competency by the frequency with which he or she is reversed, we have no authoritative way of knowing how often the judge was correct on the evidence, or on the applicable law *at the time of the trial*, and therefore no statistical means of determining whether the bench trial or the jury trial provides the greater degree of justice.

Even were we to discover a means of learning a judge's "correct" percentages, we would still have one more statistical difficulty to surmount. Judges hear a higher percentage of simple civil and criminal cases than do juries, so that their "correct" percentages *should* be higher than those of juries, which means we would have to find some way of weighing cases by their degree of complexity. At such a point, we enter an evaluation system of so many variables that to attempt the effort would almost certainly be an exercise in futility.

Therefore, expert opinion has substantial drawbacks as a research tool in studying the jury. In enumerating these drawbacks, however, we must not lose sight of expert opinion's singular virtue as a polling tool that provides evaluations of the jury by those individuals, judges and (in a few instances) lawyers, who professionally deal with juries. These are the people who, as it were, are every day in the pits with the jury, unlike the more removed, theorizing academicians. Should we find that poll after poll reaches the same conclusion, either favorable to the jury or not, we then have a verdict about juries that may be more meaningful than any other.

The Mock Jury. If expert opinion research is primarily a product approach to the jury, the mock jury is a process approach. Researchers, almost always academicians, use this method to attempt to replicate real jury deliberations through staging verdict debates by pseudo-jurors they have selected for their experiments.

Simulations come in almost as many constructions as there are researchers. Due to their ready availability, college students—especially law students—are those most frequently pressed into service by professors; only 12.5% of simulation studies use people who have been called for real jury duty.[36] Each mock panel is given some version of a case to consider, ranging from a written summary of the facts to an actual trial in progress that the mock jurors witness.

The mock technique allows researchers to learn not only how groups act when faced with an objective decision problem but also how they respond to variables. For example, two sets of mock jurors can be given the same evidence facts, but one group is told the defendant is white and the other that he is black.[37] Or, the facts stay the same but the jurors change. Anapol, for example,[38] used two sets of jurors, one consisting of college students and speech graduates, the other of members of the public who had served on a jury over the previous four years.[39] Anapol's efforts were wide-ranging. For some tests, subjects were permitted to take notes on the testimony of their mock trial; in others they were not. In another test, the subjects were given information about the lawyers' backgrounds (one being described as a graduate of a high-prestige law school, the other not) and asked to decide which lawyer they would choose for themselves.[40] Verdicts were then studied to see if mock jurors favored a high-prestige lawyer with a weak case over a low-prestige lawyer with a strong case, or high with strong, low with weak, and so on. The purpose was not to predict what would happen in reality—the reality would never happen; jurors aren't told which lawyers come from a high-prestige school, etc.—but rather to attempt to assess the effect of prestige-beliefs on a group. (The results were quite mixed.[41])

In one of its multitudinous efforts, the University of Chicago Jury Project developed still another variation of the mock technique. Tape recordings of simulated trials, based on real trials, were played for individuals who were then on jury duty. Four civil cases were used, each employing slightly different versions of the evidence. These were heard by over 100 juries, with the verdict variations then studied. Apparently, the full results of this experiment were never published.[42]

Elwork and his colleagues were after something different. At the time of their experiments, they were working on a manual designed to rephrase juror instructions into simple English.[43] To do so, they tested both volunteers and mock jurors on their degree of understanding of different versions of the same instructions. It will come as no surprise that the simpler the language became, the better the jurors understood it.

Still other mock jury studies attempt personality profiles in order to determine the importance of individual role-playing within the group, e.g., which type of person is most likely to display dominance in jury-room discussions; which most likely to try to follow the judge's instructions; which most likely to be elected foreperson, and so on.[44]

The problem with mock jury studies is that, like mock turtle soup, they aren't the real thing. No matter how seriously the pseudo-jurors take their duties, they still *know* they aren't real jurors, *know* that their deliberations are being recorded or observed[45] (sometimes through a one-way mirror), and *know* that whatever verdict they come up with has no impact on the life or fortune of any human being.

The technique has evinced other weaknesses as well. The literature of jury research reveals only one study[46] in which the mock jurors underwent *voir dire* questioning by opposing lawyers before selection to the panel. Aside from that one study, therefore, we can't assume that jurors on mock panels are typical of those chosen for real ones. The perils of asking mock jurors to decide a case based merely on a written summary of it are too self-evident to require comment; but even in more realistic efforts, such as those in which excerpted reenactments of an actual case are employed, the videotape alone creates a variable. Psychological research indicates that memory of a videotape will be sharper than memory of a live event,[47] probably because of the absence of the distractions that occur in a contemporaneous setting. The videotape trial also compresses time—and omits the typical courtroom delays, the sidebar conferences, and so on—creating another distortion of reality. For example, in one experiment, the actual trial lasted three days, the videotape reenactment three hours.[48] The shortened time frame, by itself, can give the mock jurors a vivid memory of each event that would be unlikely in a real trial. (Videotape is sometimes employed in real trials, with controversial results; see Chapter Three.)

A different problem arises during the mock jury's deliberation process. Knowing they are under observation, the subjects may select their words and arguments with a self-consciousness absent in a real jury deliberation, when they are confident of their privacy.[49]

There is still another hazard to the mock method of studying juries. Even were we generously to grant that videotapes and reenactments do not by themselves have an invalidating effect, the trial to which the subjects are exposed has its own unique set of events and legal questions which may not have any generalized applicability. For example, two of the most ambitious studies, which will be discussed further in Chapter Four, Padawer-Singer's and Hastie's, each employed dozens of panels of various compositions, with every panel in both studies seeing a reenactment of a single trial. The trial, therefore, was a constant, allowing the experimenters to compare how their various groups viewed it; consequently, we learn a great deal about how those groups reacted to the *same* information, but we have no reason to believe that given a *different* trial, they would have reacted the same way. They might have; they might not have.

For all these reasons, academic critics of jury research[50] warn that inferences about jury behavior based on mock situations must be viewed with great caution and the results of such studies should be confirmed by other sources before we generalize and apply them to real trials.

The critics are persuasive. However, this does not mean that we should disregard a jury study because it is based on a mock situation. On the contrary, when the study is well-formulated, although we may never learn from it in an absolutely trustworthy fashion what real juries do, we can gain insights about how individuals in controlled situations perform when confronted by an objective, jury-type decision-making problem. From these insights we gain knowledge that can be valuable, as long as we don't yield to the temptation to take it beyond itself.

For example, Anapol found that his college students made excellent jurors.[51] From that conclusion, one might infer—though Anapol didn't—that we would improve our juries if we limited their membership to the college-educated. On reflection, however, it becomes apparent that such a conclusion doesn't follow from the premise. College students aren't comparable to college-educated people. Students have in common their youth and relative inexperience in life, while the vast majority of the college-educated come to the jury equipped (or burdened) with views and understandings that cannot be analogized to those of the very young. To say, rightly or wrongly, that college students make excellent jurors, therefore, is *only* to say that college students make excellent jurors.[52]

Anapol, however, does provide the kind of suggestive information that can be the province of the well-formulated, simulated jury study. In his study, the subjects were required to weigh the merits of a personal injury case; he discovered that, regardless of whether they were students or those who had served on juries, they went about their tasks much the same way. Every panel, he found, first decided on liability and only then talked about damages; the members also uniformly worked on holdouts by taking turns to try to convince them. Both the students and the ex-jurors concentrated on discussing the facts, handled the various exhibits, attempted to recreate the accident, seemed somewhat influenced by the emotional ploys of the lawyers, but, all in all, deliberated with a logical consistency that Anapol found impressive.[53] From Anapol, therefore, we learn that demographically diverse groups, under laboratory conditions, have approached a jury-like problem quite similarly to one another and that their procedures are marked by orderliness and rationality. This does not mean, and Anapol would not have us think it means, that all or even most real jury deliberations are conducted the same way; however, the data indicate that this *may* happen, alerting us to an important area of jury competency to be confirmed or refuted.

A variation of the mock jury is the *shadow* jury. For it, the researcher selects jurors who actually sit through a trial from beginning to end and retire to reach their verdict at the same time as the real jurors do, with the researcher recording the shadow jury's deliberations. Therefore, the shadow jurors (unlike other mock jurors) actually experience a trial with all its frustrations and delays. Their time-and-experience frame is identical to that of the real jurors, but their *participation* frame remains different. The jurors in the box are the constant subject of attention—by words, by gestures, by eye-contact—from lawyers, witnesses, and judge. The shadow jurors are not.

The shadow jury has relatively rarely been employed by American researchers. The most extensive experiment was conducted in England and involved the use of 30 shadow juries covering that many trials.[54] A non-academic adaptation of the shadow jury was made by IBM in a California case in which it was a party. The case was settled before verdict; but while it was still in progress, the shadow jurors were regularly interviewed by IBM's research firm to get their views of the case, presumably so that IBM's lawyers could use that information to develop its ongoing trial tactics. After the case was over, the researchers interviewed the real jurors and found that they had formed sub-groups with similar views on the case, exactly as the shadow jurors had been doing.[55]

Related to IBM's use of the shadow jury in the California case is a service offered by a number of market research firms that procures mock jurors and provides facilities for litigants who want to try a dry run of their case. Those selected fit, as closely as possible, the demographics of most juries in the district in which the case is to be tried. The jurors know, in a general way, the purpose of the experiment, are paid for their services, but are not told which side has engaged them. They hear a highly abbreviated version of the evidence, acted out by people from the side that is paying the bill. For example, if the defendant is the employer, the attorney who will try the case will act as defense attorney with another lawyer from the same firm taking on the role of plaintiff's counsel, and so on. The jurors are then observed and recorded as they deliberate. That way, the attorneys presumably learn the strengths and weaknesses of their cases as they appear to the surrogate jurors and will be able to adjust their trial or settlement decision-making accordingly.

A more formalized version of the same idea is the summary jury trial, developed in 1980 by Judge Thomas D. Lambros of the United States District Court for Northern Ohio[56] and since adopted by a number of federal courts.[57] The judge assembles a summary jury when he or she thinks a case should be settled but the two sides have not reached an agreement. The summary trial has as its purpose to give the litigants an idea of what would happen if they took their case to jury trial.[58] For it, six jurors are empaneled who listen to a one- to two-hour summary of the case provided by the lawyers. No witnesses testify but exhibits can be introduced. The jurors are encouraged to bring back a unanimous verdict, but when they cannot, they fill out individual verdict forms.[59] The lawyers may then be permitted to question them about their reasoning. As the format suggests, the summary trial bears little resemblance to a real trial where jurors see witnesses and are able to assess their credibility. It does, however, succeed, just as the hired-juror format does, in giving lawyers an idea about the strengths and weaknesses of their own and their opponents' case when presented in brief to objective observers.

To summarize, the great attraction to researchers of the mock jury is that it lets them see how a series of groups will handle the same information or slight variations of it, something that cannot be done with a real jury. (For replication to occur in reality, one would have to find a representative group of plaintiffs and defendants who would agree to have their case tried over and over again—always using the same evidence in the same order—each time to a different set of jurors, a Kafkaesque, but hardly practical, premise.) The great weakness is that simulation, no matter how assiduously cultivated toward reality, is not reality; and further, even if we assume that simulation has equated reality, we still have reality only for the one case. Nevertheless, when we have well-constructed studies, and these studies produce complementary information, both amongst themselves and from studies using other methods, we can say, with some confidence but with continuing caution, that we have learned that much about how real juries, as group decision-makers, *often* act.

Statistical Analysis.   This method of jury research has a number of purely pragmatic applications. Court administrators, for example, wish to know how many people must be summoned for jury duty in order that, after eliminations are made, they'll have enough bodies to fill the required panels; statistical analysis can give them the numbers. From an academic point of view, however, the principal goal of statistical analysis is to develop comparable quantitative portraits of verdicts in the expectation that from them we gain understandings of jury decision-making in various kinds of cases. The most thorough study of this kind is the Rand Corporation's Civil Litigation Project, which analyzed jury verdicts and awards in Cook County (Chicago), Illinois, and San Francisco over a 20-year period (1959 through 1979).[60] In San Francisco, 5,300 verdicts were analyzed; in Cook County, 9,000.[61] From such a sophisticated effort, it is possible to learn, among other things, how likely plaintiffs are to win cases; whether they are likely to win some kinds of cases more often than others; how much they are likely to win for certain types of injuries; and how damage awards compare to actual losses caused by the injury. Similarly, we can find out if defendants from certain categories are more likely to win than others, and whether some types of defendants have to pay higher amounts than others for the same type of injury.

When a statistical analysis covers a lengthy period of time, as did Rand's, it can also inform us, as one with a more truncated time-span cannot, whether or not juries are performing consistently, i.e., if they are finding for plaintiffs at about the same rate and the same amount of money (in inflation-consistent dollars) at the end of the period as they were at the beginning. If they are not, or if they are performing consistently in some kinds of cases but not others, then we know we have discovered an area that requires further research.

In evaluating a statistical study, we must take into account its base limitations, quantitatively and qualitatively. A sample of a couple hundred cases by itself tells us virtually nothing, although many such small samples could tell us a great deal. The Rand study, despite the largeness of the sample, illustrates the qualitative problem.

Its subject areas, San Francisco and Cook County, are both large urban centers—which means, from the outset, we can not properly apply their statistics to rural and suburban counties. The two cities themselves also present special situations that should make us wary about extrapolating their configurations even to other cities. San Francisco's demographics—including the presence of large Asiatic and homosexual populations—differ substantially from cities of similar size such as Milwaukee and Washington, D.C. Chicago's population mix also differs from cities of comparable size (New York, Los Angeles), and—based on its 1983 and 1987 mayoralty elections—may have particularly virulent racial problems. Since racism could have an effect on jury verdicts—and, as we shall see, the Rand study tentatively concludes that is so in Chicago—the issue is not merely a theoretical one. Moreover, since the time of the Rand study, a widescale investigation into corruption of the Chicago courts has led to convictions of several judges and lawyers, giving us additional reason to question the Chicago figures, since the decisions of honest members of the bar about demanding a jury might have been influenced by their suspicions of the court's integrity.

The Rand study has another significant limitation, one it shares with *The American Jury*: the absence of comparables. Rand did not have access to information about bench verdicts,[62] so we have no way of knowing, anymore than we did from *The American Jury*, how judges rule in nonjury cases of the same type for which we have the jury analyses. Another comparable omitted by the Rand study—again of necessity; such matters are usually kept secret between the parties—was that of settlements. Access to settlement figures would allow us to test the premise that settlements are frequently predicated on the expectation of what a jury would do if it tried the case. Ideally, we should have three sets of alike cases—ones in which settlement was reached, ones that were decided by bench trial, and ones decided by jury; we could then compare settlements with the two types of trial verdicts.

This does not mean that statistics based on jury verdicts cannot be helpful; as we shall see, they often are. However, it does mean that we cannot properly use them to reach conclusions about the relative merits of the various methods of resolving a case.

Juror Surveys and Interviews. Asking jurors what they did and why they did it would seem the most obvious research approach, yet it has only been attempted infrequently.[63] The University of Chicago Jury Project undertook such a study, but the final results have never, apparently, been circulated. A preliminary report, however, was published in 1959,[64] by which time 225 jurors in 20 cases (13 of them civil) had been interviewed in sessions averaging 90 minutes each. Questions ranged from how the jurors viewed the *voir dire* to how they decided on damages. In another aspect of the same study, about 1,500 jurors were asked how balloting was employed during deliberations on criminal cases.[65]

Although it is not entirely clear why the juror interview approach has generally been eschewed, several possibilities suggest themselves. To interview jurors, either in person or through a questionnaire, it is necessary to obtain permission from a judge, and some judges don't wish to have their jurors exposed to researchers, either because they have a deep belief in the sanctity of jury room secrecy or—more likely—because they fear that information developed from the interviews could give the losing side in a case grounds for a new trial.

Even when permission is granted, the jurors themselves can present a problem. Some may not wish to cooperate so that the researcher is left only with the amenable ones and cannot know the effect the absentees might have had on the findings. (Perhaps none at all, if the only reason for not answering questions was their desire to get home; perhaps considerable, if they were angered by their experience and wanted nothing more to do with it.)

However, since almost all jurors, based on Pound's experience,[66] are willing to participate in surveys of their experience, especially if the judge encourages them, absenteeism is apparently not a serious problem with this method. Truthfulness may be. The danger is not so much that jurors will deliberately lie—although that's always a possibility—as that they will make inadvertent misstatements. For example, a juror's response to either oral or written questions can be unconsciously self-serving or made inaccurate due to blurred recall. Memory distortion can take place almost immediately after an event, as experiments with eyewitnesses in simulated situations have shown,[67] and unquestionably the more time goes by, the greater the loss of accuracy. From the researcher's view, the crucial question is: How much time is too much time for the juror? Considering how unusual the experience of a trial is for most jurors, one would expect their retention period to be longer than it is in their more mundane affairs, but we have no reliable guidelines to go by.

Despite these problems, the written survey and the personal interview techniques have the very considerable merit, lacking in the other procedures that have been described, of developing firsthand information. If blurring occurs, at least it is not the more substantial blurring caused by the secondhand judgment of experts or the secondhand simulations of the mock jury technique. The best way to get accurate information, according to traditional investigation, is to go to the people who know the most about the situation. That could well be true of jury investigation as well.

The survey method was undertaken by the Roscoe Pound Foundation for its jury study. The information was primarily developed from two questionnaires answered by jurors who served in civil trials that reached verdict in southeastern Pennsylvania. Respondees included federal court jurors, those who served on big city (Philadelphia) and suburban (Montgomery County) juries. The shorter of the two questionnaires (46 items) was answered by the jurors in the courtroom immediately after trial, and the longer (78 items) was completed by them at home. In total, 352 jurors answered at least one of the two questionnaires.

The findings of the study are generally discussed throughout Chapters Three and Four. A detailed statistical analysis of the results, written by the project's research director, Bettyruth Walter, PhD, Post-Doctoral Fellow, Law School of the University of Pennsylvania, is to be found immediately following the conclusion of the text.

Pound also was able to develop a smaller sampling of seven juries that served to verdict in civil cases in Columbus, Ohio; these jurors answered the short questionnaire only. In addition, it became possible to undertake a phone survey of jurors in civil cases in Phoenix, Arizona, reaching 98 individuals who served on panels that reached a verdict. Both the Columbus and Phoenix backup studies confirmed, with only insignificant differences, the findings of the much larger southeastern Pennsylvania study.

In many respects, as will be seen, Pound, using the survey questionnaire, also confirmed results of some studies using other methods, adding in that fashion to our store of independently replicated information about the jury system. Pound also delved into a number of areas hitherto largely or entirely untouched by jury research, and its pioneering findings must be viewed with caution until and if subsequent studies provide confirmation. The following text will make clear when Pound is the only, or virtually sole, source of our knowledge.

PART 1

Chapter 1
Bushel's Case

The case began on a Sunday, August 14, 1670, in London, England, when a squad of constables pushed their way through a crowd gathered at the corner of Gracechurch and Lombard Streets and arrested two men. The indictment that quickly followed charged that the younger of the pair, 26-year-old William Penn, had, with the abetment of co-defendant William Mead, taken "upon himself to preach and speak . . .by reason whereof a great concourse and tumult of people in the street . . . a long time did remain and continue, in contempt of the . . . Lord the King, and to his law; to the great disturbance of his peace, to the great terror and disturbance of many of his liege people and subjects . . ." which meant, when the rotund wording was parsed, that the defendants were charged with sedition and fomenting rebellion, serious matters indeed.

Both Penn and Mead were members of the pacifist Society of Friends or Quakers (so-called because of their admonition that all should quake before the work of God). The principal defendant, Penn—the 42-year-old Mead seems to have been arrested solely because he was standing next to Penn—was a recent convert and an important one, son and heir to the powerful and wealthy Admiral Sir William Penn.

Young Penn and Mead's trial by jury the following month was to establish a principle of justice that to this day protects both Englishmen and Americans from tyranny in their courts. The trial would also teach a lesson—one that Penn and his jurors understood but which all too easily can be forgotten—and this is that human rights, once gained, must be zealously guarded, for when they are not they tend to become mere privileges which those in power can remove when they find the conferring of them no longer convenient to their purposes.

1

I

The Athenians, as far as we know, were the first people to come up with the idea of the jury, about 400 years before the time of Christ. The Athenian law, as Aristotle explained it, was that those accused of wrongdoing should be allowed to argue their cases before a tribunal of their peers, who had as their duty not to interpret the letter of the law but, rather, to apply their understanding of "general justice,"[1] that which we would now call the conscience of the community. The jurors or *dicasts*, as they were known, were chosen by lot (only males over the age of 30 were eligible) numbering from 501 to 1501 in criminal cases and 201 in civil—the odd numbers to guarantee a verdict by majority. Their judgment was final, although the loser did have the right to bring a private suit against any witness he charged with perjury. In criminal cases, punishment followed directly upon the announcement of the decision, with accusers at risk as well as defendants. Thus, when in 330 B.C. the orator Demosthenes was charged by his archenemy Aeschines with bribe-taking and cowardice in battle, the jury of 501, finding in favor of Demosthenes, ordered Aeschines into exile. In civil cases, the jury had no such enforcement power; the victors in civil matters had to find the means they could to collect the judgment they had won.

When the Athenian world was swept away by Roman might, so temporarily was the idea of the jury, although references to its continuing use in capital cases in Greece can be found as late as the reign of the Emperor Augustus.[2] The Romans were indefatigable writers of laws, designed to cover every conceivable situation that might occur in their governmentally complex and far-flung empire. Their courts served to apply the statutes, not interpret them, and for that no ordinary citizen input was required. A compendium of Roman law, *Corpus Juris Civilis*, was codified under the direction of the aptly named Emperor Justinian between 528 and 534 A.D. and became the basis of legal systems still in effect in many European countries, most of those in Asia and nearly all in South America, but none of the British Commonwealth nations or the United States. Among democracies practicing Roman law, the jury has made only occasional, and frequently temporary, appearances, and it is never to be found in authoritarian states, whatever the basis of their justice code. (One of the first things the Nazis did when they occupied France in World War II was to abolish the jury there.)

By Justinian's time, the Western Roman Empire had fallen, and the capital had moved far to the east to the city of Constantinople. The barbarian tribes which sacked Rome and took over its richest domains had no use for a sophisticated justice system, although Roman legal modes did remain in effect, here and there, in corrupted forms[3] that departed further and further from the original with successive centuries of the Dark Ages. Even in the city of Rome itself and its surrounding Italian provinces, law became largely a matter of local traditions and superstition, with the arbitrary and brutal rule of the Coliseum more likely to be applied than that of the old courts. That the customs Justinian sought to preserve were kept alive at all was due primarily to the early Christian church, which adapted portions of the old law for its canonical statutes.[4] However, it was not until the 12th century that the Roman law was revived for secular matters by university scholars in Italy.

For about a hundred years after the fall of Rome, statements of secular law continued to be published occasionally, principally in Gaul and Spain, but they were largely in the form of listings of offenses and tariffs.[5] Of the law of the conquering, German-speaking peoples we know little. Leaders of greater and lesser power came and went, ruling as they could by the sword; and it is likely that local, village-level disputes were settled by councils of elders, although among the Scandinavians, a crude form of the jury may have been involved in some decision-making.[6] However, in most places each kindred group probably had its own law—one family guided by one set, its neighbor by another. The resultant anarchy in mainland Europe only began to subside in the last quarter of the eighth century when, among the Franks under Charlemagne, a sense of nationhood began to reemerge and with it attempts to fabricate a unified civil governance.

Matters proceeded somewhat differently in the British Isles. Roman governors had departed in 407 A.D., taking with them their law which had never succeeded in making much of an impact on the ways of the heathen Angles and Saxons or the Christianized Celts. For the next 200 years, the English tale is one of kings (some of whom, like Arthur, perhaps existed only in legend), doing battle against one another and an assortment of foreign invaders. Out of all this turbulence, the main victor was the Christian church which brought with it a growing body of ecclesiastical law. Few statutes of the early kings survive, and those that do may give a distorted impression of how justice was rendered, since in those days rulers apparently only put into writing those edicts that were designed to cover extraordinary circumstances;[7] as a result, we know next to nothing about formal regulations that governed daily life. Of folk customs, however, we do have some knowledge, primarily derived from later documents. One was the family vendetta or blood feud,[8] which could continue for centuries, long after the original cause had been forgotten. Random crimes, which could set a new blood feud into motion, were typically resolved at the village level through the hue and cry. In it, a witness, truthfully or not, would give call that a crime had been committed and by whom, whereupon the people of the village would join together, hunt down the accused, and kill him on the spot. In some districts, the mass manhunt gave way to the *posse comitatus*,[9] a group of locals selected by the sheriff, who was a powerful figure in ancient England. We aren't certain how long justice-by-mob continued, although references to the hue and cry can be found as late as the mid-13th century;[10] then, a person caught with the fruits of his crime or its instrument—such as a bloody knife—could still be considered guilty without trial and executed on the spot, as could the forger of a document.[11] During the Anglo-Saxon period (prior to 1066), the most common crimes and those most likely to lead to a lynching were cattle rustling and horse stealing (the same would be true centuries later in the American West).[12] For some lesser forms of theft, the perpetrator's life might be spared but he and his entire family would be punished by being placed into slavery.[13]

During the Anglo-Saxon era, there were almost certainly attempts by kings and nobles, and probably by the priest-class, to impose some order on the ways of the people, although the first documentation we have is almost 200 years after the Roman departure. At that time, King Ethelbert (552?-616) proclaimed a set of fines to be imposed on those who caused others injury. The genesis of our modern laws of negligence, Ethelbert's system, and succeeding ones, ignored the possibility that the victim might have helped cause the mishap and levied fines regardless of whether the injury was deliberately or accidentally inflicted,[14] although, if not in Ethelbert's time then soon after, the penalties for intentional acts were the higher.[15] Ethelbert's list got quite specific, too, ranging from sums to be paid the crown for injuries ranging from loss of an eye to loss of a toenail.[16] Fines assessed for inflicting injuries upon the nobly-born were considerably higher than those for injuring commoners. And Ethelbert—a great believer in the power of financial deterrence, especially when it came to himself—made injuries to the king the most expensive of all. (The rule, however, cut both ways; if a noble injured someone, he would be fined more than would a person of lower standing.)

Around this time, steps were also taken to curb the blood feud through the *wergeld*, which can loosely be described as a mediation system employing the Ethelbertian scheme of graduated fines.[17] But, as with mediation today, it only worked when the two sides agreed to bring their grievances before it, and then only if they happened to agree with the verdict.[18] When they did, compensation due from the wrongdoer could be paid in stages, and it may be that at times family members were given as hostages until the debt was satisfied.[19]

Eventually—we don't know exactly when—the voluntary nature of the wergeld was replaced by compulsion, which meant that any man who refused to submit to adjudication could be deemed *outlaw*, along with any male members of his family who continued to side with him. (Women could not become outlaws, since they had no legal rights to begin with.[20]) Those ordered into outlawry could be hunted down by any member of the community (later by the king's forces), slaughtered on sight, their property destroyed.[21] As ominous as that sounds, a proclamation of outlawry often had no consequence. The person named might be one who did the bidding of a lord rival to the king—sometimes the bidding of a rival king—so that he and his family enjoyed the protection of the patron, occasionally within the very district where the prosecuting king claimed to rule.[22] We don't know the early statistics, but by the 13th century for every 10 men outlawed, only one was ever caught and hanged.[23] (There was an ecclesiastical version of outlawry, too, though a milder one, excommunication. A person who suffered this was not in danger, at least not directly, of loss of life or property, but was to be shunned by the God-fearing. He was not to be prayed with, spoken to, or sat at table with to dine; as with outlawry, excommunication proved easier to announce than to carry out.[24])

Nearly 300 years would pass from the time of Ethelbert until the next significant figure in English legal history made his appearance. He was King Alfred (849-901), called "the Great" because of his success in turning back the invading Danish hordes. In between raids, Alfred occupied himself by compiling the extant law of the land, and adding to it, in his Book of Dooms. Beginning his work with a recitation of the Ten Commandments, Alfred used as his guiding principle the Golden Rule. "What ye will that other men should not do to you, that do ye not to other men," was his version,[25] to which he added: "By bearing this precept in mind, a judge can do justice to all men; he needs no other law books. Let him think of himself as the plaintiff, and consider what judgment would satisfy him," a line of reasoning that may not have been comforting to defendants. Although Alfred's rules appear to have gained a considerable measure of acceptance, British kings, even in his day, had not gained the absolute power they were to wield later—nor was there a centralized justice system to carry out *anyone's* laws uniformly.

Such regular courts as existed were local. One was that of county or shire and another that of vill (village) or "hundreds."[26] Neither of these early Anglo-Saxon judiciaries initially were particularly effective; they had no way of compelling attendance or of enforcing their orders, although sometimes an expedition would be sent out to capture a particularly desperate character.[27] Much more potent were the private manor or seignorial courts[28] presided over by the local earl who could force attendance by his tenants accused of misdoing, and have the fines collected by his reeve or sheriff; apparently the fines were kept by the earl who enriched himself at the expense of the people whose toil was already enriching him. (In Anglo-Saxon times, all nobles were known as earls or eorls; it wasn't until about the 10th century that the word began to refer to a specific ranking in the peerage.[29]) During the Middle Ages, the manor courts became increasingly powerful[30] and so did the barons—as they were now known—who presided over them. However, the tribunals of shire and vill would have the longer and more important history, developing into the borough and city courts,[31] and thereby serving as models for the modern British court system.

Although imposition of a fine was commonplace for resolving minor matters, the punishment for a serious offense could be either mutilation or execution. (Oddly enough, considering the brutal times, capital punishment was abolished in England in the 11th century as inhumane, only to be reintroduced in the 12th and become widespread again by the 13th.[32]) For these serious matters, ranging from witchcraft to murder, the favored method of trial for commoners, in Anglo-Saxon days, was the ordeal. It was practiced not only in England but also throughout Europe, always under a religious aegis and with a priest presiding, under the theory that only God's hand, not man's, could point out the guilty. (The idea was not original to the Roman Church; references to trial by ordeal can be found in Hindu chronicles from a thousand years before the time of Christ.[33])

In ordeal, God's hand could touch quite painfully, both the guilty and the innocent. One common method was to have the accused hold hot irons in bare hands or plunge hands to the wrists in boiling water, and up to the elbows when the charge was treason.[34] If, after several days, the priest, following his inspection, declared the wounds were healed, the accused was found innocent. Still other defendants were thrown into the water, and if they stayed down, were innocent, albeit dead; if they succeeded in floating, were alive, and guilty. As horrifying and unjust as the trial by ordeal may seem to modern sensibilities, in context it marked a notable improvement over the hue and cry, and appears to have been attractive to both the ruling class and the clergy as a means of controlling the bloodlust of their subjects. The accused, in that sense, played the role of popular scapegoat as well as defendant; the trials were a time of holiday, of priestly pageant and popular drama, for villein and serf.

At times, the result of a trial by ordeal was foreordained, and not by God but by money. On these occasions, the priest or the royal torturer was bribed to assure that the trial method would be either hot irons (which were not very hot) or boiling water (which was actually lukewarm).[35]

Although records of ordeal trials are scant in number, those we do have suggest that a sizable percentage of the defendants were female,[36] perhaps indicating the fear that men had of the magical powers of the women they kept powerless. A woman forced to grasp hot irons provides an eerie precursor to the witchcraft trials of later centuries, and the ordeal by water foreshadows the dunking stool subsequently used to punish female gossips.

There was a second method of trial. It was called compurgation, from a Latin word meaning "to purify," and was largely reserved for the benefit of members of the upper classes. When such a person was accused of a crime or an offense we would now call civil, he was required to bring with him individuals, usually 12 of them,[37] known as oath-helpers. A failure to bring the proper number of helpers could cause the defendant to be bound over to ordeal.[38] A compurgation trial began when the accused swore that he was guiltless of the charge, after which the helpers—who had to be men of standing in the community—would avow that the accused was a person of good reputation and would never tell a lie. Ordinarily, that testimony would satisfy the court and the defendant would be found not guilty. That is, he'd go free unless an oath-helper forgot some of the words of the complex oath or stumbled over even one of them; this was taken as a sign that God had struck the speaker's tongue and proved the accused's guilt.[39] Off to ordeal he would go.

In cases in which the dispute was between individuals, the accuser would similarly swear, bringing his oath-helpers to do the same. The side that made the fewest mistakes in swearing emerged victorious. Exactly how often the judge would ignore stumbles is unclear, but we can speculate it was exceedingly rare for a member of the nobility to be found guilty, no matter how stammering his oath-helpers, unless the person accusing him was even more noble.

When William the Conqueror defeated the British at the battle of Hastings in 1066, he brought with him from Normandy another form of trial, that of battle.[40] In it, accused and accuser would whack at each other with axes or sometimes, apparently, fists,[41] and the victor—or survivor—would be declared the innocent party. (In civil cases, the combatants were permitted to hire mercenaries to do their fighting for them.[42])

Trial by battle never became well-accepted among the English, perhaps because they recognized that the strongest and most adept in battle always won. It was hard to see God's hand in that. It was also possible and maybe more likely that they disliked the practice because the hated Normans had foisted it on them. (Trial by battle hasn't completely disappeared, as witness the head-butting contests by some Eskimos to settle disputes.[43])

It is unclear whether William also brought with him from Normandy any ideas of justice that went beyond the sword; written law did not exist among the Normans[44] as it did elsewhere in France,[45] at least to some extent, to say nothing of England itself. Among the Anglo-Saxon laws and customs were two that can be considered ancestor to the jury. For one, William had available to him the king's *witenagemot*, an assembly of wisemen which could include landowners and priests, to which came those who said they had been denied justice in the local courts.[46] From that basis, William developed the King's *Curia Regis*, or royal court, with the witenagemot sometimes impaneled as a kind of grand jury or king's factfinders.

William also inherited a more rarely used protocol known as the *recognition*; in it, neighbors who might have knowledge of the facts of a dispute were called upon to say what they thought was true.[47] Even more like the modern jury was the 12-man body instituted in Wales in the year 725 by a king named Morgan of Gla-Morgan, but it is doubtful if it ever spread beyond its original borders or would have been remembered by anyone in William's time.[48]

Fresh in memory, however, would have been the laws promulgated by the Danish king Canute who had briefly reigned over his homeland and England shortly before the Norman invasion. Like Alfred's, Canute's philosophy of the law was a gentle one for the times, influenced by underlying Christian principles that the church itself, by then, was often ignoring. The Danelaw which Canute had attempted to impose contained a form of the grand jury in which the 12 elders of each village were required, on a certain holiday, to swear out accusations against misdoers,[49] but there is no evidence that they or anyone else among the common people were subsequently enlisted to try the cases.

More directly antecedent to the jury[50] was another custom of which William and his Norman advisors might have had knowledge. Called the *jurare* and *inquisitio*, it had been developed in the Carolingian period by Charlemagne and his successors, and seems to have disappeared around the year 900, although it may have reemerged around the time of William.[51] A jurare was a group of wellborn citizens of a district who occasionally would be brought together by the king to inform him or his visiting representative of any local crimes and to state which of the claimants to a piece of land had the right to it—perhaps the king himself, the local lord, or sometimes the church. It would seem, as the king's appointees, that jurares would hardly rule against him, yet they frequently did so and apparently with impunity. It may be that the Carolingian kings, whose power was often shaky, felt it good politics to give the local gentry this form of freedom of decision-making, permitting barely loyal lords and unruly bishops small victories over small pieces of land.[52] As a consequence, not only were rebellions less likely to break out (bishops were particularly good at fomenting them), but, also by the very act of submitting a dispute to the king's jurare, the lords and clerics were implicitly admitting the king's right to act as primal authority.[53]

William, in England, had the same goal for himself. Upon his victory, he had taken a first step by dispossessing the Anglo-Saxon nobility and replacing them with his Norman kinsmen. That got rid of the rebels, but it also gave power to those who, based on the disputatious history of Normandy, were likely eventually to use their new power against its grantor. (Gratitude was as rare a commodity in politics then as it is now.) William acted quickly to assert his authority over all his enemies, real and putative. In 1086, he appointed a commission of royal fact finders[54] to take a census for tax purposes of who owned exactly which land and exactly what was on it: how many mills, how many fish ponds, how much woodland, how much meadow. That such a monumental task could be carried off makes the Domesday Book one of the truly impressive accomplishments of medieval history, but politically it was even more impressive. By cajoling or forcing everyone to cooperate—when many must have feared the king's real plan was to steal their lands through taxation—and doing so without bringing about a rebellion, William showed how a king could rule not only by force of arms but also through the establishment of civil authority.

Although the English jury system would eventually do much more than the Domesday Book to consolidate power in the king's hands, it would seem, in the context of a feudal society, a most unlikely vehicle to achieve that goal. Congenial the jury may have been to the democratic soul of Athens but hardly to a world in which the nobility and the priesthood were the self-announced, exclusive vessels for carrying out the will of God. It was not that the non-anointed couldn't participate in meting out justice; they had done so in pre-feudal days through the hue and cry and the wergeld, and it is apparent from the hue and cry's sporadic continuance well into the Norman period that even if a king had wanted to stop it he probably couldn't have. Both the recognitors and the jurare emerged with feudalism but were consonant with its principles, in that members served only at the pleasure of lay or ecclesiastic rulers (the Frankish church had its own version of the jurare).[55]

As occasional and advisory instruments of power, the pre-jury formulations were not, nor were they ever intended to be, crafted into a justice system as a permanent part of its functioning. For that to occur, a ruler was required who had imagination, who had an interest in the law and the cleverness to understand how an act that was seemingly disinterested would, in fact, serve his own political goals. This particular combination of acumen has proven rare at any time in history, but it was to be found at its pinnacle in the person of King Henry II (1133-89).

II

Stocky, bull-necked, probably not much more than 5 feet tall in an era when the average man stood 5 feet 6 inches, the French-born Henry—he never did learn to speak much English—could be a boon companion one moment, heartless and vile-tempered the next. Today, he is largely remembered (and mostly misremembered) for his love affair with and marriage to Eleanor of Aquitaine, and for his dispute with Thomas à Becket, the Archbishop of Canterbury who was murdered in his own cathedral. Henry had a harried domestic life; Eleanor plotted against him as did his four sons, most notably the bloodthirsty Richard and the double-faced John (that is, they all plotted against Henry when they weren't plotting against each other). These problem's of Henry's are of no great moment to our story, but his clash with Becket is.

We have already referred to the part the church played in the Anglo-Saxon justice system through the institution of trial by ordeal. But its role—both that which it held and that which the Papacy sought for it—went far beyond dipping people's arms in boiling water. By Norman times the ecclesiastical courts ruled over much of secular daily life, with bishops regularly sitting in judgment at the manor courts.[56] All offenses against morals (including incest) and religion (heresy, sorcery) and most marriage and inheritance matters were tried in church courts as were any crimes committed by clerics. Final appeal from the church tribunals was to the pope not the king. William had attempted, without success, to bring the ecclesiastical courts under royal aegis. Henry set out on the same tack, his first goal to gain the right to try clerics accused of felonies. In so doing, he was talking about a considerable part of the population. By the 12th century, one of every six Englishmen had taken holy orders of one kind or another.[57]

Although Becket, once Henry's protege, almost certainly was not assassinated at Henry's order, his many public attacks against the king and Henry's enraged rebuttals undoubtedly had encouraged the deed, as Henry himself admitted with many an expression of pious sorrow. (He even had himself publicly scourged.) Whether Henry felt contrite or not is uncertain, but the martyrdom of Becket—he was canonized two years after his death—had brought with it the wrath of Rome and the possibility of excommunication, which would virtually guarantee war against him.

Thus, in death, Becket triumphed.[58] In the compromise that was finally struck by Henry with the Pope, the ecclesiastical courts not only continued to have total authority in cases involving clerics—except treason, which had always been under the king—but also had their suzerainty formally recognized for personal property claims, all marriage matters, and new significant powers in contract cases.[59] In the noncriminal area, the various lay courts—not only the king's—had reserved to them the very large category of land ownership disputes over title and occupancy.[60]

Henry's failure[61] to curb the growing political power of the church—and politics is what the quarrel with Becket was really about—did not deter him from attempting to expand his secular rule. Standing in his way were the Norman nobles who had proven as untrustworthy as William had feared. Under the feudal system in England, freemen could choose the lord they wished to serve in peace and war, with that personage—at the highest level a baron—protecting them in return, including, ordinarily, in the courts of law. Although formal allegiance was sworn to the king, vassalage meant, in practice, that loyalties were divided, with the king's ability to wage war dependent upon the good will of those who could supply troops and money to support the cause.

Henry's immediate goal, therefore, was to provide a reason for some vassals and the population in general to turn to him for protection rather than to the barons. The time, in that sense, was propitious. The reign of Henry's amiable but weak predecessor Stephen had been marked by civil wars, and there was some feeling, even among the barons, that a time had come to recuperate, a time for law and order. A lesser man, sensing this, might simply have attempted to impose his rule, but Henry—perhaps learning from his experience with Becket—decided to avoid direct confrontation with the barons.

His basic tactic became to widen and then implement the power he was already recognized to have in nonecclesiastical matters.[62] Proving immediately useful to him was the ancient Anglo-Saxon concept of the King's Peace, the same term that would turn up in the William Penn indictment 500 years later. Until Henry's reign, the King's Peace referred only to offenses actually committed in the king's sight or on the highways under his control.[63] Bit by bit, Henry managed to alter the concept so that it applied to almost any kind of criminal offense,[64] ranging from treason to stepping on a blade of grass on someone's property.[65] To seize a controlling interest in property cases, he employed another established right of the king, that of hearing appeals in land ownership cases in which justice had been refused. However, these thrusts by Henry did not necessarily vitiate the power of the manor courts, in which the legal rules varied from place to place and often from one lord to his successor. In other words, although the king might have the right to hear the cases, his problem was getting customers.

It was on this point that Henry's considerable ingenuity came to the fore. Litigants would come, he reasoned, if the King's court provided a better quality of justice than was available at the manorial courts. To have the king's judges preside over cases was likely to be more appealing to most people than placing themselves at the mercy of the lord of the local manor who—questions of ignorance to one side—would invariably favor his closest allies. Of course, these allies were likely to prefer the manor courts for this very reason. Also, since Henry's judges reported to Henry, no doubt litigants would fear to bring a case in which they perceived the king had an interest. But in the main Henry proved right. Litigants came because the king's justice was better.[66] Poor plaintiffs had a chance of winning over rich defendants, an event hardly likely to occur with the barons. In fact, so highly regarded did Henry's courts become that their fame spread abroad; at one point the kings of Navarre and Castile elected to have their boundary dispute settled by one of Henry's judges.[67] Not only was Henry's justice better than the local variety, it was also swifter (manor courts were not famed for the regularity with which they met). Moreover, because of the king's prestige, his court's rulings were more likely to be enforced than those of the local tribunals.[68] Today's common law had its origins in the rulings of Henry's courts,[69] which became accepted as "common" to all of England, something that never happened with the parochial and inconsistent judgments of the manor and shire and vil courts. (The term "common law" came into usage in the 13th century; our earliest references to it are found not in secular but in ecclesiastical court decisions.[70])

The consolidation of Henry's law took place at the great Assize of Clarendon in 1166, 100 years after the Norman conquest. We know little authoritatively of what was said and done there, although we can imagine the trumpets, the banners, the priests and archbishops in their grand robes, the knights in armor clanking onto the scene on horseback, hooves kicking up dust. And in his tent the stocky unimpressive young king, only 33 years old, accepting homage both sincere and insincere. What he set forth may have been done by decree or quite possibly by the dropping of the right word,[71] but however it happened, when it was done, the jury had come into existence as an integral part of the English justice system.

From the beginning, Henry's juries had independent fact-finding powers for noncriminal cases—we'll get to the more limited criminal jury later—an aegis that soon included cases brought at shire and vil where juries were invoked primarily to decide tax cases when a property owner would claim his assessment was too high.[72] (Henry had neither the power nor the will for such a political risk as disestablishing the manor courts, which continued as before.)

Although Henry left no writings to explain his reasoning, we can infer from his other political and judicial actions at the time that he must have seen that a jury system would have two singular virtues. First, since it would give people the chance to help decide their own affairs, its presence was likely to add to the popular support he was seeking for his royal courts over the baronial ones; secondly, and at least as importantly, the jury would provide a justice-dispensation method which the church could not readily control. Its mettle in that direction had already been proven, at least in a limited way, beginning two years before Clarendon. Land disputes had grown common in which the church and the owner of record would argue whether or not a piece of property had, sometime in the past, been dedicated or donated to religious use.[73]

If the land had been so dedicated, the litigation would be handled by the church courts, where the outcome was certain. To protect landowners and prevent more and more land from disappearing into the hungry maw of the church, Henry intervened by appointing panels of 12 lay recognitors to determine if dedication, in fact, had taken place. If they said not, and Henry's satisfaction with the system suggests they usually said not, then the church, if it wanted to pursue the matter, had to do so in a secular court, where its chances of winning were poor.[74]

In instituting the jury, Henry did not abolish either the ordeal or the battle as a trial method. Both remained for some years as options that a defendant (and sometimes a plaintiff or accuser) could choose instead of the jury,[75] which was popularly known as "going on the country." Henry did banish compurgation from the royal courts,[76] but it is unclear if that had anything to do with his jury innovation; compurgation would make a brief reappearance in the 13th century at the king's principal court at Westminster[77] and then vanish entirely from the secular law scene.

The creative leap that Henry took at Clarendon, therefore, was not revolutionary, since the old board was not swept clean, nor was it one of innovative form, since the jury in that sense already existed, nor one of magisterial purity, since the motivation was primarily political. But it was, nevertheless, of awesome magnitude. By it, for the first time since the heyday of Athens—of whose jury system Henry almost certainly would have had no knowledge—those seeking redress of their grievances could have their case settled not by king, not by baron, not by priest, not even by the king's judge or the king's commissioners, but by their own peers.

Before describing Henry's civil and criminal jury systems, a caveat is in order. In the 12th century, and for several centuries thereafter, definitional distinctions between the tortious and the criminal act were incompletely drawn, despite the awareness we saw dating from Ethelbert's code, or shortly thereafter, that accidentally inflicted injuries should not be penalized as heavily as deliberate ones. By the time of Henry's reign, and perhaps before, land-title cases had begun to fall into the same vaguely noncriminal category as accidental injuries, or, at the least, were being treated in a formulaic way in which we can see the rudiments of the modern damage suit. Therefore, although Henry probably didn't think of his "civil" jury by that name—it was more of a land-dispute resolution device—his act in creating it as a separate justice entity did much to forward the concept of the civil law as distinct from the criminal.

In Henry's civil system then, the litigation process began with a writ prepared for the plaintiff by the office of the King's chancellor. The chancellor was a bishop, the clerk who did the writing a cleric. (Henry may not have been fond of the church, but he would have had no choice in the matter; few people outside the priest-class, even among the nobility, were literate.) The writ contained a brief outline of the plaintiff's case and was served on the defendant by a royal sheriff. (Sheriffs to this day carry out a similar function in property cases in many jurisdictions.) Once service was completed—and assuming the defendant was willing to appear (some were not, in which event, in the early days, a trial could not be held[78])—four knights of whom there were aplenty were summoned. They chose 12 jurors—freemen, for this was not a job for serfs—of good reputation and who had knowledge of the facts of the case or, if they didn't, were expected to investigate the facts prior to the trial.[79]

At the trials, there were no witnesses, no lawyers, no evidence as we now know that term; at the most a document might be presented to show it bore an official seal. The judge explained the law to the jurors, who were the final determiners of both it and the verdict.[80] In the very early days, the number of jurors might exceed 12, but no verdict was possible until that many had agreed.[81] Although the unanimous verdict did not become a statutory requirement in civil and criminal trials until the year 1367,[82] almost from the beginning[83] a non-unanimous decision was nearly unheard-of, and unanimity always clearly had been the expected result. The emphasis on agreement, it has been argued,[84] emanated from the medieval belief that there could be only one correct view of any event, so that a nonunanimous jury was a legal and logical non sequitur; or, more simply and more likely, the reason was that a verdict had a greater ring of authority when it emanated from all 12 throats rather than a mere majority.[85]

The laws governing land possession generally favored the person who held the property at the time of the complaint over the one who may have had original title or was attempting to seize it back from the one to whom a life tenancy had been given.[86] This concept, which went back to pre-Norman times,[87] may be the basis of the popular notion that possession is nine-tenths of the law. It was also a doctrine that served Henry's political purposes, or else he might have changed it. In effect it made it virtually impossible for descendants of Anglo-Saxon property-holders who had been dispossessed by their Norman conquerors to reclaim the familial estates, thus serving the interests of the ruling class. But even when such ancient matters weren't involved, the possession rule had great popular appeal since it promoted stability in land usage by the actual users, the gentry whose support was important to Henry in his battles with his various enemies. The possession rule, however, by no means made the results of every jury trial foreordained; in many instances, the issues were quite complex legally, even by modern standards, and this was particularly true when the quarrel was one between heirs or when the terms of a tenancy were ambiguously worded.[88]

At the end of the trial, the party that lost could be fined or imprisoned for having asserted a false claim.[89] When the defendant lost, he was, in addition, required to pay money to the plaintiff. These "damage" assessments, as they came to be called, fell into two categories: those to cover any out-of-pocket cash loss the plaintiff may have had, and—in a word that appears in virtually every civil suit from the early 1200s onward—those for the "shame" that the defendant's action caused the plaintiff. Shame was an ancient concept in England, going back to early Anglo-Saxon times, although apparently it had originally come up only in name-calling. (For example, one old statute required a person who "shames" a woman by wrongfully calling her a harlot to pay her 45 shillings.[90]) It is from this concept of "shame" that today's jury payments for pain and suffering and mental anguish are derived.

Although the land cases, where the king had undenied jurisdiction, were by far the most common of the civil jury trials of Henry's day, and for some time thereafter, by the 13th century civil cases alleging fraud and deceit began arriving in the secular courts. And by the 14th century, slander made its first appearance as a case for jury rather than fine.[91] The day of the negligence case, however, was still centuries away.

By his use of the civil courts and the civil juries, Henry succeeded, as one observer has noted, in bringing an end to most of the violent quarrels over land; by developing the authority and legitimacy of his courts, he kept the powerful barons in check; and, by requiring filing fees and imposing fines, he not-so-incidentally filled the royal coffers.[92] But, perhaps most importantly, he set into motion, through his land dispute trials, the idea that for every wrong there should be a remedy,[93] and that the jury was the source to find it.

For criminal matters prior to Henry's rule, at regular intervals the sheriff,[94] in a carryover from Danelaw, would call 12 freemen of each vicinage to swear oaths that certain individuals were believed guilty of crimes.[95] The swearers—and the word "jury" means "to swear"—were not necessarily stating they had firsthand knowledge of a person's guilt, but only that the person had such a reputation. The sheriff would then make the arrest, and, if the matter were a misdemeanor, the defendant was said to be "in mercy" and turned over to the local magistrate who, without further trial, would institute a fine.[96] Those charged with felonies were dispatched to ordeal. (The term felony was in use around Henry's time and covered most of the same offenses it does today.)

Henry's system was relatively more sophisticated, although it was still essentially an informational one. As an example, let us say that a murder had occurred; in that event, four men from each of the villages most nearly north, east, south, and west of the scene of the crime would be summoned to tell what they knew of it. Since these individuals were usually serfs or villeins, as were those they accused,[97] their lowborn word was not considered sufficient for an arrest. Instead, the villagers swore to what they knew before a jury consisting of 12 knights or other notables of the shire[98] who questioned the village jurors and, if they believed what they were told, ordered the person accused put to ordeal.[99] In effect, the 12 notables acted as an indicting grand jury or, when there was a question about the cause of death, as a coroner's inquest.

Then, in the year 1215, Pope Innocent III at the Fourth Lateran Council brought ordeal to an end throughout Europe by forbidding priests from any longer participating in it.[100] In England, the overnight disappearance of ordeal meant that, temporarily, there was no effective way to try serious criminal cases.[101] Trial by magistrate had always been only for minor matters and judges weren't eager to try hanging offenses for fear of finding themselves murdered by a defendant's family. Compurgation had virtually vanished and nobody was interested in resurrecting it. Trial by battle was now limited to private combatants. And the jury was intended only for indictment purposes. Since, however, the jury was also already trying cases in the civil arena, it became the obvious choice to replace ordeal as the new trial mode, and so it was done.

The transition, however, was slow. At first, emphasis continued to be placed on the indictment process, quite possibly because that was the juror function most familiar to judges. In some or perhaps all the courts of shire—our records are by no means definitive, and it is likely that not all courts functioned in exactly the same way—as many as three indicting juries could be empaneled for a single case: one consisting of 12 knights, one of commoners selected from the hundreds, and another, as in the old system, of four jurors from each of the four nearest villages who were supposed to be knowledgeable of the crime and who had committed it.[102] As with the first civil cases, indictment in the criminal cases didn't require a unanimous decision; either a simple majority or one less than unanimous was sufficient.[103] The accused apparently was permitted to be present at the indictment proceedings, and at some point was allowed to have a "pleader" or lawyer present, but it does not appear that the accused was permitted to speak.

Although the indictment phase was both lengthy and unwieldy, it represented a marked improvement in two regards over previous systems for the administration of justice. First, evidence (not merely allegations of bad reputation as earlier) had to be presented and taken down in writing before a person could be held for a crime. Secondly, both the accuser (usually the Crown) and the accused had the right to challenge and remove jurors who they believed might be unfair,[104] a right that apparently was extended to the trial itself and which, around the same time, was also available to litigants in civil cases. One result of the challenging process was that individuals who had been called for one trial, because of their supposed knowledge of the case, would be pressed into service to vote on an indictment or render judgment on a matter of which they were ignorant.

For the trial itself—which seems to have been treated almost as an afterthought in the early years—the jurors were either entirely or in part selected from among those who had brought the indictment and who, hence, believed the defendant was guilty before the trial began.[105] Because defendants were certain they would be convicted by a jury chosen in such a fashion, many of them—no doubt mourning the passing of the ordeal and all its useful corruption possibilities—refused to enter a plea, which meant under the existent law that they couldn't be tried. This was a serious matter for the crown; a refusal to enter a plea meant not only that a criminal might escape justice, but also, perhaps more importantly, that the state couldn't seize his property, since, for that to happen, a guilty verdict was required. As a consequence, "notorious felons," if they could be caught, were placed in "strong and hard"[106] imprisonment to encourage them to plead. They and anyone else who was indicted, if they continued to prove recalcitrant, were subject to having stones or irons placed on their bodies; some defendants, the old records showed, allowed themselves to be crushed to death rather than face trial in order to save their families from disinheritance.[107]

As the centuries wore on, torture to force trial was gradually abandoned, although an instance turns up as late as 1734 in English court records, and the rule was not repealed until 1772.[108] In its place, refusal to be tried came to be considered an admission of guilt and was dealt with accordingly. The American system, in which a failure to enter a plea is deemed a denial of guilt, was not adopted in England until 1827.[109]

Despite defendants fears that their jury would be stacked against them, by the last years of the reign of Henry's grandson, Henry III (1207-72), not-guilty verdicts were outnumbering the convictions. How this seemingly anomalous result came about our sources don't tell us. We can assume the bias challenges played a role, but it seems likely that a rapid decline in the importance of indictments[110] was much more significant. Before the 13th century ended, the multiple-jury approach to indictment had begun to fade away—possibly in large part because of its cumbersomeness—and be replaced by a system in which an information was filed against a party in a more sophisticated format than in Henry II's system. Here we can see the outlines of the contemporary concept that a *prima facie* case has to be made before an indictment can be issued. The change meant the indicting jurors were taking on an essentially rubber-stamp function and not, as they had been, virtually declaring the defendant guilty by charging him.

Whether the eventual exclusion of the indicting jurors from the trial juries (a change that came about in the mid-14th century) had any impact on the number of not-guilty verdicts is unclear, although, apparently coincidentally, by then the guilty findings were vastly outnumbering those of innocence. No doubt a number of reasons led to this turnabout: changes in application of the law, changes in pleading methods, variations in record keeping, and so on.[111] But one reason that was probably quite significant was the growing awareness by jurors of what might happen to them if they found against the judge's wishes.

When a judge or some other royal authority disagreed with a jury verdict, a writ of attaint (i.e., a claim that the verdict was tainted) could be issued and a new jury of 24 summoned to reconsider the case and try the original jurors for perjury rising from their "false" verdict.[112] Should the second jury decide the first had done wrong—which usually meant it decided that bribery had taken place—the punishment meted out to the attainted jurors could be a heavy one.[113] As Sir John Fortesque summarized in 1470: "All of the first jury shall be committed to the King's prison, their goods shall be confiscated, their possessions seized into the King's hands, their habitations and houses shall be pulled down, their woodland shall be felled, their meadows shall be plowed up and they themselves forever thenceforward be esteemed in the eye of the law infamous."[114]

The prospect of an attaint being issued made many juries reluctant to reach any verdict. Realizing that, judges would try to force them by refusing them food or drink while they were deliberating, or else, as a 14th-century chronicle tells us,[115] have them hauled about town in open tumbrils in all manner of weather, to force a verdict. Since a guilty finding was the one the judge (or the Crown) usually wanted, the jurors, under such persuasion, were likely to bring it.

With the gloomy prospects of attaint or public humiliation in mind, few were eager to become jurors, and those able to do so purchased exemptions.[116] Nevertheless, as long as someone else was doing the work, most people from the earliest days onward favored the jury system. The English people proudly perceived it both as a right that made them a free people in a way that others weren't[117] and as a protection they enjoyed against the might of the king and his minions. The combination of its popular acceptance and the gradual disappearance of alternate methods of trial meant that by the end of the 13th century virtually every felony and civil case that rose above the summary judgment level was being resolved by jury verdict.[118] An exception was in church courts where the priests had never seen the need of lay people to teach them the way of God; there, criminal trials against clerics continued to use the otherwise-discarded compurgation, with defendants who failed the test likely to be stripped of their orders and perhaps imprisoned in a monastery.[119] The power of the church courts to hear lay cases gradually eroded throughout the late Middle Ages with the split between Henry VIII and Rome in the 16th century ending it altogether.

As jury usage expanded during the Middle Ages, the method of selecting jurors on the basis of their knowledge of the case did not change, at least in theory, but there were some practical exceptions. We have already mentioned that challenges to jurors on a criminal case could lead to the addition of outsiders. The physical difficulty of getting to court could have the same consequence for civil cases. In the early years, such cases were heard at the king's court at Westminster,[120] which meant that the parties to the trial, including the jurors, could have a long and frequently dangerous trip to make. (The land was cluttered with outlaws, very few of whom, as we have seen, ever got caught.) As a result, some jurors never arrived and, quite likely, some never set out. Rather than postpone a case to an uncertain date when all the jurors might get there at once, the litigants, who had also had a hazardous trip, usually agreed to ask jurors who were on hand for other cases to serve along with the knowledgeable jurors who had shown up for theirs. Those who knew the case would then explain it to the newcomers, and the total body would render its unanimous verdict.[121] The so-called bystander juries in both civil and criminal cases established the idea that fact finders didn't necessarily have to possess prior knowledge of an event in order to render a verdict on it—a legal principle that was to become increasingly important.

Throughout the medieval period, we also find instances in which jurors were never expected to have information about the particulars of a case but were chosen, instead, for their expertise in its *subject*. A decision rendered in 1280, for instance, required that Florentine merchants living in London should serve on a jury in a case involving an act that occurred in Florence.[122] In at least one case, Jews were empaneled to try a Jew, and it was not uncommon for cooks to be summoned as jurors when the charge was selling bad food.[123] This system lives on today as the "special" or "blue-ribbon" jury.

The gradual erosion during the late medieval and early modern period of reliance on the knowledgeable juror—whether knowledgeable of the facts of the case or of its subject—does not appear to have been caused by any new, emerging philosophy of justice but rather by the growth of England's population and, specifically, its rapid urbanization. In Henry's time, most people lived on farms or in the small villages clustered about them, and it was likely that jurors would, indeed, have some awareness of the case (for instance, that the defendant had a bad reputation or that the land in question did belong to the plaintiff). As cities began to grow, finding such jurors became increasingly difficult. A medieval Londoner, for instance, was much less likely to know (or care) who held title to a house a block away than would a rural dweller about a farm a mile from him. It was even less likely for the city dweller to be privy to the reputation of someone accused of a crime, unless he lived near him, which might mean he was a member of the criminal class himself, not exactly what the authorities had in mind when looking for knowledgeable juries. As a result, jurors who didn't know the facts (or the rumors) of a case became increasingly commonplace, leading to the necessity of acquainting them with the facts through witness testimony. We don't know precisely when witnesses, other than plaintiffs and defendants, were first permitted to testify; occasional references to them can be found as early as the reign of Henry III[124] in the 13th century, although the practice appears to have become common only in the 15th or early 16th century.[125] Even then, however, jurors didn't have to listen to witnesses if they didn't wish to, and they were still expected to draw on their own knowledge of the case or what they could learn about it outside the courtroom.

It is not until the early 17th century that we find that jurors were expected to be chosen on the basis of their impartiality,[126] although selection was still to be made from the locality in which the incident, civil or criminal, occurred, because "[T]he Inhabitants whereof may have the better and more certain knowledge of the fact."[127] The transition that occurred, therefore, was from jurors who were accusers to those who *might* have knowledge of the event but asserted they had the capacity to render a judgment based only on what they heard from others in the courtroom. By the latter years of the 17th century, it had become so rare to have knowledgeable jurors that one scholar urged that, "if a jury gives a verdict of their own knowledge they ought to tell the court so that they may be sworn as witnesses."[128]

When we reach the early 19th century, we find that even indirect awareness of the facts of a case could excuse a juror. In the United States, that rule was enunciated by Supreme Court Chief Justice John Marshall in the Aaron Burr treason trial in 1807 when he held that knowledge of a case *gained by secondhand information* (such as newspaper accounts) would not serve *by itself* to exclude a juror, but a predisposition against one side or the other because of that secondhand knowledge would.[129] Also falling by the wayside was the expectation that jurors investigate cases on their own; those who might attempt to do so today would risk being jailed for contempt or, more likely, risk their lives while pursuing inquiries in some of the murkier neighborhoods of our great cities.

While all these changes were taking place, the jury number requirement held firm, which brings up a question that would sorely vex the United States Supreme Court 800 years after Henry II's time: Why 12 of them?

It probably never crossed Henry's mind to choose another number. He already had in place before him the 12 recognitors[130] and the 12 oath-helpers, the number commonly required in compurgation trials[131] in which the defendant might also be required to do his swearing in 12 churches on the theory that no man would dare risk the wrath of God by perjuring himself that often on sacred grounds.[132] The selection of 12 as the proper number almost certainly had its direct origin in the 12 apostles of Christ who gave witness to his truth just as compurgators and jurors were to do for their cases. Indeed, Morgan of Gla-Morgan's eighth century jury system was deemed by him the "Apostolic Law" because "[a]s Christ and his 12 apostles were finally to judge the world, so human tribunals should be composed of the king and 12 wise men."[133]

The number 12 itself throughout ancient history was considered a "good" magical number. The first Roman law was that of the Twelve Tables,[134] while in the Old Testament we learn of the Twelve Tribes of Israel, the 12 patriarchs and the 12 officers of Solomon,[135] which may suggest, to those who don't believe in the literal truth of the New Testament, why Christ was given 12 apostles. That the 13 lunar months have been crowded into 12 calendar ones exemplifies not only the good magic of 12 but the "bad" of 13, which may have become evil because it followed 12. Even today we see vestiges of the rule of 12; we buy eggs by the dozen, have 12 inches to the foot, which when multiplied by three—another good (holy trinity) number—gives us a yard. The magical properties of 12 are further reflected in some of our earliest numbering systems which were duodecimal, including that Canute brought with him to England.

Continuance of the jury system itself in its early years was not nearly as inevitable as the choice of the number 12 as the only proper one for juries. Popular the jury might be, but what one king put together, another could lay aside—and replace it with exclusive rule by judge. That such would not be the jury's fate came about, by accident, on the meadow of Runnymede on June 15, 1215. There was an irony to this moment in history: Henry had introduced the jury, in part, to weaken the barons, and now the barons were about to strengthen the jury in order to weaken Henry's son, John.

Shifty and wily, John was the kind of person who today would be described as too smart for his own good. All of his plans to cement his kingly power were clever and all of them failed. They were punctuated by a series of military defeats, religious quarrels—at one point, he succeeded in having all of England excommunicated by the Pope—and accompanied by ruinous taxation policies. In May of 1215, the barons renounced their homage to him. Civil war seemed certain unless John agreed to a series of demands the barons were making upon him. At Runnymede, he did.

In presenting the document that became known as the Magna Carta, the barons were acting purely in self-interest, and they doubtless would have been amazed and horrified if they could have foreseen the uses to which their Charter would eventually be put. That was the major difference between them and Henry. Although Henry hardly ever absented his own benefit from his calculations, he, unlike the barons, had a genuine interest in the law and wished to create a justice system that would be marked by fairness—and, indeed was, by the lights of his time. For their part, the barons simply wanted to strip the king of as many of his prerogatives as they safely could. (Their principal ally among the religious, Stephen Langton, the Archbishop of Canterbury, was a leavening influence upon them, insisting on wording that would pay respect to ancient customs and the existent law.[136]) Thus, when the barons in the Magna Carta referred to trying cases by the ''judgment of peers,'' they meant that barons were to be judged only by barons, and not, by any stretch of their imagination, by the freemen eligible to serve on Henry's juries.[137]

Despite what they apparently intended, their Magna Carta incorporated a principle that was to become the cornerstone of the English democracy, the principle that the law is superior to all men.[138] Since it was John who had been acting superior to the law, the proposition must have seemed a good one to the barons, but as time went on, it seemed an even better one to Englishmen of any rank or birth. They could claim the Charter of Runnymede as their written document of protection against all tyranny, whether that came from king or baron or church or parliament.

The Magna Carta consists of 61 chapters or clauses. Several deal with situations that must have been considered of transitory importance even then, while others hold interest today only because of how they depict the mores of the era. Chapter 54, for instance, in its entirety reads: ''No one shall be arrested or imprisoned upon the appeal of a woman, for the death of any other than her husband.''

But then there are those other chapters that do limn the landscape of freedom. Chapter 10, for instance, refers to the ''day of assizes'' where there shall be present knights and freeholders ''as many as are required for the efficient making of judgments.'' In an apparent direct reference to the jury, Chapter 40 notes that justice shall not be delayed nor denied (the basic concept of due process), while Chapter 52 requires that without the ''judgment of peers" no one can be dispossessed of property. But it was Chapter 39, as subsequently interpreted, that gave the specific imprimatur to the jury: "No freeman, shall be taken or/and imprisoned or disseised or exiled or in any way destroyed, nor will we [the king] go upon him nor send upon him, except by the lawful judgment of his peers or/and by the law of the land."

John, it will come as no surprise, had no intention of carrying out the Charter that the victorious barons had foisted on him. Through his agency, his new ally and onetime enemy, Pope Innocent III, condemned it and war broke out. But following John's death in October 1216, the Great Charter was reissued and soon took on the authority of statute as 9HenryIII.[139] Near the end of the century, Kind Edward (1239-1307) specifically declared that the right to trial by jury was henceforth to be considered a part of the common law.[140]

By establishing, advertently or otherwise, the concept that the "law" was superior to all men, the Magna Carta laid the groundwork for the eventual emergence of statutory enactments, such as 9HenryIII, as the preeminent legal force in England. It was not a development that came about easily. The ecclesiastical courts still considered themselves supreme in their sphere, as did the common law, or common pleas,[141] courts in theirs. Each disliked the thought that rules put together by mere legislators, unlearned in the law, could have suzerainty over both.

The British Parliament—which was to become the law enactment body—came into existence gradually in the 13th century as a series of irregularly held "parleys" (hence the name) between the king (or occasionally the barons) and members of the landed gentry and the rising merchant class (burgesses) of cities like London. The typical reason for these meetings was to help the king raise money or rally support, usually for one of his military enterprises. After being given the flattering opportunity to mingle with the mighty, the enspirited parleyers presumably went back home to fulfill the tasks assigned them. Before departing, however, the guests were likely to make requests of their own which the king would usually find politic to grant.[142] During the latter years of the 13th century, King Edward established three meetings of Parliament each year, and gave the body the right to pass laws. For Edward, who always needed money for war, this was a good trade-off. By permitting the lawmaking, he gained allies among the gentry and in the process separated them from the barons.[143] During the course of the 14th century, Parliament began to take on its present form with both elected and appointed members, which led to the separation of the House of Commons and the House of Lords. The Tudor kings, who came into power in 1485 when Henry VII defeated Richard III at the battle of Bosworth, further strengthened Parliament as a bastion of royal support against the barons, with the result that by the 16th century the barons were finally passing from the scene as a political force in England.

Although the 16th-century split with Rome had marked the end of the power of the church over lay matters, not all the English courts which were presided over by ecclesiastics had always been under Rome's control. By as early as Henry II's time, as we have seen, the King's Chancellor was a bishop who oversaw any royal matter that required writing. The scrivening of plaintiff writs was part of that function, but soon another element was added. The king, since the days of William the Conqueror, had reserved to himself the right to hear appeals, regardless of their court of origin, with such pleas for "equity," as it was known,[144] probably originally handled by the supplicant coming forth to the king, who decided the matter on the spot. Quickly, the burden of these cases became heavy, and the entire process, which now included the writing of appeals, also became the province of the Chancellor's office which became known as the court of Chancery or Equity.

As the Chancery courts were developing, so were those of common law. They now had their own clerks to prepare writs for civil suits and handled their own trials without interference from Chancery, so that each system seemed to have its own independent realm: the Common Pleas courts for trial, Chancery for appeals. The two systems, however, were soon on a collision course with each other.

The problem began in the common courts. By the 14th century, their writs had become highly formalized, requiring the services of pleaders or serjeants, as lawyers were first known,[145] to help the litigants through the legal thickets. But sometimes it seemed that nothing could be done; if a writ didn't already exist that fit the circumstances of a new case, that case could not be brought. It couldn't, that is, unless some selective bribery took place to stretch the meaning of a form to meet the briber's needs. Corruption, in this way, became common in the common courts. When bribing the judge didn't work, a well-to-do plaintiff or defendant would hire the sheriff to bring in a panel of jurors paid to reach the desired verdict, with the possible consequences to the jurors that we have already described. In the face of both the venality and the nearly impenetrable bureaucracy, people began to turn increasingly from the common courts to the Chancellor's office. Soon, the Chancery not only was receiving appeals from allegedly inequitable decisions in the Common Pleas courts, but also was asked to accept original jurisdiction on the matters that didn't fit one of the common court forms. The Chancery was hardly reluctant to take on these cases; from them, it got fees that otherwise would have gone to the trial courts.[146]

The common courts were ineffective in another way as well. Although such courts could assess damages once a harm was done, they had no way of preventing one. Chancery, by its power to issue injunctions, could do this. For example, a person might assert that someone was attempting to gain control of his land illegally or was refusing to carry out an agreement. He could then apply to Chancery which could issue an order requiring the alleged wrongdoer to cease what he was doing until the matter could be decided at trial. Should the defendant refuse to obey the injunction, Chancery had the right to imprison him until he did. Similarly, if a defendant defaulted in a judgment made against him, a "commission of rebellion" might be issued by Chancery since such a person was considered in direct disobedience of the king who had appointed the Chancellor.[147] He might also then be jailed until he or his family made good on the debt.

Like the Common Pleas Courts, those of Chancery at first worked quite well. "Equity and a good conscience," it was said was all the law a

chancellor needed, and that often proved sufficient. However, the good conscience of one Chancellor might not be the twin of his successor, so that
rulings by Chancery tended to be much more unpredictable than in the
common courts, where judges by now were beginning to instruct juries on the
law as it had been established in previous cases.[148] But even this problem
seemed to come to an end. Henry VIII's split with Rome had resulted, by the
time of his daughter Elizabeth's reign,[149] in the removal of ecclesiastics from
the Chancery court. Their place was taken by lawyers, who, being the tidy
sorts they are, began to publish Chancery decisions, creating, as with the
common law, a body of jurisprudence to serve as precedent for future cases.

As Chancery gradually ceased to be purely a court of appeals, it did not, at
the same time, incorporate the use of the jury in its new functions, even
though these cases would have been tried by a jury had they remained in the
common courts. Although we are not certain of this, the probable reason for
the exclusion of the jury rose from the perception that Chancery's new cases
were appeals as well, in the sense that litigants "appealed" to Chancery to
take over jurisdiction when the common courts proved incapable. Therefore,
since appeals were never heard by a jury, there was no reason these otherwise
jury-triable cases should be, either. (Juries were not entirely excluded from
the Chancery courts; a Chancellor could empanel one when he wanted a lay
view of the facts of a case, but the role of these jurors was entirely
advisory.[150])

The large number of cases now reaching Chancery produced, as in any
burgeoning bureaucracy, a matching blizzard of paperwork; as a result,
Chancery's operation, in complexity and slowness, began not only to rival
but also sometimes to surpass that of Common Pleas. Cases were known to
linger for 10 to 20 years before a chancellor would get to them, and when a
case was expedited, it was often because the chancellor or one of his aides
had been paid. (In 1681, when King Charles II granted William Penn a
charter for his colony in the New World, Penn, in order to get the document
through the Chancery, was required to spend £10,577 in bribes.) It was not
unusual for a chancellor to sell offices in his court for sums that could be
counted in the hundreds of thousands of present-day dollars, indicating how
profitable these positions could be for those who held them. Then there were
the clerks who wrote the writs or appeals for litigants. They charged by the
page, and soon learned the lucrative habit of writing in large hand, with wide
spaces between the lines, and wider margins yet.[151] Chancery had become the
kind of justice the poor couldn't afford to buy.

By the end of the 16th century, Common Pleas judges, who had long
chafed under the oversight function of Chancery, were becoming increasingly embittered by the ways in which Chancery was seizing original jurisdiction
from them. The crowning blow occurred when Chancery also took upon itself
the right to issue injunctions to prevent a party from pursuing an "unjust"
claim in Common Pleas court. Opposition from the 12 Common Pleas
justices—there's that magical number again—was led by Sir Edward Coke
(1552-1634) whose dissertations on the common law were to become
textbook matter for generations of lawyers and judges in England and

America. Coke bluntly declared he'd release from prison anyone put there by a Chancery injunction. In 1616, the quarrel was placed before King James I.

Desirous of reasserting the Divine Right of Kings, James mistrusted and feared the common law courts where juries often defied the rulings of the judges the king had appointed.[152] The commission James named to decide the matter was led by Sir Francis Bacon—a brilliant legal theoretician and an eminently practical man—who knew what the king wanted and gave it to him: Rulings by the Courts of Chancery henceforth were always to be considered superior to the common law. As politically astute as that decision may have been, in practice nothing was decided. The functions of the two systems continued to overlap,[153] to the increasing confusion of litigants and their lawyers—and with such results that an action might be brought in one court, with the parties only discovering, after several years, that they should have been pleading it in the other. The division that was eventually worked out—i.e., Common Pleas with its juries got cases in which there was a demand for money, Chancery those calling for the settlement of accounts and estates—helped a bit, but much overlapping and confusion remained. (As we shall see in Chapter Eight, the ancient battles between Chancery and Common Pleas were to provide grounds for a modern attack on the jury system.)

Coke, having lost to the king's courtier, Bacon, shifted ideological horses in midstream. Resigning from the Common Pleas bench, he got himself elected to Parliament, which he now declared to be a lawmaking body superior to both the common law and Chancery. To Parliament, growing restive under the autocratic rule of James and his son Charles I, this was heady stuff indeed. Resurrected for the cause was the Magna Carta, which was now—for the first time in any significant way—declared to be the sacred guarantor of the rights of all Englishmen. It became the bloody shirt of a revolution that would cost Charles his head.

Playing a role in bringing about that revolution was still another court, and in it, as in Chancery, juries were not permitted. Called the Court of Star Chamber, it was initiated in 1487 as a means of bypassing the frequently corrupt and ineffective common law courts in criminal cases. The Star Chamber—appointed by the King's Council—was given exclusive jurisdiction over such felonies as forgery, perjury, rioting, fraud, libel, and conspiracy, the latter the great catchall that prosecutors have ever since wielded punitively when they lack the evidence to make any other charge stick. The Star Chamber, using methods of discovering guilt learned not from British law but from the Spanish Inquisition, soon extended its rule to all manner of political crimes. Among those brought before it for punishment were jurors who had decided against the Crown.

The same Parliament that had seized on the virtues of the Magna Carta also seized on the Court of Star Chamber and in 1641 abolished it. But the memory of it and its excesses was still fresh in the minds of many, including young William Penn when he was brought to trial on the third of September 1670.

III

The Conventicle Act, the basis of the arrest of Penn and Mead, was enacted shortly[154] after Charles Stuart acceded to the throne of England in 1660 as King Charles II, following 11 years of Puritan rule under the Cromwells. It was a time of deep religious division in England, with the Puritans, on the one side, and the Church of England, on the other, agreeing on very little save that the greatest threat to the nation emanated from the Papacy. The new king, whose return had been without welcome in many quarters, was endangered by that belief; he and his family were rumored to be secret Catholics. Whether or not the king would have anything to do with it, a Popish invasion—no doubt emanating from the fiendish French—was feared at any moment, with the groundwork at home to be laid by a fifth column of Papal agents. The Conventicle Act was intended to forestall such an internal calamity by "providing . . . speedy remedies against the growing and dangerous practices of seditious sectaries, and other disloyal persons, who, under pretense of tender consciences, have or may at their meetings contrive insurrections, as late experience hath shown." Specifically outlawed was the presence of "any subject of this realm" who was 16 years or older at any "assembly, conventicle, or meeting, under color or pretense of any exercise of religion, in other manner than according to the liturgy of the Church of England." The law provided for a series of escalating fines which, if unpaid, eventually could cause the convicted person to waste away the remainder of his life in debtor prison.[155]

Although the Conventicle Act was overtly aimed at Catholics—who were, for the most part, quite careful to practice their religion in secret, even before the law was passed—it principally affected the Quakers who practiced their beliefs openly. Not that they were an accidental target. Accusations abounded, apparently fed by the prelates of the Church of England, that the Quakers were secret Papists themselves. In the reasoning of the time, both the hysterical and the well-calculated, the charge could seem to make sense. The Quakers spoke for freedom of religion: Did not that mean freedom for the Catholics? Worse yet, the Quakers advocated pacifism: And what could be more calculated to weaken England and make it ripe for invasion? A plot could even be discerned in the rapid growth of the Quakers: Didn't that mean they had to be financed by Rome? (Founded in 1640 by George Fox, the Society of Friends in 30 years gained more than 40,000 adherents, many of them influential merchants.) Now, having subverted young Penn to their cause, the Quakers had snared the son of an admiral who was a favorite of none other than the suspected king himself! The best thing about conspiracy theories is that they don't have to be true to be effective.

Penn's arrest on the charge of "seditiously" causing a tumult was, therefore, no small matter. It represented a coup for the king's enemies, and the king, sensitive to the Popish allegations against him, was hardly likely to try to intervene. On the day of trial, Mead— a linen draper and a former Puritan who had fought with Cromwell[156]—and Penn appeared before Sir Samuel Starling, the lord mayor of London and no friend of the Crown, along with a Recorder, five aldermen, three sheriffs . . . and a jury of 12 citizens.

Although the officials were united in their plan to convict Penn—which, they presumed, would harm the Quaker cause and embarrass the king at one and the same time—the jury was a problem. Most Londoners had remained unimpressed by the charges against the Quakers whom they perceived as the most peaceable of people, hardly likely to frighten anyone, much less "tumultuously" and "with force and arms." Nevertheless, the judge and his colleagues had great hopes for the jurors, who, though they might respect the Quakers, would also know the long history of jurors being treated as criminals when they did not come up with the desired verdict in a sensitive case. And this was a sensitive case.[157]

Just as the trial was getting underway, Sir Samuel, acting as judge, observed that the defendants were not wearing their hats which had somehow gotten lost.[158] Since Sir Samuel knew it was the Quakers' custom not to bare their heads before any temporal authority, he ordered a bailiff to put hats on them and then fined them 40 marks each for wearing them. To that, Penn responded: " . . . it may be observed that we came into the court with our hats off and if they have been put on since, it was by order from the Bench and therefore not we, but the Bench, should be fined." Despite this persuasive logic, the fines were not rescinded and the court proceeded to the evidence which came from three men who said they had seen Penn preaching but could not hear what he said.

Penn then declared that their assembly had been for the purpose of "reverencing and adoring our God, who made us," which led one of the court officials to snap that the defendants weren't on trial for worshiping but for breaking the law. Penn asked what law, and although it was clear from the wording of the indictment that the Conventicle Act was being invoked, the Court told Penn he was being charged "on common law." The shift was a tactical one by his prosecutors who knew that Penn could readily afford to pay the fine to which he'd be liable under the Conventicle Act whereas conviction under the matching common law offense, unlawful assembly, could lead to a prison sentence.

Sniffing out what was afoot, Penn demanded to know which common law and the Court refused to say. To that, Penn, never at a loss for words then or later in life, observed: "Certainly, if the common law be so hard to be understood, it's far from being very common; but if the Lord Coke, in his Institutes, be of any consideration, he tells us, that common law is common right; and that Common Right is the Great Charter Privileges." Still, the court refused to produce the law he supposedly had broken, leading Penn to conclude that "you do at once deny me an acknowledged right, and evidence to the whole world your resolution to sacrifice the privileges of Englishmen to your sinister and arbitrary design."

That plain statement of the situation did not please the Court and the Mayor ordered Penn put in the bail-dock, a locked enclosure. It was now Mead's turn. Turning from the court, he said to the jurors: "You . . . who are my judges, if the recorder will not tell you what makes a riot, a rout, or an unlawful assembly, Coke . . . tells us . . . a riot is when three or more are met together to beat a man, or to enter forcibly into another man's land, to cut down his grass, his wood, or break down his pales." For that accurate summation, the Lord Mayor informed Mead ''you deserve to have your tongue cut out'' and ordered him locked in the bail-dock as well.

With the prisoners safely in their cages, the Recorder turned to the jury, summarized the evidence—that Penn had been seen preaching and ''that Mr. Mead did allow of it''—and concluded by saying, ''Now we are upon the matter of fact, which you are to keep and to observe, as what hath been fully sworn, at your peril.''

The jurors would have recognized the threat of those last three words, and even as they took the message in, Penn was shouting through the bars of his cell to remind them ''that I have not been heard . . . [and] I appeal to [you], and this great assembly, whether the proceedings of the court are not most arbitrary and void to all law, in offering to give the jury their charge in the absence of the prisoners.''

Mead agreed through his bars, describing the proceedings as ''barbarous and unjust,'' causing the Recorder to order the prisoners to be locked in ''the stinking hole'' while they awaited their verdict. After 90 minutes, the jury members—their names are to be found at the beginning of this book—stood eight to four for conviction. One of the aldermen knew one of the jurors, Edward Bushel, and, suspecting he was one of the holdouts, declared, ''[Y]ou deserve to be indicted more than any man that hath been brought to the bar this day,'' after which Bushel was threatened by Starling with branding.

Following the exchange, the jury was sent back to reconsider its verdict, and this time it came up with one: William Penn, they said, was ''guilty of speaking in Gracechurch Street.'' That was not what the judges wanted to hear. They couldn't send anyone to prison for that. ''Was it not an unlawful assembly?'' demanded the judge. ''You mean he was speaking to a tumult of people there.''

The foreman of the jury: ''My lord, this was all I had in commission.'' The court then declared that the jurors were not to be released until they had given a verdict. They replied that they had. That did them no good, and they were ordered to go and reconsider; after another half-hour, they were back again, repeated the verdict as to Penn but this time added that Mead was found not guilty of ''the said indictment.'' Cried the Mayor, outraged: ''What will you be led by such a silly fellow as Bushel?'' to which the Recorder added, ''Gentlemen, you shall not be dismissed, till we have a verdict that the court will accept; and you shall be locked up, without meat, drink, fire and tobacco; You shall not . . . thus . . . abuse the court, we will have a verdict by the help of God, or you shall starve for it.''

Once more they were ordered to their room. Before they left, Penn managed to break through long enough to say: ''The agreement of twelve men is a verdict in law, and such a one being given by the jury, I require the Clerk of the Peace to record it . . . And if the jury bring in another verdict contrary to this, I affirm they are perjured men in law.'' Then, turning to the jurors, he shouted: ''You are Englishmen. Mind your privilege. Give not away your right.''

The following morning back they came with the same verdict, causing the Lord Mayor to threaten to cut Bushel's throat. Penn, thereupon, asked the court to free Mead since he had been fully acquitted, but the court declared that since Penn and Mead had been indicted for a conspiracy (i.e., under the Conventicle Act), there could be no verdict until they were both convicted. "If not guilty be not a verdict," Penn opined, "then you make of the jury and Magna Carta but a mere nose of wax . . . What hope is there ever of having justice done, when juries are threatened, and their verdicts rejected?"

The jurors spent still another night locked away, and at seven the following morning, they trooped back into court and asked to have their written verdict returned to them. To the Lord Mayor and his henchmen, this could mean only one thing: They had won. Magnanimously, the judge told the jurors: "That paper was no verdict and there shall be no advantage taken against you by it." He was in for a surprise. "How say you?" inquired the clerk. "Is William Penn guilty or not guilty?"

"Not guilty," said the foreman.

At that point, the judge gave up trying to force the verdict he wanted. But when Penn demanded his liberty, he was ordered hauled away to jail as was Mead in lieu of paying fines for contempt of court. The judge then turned to the jurors and fined them 40 marks each, and when they refused to pay, they too were sent off to Newgate Prison.

Despite his belief that the court was violating the Great Charter, Penn was not interested in staying in prison on principle, and when his father paid his and Mead's fines, gladly the two men left. Eight of the jurors soon gave up and their fines were paid as well. But four didn't. Edward Bushel did not, and neither did John Baily, John Hammond, and Charles Milson.

With Bushel acting as their leader, they stayed in Newgate, retaining lawyers to argue on their behalf in what became known as *Bushel's Case*. Eventually, the Court of Common Pleas granted them bail, and after nearly a year a verdict was rendered: The fining and imprisonment of the Penn jury was declared illegal; no jury, concluded Chief Justice Sir John Vaughan, can be punished for its verdict.

Bushel and his colleagues—men otherwise anonymous but distinguished in the history of freedom—had made it possible for all juries that came after them to render their verdicts without fear and as they, not the judge, saw the equities. The jury of one's peers that the barons had provided had at last become what the barons never wanted it to be, a democratic parliament of 12.

IV

Twelve years later, in the Frame of Government he wrote for the inhabitants of his new colony in America, Penn extended rights not yet known in England, including that of freedom of religion, along with a humane penal system which contained but two causes for capital punishment: first degree murder and treason. (There were dozens on the books in England and elsewhere in America; in Puritan Massachusetts, for example, to be a Quaker was a hanging offense.) One British statute, however, which Penn left undisturbed was that forbidding criticism of public officials. Anyone who did so could be charged with seditious libel. It was a law that was to cause problems for William Bradford, a 22-year-old Quaker who arrived in Pennsylvania in 1685, bringing with him the colony's first printing press.

In 1688, Bradford was arrested by John Blackwell, Penn's governor in the colony, for printing a piece mockingly describing Penn as a "Lord." When Blackwell was recalled to England for unrelated reasons, the case died, but not before Bradford had declared he would print what he pleased. Several years later, Bradford was again arrested on seditious libel charges—for printing speeches by George Keith, a Quaker dissident—and this time Bradford argued that, although the law might say he was guilty, he had the right to a jury to determine that. He got what he wanted; the jury couldn't reach a verdict, and Bradford, discouraged by the censorship he was encountering, moved to New York City.

There, no longer a rebel, he soon became the Royal Printer and eventually publisher of a weekly newspaper, the *Gazette*. In 1711, he took on as an apprentice, a 14-year-old German boy who had come to America from the Palatinate a year previous. His name was John Peter Zenger, and he remained in Bradford's employ until 1719, after which he moved to Maryland, returning to New York in 1722. Briefly, in 1725, he was Bradford's partner but soon decided to go into business for himself, eking out a living printing religious tracts until 1733.[159] At that point in his career, Zenger seemed a nice enough, respectable man, who added to his meager earnings by playing an organ in church. Nothing indicated he was destined to become one of the pivotal figures in American history.

What set Zenger's fate in motion was the arrival in New York of a new royal governor, William Cosby. Although it is uncertain that Cosby was a thief, he was a grasping, avaricious man who demanded huge sums in payment from the New York council for his services, and attempted to force the prior interim governor to turn over to him half the salary he had been paid. The ex-governor, Rip Van Dam, thriftily and courageously refused. When Cosby then instituted suit against Van Dam in Chancery—he knew he'd lose in Common Pleas before a jury—a sizable number of the colony's wealthier gentlemen closed ranks around Van Dam. To propagandize their detestation of Cosby—a cause popular among the masses as well as the rich—Cosby's enemies turned to Zenger, knowing they could expect no help from Bradford's *Gazette* (not if Bradford wanted to continue to be Royal Printer). They offered to finance a newspaper for which Zenger would act as editor-publisher.

Zenger's *New-York Weekly Journal* made its first appearance on November 5, 1733, and, unlike the Bradford sheet, was hardly dry reading. With many of the scorching editorials written by a Van Dam ally, attorney James Alexander, the *Journal* quickly drew attention, though perhaps mostly for its mock advertisements. In one of them, Francis Harrison, a Cosby lackey, was described as "a large Spaniel, of about 5 feet 5 inches high . . . lately strayed from his kennel with his mouth full of fulsome panegryricks." The sheriff found himself described as a "monkey . . . lately broke from his chain and run into the country." Song sheets stronger in their invective than their scansion followed. ("The petty-fogging knaves deny us rights of Englishmen. We'll make the scoundrel raskals fly, and ne'er return again.") None of this set well with Cosby and his cohorts—one of whom apparently threatened Alexander's wife[160]—and on November 2, 1734, Cosby ordered that four issues of Zenger's paper be burned by the common hangman. The hangman refused. The sheriff then "delivered the papers into the Hands of his own Negroe" who carried out the conflagration.

Fifteen days later, Zenger was arrested, charged with "presenting and publishing several seditious libels . . . influencing [the people's] Minds with Contempt of his Majesty's Government," the same charge against which Bradford had fought more than 40 years before. Zenger was confined to the dungeon of the old City Hall, which housed the courts, on £400 bail, a prohibitive amount. (It was the bail placed on Zenger that would influence the writing of the Eighth Amendment of the United States Constitution, forbidding excessive bails and fines.[161]) Cosby's next step was to have Zenger's lawyers, William Smith and Alexander, disbarred when they argued against the bail. John Chambers, a member of the Cosby party,[162] was appointed to defend Zenger, who, dictating editorials to his wife through the dungeon door, missed only one issue of his newspaper while in prison.

Despite jury lists that seemed rigged in Cosby's favor, eventually a panel was obtained that contained seven Dutch-descended New Yorkers, among whom anti-British feeling was strong. Even so, there seemed no likelihood that they, any more than the jurors in Penn's trial, would cause a problem. Under the law, if Zenger admitted he had published the articles, the jury would have to find him guilty, and it would then be up to the judge to determine if the articles were seditious and libelous which, as a Cosby minion, he would.

Unknown to the Cosby forces, Zenger's allies had not been quiet, and the fruit of their endeavors, a 60-year-old man, was sitting in the audience as the trial began. Now he arose and, to the dismay of the judge and prosecutor, identified himself as Andrew Hamilton of Philadelphia, the most famous advocate in the colonies. (It was Hamilton's role in the Zenger trial that gave coin to the phrase, "when in trouble get a Philadelphia lawyer.")

Chambers, in a difficult spot, gladly stood aside, leaving the defense in Hamilton's hands. From the start, Hamilton admitted Zenger had printed the papers, but observed that for a libel to be proved it must be both false and malicious. "It is a right," said Hamilton, "which all freemen claim, and are entitled to, to complain when they are hurt; they have a right publicly to remonstrate against the abuses of power in the strongest terms, to put their neighbors upon their guard against the craft or open violence of men in authority"—a function for a newspaper to perform—"and to assert with courage the sense they have of the blessings of liberty."

The Court, however, quoting from decisions of the notorious Star Chamber, stated that it was no justification of a libel that it be true; on the contrary, the judge said, ". . . the greater appearance there is of truth in any malicious invective, so much the more provoking it is." The ruling meant that Hamilton was forbidden to put on witnesses who would testify to the truth of the *Journal*'s articles, testimony that Cosby very much wanted to avoid.

Unable to present his evidence, any more than Penn had, Hamilton's only chance to acquit his client was through his summation to the jury. He began by pointing out that "the suppression of evidence ought always to be taken for the strongest evidence," and from there on he got tough, referring to the inequities of "corrupt and wicked magistrates," the evils of the Star Chamber and its forbiddance of trial by jury, before coming to his peroration: "I am truly very unequal to such an undertaking on many accounts. And you see I labor under the weight of many years, and am borne down with great infirmities of body; yet old and weak as I am, I should think it my duty, if required, to go to the utmost part of the land where my service could be of any use in assisting to quench the flame of persecutions upon informations set on foot by the government to deprive a people of the right of remonstrating of the arbitrary attempts of men in power. Men who injure and oppress the people under their administration provoke them to cry out and complain; and then make that very complaint the foundation for new oppressions and prosecutions . . . Gentlemen of the jury . . . it is not the cause of a poor printer, nor of New York alone, which you are now trying. No! It may in its consequences affect every freeman that lives under a British government on the main of America. It is the best cause. It is the cause of liberty; and I make no doubt but your upright conduct this day will not only entitle you to the love and esteem of your fellow citizens; but every man who prefers freedom to a life of slavery will bless you and honor you, as men who have baffled the attempt of tyranny . . ."

As Zenger himself later noted: "The jury withdrew, and in a small time returned, being asked by the clerk whether they were agreed of their verdict, and whether John Peter Zenger was guilty of printing and publishing the libels in the information aforementioned, they answered by Thomas Hunt, their foreman: Not Guilty. Upon which there were three huzzas in the hall, which was crowded with people and the next day I was discharged from my imprisonment."

Zenger quickly published the transcript of the trial, and his and other printings—one by Benjamin Franklin—soon spread word of it around the American colonies and into England. From the day of the jury's verdict, although the seditious libel laws were not repealed, prosecutions under them in America ceased. Through the forensics of Hamilton and the courage of Zenger's jurors—who, as in Penn's case, refused to give the verdict the crown demanded—the right to a free press was established.

More salient to the purposes of this discussion, the verdict in the highly-publicized Zenger trial impressed thousands of Americans with the importance of the right to jury as a bulwark against official oppression, leading Gouverneur Morris, one of the framers of the United States Constitution, to describe the case as "the morning star of liberty which subsequently revolutionized America."[163]

A denial of the right to jury helped force that revolution into existence. The stage was set through the passage by Parliament of the Stamp Act of 1764, a tax on paper that was considered a form of censorship by many newspaper publishers. It proved difficult to enforce. To gain convictions of violators, the British government switched prosecutions under the statute from the Common Pleas to the Admiralty courts where, as in Chancery, juries—which would have freed the Stamp Act protestors—were not permitted. The Stamp Act Congress, held in New York in 1765, specifically condemned this abrogation of the jury trial,[164] but Parliament, at least initially, was unimpressed by the complaints. However, they were soon impressed by the activities of another William Bradford, the grandson of Cosby's printer. Himself a newspaper and book publisher, the younger Bradford and some of his colleagues formed the Sons of Liberty, whose ideas of justice had little to do with trials or juries. Instead, they visited the homes of the royal tax collectors and after admiring the fineness of a building's construction and the handsomeness of its furnishings, thereupon observed how sad it would be to see such elegance burned to the ground. The collectors got the message. The Stamp Act tax became virtually uncollectable, and Parliament, its tail well-pulled, repealed it.

The denial of jury trial under the Stamp Act, followed by similar prosecutions brought under the Navigation Acts, continued to nettle the growing number of patriots. In 1774, the First Continental Congress raised the jury issue directly with Parliament when it declared: ". . . the respective colonies are entitled to the common law of England and more especially to the great and inestimable privilege of being tried by their peers of the vicinage, according to the course of law."[165] By July 1776, England's refusal of the right to jury had become one of the specified causes for revolution listed by Thomas Jefferson in the Declaration of Independence ("for depriving us, in many cases, of the benefits of trial by jury . . .").

When the Constitution was written 11 years later, jury trial in criminal cases was the only civil right specifically guaranteed (Article Three, Section 3: "The trial of all crimes, except in the cases of impeachment, shall be by jury . . ."). The omission of the right to jury trial in civil cases provoked immediate and powerful opposition to ratification of the Constitution.[166] The battle was led by Jefferson who had not been present at the Constitutional Convention—he was ambassador to France at the time—and who believed the civil jury was necessary to frustrate the enforcement of unwise legislation, to protect the citizenry from oppressive judges, and to assure fair trials in private actions brought against the government.[167]

Jefferson, joined eloquently by Patrick Henry and by other early leaders of the Revolution, also demanded that the right to criminal jury trial be stated in language stronger and more precise than offered in Article Three. Only when agreement was won by the Jeffersonians on both points from their Federalist opponents, was ratification of the Constitution assured, with the jury rights spelled out in the sixth and seventh of the 10 amendments known as the Bill of Rights. "In all criminal prosecutions," according to the Sixth Amendment, "the accused shall enjoy the right to a speedy and public trial, by an impartial jury of the state and district wherein the crime shall have been committed . . . be informed of the nature and cause of the accusation . . . be confronted with the witnesses against him . . . have compulsory process for obtaining witnesses in his favor, and . . . the assistance of counsel for his defense." The Seventh Amendment in its entirety reads: "In suits at common law, where the value in controversy shall exceed twenty dollars, the right to trial by jury shall be preserved, and no fact tried by a jury shall be otherwise re-examined in any court of the United States, than according to the rules of the common law."

The wording of both articles seems explicit enough to preclude conflicting interpretations, yet that has not proven to be the case. In interpreting the

Sixth, the United States Supreme Court in 1904 and again in 1970 has ruled that when the framers of the Bill of Rights said "all" they did not mean all, but only some, crimes. If the maximum sentence was five months, no jury could be demanded; if six, one could. (This was not the only instance, as we shall see, in which the Supreme Court found a distinction between six and five; belief in the magic of numbers has apparently not disappeared.) Similarly, the apparently absolute right to counsel in criminal trials had been forbidden to many indigent defendants until the Supreme Court ruled in *Gideon v. Wainright* (1963) that the Amendment, in this instance, did mean what it said. But not quite: If a charge cannot possibly result in a prison sentence, or if a judge declares in advance that no jail time will be imposed, or if the maximum sentence is less than six months, or if a fine of no more than $500 can be levied, then a defendant may still be tried without benefit of legal counsel.[168]

In the case of the Seventh Amendment, the phrase "in any court of the United States" has been interpreted to mean federal, not state, courts; however, every state, in its constitution, has followed the Seventh Amendment by permitting civil jury trial in common law cases.

The jury's conclusory powers in civil matters, however, have been restricted by the interpretation given to the final words, "according to the rules of common law." The common law is pretty much what judges say it is, and thus the prohibition against reexamination of any jury's verdict, apparently established by Bushel's Case, has given way to the practice of permitting judges—in some circumstances—to set aside civil verdicts, or to reduce the amount awarded and at times not permit the case to go to jury. The standards to be applied in determining whether a jury's verdict can be overturned have never been unambiguously established and differ from jurisdiction to jurisdiction, sometimes from one judge to another within the same jurisdiction.[169] Many judges have held that the jury's verdict stands if there is *any* evidence to support it, but others that it can be reversed when the evidence to the contrary of the verdict is overwhelming, even though *some* evidence supports the jury's view.[170] Finally, a verdict can be reversed when it is contrary to evidence that is undisputed by both sides.

A judge may also direct a verdict in civil cases, taking it out of the jury's hands when the evidence isn't sufficiently in dispute for a jury to consider. (A Chicago study found this happens about 13% of the time in injury cases.[171])

The wording of the Seventh Amendment also makes clear that *only* cases at common law—essentially those in which legal rights, including monetary payment for injury, are demanded—are triable by jury while others are not, an adoption of the British chancery system as it developed. Also inherited from England was the practice of having the equity (chancery) courts separate from the common pleas ones, each with its own judge. Matters remained that way until 1848. That year the New York legislature passed a new code of civil procedure, written by David Dudley Field, by which a single civil court system was created, with the same judges now permitted to hear both equity and common law cases. Field's code, which also simplified some of the legal hairsplitting and reduced the chasing of cases from one court to another, was soon adopted throughout most of the United States.[172] (England finally got around to abolishing its dual system in 1873.)

Although the courts were no longer separate, the two kinds of actions still were, with equity powers in the United States, even after the Field reforms, remaining largely what they had been. Thus, a judge still could issue an injunction, using the Chancery power, to prevent picketing in a strike and if it continued, throw the offenders in jail. Just as in England, going back to the old ecclesiastical courts, most matters concerning trusts and estates—including protection of minors who were heirs—came under equitable rather than common law jurisdiction, as did other legal matters involving accounting of assets and debts. Once a case had been filed under equity jurisdiction and accepted by a judge as properly belonging there, it remained in that status regardless of how the case developed. For example, during the course of a business partnership dissolution, the accounting might produce evidence that one partner was defrauded, but that person, because the case was already under equity jurisdiction, was not permitted to sue for damages under common law. As a result, many lawyers who wanted to avoid juries—either because they thought they wouldn't be able to understand the case[173] or (frequently) because they feared their client's action, though legally defensible, would shock jurors—did their best to get their cases accepted under equity.

These jury-avoidance schemes began to run into trouble in 1938 with the adoption of the Federal Rules of Civil Procedure which permitted parties to claim both equitable and common relief in a single suit.[174] The provision, strangely enough, was not tested in the United States Supreme Court until 1959, when, in *Beacon Theatres Inc. v. Westover*,[175] the Rules were upheld in an opinion by Justice Hugo Black,[176] establishing that when a case has both equitable and legal issues, the latter, though not the former, may be tried by a jury.[177]

Jefferson's wisdom in promoting the right to trial by jury was proven more quickly than he might have wished. Hardly was the ink dry on the Bill of Rights than his Federalist opponent, President John Adams, succeeded in getting Congress to pass the freedom-limiting Alien and Sedition Acts. Judges seemed ready to carry out their draconian provisions, but not juries. Like Zenger's jury, they refused to convict and the laws were soon repealed. (See also Chapter Nine.)

Juries, not judges, were also responsible for helping put an end to unjust laws in England. By the early 19th century, the British criminal code countenanced more than 230 hanging offenses[178]—pickpocketing included—with the result that capital convictions for minor crimes were becoming impossible to obtain. As the jurors of London put it in a letter to Parliament in 1831: ". . . the penal consequences of the offenses excite a conscientious horror in their minds, lest the rigorous performance of their duty as jurors should make them accessory to judicial murder."[179] The victims of crime sometimes felt the same way. A year earlier, the bankers of England had also addressed a petition to Parliament, asking that forgery be removed from the fatal list. Juries were regularly freeing forgers rather than send them to the hangman; the crime was becoming rampant as a result, and the bankers hoped that replacing death with a prison sentence would make jurors more prone to convict.[180]

Although there seems to be no causal connection during the same period that British juries were acting to nullify the extremes of the British criminal law, their right to hear civil cases came under attack. Until 1854, the jury was the only method employed in England to resolve common law cases, but that year Parliament passed a statute permitting civil juries only upon the consent of both parties. In 1873, trial by judge, rather than by jury, was extended[181] to cases involving "prolonged examination of documents . . . or any scientific or local investigation." In 1883, the right was further circumscribed to permit juries only in cases of libel, slander, false imprisonment, malicious prosecution, seduction, and breach of promise of marriage, although in most other civil matters the jury still had to be given when asked for.

That's how the law stood until 1918 when, in response to the World War I manpower shortage[182] (women then rarely served on juries), another act was passed which forbade juries in civil trials except for the infrequent categories enumerated in the 1883 law, plus fraud. This statute was supposed to remain in effect only until six months after the conclusion of hostilities, but in 1920 the 1918 law was reenacted, only to be repealed in 1925, which meant the 1883 rules were back in effect and juries in civil cases again became prevalent.[183] The next turnaround occurred in 1933 when Britain went back to the 1920 version, with a little twist added; now in civil fraud cases only the accused had the right to ask for a jury, although a court could always order one.[184] Finally, the Emergency Provisions of 1939, in response to the start of World War II, put a virtual end to civil juries and although the Provisions were finally repealed in 1951, by then the use of the civil jury had been virtually abandoned.[185] Statistics illustrate the history: In 1913, 55% of all civil trials were before a jury, by 1933 only 12%, and today less than a fraction of one percent.[186] (These figures do not include Northern Ireland where industrial accident cases are usually tried before a jury.[187])

Whether or not the British were wise in virtually abolishing their civil jury system—one reason was the widespread belief among judges that the system was costly[188] and jurors were incapable of assessing damages fairly—the ease with which that abrogation was accomplished points up a significant difference between the English and American systems of justice and governance.

In both nations, statutory law is deemed superior to judge-made law, and when there is a conflict between the two, statute prevails. (Parliament's victory over Charles I established that, though it took some more fighting to assure it.) However, a major reservation to that principle occurs in the United States: The American Constitution gave courts the right to decide whether or not a statute is in conflict with a primal document (either the federal or a state constitution) and to declare acts ruled "unconstitutional" void. In England, on the contrary, there is no constitution, no separation of powers. There is only, ultimately, Parliament, and its decimation of the trial by jury in civil cases, good idea or not, exhibits the manner in which any civil right can be abolished—without appeal—whenever the power of the legislature is absolute.

As this analysis suggests, the right to trial by jury in the United States is not sacrosanct either. Repeal of the Sixth and Seventh Amendments is theoretically possible, and it may be that individual state legislatures could remove the right to jury in civil cases through revisions of their constitutions without running into problems with the Seventh Amendment. (In other words, juries would still be permitted in federal cases but not in state courts where the right had been repealed.)

Nevertheless, despite what could be done theoretically, the stature given the civil jury through the Seventh Amendment of the federal constitution provides it with a potent basis in law and not merely in custom, as was true in England. In the American system the judiciary is an independent branch, with the jury under its aegis, and thus if the right to civil jury is to be restricted or eliminated here, it is highly likely to occur through the courts, where legal principles are enunciated and constitutions interpreted, not through legislative action as in England. Looked at that way, the continuation of the public's only direct say in the working of its justice system is less in the hands of its elected representatives than of its judges, against whose possible authoritarian excesses[189] the jury stands as a safeguard.

Some limitations on the right to jury in the United States in addition to those already noted have occurred, notably beginning in the early 1970s, following the accession of Warren Burger to the post of Chief Justice of the Supreme Court. In the criminal arena, in 1971, that body determined that juveniles had no right to jury trial under the Sixth Amendment even though they were charged with the same crimes as adults.[190] In 1973, in *Alexander v. Virginia*, the Supreme Court ruled that jury trial was not required in cases involving the "community standards" test for determining obscenity, an apparently logical non sequitur since it would seem that jurors from the community would be the only proper body to determine such standards, assuming they can ever be determined.[191] In a 1973 case, *Muniz v. Hoffman*, the Burger court appears to be saying that a corporate defendant is not permitted a jury when the only sentence that can be imposed is a fine.[192]

Limitation on the right to jury in some civil cases was upheld by the Supreme Court in 1977 in *Atlas v. Occupational Safety and Health Review Commission* (OSHA). This case involved federal legislation that permitted the government to investigate workplaces for the purpose of discovering hazardous conditions and to impose fines to force their remedy. The Supreme Court decision held that in public-rights cases—in this instance, the right to safe working conditions—no jury was to be permitted when Congress decided on an administrative fact-finding body[193] as the exclusive dispute-resolution forum, as it did in the OSHA legislation. The jury right, however, continued to be available to private individuals who alleged injury from the hazards.[194]

Removal of the right to jury in civil cases involving complex legal and fact issues has also been urged in many quarters, an issue that will be discussed separately in Chapter Eight.

Although from the jury's history we learn why it came into existence and the purposes it is supposed to serve, from such chronicling we do not learn, save by inference, how it is perceived and employed by the practitioners of today's American justice system. Chapter Two describes how that system operates and the jury's role as one decision-making device within it.

Chapter 2

Justice, Juries, Choice & Chance

One way to think of the American justice system is as a construct with a series of functions that occur in a dual fashion. It has two sets of courts, federal and state, which hear two kinds of cases, civil and criminal. The civil ones are divided into those of equity and those of law, the criminal into those of felonies and misdemeanors. Trial decisions can also be derived in two ways, either by a jury or by a judge in a so-called bench trial. There are even two kinds of juries, *grand* to issue indictments, and *petit* or trial juries which are the subject of this book.

The duality can further be perceived in the enforcement and persuasion arms of the system. As persuader, the courts have available two modes, mediation and arbitration, used to keep civil cases out of the enforcing courtroom. (See also Chapter Five.) As enforcer, the courts have in criminal cases police to make arrests, trials, and judges who can sentence the convicted either to probation or prison. The prison system simultaneously enforces, by locking people in cells, and tries to persuade them, by offering parole to those who make life easier for the enforcers by obeying their rules.

Duality also exists in the cross-checking protocols that have been developed. The police can arrest, but rules exist to protect the rights of the accused. The trial courts dispose, but the appeals courts can reverse the disposition (save for a ''not guilty'' finding in a criminal case).[1]

In the world outside the justice system each day events occur which could thrust the system's machinery into action. Whether they will or not depends largely on two factors, those of choice and of chance.

I

Turning to the role choice and chance play in crime first, currently approximately 220 million incidents occur in the United States, or about one per person,[2] in which the individual recognized that he or she was the victim of a crime. Of each 100 victims, however, only 37 reported their misfortune to the police.[3] Non-reporting occurs for many reasons: the belief that the incident wasn't important enough (typical of minor thefts); that nothing could be done about it (no way to catch the perpetrator); it was a personal matter (e.g., domestic violence); and concern about reprisal (especially prevalent in rape cases).[4] The "not important enough to report" category frequently masks an underlying worry by the victim that if someone is arrested, the result will be repeated court appearances that may be more costly for the victim, in terms of lost wages, than was the crime itself.

As this description suggests, the nation's crime statistics (the number of reported crimes) are the product of choice and chance. We have, for instance, Shopkeeper A who will always choose to report a theft, Shopkeeper B who will sometimes, Shopkeeper C never, and so on. Consequently, the criminal who by chance only steals from Shopkeeper C keeps the (known) crime rate down and himself out of prison. Even those who steal from Shopkeepers A and B have an excellent chance they won't be caught, either. In a typical year, only about 19%[5] of all victim-reported crimes result in an arrest.

In addition to the victim-reported crimes, we have those that become known through police action that is unsolicited by the public. Arrests for victimless offenses—prostitution, vagrancy, gambling, public drunkenness, drug usage—are almost invariably police-initiated, although those for almost any felony or misdemeanor can be.

Of the approximately 11 million arrests that occur each year, about half are of the police-discovered variety, and for these choice and chance can also play a role. It is a matter of chance, for example, that a patrol car goes by at the precise moment that a burglar attempts to break into a house; a minute earlier or later and he would not have been apprehended. Choice plays its role when the police decide which laws they will enforce and which not. Thus, today the prostitute plies her trade free of interference; tomorrow, because of a shift in policy, she is arrested. A numbers writer may find himself arrested three times in one month and not once in three years, even though the frequency of his illegal activity never varies.

Choice and chance can also determine which kinds of offenders are most likely to be arrested. Juvenile caseworkers have reported[6] that gang leaders, who are usually the brightest members, choose their duller and less experienced followers to carry out crimes in which the chance of getting caught is great. Along the same line, as any defense attorney will confirm, stupidity is the curse of the criminal classes; those who get arrested, and especially those who get arrested repeatedly, are those who carry out their crimes with a maximum lack of intelligence and planning. Their chances of getting before a judge are quite good.

Although it is highly likely that anyone who repeatedly commits crimes will eventually be caught—and for the least cunning criminal and most obvious crime, caught frequently—it is apparent, from the choice and chance factors, that the success rate per crime is quite high. There is no precise way of knowing how high; for example, of every hundred people who *could* be arrested for drunk driving, how many are? how many drug dealers? how many numbers writers? prostitutes? and so on. But if the non-victim-reported apprehension rate is roughly the same as for those incidents that are reported to police (i.e., 19% apprehended of the 37% reported), then our ballpark figure is seven arrests for each 100 commissions.

Relatively few of those who are apprehended will ever have their cases tried before either a judge or a jury. At the outset, one sizable deduction must be made from their numbers: juveniles. Though the national statistics are not entirely reliable, somewhere around 25% of all arrests in the United States each year are of youths under the age of 18.[7] A tiny handful of them will be certified for trial as adult; the majority of the remainder will have their cases "adjusted" (i.e., dismissed) by a professional other than a judge, with the rest receiving an "adjudication" hearing—not a trial—before a judge. (Its average length is less than five minutes.[8]) Subtracting the juveniles, we are now left with about five of our original seven eligible for a real trial.

Not all of them get there either. In many cases, the charge is dropped. Among the reasons: lack of evidence to convict; unavailability of witnesses; an illegal arrest; and a very large category known as prosecutorial discretion. Under that rubric, we would have cases that are *nol-prossed* (prosecution dropped) because they involve very minor offenses—turnstile jumping, loitering, etc.—and those in which the arrested person has never been in trouble before and is offered a pretrial probation period after which, if he or she keeps out of trouble, the charge is dropped. Based on a study of 15 states, the dismissal rate is about 25%,[9] although perhaps double that in a number of our major cities,[10] where many minor and doubtful cases are diverted from the system solely to keep the backlog manageable. Using the 15-state figure, we find, therefore, that after dismissals we have about four prospects for trial from our original 100 criminal incidents. (We are not even considering here the fact that for some incidents more than one person is arrested, so that our four prospects often represent fewer than four crimes.)

The majority of the four—51% to 60% by various estimates[11]—will plead guilty,[12] which means they don't go to trial but, rather, appear before a judge who accepts the plea and pronounces sentence. That leaves about two of the alleged perpetrators—the police don't always get the right person—who ever find themselves at trial.

Despite these reductions, the number of trials annually is still quite considerable, although again we have no firm statistics. One source[13] estimates 300,000 a year, without differentiating between criminal and civil. (The reasons why our statistics are so unsatisfactory will be discussed in Chapter Six, but the basic cause is that no two states seem to keep their figures the same way.) A federal government study doesn't offer specific numbers, but its tables can be interpreted as meaning 300,000 criminal trials alone each year, and probably more.[14]

Of the two kinds of crimes, felonies are about five times as likely to reach trial as are misdemeanors,[15] and also more likely to be tried by a jury than a judge. Juries hear about 60% of all felony cases in state courts and 57% of those tried in federal court.[16] The vast majority of all arrests, however, are for misdemeanors, about three-quarters of the federal caseload[17] and more than 90% of those that reach state courts.[18] Less than 1% of all misdemeanors in federal court are heard by a jury[19] and not much more than that in state court, based on the sketchy figures available.[20]

Ordinarily, in theory anyway, the defendant chooses whether his case—and more than 80% of the time the defendant is a "he"[21]—will be decided by a judge or a jury, although in some jurisdictions the prosecutor may demand a jury even when the defendant doesn't want one. In the real world, however, the defendant rarely makes the choice; it is made for him by his attorney.

Considering the raw statistics only, it would seem a lawyer should always opt for a jury trial, since (based on 1978 data) judges convict 78% of the time and juries only 65%. The picture changes dramatically, however, when the defendant is accused of a felony. In those cases, juries convict in 79% of the cases and judges 58%. For misdemeanors, the figures are almost directly the opposite, with judges convicting at a 79% rate and jurors 54%.[22] (Even though jury trials in misdemeanor cases make up little more than 1% of the total, they have a statistical impact because of the huge size of the misdemeanor category.)

No studies have been done to explain these startling differences in conviction rates. However, a few hypotheses can be offered. It may well be, as has been suggested,[23] that in some minor cases—a fistfight between neighbors or a bar serving an underage soldier—juries consider the offense too trivial to burden someone with a criminal record over it. The higher percentage of judge convictions in misdemeanor cases may be the product of the wholesale nature of the proceedings, in which the typical judge will hear 20 or more cases in a day at an average of about 15 minutes each, with the arresting officer's word usually treated as Gospel, reasonable doubt a virtually forgotten concept, and "justice" created by finding virtually everyone guilty but sending virtually no one to prison. When we turn to felonies a different dynamic is involved, emanating from a choice made of necessity by the defense lawyer. Should the lawyer be convinced, based on the facts of the case, that a judge would undoubtedly convict, then the jury is chosen as the only means of giving the client a chance for acquittal.[24] As a consequence, juries, for felonies anyway, hear more cases than do judges in which the likelihood of conviction is overwhelming, and apparently they respond accordingly.

However, there can be times when, even though the evidence is overwhelming against the defendant, his lawyer will choose to have a bench trial. Typically, this happens when the case contains technical legal issues in the defendant's favor that a judge can't ignore but a jury, considering only the evidence, will. The reverse can occur when there is a sympathetic defendant, such as an abused woman who has slain her brutal spouse, whom a jury may acquit but a judge, bound to apply the laws governing homicide, cannot. Very often, the lawyer, if not the defendant, knows that no matter what happens the defendant is going to be found guilty, so that the choice then becomes in which forum, judge or jury, is the *lower* degree of guilt likely to be reached. In such a case, if the judge is known as a lenient sentencer, the chances are, regardless of any other factors, it will become a bench trial; if the judge is known as pro-prosecution and a stern sentencer (the two go together), then almost certainly the jury will be chosen.

Not all choices between bench and jury trial, however, rise from the lawyer's strategic speculations. The lawyer may also be responding to pressures and choices applied by the justice system itself. It comes about in this way. Courts generally want to keep the number of criminal jury trials to a minimum because of the amount of time they consume. (The average criminal bench trial requires 45 minutes to an hour;[25] selecting a jury can take a day by itself even in a routine felony case.) When the number of jury trials escalates, the time-consumption presumably causes the backlog to rise, increasing the risk that some defendants, including dangerous ones, may go free because they were denied their right to a speedy trial. Consequently, in many jurisdictions—and particularly in big cities with their heavy load of street crimes—the courts make it attractive for defense lawyers not to ask for juries by assigning judges with reputations for leniency to many of the criminal courtrooms.

Jury trials are also discouraged in another way. About 70% of all individuals arrested each year are too poor to be able to hire a lawyer, so their counsel is appointed by, and paid by, the court system. The fees for this work are wretched by lawyers' terms; $15 an hour and a maximum of $500 for most cases would not be uncommon, regardless of how much time the lawyer spends in preparing and trying the case. Although the pay would cause few lawyers to reject a jury trial when they felt it was clearly the only way to go, the remuneration system can cause them to veer toward bench trials, since jury trials, especially a series of them, are a losing proposition for lawyers financially. However, in most jurisdictions the large majority of indigent defendants are represented not by court-appointed lawyers but by salaried members of a taxpayer agency set up for that purpose. Although the attorneys who work for these agencies get paid the same amount whether they try their cases before a jury or a judge, the tendency again for them will be toward bench trials. This occurs in part, because of the time-demands on limited staff caused by jury trials and—at least in some places—because of an implicit understanding that the defender association, as a public agency, should not slow the orderly process of justice (and increase its cost) by demanding too many juries.

II

Well over a hundred million incidents occur each year in the United States that could lead to a civil action. To begin with, each of the 45 million annual reportable crimes might lead to a civil action, since every criminal offense has its civil counterpart. The robber can be sued for assault, the burglar for trespass, and so on. Civil suits of this kind are rare—not many people are keen on trying to collect a judgment from a thug—although, in some situations, both criminal and civil actions are taken, or a civil rather than a criminal. Fraud cases provide one example.

Civil actions, however, don't ordinarily coincide with the world of crime. Most instances of property damage (a fender-bender, for example) do not involve crimes and neither do most injuries unintentionally, if perhaps carelessly, inflicted; cases based on these allegedly negligent actions are called torts. The non-tort cases run a vast gamut, ranging from disputes arising from divorce proceedings—perhaps the largest single category[26]—to those multimillion-dollar affairs in which high-powered corporations are pitted against one another.

In terms of who sues and who gets sued, almost all civil cases fall into one of the following groups: individuals suing individuals (anything from an injury to a bad debt); individuals suing businesses or institutions (such as a hospital for malpractice) or being sued by them (e.g., attempts to collect unpaid student loans); businesses suing businesses; businesses or individuals suing or being sued by government agencies (the latter again usually collection cases); and legal actions by groups, almost always against government or business (typically civil rights or environmental-protection cases). In the overwhelming number of suits, the plaintiff is acting independently, although occasionally parties with like demands or like injuries join together as a class.

From a study published in 1983 by the Civil Litigation Research Project (CLRP) of the University of Wisconsin Law School,[27] a picture emerges of the frequency with which dispute-situations lead to some kind of civil court action when the aggrieved party is an individual.

The CLRP found that 71.8% of those who believed they had a legally contestable civil grievance registered a complaint—even if they did nothing else—with the party they believed caused the situation. A number of reasons suggest themselves for non-action: the incident was so minor it did not seem worthwhile doing anything; fear of getting involved in the legal system; the injuring party had no assets or insurance (was suit-proof); or the injured party was worried about the consequences of taking action (e.g., the employee who risks losing a job if entering suit against his or her employer).

Of the 71.8% who notified someone of a grievance, 63% saw the merit of their grievance disputed by the allegedly offending party, according to the study.[28] Therefore, out of 100 instances in which there could have been a dispute in only 45 of them did one actually occur, i.e., 63% of 71.8%. (We are not considering here all those instances in which there might have been grounds for civil action but in which none was taken because the putative plaintiffs didn't know they had a legal right to do so.) Looking at the same figures another way, we see that 37% of the time (100% minus 63%), the dispute, once lodged, somehow got resolved with no further steps taken. Perhaps there was a satisfactory explanation, perhaps a palliative action was taken (e.g., the landlord fixed the pipe and the tenant paid the rent that had been held back), perhaps a payment was made to smooth matters over, or, again, the aggrieved party simply decided to do nothing further for whatever reason.

Of those 45% of the cases in which the dispute isn't resolved after being brought to someone's attention, only 11.2% of them, according to the CLRP study, eventually lead to the filing of a formal legal action of some kind.[29] Some of the dropouts can be explained for the same causes we have just mentioned; however, it is at this point—the dispute lodged and nothing done about it—that insurance companies may enter the picture. This most commonly occurs in injury and property damage cases when the prospective defendant informs the insurer of the "claim," as it is now called. The insurance company's adjuster negotiates with the claimant, the matter concluding if the claimant accepts a sum of money in return for a signed agreement not to sue. The claimant, by then, may or may not have engaged the services of a lawyer, and ordinarily gets more money if he or she has.

When a legal filing in a civil matter occurs, it can take the form of a lawsuit (which could be tried by a jury) or an action in equity (which can't be, as we saw in Chapter One, unless it also has a lawsuit component). Based on the Rand Corporation study of jury trials in Chicago, about 25% of all defendants in cases brought by individuals are business firms, 10% hospitals or nonprofit organizations, the remainder private parties; the overwhelming number of defendants in each category are represented by insurance companies.[30] (It is also common for the plaintiff to be an insurance company seeking reimbursement from a defendant insurer for a claim it has already paid to one of its customers.[31])

After filing, nothing further might happen if the claimant—now formally known as the plaintiff—decides to drop the matter, or has it dropped against his or her wishes when a judge decides no legal cause for an action has been established. Suits can also be lost before trial when the defendant proves to a judge's satisfaction that the action wasn't filed before the running of the statute of limitations. (The deadline varies from jurisdiction to jurisdiction and by type of claim, but usually the plaintiff has one to two years to act from the time he or she knew or should have known—that's the tricky part—of the grievance.) Of the injury suits that don't fall by the wayside for reasons such as these, somewhere between 85% and 95% are settled by a payment from the defense. Included in this figure would be settlements arrive at by court-administered arbitration and mediation programs, either directly or because the figure suggested by the referee becomes the basis for the eventual agreement.

Cases not likely to be settled include those initiated or supported by public-interest groups in which money is not the issue. The school desegregation case, *Brown v. Board of Education* (1954), would be an example from that category. Settlements occasionally are also refused, even generous ones, when the plaintiff has been so outraged by the event that nothing will do but to get the defendant into court, preferably before a jury and have the wrongdoing publicly exposed.

In a civil case, either side can demand a jury, and the reasons for selecting one rather than a bench trial are generally similar to those for criminal cases, i.e., the legal facts of the case, the kind of person involved, beliefs about the judge's predilections. (For a further discussion of the important role played by the litigants' views of the judge, see Chapter Seven.)

Principally because of settlements, but also because of the number of cases that are lost along the way for the other reasons we have given, the same shrinkage, through choice and chance, occurs in civil cases as in criminal, with about 1 to 2% likely to be heard by a jury.[32] Although we have a good idea how many civil trials are begun each year—a subject that will be discussed in Chapter Six—we do not know how many are finished either in state or federal court. The likelihood, however, is that a substantial majority, whether tried before a judge or a jury, don't reach verdict, since settlement negotiations between the two sides ordinarily continue throughout the trial, which is aborted if an agreement is reached.

The availability of the jury in most civil cases plays a major role in reducing the number of suits that go to trial. The reason lies in the belief held by lawyers and by insurance companies that juries are more unpredictable than judges; consequently, when one side or the other files a formal demand for a jury, it is acting to force the opposition to negotiate seriously, even though the side asking for the jury may want to avoid its uncertainty, too. At times, the jury-demand, as a settlement stratagem, acts to the benefit of the plaintiff: Since juries are also widely believed to be more generous on the whole than judges, the defense might make a higher offer than it would were there no juries. On other occasions, the defense can use its jury right as a bargaining tool. For instance, the defense may believe the plaintiff is someone a jury is not likely to believe or else the defendant belongs to a group—doctors in malpractice cases would be one example—that historically has fared well before juries. Should the plaintiff's counsel reach the same conclusion, the case again may be settled, but now for a small rather than a large amount. (The defendant insurer, in the vast majority of cases, will make at least a token settlement offer, no matter how confident it is of the verdict, simply to avoid the expense of trial and the risk that the unpredictable jury might disagree with its analysis of the case.)

The values that the jury has for lawyers and their clients, in both civil and criminal cases, are well-perceived by those who administer the justice system, and they see special advantages for themselves from it as well. To judges, from the Middle Ages onward,[33] one of the great attractions of the jury has been that it acts as a lightning rod[34] to protect them from public outcries. An example of that phenomenon occurred in the trial of John Hinckley, charged with attempting to assassinate President Reagan; a jury found Hinckley not guilty by reason of insanity, and although the jurors were the subject of intense criticism from many quarters for that verdict, they were soon able to fade back into anonymity, while if the judge had come to the same decision, quite conceivably the only proper one, he very likely would have been hounded from the bench. Somewhat analogously, it is widely stated by those within the justice system that juries make the law more acceptable,[35] their availability giving the public a belief that it has an input into a system that otherwise could be considered arrogant and arcane due to its domination by a hierarchical legal priesthood.[36] (The public participation argument is also used as a reason for electing judges rather than appointing them.) Further, the jury is seen by some within the system—including many legal scholars and judges[37]—as having a liberating effect upon the law in that a jury when rendering a verdict can ignore a law it considers stupid or counterproductive, while a judge, who may feel the same way, has no choice but to enforce that law. (See also Chapter Nine.) As one judge has observed, juries assure that people get the justice they want, not what the experts want for them.[38]

III

Because the operation of the justice system and the jury within it is largely a response to the random influence of choice and chance, the law itself necessarily will always be incomplete. Issues constantly lap at it that have not yet been decided and may never be decided (or, once decided, re-decided as when *Brown v. Board of Education* reversed a Supreme Court decision of a half-century earlier which had permitted segregated schools). Rare is the trial lawyer who doesn't have a story to tell of a case involving a new constitutional or legal issue that never got to trial, not infrequently because the other side dropped the case precisely because it feared the consequences of the issue being decided. In civil cases, settlement can be the great intervenor that ends the great challenge; the plaintiff may be interested in principle but, in the end, decides principal is more important.

As a result, although the amount of law that has been laid down is probably beyond calculation—as any visitor to a law library, viewing books thick with nothing but decisions, will attest—the law that hasn't been enumerated may be more vast still, so that each case, no matter how mundane it appears on the surface, can be fraught with both the peril and the excitement that somehow out of it will pop the previously undecided issue, or the refinement (with a twist) of the issue that everyone had thought was resolved once and for all. Going to law is a chancy business.

Should the case arrive before a jury, the sense of choice and chance is magnified. A litigant will rightly wonder: Which of these strangers shall I choose? Which will improve my chances that my cause will be sympathetically heard? Those issues of choice and chance are the subjects of the next two chapters.

Chapter 3
Trial By Jury

Persons who serve on a jury find they undergo two distinct stages of participation. The first, during which they are primarily acted upon rather than active themselves, begins with the day they receive their jury summons and concludes when the judge gives them their instructions at the end of the trial. They then enter into their active stage, which begins with their secret deliberations and finishes with the reading of their verdict. This chapter will be concerned with the events of the first stage; Chapter Four will focus on the second. (Various findings of the Pound study are summarized in these Chapters. For details and a statistical analysis, see Addendum beginning page 283).

I

The Summons to Jury Duty. A jury is supposed to be composed of a representative cross section of the people who live in the community in which the trial is held. If 10% of the population is black, so should be 10% of the jurors; if 52% female, so that many of the jurors; if 50% of the population consists of blue-collar families, it would be similarly unrepresentative to have juries consisting 90% of white-collar workers, and so on. But even if we assume representativeness is possible theoretically, the methods used for selecting those who serve have virtually eliminated its occurrence.

In some jurisdictions, deliberate efforts have been made to avoid the cross section. Although it has been illegal to overtly exclude blacks from juries since 1880,[1] in the south for many years they were never or rarely called for duty, through the employment of a number of expediencies,[2] the most common of which was to limit jury lists to registered voters at a time when blacks weren't permitted to vote. In a 1975 Georgia case, a jury commissioner explained the exclusionary policy this way: "Well, you just can't put the mules in with the horses, can you?"[3]

Overt discrimination in jury selection, however, has never been limited to the south nor to blacks. In some places, including New York City[4] until relatively recent years, juror names were recommended to the court by individuals of standing in the community, the so-called "Key Man" list,[5] eliminating all those who might not move in such rarefied orbits. In a district in California, prospective jurors were required to take an intelligence test which they automatically failed if they didn't complete it in 10 minutes. As a result, 14.5% of jurors from upper income brackets and 81% of ghetto residents were eliminated. That law was declared unconstitutional in 1968[6] as have similar ones elsewhere;[7] however, elimination of jurors on the basis of lack of education is apparently permissible.[8]

Still empaneled in a few jurisdictions are "special" juries for certain kinds of complex cases; their members tend to be upper-middle-class, well-educated white males.[9] In some districts, prospective jurors are sent questionnaires and not called for service if they don't respond. A 1974 study in Chicago, for example, showed that 23% of those who were sent the questionnaire by the state courts didn't return it, including 42% of those living in predominantly black areas. In the same district, only 2% of prospective jurors for federal court cases didn't answer, because that system followed up on those who didn't reply to the first notice.[10]

The voter list is the most commonly-used mechanism for assembling citizens for jury duty, though this has been declared illegal in California.[11] Its employment furthers non-representativeness:[12] Studies estimate that voter lists automatically exclude about one-third of the adult population, tipping the prospective juror pool toward the elderly, toward the relatively affluent, toward the self-employed and government workers, and away from minorities,[13] including women, blacks, and Hispanics.[14] To avoid this distortion, the federal courts and some states[15] have replaced voter rolls with the telephone book or supplemented it with other lists, including public utility customers, all people who hold drivers' licenses, and those on welfare.[16]

Regardless of how broad-based a prospective juror panel becomes, true representativeness cannot be obtained because of exemptions. Some are occupational (e.g., police officers for criminal cases) while others are given for reasons of health and—probably the largest category—to those for whom jury duty would entail a personal or financial hardship.[17]

Exemptions from jury duty in federal court have been sharply restricted[18] since 1978 when the Jury System Improvement Act was passed. In addition to the stick of toughened regulations, the Act also offered the carrot of increased compensation and travel allowances and forbade employers from firing jurors or causing them to lose seniority as a result of their service.[19]

In state courts, the exemption system varies so much from jurisdiction to jurisdiction and is so frequently the consequence of political influence—in many places, the best way to get a "hardship" exemption is through a call from one's ward leader—that no meaningful general statements about its influence on the representativeness of the pool can be made.

When, one way or another, the exemption process is completed, those who remain in the pool will eventually be called to the courthouse where it is possible they will be required to serve on juries for a full term, which could be a matter of weeks or months. This lengthy service is much less common now than it used to be. By 1984, 39 states[20] had adopted the "one day/one trial" rule. Although the details of its operation vary a bit from place to place, under this system the prospective jurors report for one day and if they aren't selected, they are excused; if they are chosen, that jury is the only one on which they are required to serve.

Voir Dire.   During the voir dire, lawyers on both sides are permitted to remove from the panel of prospective jurors, known as a venire (literally, "you are called to come"), any they think may be biased. The challenges issued are of two kinds: *peremptory,* for which a lawyer doesn't have to give a reason, and *cause,* for which a basis must be stated and approved by the judge. A ground for a cause challenge, for example, would be an admission by a venireman that he or she has personal knowledge of one of the parties in the case or displays prejudice of some sort. A cause challenge, however, cannot be based solely on a venireman's statement that he or she has heard about the case or even has formed an opinion of it; rather, if the venireman asserts that he or she can rise above any pre-views of the case and decide it impartially,[21] and the judge believes the assertion, such a person can be accepted as a juror. (To eliminate all those who had an awareness of an especially notorious case—such as the Hinckley attempted assassination of President Reagan—would be virtually to guarantee a jury of the utterly ignorant and mentally incompetent, a view expressed by the United States Supreme Court in *U.S. v. Haldeman* [1977].[22]) A lawyer, however, who wishes to do so, can eliminate knowledgeable and opinion-holding prospective jurors through peremptory challenges. But that effort will go only so far, since the number of them, unlike that of the cause challenges, is always limited—perhaps as few as six to a side—in order to prevent a party that wants to avoid trial from using the peremptories to make jury selection impossible.

Though no reason need be given for them, peremptory challenges have themselves frequently been challenged by the loser in a case on the ground that they were prompted by ethnic or gender bias. A number of these appeals have reached the United States Supreme Court,[23] most often in criminal cases, with the issue raised by defendants. The decisions resulting from them provide a precedential framework when similar issues arise in the civil sphere.

In *Swain v. Alabama* (1965)[24] the Supreme Court showed little sensitivity to the ethnic problem when it ruled that prosecutors had the right to strike blacks from juries unless it happened in virtually all the cases in the district,[25] despite the West Virginia case in 1880 and a 1940 one in Texas which forbade exclusion of blacks from indicting grand juries.[26] In 1975, in *Taylor v. Louisiana*, the issue went somewhat differently when the Court held that the pool from which the jurors were chosen had to be representative of the population.[27] Similarly, from a civil case,[28] and other later rulings, we learn that a venire which excludes members of a group can be quashed, but that rule does not apply to an individual jury. Four years after Taylor, in *Duren v. Missouri* (1979), the Supreme Court now held that for a defendant to show venire bias, it must be proven that (1) the group that was excluded was a distinctive group (such as blacks); (2) that the number of representatives of the group in the venire was not fair in terms of its presence in the community;

(3) that the exclusion of the members occurred systematically during the selection process.[29]

By 1986, at least five states—California, Delaware, Florida, Massachusetts, and New Mexico—had ignored the Supreme Court's tapdancing on the subject and had passed blanket rules that forbade challenges based on ethnicity. In April 1986, in *Batson v. Kentucky*, the Supreme Court belatedly joined with those states by overturning *Swain* and ruling that use of peremptory challenges to remove blacks from any single jury was unconstitutional, though the decision left unclear how courts were to monitor the new rule or the remedy that was to be applied if a judge decided racism was involved.[30]

An early Supreme Court decision on gender occurred in 1941 in *Glasser v. U.S.* in which it was held that excluding all women, except members of the League of Women Voters, from federal jury lists was *not* unconstitutional.[31] But 34 years later, in *Taylor v. Louisiana*, the Court stated that women generally cannot be kept off juries because "a flavor, a distinct quality is lost if either sex is excluded . . . [making] the jury less representative of the community."[32] (At that time in Louisiana, a woman was called for jury duty only if she filed written notice of her desire to serve.[33]) *Duren* also delved into women on juries, holding that an "appropriately tailored" exemption for women was permissible in order to safeguard "the important role played by women in home and family life," but that the "preclusive domestic responsibilities of some women is insufficient justification for their disproportionate exclusion" from juries.[34] That language seems capable of encompassing almost every possible interpretation.

Whatever its legal standing, racism, if not gender bias, is still very much a part of our court system, particularly in criminal cases,[35] and particularly on the part of prosecutors. A study published in 1977[36] discovered that the primary defined reason for prosecutors removing a prospective juror from a panel was because he or she was black (10.9% of the total), whereas not a single venireman was challenged by a prosecutor because he or she was white. No veniremen were removed by criminal defense lawyers because they were black, and only 2.2% of whites were; a 1986 study in Dallas, Texas, reached the same results.[37] The challenging of black veniremen by prosecutors may have its most salient—and deadly—effect in capital cases; prosecutors are especially eager to get rid of them there since blacks, as a whole, are more opposed to the death penalty than are whites. The result is that so-called "death-qualified" juries tend to be particularly unrepresentative of the community, veering toward a nearly exclusive white, middle-class composition.[38]

Jurors and lawyers are not the only ones to exhibit biases. So do judges. In *The American Jury*, a southern judge is quoted as speaking of the "lack of moral sense" of blacks.[39] Still another judge, a northerner, described blacks as "cannibalistic; it is in their genes and this is proven by the way they are devouring each other."[40]

Ferreting out bias (or attempting to create it), however, is not the only purpose[41] of the voir dire. Studies show that when lawyers rather than the judge conduct it, both sides use it to try to teach the jurors about their view of the case—somewhere between 40% and 80%[42] of the time. This indoctrination aspect worries some critics, yet it is often difficult to separate it from the legitimate goal of seeking fair-minded jurors. For example, in a case in which eyewitness identification is crucial, the identified person's lawyer may want to ask prospective jurors if they haven't ever seen someone on the street they thought they knew, only later to realize it was a stranger. By so doing, the lawyer is preparing *all* the jurors for the misidentification strategy that will be used at trial; but he also has a "fairness" reason for asking, since someone who would deny ever having this very nearly universal experience might well be an undesirable member of the panel.

The voir dire also acts to introduce the prospective jurors to a social situation that is new to most of them, a rite of passage which because it takes place in a courtroom—often with a judge present—has an inherent solemnity that presumably inculcates the members with the gravity of the task they may be asked to perform.[43] For most of the veniremen, the voir dire will be their first direct engagement with the trial process, and from the questions put to them they may also gather their initial impressions of fundamental legal concepts, such as due process and reasonable doubt. We have almost no information about how veniremen feel about the voir dire process.[44]

The voir dire can be conducted several ways. All the veniremen may be questioned at once, or only the number that will ultimately be required (six, eight, ten, twelve) enter the jury box at one time, with new ones added as eliminations take place. An alternative is the so-called "struck" jury.[45] In it, after challenges for cause are completed, the panel consists of the number of jurors that will eventually be chosen plus as many more as there are peremptory challenges permitted.[46] Thus, if there are to be 12 jurors and each side is permitted seven challenges, the size of the panel will be 26, so that the jury consists of those left over when the 14 peremptory challenges have been exhausted. A number of studies, based on mathematical theories, have concluded that the struck jury system is the one most likely to produce an impartial jury[47] and it is, in any event, the system most frequently used in federal court.[48]

Occasionally, veniremen will be questioned privately, particularly in cases about which there has been widespread media coverage.[49] The private voir dire serves to avoid contamination in cases in which open questioning is likely to be prejudicial. For example, let us suppose we have a famous murder case in which newspapers have reported that the accused signed a confession, which has since been suppressed with the defendant now pleading not guilty. To question each venire member publicly about his or her knowledge of the reported confession would inform those panel members who didn't know about it and quite probably bias them against the defendant. (In some of these situations—even with private voir dire—it will be impossible to obtain an impartial jury, forcing a change of venue for the trial.)

Depending on the jurisdiction, and sometimes upon individual judges within a jurisdiction, the questioning will either be done by the opposing lawyers, by the judge, or by both the lawyers and the judge. In judge-conducted voir dire, the judge may (but doesn't have to)[50] accommodate the lawyers by asking questions they have submitted prior to voir dire. Even when they aren't permitted to do the questioning, lawyers retain their right to make eliminations through challenges.

The scope of the questioning, regardless of who is conducting it, is also determined by a court's or a judge's own rules.[51] In some places, lawyers are permitted a wide range of questions into the attitudes of veniremen, but in others the prospective jurors can only be asked if they have direct knowledge of the case, know or are related to one of the parties or some of the lawyers, or have a financial interest in the case's outcome.

Judges usually permit extensive voir dire questioning in criminal cases, apparently because a person's freedom is at stake in them. Severely limited questioning is typical of the civil case, which is, by this definition, less serious because only money is at issue. Judges who hold to that reasoning are, therefore, saying that a quadriplegic seeking redress for his or her injuries has a less important case—one less worth spending time and taxpayer money putting together a jury for—than has the shoplifter accused of petty larceny.

That limited voir dires do save time and money, there is no doubt. A federal court study revealed that judges require an average of a half hour to put a jury together when they conduct voir dire alone,[52] whereas, based on New York statistics, lawyer-conducted voir dires average 12.5 hours, some of them up to six weeks, and as long as the trial itself in 20% of the cases.[53]

Another study found the average differences less striking but still considerable: 111 minutes for lawyer-conducted and 64 for judge-conducted.[54] Time, however, can be looked at another way. Each hour the judge uses to conduct a voir dire is an hour that won't be spent trying a case in another courtroom.

Those who favor judge-conducted voir dire have another argument. As they point out, when the judge is in charge, lawyers have no opportunity to woo the veniremen, so that those who are eventually selected have few or no preconceived notions about which side is in the right.[55] Based on the Pound study, however, the "wooing" worry lacks merit. In more than half the Pound juries, the voir dire was lawyer-conducted and in these, as in the judge-conducted ones, almost to the same percentage, the overwhelming majority of jurors reported having no feelings about the merits of the case as a result of the selection questioning. In total, 88% came out of voir dire with neutral feelings about the case; 2% couldn't remember the view they might have had; 6% leaned toward the plaintiff; 4% toward the defendant.

When we consider the prime purpose of the voir dire—to root out prejudiced jurors—the evidence strongly suggests that, if anyone can do it, lawyers are generally better qualified for the task than are judges. Because judges don't know the issues of a case as well as its lawyers do, their questioning—even when it is not limited to the basic inquiries—tends to be superficial,[56] as can be inferred from the 30-minute average uncovered by the federal court study. Jurors may also tend to be intimidated by the presence of the judge and want to make a good impression on him or her, and therefore are less likely to admit to biases than when lawyers—of whom they are much less in awe—do the questioning.[57] Studies also indicate[58] that lawyers, by their willingness to ask more threatening and probing questions[59] than will judges, are more effective at rooting out biases that even the jurors didn't know they had.

Evidence favoring lawyer voir dire also comes from a study undertaken in a federal district court which, until then, had permitted only judge questioning. In the experiment, when lawyers were allowed to be in charge of the voir dire, the judges agreed that this was an improvement over the prior system in 19 cases, somewhat helpful in six, and not helpful in 11. Plaintiff lawyers and prosecutors approved lawyer voir dire, in the same experiment, by a 15 to two count, and defense attorneys by 12 to three.[60] Although the sample was a small one, the judges' approval percentage—since it involved giving up a power they had hitherto enjoyed—is significant.

If we conclude—as we should—that the lawyer-conducted voir dire is, in terms of serving the prime purpose, the preferable method, this does not mean that lawyers are always going to be more successful in discovering bias than are judges. Time limitations on interrogation, which are sometimes imposed, may not allow for the lengthy probing by the lawyers that could lead to revealing replies. Moreover, although veniremen may be less frightened of lawyers and less likely to tailor their replies to them than they would to a judge, they are, nevertheless, in a situation in which they have to answer questions posed by a stranger with other strangers listening to their replies, hardly the ambiance in which people are likely to reveal their innermost thoughts or prejudices. Lying, not so much out of malice as out of a desire to come up with an acceptable answer, can be commonplace, as when a venire member will piously assert that he or she knows absolutely nothing about the case which has been headline news for weeks.[61]

The way a lawyer poses a question can also make a revelatory answer unlikely or impossible, with those requiring a "Yes" or "No" response usually the least effective.[62] One former juror, for example, recalls that during voir dire he was asked if he had ever owned a certain make of clothes drier, to which he replied "Yes." He was not, however, asked how well the drier had performed; had he been, he would have replied it was a lemon and that he would never buy a product from that manufacturer again. Since alleged failure by the appliance was at the heart of the suit, the lawyer for the manufacturer, by not asking an open-ended question—"How did you like my company's products?"—risked allowing a biased member on the panel.[63]

The experience related by that juror raises the question of what happens when the opposing lawyers are unequal in ability. As advocates of judge-conducted voir dire point out, and most attorneys admit,[64] the real reason lawyers like to do the questioning is to get, not impartial jurors, but rather ones they think will be favorable to their side, so that if the one lawyer is much more able than the other, presumably the jury eventually selected will lean in his or her direction. On the other side, it can be argued that when lawyers are more or less equal in ability, each will cancel out the other's favorites, so that a relatively impartial jury will result—or at least a balanced one—something much less likely to occur under the superficial judge-questioning.

During the voir dire, folklore beliefs often guide the questions and the selections ultimately made by the lawyers. It sometimes seems there are as many of these beliefs as there are lawyers, but the following maxims, selected from those which have appeared in print, give a flavor of the legal legendry:

Beware of female jurors if your client is a young and attractive female,[65] although married women make good jurors for civil plaintiffs and criminal defendants.[66] If your client is the plaintiff, don't permit anyone who had been a defendant in a civil case on the jury, and by all means get rid of police officers and nurses because they have become callous to injured people from having seen too many of them.[67] Property owners should also be avoided by plaintiffs because they'll fear that a plaintiff verdict will drive up their insurance rates.[68] Avoid wage earners if your client is accused of tax fraud.[69] In criminal cases, young people with few ties to the community are better than more mature ones who hold executive positions.[70]

Irish jurors, or so it is said, will be unfair to English litigants and vice versa; Germans will be unfair to Jews and vice versa, although ordinarily members of minorities—including Jews—are good for plaintiffs, with black jurors especially good for plaintiffs in police brutality cases. However, utility workers—apparently including black ones—are bad for plaintiffs because their bosses have indoctrinated them against believing people claiming injuries.[71]

While they're at it, plaintiff lawyers should avoid (and defense lawyers seek) those who have had injuries similar to those claimed by the plaintiff because, if such jurors got small awards in their cases, they won't want to give the plaintiff any more than they got. As for jurors who have sat on two or more previous cases, it's probably a good idea all around to excuse them because they've been "to the well too often."[72]

Religion, according to the folklore, can also be a factor. Clergymen and their spouses make poor jurors because they are too opinionated.[73] Presbyterians are bad for defendants in criminal cases and plaintiffs in civil ones because they are too cold, yet all those warm-blooded Baptists are worse, but then again there are the Unitarians (if you can find one) who are just fine,[74] except all religious people should be avoided by defense lawyers in obscenity cases.[75]

In criminal cases, Dallas, Texas, prosecutors were warned in a 1963 guideline to avoid selecting "Yankees . . . unless they appear to have common sense" and "anyone who has ever lived in California."[76] In criminal trials, too, engineers, scientists, and accountants, because of their obsessive personalities, are good for defendants when the evidence is circumstantial but dreadful when there are appeals to the emotions.[77] For clients who are wealthy, get jurors who believe in material things,[78] unless your client is up on a criminal charge and the materialist has an authoritarian personality.[79] Always avoid a smiling juror.[80]

While the lawyer is keeping all this in mind during voir dire, he or she should also be alert to body language, or so the folklore says. Pupil dilation on the part of a venireman—one assumes the lawyer will be close enough to observe that—indicates deception, while crossing of arms is a defensively negative gesture.[81] Some studies also indicate that jurors who regularly pause before answering, who change their breathing patterns or their vocal pitch don't favor the lawyer asking the question and should be dismissed.[82] Criminal defense lawyers are especially well-advised to excuse a prospective juror who looks to the judge or the prosecutor for approval before answering their questions.[83]

The truly conscientious lawyer, however, doesn't wait til voir dire to begin observing the venire members. Rather, that lawyer will stealthily prowl the halls of the courthouse observing those who have been called for jury service, noting the newspapers, the books, and magazines they purchase, whenever possible eavesdropping on their conversations, thus providing the good lawyer—or so it is said—with tipoffs that can spell the difference between winning and losing.[84]

Some lawyers don't rely entirely on their own ability to spot biased jurors. Rather, when they have clients that can afford to pay the tab—$5,000 to $20,000 and up, according to one trial attorney[85]—they hire jury selection experts. These individuals first appeared on the scene as advisers to defense attorneys in cases with political implications, beginning with the Harrisburg Seven trial in 1971, the Angela Davis trial in 1972, the Daniel Ellsberg and Anthony Russo trials the same year, and—on the other side of the political ledger—the Maurice Stans-John Mitchell-Robert Vesco trial at the time of Watergate.[86] More recently, "scientific" jury selection has been associated with major civil litigation at a pre-voir dire stage. The dry-run trials organized by market research firms not only tell the clients which arguments are most likely to impress jurors but also presumably develop, based on the mock jurors' responses to the arguments, a profile of who should be sought and who avoided for the jury when the real trial comes.

More common than this approach is to hire an expert such as Margaret Covington of Houston, a lawyer with a PhD in psychology, who acts as a consultant for other lawyers in jury selection. She has written about her efforts on behalf of Richard "Racehorse" Haynes when he was acting as defense counsel for Texas millionaire T. Cullen Davis who stood accused of murder. Covington devised a full panoply of psychological and statistical techniques to draw up profiles of the kind of person who would be an ideal juror in the Davis case. For example, because the defense was a complex one, intelligent jurors were sought, just as they might be anathema, one assumes, in another case. A sophisticated attitudinal analysis of the community from which the jurors were going to be drawn was undertaken, topped by an on-site evaluation of the homes of 500 prospective jurors. Bumper stickers on cars were observed, the presence or absence of burglar bars on windows, the upkeep of lawns, and so on, with the information inevitably fed into a computer. From all this, the ideal juror became known, but, leaving nothing to chance, Covington was also present during voir dire to identify body language that she believed might reveal whether a prospect should be included or excluded. Jury selection ultimately took six weeks; Davis, who was accused of killing his 12-year-old stepdaughter, was acquitted.[87]

Despite such apparent victories, jury selection experts have received, at best, mixed rating from attorneys and will be of little use, for good or ill, when the judge controls the voir dire. Some lawyers praise them highly,[88] although at least one trial attorney dismisses them as modern "snake-oil" salesmen.[89] A federal study found that most lawyers interviewed who had used "scientific" experts expressed negative comments about their abilities, but the sample was a very small one,[90] as was that for another survey in which opinions were about evenly divided.[91] Even lawyers who have little or no faith in the "science" of the experts may find themselves hiring one, for fear that if they don't and the client loses, the client will then charge them with ineffective assistance of counsel.[92]

The siren call of the jury-selection expert, therefore, is a simple and seductive one: I'll get you the right jurors and that way you'll win your case regardless of the evidence against you. The doctrine of the preprogrammed juror is one promulgated not only by those who are in the business of selling their expertise but also by some lawyers.[93]

A more conservative version of that hypothesis, one upon which there would probably be more general agreement by attorneys, is that adept jury selection (by lawyer or by "scientific" expert) helps create a favorable trial climate for one's client but that the presentation of the evidence remains the key factor in winning or losing. The Pound study throughout strongly confirms this belief. (See especially the discussion of key trial events below.)

In attempting to evaluate the ability of lawyers (with or without expert assistance) to select "winning" jurors, we can hardly denigrate either the folklore advice or the more "scientific" sanctions that lawyers splash across the pages of the texts they publish. Such authors, after all, are successful trial attorneys; presumably they know what they are doing and even if what they say, at times, expresses a near awe-inspiring bigotry, that doesn't by itself invalidate their pronouncements. (It also doesn't necessarily mean the authors are themselves bigoted; rather, they are presumably only assessing, for their clients' sakes, bigotry they have perceived in others.)

Nevertheless, the do/don't lists engender credibility problems. Often, we don't know the origin of the reasoning. For example, when an author recommends that ethnic-Irish jurors be eliminated when one has an ethnic-English client, is that advice based on the lawyer's trial experience or is it an assumption based on his or her lay knowledge of historic antipathies between Ireland and England? The very broadness of the stereotyping also eliminates consideration of the more refined nuances of prejudice, e.g., is it not possible that some Irish (under the theory of what familiarity breeds) will be more anti-Irish than any Englishman, or that some cold Presbyterian wouldn't trust another equally icy one to tell the truth if his life depended on it, and so on? But perhaps the most hobbling credibility aspect of the do/don't lists is the lack of agreement among lawyers, not only as to the particulars—no two lists are the same—but also to the general concept. For while it is true that some very successful attorneys subscribe to do/don't lists, others equally successful hardly ever challenge a prospective juror for any reason.[94]

One academic study[95] appears to provide a measure of confirmation for the belief that adroit questioning during voir dire can affect the outcome of a case. In this study, conducted by Zeisel and Diamond, shadow juries were formed of veniremen who had been rejected by defense lawyers in a dozen criminal cases because they allegedly exhibited a pro-prosecutorial bias during the voir dire. These supposed pro-prosecution veniremen then watched the actual trials. In four of the 12, based on first ballot preferences elicited from them by the experimenters, they would have either probably or definitely convicted, while the real jurors in these cases found the defendant not guilty.[96] In three of these four trials, the judge declared that the real jury's verdict was without merit, the only instances out of the twelve cases in which that criticism was leveled. (In the fourth case in which the shadow juries disagreed with the real juries, the judge said the verdict was a tenable one for a jury to reach but one with which he disagreed.[97]) In essence, therefore, in three cases, possibly four, the judge was saying the shadow jurors were right and the real jurors wrong, indicating that the defense attorneys in those cases had won because they had succeeded in identifying and eliminating pro-prosecution jurors from the venire.

But we cannot be sure of that. In the disputed cases, there was never unanimity among the shadow jurors on the first and only polling that was taken of them[98] so that we do not know how they would have finally decided had they been exposed to one another (rather than to a professor) in the give-and-take of a deliberation debate in which their verdict would have had a real meaning.

We also lack information about the three judges involved in the experiment. We are not told, for example, whether the "without merit" assessments came from a single judge (which might indicate pro-prosecution bias on his part) or were spread among all three. Moreover, although the real jurors were interviewed by phone a month after the trial,[99] they were only asked to recall the first ballot in their cases, so that we learn nothing about their reasoning, which would have been especially helpful to know for the three "without merit" juries. Had in-depth questioning taken place, the researchers might have discovered that the non-meritorious jurors had meritorious reasons for their verdicts that didn't occur to the judge, or that their reasoning was non-meritorious but had nothing to do with their supposedly pro-defense bias (e.g., a simple misunderstanding of the evidence).

Other academic research studies of the effectiveness of voir dire questioning have come to conclusions that either contradict one another, or that provide no corroboration[100] for the selection methods espoused either by lawyers or "scientific" experts.

For example, several academic studies agree with lawyers that "authoritarian" personalities—i.e., those who tend to accept the word of any person in authority—tend to favor the prosecutor in criminal cases,[101] yet other studies have not found that to be true.[102] On demographic predictors—sex, race, educational background, occupation, and various attitudinal measuring scales—we either have the same contradictory results, or, more often, the studies (see also Chapter Four) find little or no correlation between the background of a prospective juror and his or her performance on a jury.[103]

As one study summarized it, jury research has developed "little systematic evidence that personality variables . . . provide the predictive power to detect . . . biased jurors."[104] Another study put it even more strongly when it concluded that juror verdicts could not be forecast based on the members' personal beliefs and attitudes.[105]

While it is undoubtedly true that people don't forget their prejudices just because they become jurors, events within the trial and deliberation processes act as reductive factors. The solemn oath that all jurors take to be impartial in the matter before them can hardly be without some impact on many of them.[106] Perhaps the reason why several studies, including Pound, have failed[107] to find obvious instances of prejudice during deliberations is that the biased juror does not want to express such views in front of strangers; and there is even some indication that bias can act as an anti-factor when the juror recognizes it in himself or herself and compensates by favoring the side which the bias, in prospect, would be expected to harm.[108]

It seems probable, therefore, on the issue of bias, that voir dire questioning—particularly when conducted by the lawyers—can lead to identifying overtly prejudiced jurors, and that the procedure should ordinarily catch out those who have already formed an opinion of the case. That, in itself, is no small accomplishment. However, we have no reason to think, from jury studies, that any selection system can guarantee or even make especially likely a "winning" jury.

One conclusion, however, does suggest itself from the research on jury selection, namely that *the more heterogeneous the jury's composition, the greater the likelihood of rich and unbiased performance*,[109] largely and apparently due to the great variety of life-experiences and points-of-view that will come into play from such a body when the time for deliberation arrives.

II

Efforts to prevent bias from seeping into the jury continue throughout the trial itself. During the day, when not in the jury box, the members are accompanied by a court officer to protect them from outside influence; they are required to report anyone who speaks to them or to one of their fellow jurors. They are supposed to avoid exposure to published or broadcast accounts of the case they are trying, and each day of the trial are told by the judge not to discuss the testimony amongst themselves or with anyone else. In the rare sensational case, they may be sequestered in a hotel under guard to make sure no news of the trial reaches them.

Each of these means to keep the jury germ-free is susceptible to some measure of policing by court officials or the jurors themselves. However, one order they receive, at the beginning of the trial and at the end of each day's session, is not open to control and it may be the most important of all; the instruction to avoid drawing any conclusions in their own minds about anything they hear until all the evidence has been presented. We have no way of knowing the exact frequency with which jurors try to obey that injunction—those who didn't would be hardly likely to admit it—but in theory it would be surprising if the *attempted* compliance rate were not high. By and large, jurors know, probably mostly from their exposure to television and the movies, that trials are supposed to have a Rashomon-like quality, so that it is likely they will expect that a version of the story told by a witness from one side will later be countered by a witness from the other, or else battered down through clever cross-examination. The judge's instruction on open-mindedness, therefore, will appear to jurors a reasonable one. Moreover, since our studies suggest that jurors generally attempt to follow all other instructions the judge gives them, it seems hardly likely they would not wish to comply with this one.

Nevertheless, by the beginning of deliberations, 96% of the jurors, according to Pound, have reached a verdict preference which about half the time was described by them as "leaning" rather than "definite." (Jurors were given only these choices.) Unless there is some marvelous synapse period for judgment that occurs between the close of trial and the beginning of deliberations (which no researcher has yet discovered), it would therefore appear that the jurors form in-trial opinions—though not necessarily conclusions—even when they attempt not to do so. That this occurs does not invalidate the open-mindedness instruction. On the contrary, the instruction militates, by its nature, against the formation of early, intransigently-held views of the kind that no later testimony will sway, and may also have the unintended but salutary effect, by its constant repetition, of making jurors more willing than they might otherwise be to listen to the opinions of others during deliberations. The Pound findings inferentially confirm this hypothesis. (See *Jury Discussions* and *Changes in Verdict Preference* sections in Chapter Four.)

Lawyers, understandably, are eager to learn how the jurors' pre-deliberation views are formed, so that they can tailor the presentation of their cases to them accordingly. As a consequence, the many textbooks that have been published by lawyers describing jury trial tactics have found an eager audience from among their peers.[110] Whether the authors of these texts are aware of it or not, the principles they enunciate are, for the most part, consonant with approaches considered sound psychologically by those who purport to be expert in opinion-molding techniques generally. For example, from the attorney-authors we learn that witnesses who talk too much aren't persuasive to jurors; that those who narrate their stories with few interruptions are more likely to be believed and remembered than those who are constantly interrupted; that those who overdramatize their stories may be viewed as insincere; that angry witnesses make a poor impression.[111] Occasionally, however, the advice reaches the stereotyping level that we found prevalent in the folklore recommendations for selecting jurors, as when authors F. Lee Bailey and Henry Rothblatt expound on the problems of presenting female witnesses: "Women, like children," they note, "are prone to exaggeration."[112]

In the textbooks, lawyers are also often given advice about their own demeanor, usually stated in absolutes. A favorite: Keep a poker face at all times.[113] Similar helpful instructions are provided for framing questions, e.g., never ask one to which you don't already know the answer. Although this last homily has nothing specifically to do with either impressing or alienating jurors—the unexpected answer can ruin a case just as easily in a bench trial—it points up the problem inherent in this kind of laundry-list approach. The fact is that asking a question to which the answer is unknown sometimes produces beneficial results, and may be the only intelligent approach an advocate can take. For example, a criminal defense lawyer recalls a case[114] in which her client was accused of murder and an expert witness for the prosecution testified that the trajectory of the fatal bullet was consonant with an assailant of her client's considerable height. On cross-examination, having no idea how the witness would respond, but aware how damaging his testimony would be if unchallenged, the lawyer asked him whether the bullet could have been fired by someone a little shorter than her client. To her relief, the witness said that was "possible." Encouraged, the lawyer pressed ahead, inch by receding inch, until the expert finally admitted that the shooter could have been anyone "taller than a midget."

In summary, the legal texts offer much advice that is in keeping with our knowledge of the art of persuasion, and—considering the experience of those who offer it—such advice is not to be lightly regarded.

The lawyer texts, nevertheless, do not rest upon the kind of measurable and comparable data that can be provided by formal research, and it is these studies, including Pound's, that will be the focus of the discussion that follows. Before beginning, however, two caveats are in order. First, almost without exception researchers who employ jury simulations have not made use of trials of substantial legal and evidentiary complexity, and—by the luck of the draw—that was also true of all but one of the trials that made up the Pound basis (according to the presiding judges). Consequently, the inferences that can be drawn *may* be true of jury response in highly complicated cases, but we cannot conclude that with confidence. (For a discussion of the jury in complex cases, see Chapter Eight.) Secondly, simulated trials cannot give us reliable information about the trial-in-progress since their "jurors" with rare exceptions have not witnessed a real trial. Most of our best information about the trial-in-progress, therefore, comes from Pound and the handful of other studies that have surveyed real jurors, although, in a few areas (such as ability to understand judge instructions) it is possible to derive useful information from tests employing non-jurors.

Lawyer Speeches to the Jury.   The lawyer's opening statement to the jury has been described as a "potentially awesome opportunity . . . to describe [the] client's case in a convincing and persuasive manner," the time "for attempting to focus the jury's attention on those few issues which when resolved by the jury in his or her client's favor, will return a favorable verdict."[115] That may well be true, but the impact of the opening speech prior to Pound has only been cursorily analyzed in jury research. A frequently quoted study from the University of Chicago project[116] indicates that 80% of the time the verdicts juries reach are the same as if they had based them solely on their view of the case following opening statements. This study has been interpreted as meaning that opening speeches control verdicts, but all it is really saying is that the side that presented the strongest case *in prospect* through the opening speech subsequently produced the strongest evidence 80% of the time. Another author claims that in 80 to 90% of all cases the jurors make up their minds after the opening speeches and the lawyer who hasn't "hooked them by then" might as well forget about winning.[117] The article containing this claim emanated from a company that sells jury selection and manipulation services to lawyers[118] and provides no research backing for its assertions.

Pound's findings were quite different. In this study, when jurors were asked to try to remember their feelings about the case after opening speeches, 60% said they had no strong views one way or the other, 27% favored the plaintiff, 13% the defendant, with some of the "favoring" jurors changing their minds by the end of the trial. Among those who held outset preferences, feelings for the plaintiff were much stronger in big city courts than in suburban—12 to 1 vs. 2 to 1—and were evenly divided in federal, but in all three the percentage of undecided was substantially the same. (See also *Geography and the Jury* section in Chapter Four.)

In summary, Pound depicts a gradual process of opinion formation, from 10% of jurors having views following voir dire to 40% following opening speeches to 96% at the conclusion of trial, although, even then, about half the jurors still described themselves as "leaning" toward rather than "definitely" for one side or the other. From the Pound scenario, therefore, we have no reason to believe that jurors are "hooked" following opening speeches or anywhere else along the line. The strongest influences on them are the trial events.

Another trial event that presumably can influence verdict-preferences is the lawyers' closing speeches. All lawyers seem to agree they are "important" or "extremely important"[119] yet Anapol discovered that omitting them for some of his mock juries and including them for others made no difference in the verdicts.[120] Quite similar results were found in a 1984 study of criminal cases[121] by Walter-Goldberg in which real jurors were surveyed; nearly 90% of them stated that lawyer summations did *not* change their verdict preferences,[122] and Pound confirms. The respondents in the 1984 study, however, generally agreed that the closing speeches had been important to them; among reasons given: because they refreshed their memories, clarified issues, and helped summarize the trial.[123] If the summations accomplished all that, it seems difficult to conclude that they did not, in fact, also influence verdicts more often than the jurors thought.

The 1984 study further discovered that prosecutors' closing speeches tended to be better remembered and were more interesting to jurors than were those of the defendants' lawyers.[124] Since prosecutors enter the trial with the mantle of the state wrapped around them and since the jury is usually going to find the defense lawyer's client guilty, the high regard for the prosecutor's speech is predictable and, in any event, cannot be analogized to the summations for the two sides in a civil trial. For that, we turn to Pound, which found no reason to believe that jurors are more likely to be swayed by the speeches of one side than the other.

Juror Reactions to Lawyers and Witnesses During Trial. In *The American Jury*, Kalven and Zeisel learned that marked disparity in the ability of opposing counsel did not appear, of itself, to be sufficient to sway jurors.[125] In his study, Hastie observed that attorney ability to develop arguments with clarity and succinctness permitted jurors to do the same during deliberations, leading him to conclude that "good attorneys make good jurors."[126] This may be a useful general precept to discover, but one which it might ill-behoove a lawyer whose case might become a sure-fire loser when presented with such succinctness and clarity that the jury *does* understand it to follow.

Several studies focusing on criminal trials have concluded, just as legal folklore would have it, that the degree of a jury's "liking" for a defendant is a substantive factor in verdicts,[127] although only in terms of leniency, i.e., the likable defendant is more often found guilty of the least serious charge against him than the unlikable one. Other studies, however, disagree.[128] Pound uncovered in civil trials a correlation between likability and verdict, in that jurors who reached a plaintiff decision usually found the plaintiff more likable than the defendant, and the plaintiff's lawyer more likable than the defendant's, with the same holding true for winning defendants.

From the Pound results, however, it would be improper to assume that a likability factor toward litigants and their attorneys is significant in developing verdicts, since it is perhaps more plausible to conclude that when a jury decides one side lacks credibility, that side becomes less "likable" for that reason and the opposite side more so, a belief for which Pound provides some statistical evidence (see *Jury Discussion Content* section in Chapter Four). In any event, to the extent "likability" of litigants (not lawyers) who testify plays a role in decision formulation, it is not necessarily an improper criterion for jurors to use, since they have been told by the judge that they are to consider the demeanor of all witnesses, not merely what they say, in evaluating testimony.

Pound also attempted to test credibility by asking its jurors how plaintiff and defendant testimony affected them. Nearly half (47%) of the jurors said that after the plaintiff was done testifying, they had a lessened belief in the validity of his or her case than before, and very nearly the same percentage (45%) were similarly affected by defendant testimony. Both results are quite probably a tribute to effective cross-examination. Credibility differences could be discerned by court location. In both federal and suburban courts, defendants were assessed more credible after testimony 60% of the time, although defendants eventually prevailed only 46% of the time. Plaintiff credibility was seen as improved 64% of the time in big city courts in which 70% of the verdicts were for plaintiffs. The differences are striking but the conclusions, if any, to be drawn are unclear. The high credibility ratio for plaintiffs in big city courts may only mean those jurors were hearing stronger plaintiff cases than those elsewhere did. For a discussion of why this may be so, see *Geography and the Jury* section in Chapter 4 below.

According to some authorities, the believability of any witness—not only to jurors but to the judge in a bench trial—can be enhanced or diminished by factors other than likability, demeanor, and the effectiveness of cross-examintion. Not only what is said but how it is said also presumably can have an effect. The persuasiveness of speech patterns has been studied by experts in linguistics, and by O'Barr, an anthropologist who has published a book on the subject.[129] In one of his principal experiments, university students[130] listened to tape recordings of actual witnesses and of actors impersonating witnesses,[131] the latter making various revisions of the original speeches, changing them not in content but in manner of expression. From these experiments, and based in part on earlier studies, O'Barr identified two speech modes, the "powerful" and the "powerless."[132] As the term suggests, powerful speech was assertive, non-hesitant, confident, and—O'Barr found—principally the province of male witnesses. Powerless speech incorporated "hedges" (e.g., "I think . . . If I'm not mistaken"), was repetitious, made use of direct quotations from others "indicating deference to authority," used rising intonations (e.g., "around 9:30?" rather than "around 9:30."),[133] and was most often to be found in female witnesses. Speech modes not only were sex-linked but also frequently appeared to be a product of social class, with lower-class witnesses much more likely to use powerless formations.[134] For example, a female physician, who was a witness in one of the trials O'Barr observed, used almost no powerless speech patterns while a housewife and a male ambulance driver did. Not surprisingly, O'Barr's collegiate auditors generally found the powerful speakers more credible than the powerless ones.[135]

Prospectively, lawyers drawing on the O'Barr finding might decide that they want to correct powerless speech when they prepare their witnesses for trial. The danger, of course, would be in making the witnesses so conscious of the powerless speech they've always used that by imitating "powerful" modes they will only succeed in coming across as artificial to the jury, thereby canceling out any benefit of their re-training. Nevertheless, based on O'Barr's conclusions, coaching on the wording of key phrases would seem to be advisable most of the time.

However, before lawyers decide it is their duty to turn out phalanxes of powerful speech witnesses, they might want to bear in mind that the auditors who were so impressed with powerful speech were college students, an atypical population segment in terms of presence on juries, and that these auditors only *heard* the witnesses and actors, and did not have (as real jurors do) the opportunity to assess simultaneously their demeanor and body language. Consequently, although O'Barr's findings may well be correct and appear logically probable—we are more likely to believe someone who seems certain of the facts than someone who doesn't—the basis we have for drawing that conclusion is skimpy at best. Moreover, O'Barr himself raises the possibility that there might be situations when powerless speech is more effective than powerful.[136] For instance, when the helplessness of a victim of a crime or of a negligent injury is key to the case, employment of powerful speech modes by that person could, theoretically, be counterproductive.

Of perhaps greater value to lawyers were O'Barr's experiments with verbal interplay between lawyers and witnesses. He learned that lawyers create favorable impressions of their own witnesses on jurors when they permit them largely uninterrupted narrative responses,[137] thus confirming one of the most frequent pieces of advice offered in the attorney-written texts. O'Barr, however, found a different reason for reaching that conclusion than that of the lawyer-texts. These texts consider the lengthy response by one's own witness effective because it is easier for a jury to follow than the fragmented one which, some lawyers fear, may make the jury think the witness has been coached. O'Barr, while not disagreeing with that analysis, learned that when a witness was frequently interrupted by his or her own attorney, his mock jurors felt the lawyer considered that witness to be less intelligent than the one permitted freer rein in response[138]—leading to the corollary that if the lawyer thinks the witness is unintelligent, the jury will think so too and the witness's believability, at least in many situations, suffers. O'Barr further found—contrary to the advice usually given in the legal textbooks—that lawyers who frequently interrupted witnesses they were cross-examining were perceived by O'Barr's students as less in control of their own case and less "fair" than lawyers who permitted lengthy uninterrupted answers.[139] Even if O'Barr is correct on this point, it is doubtful that most lawyers would, as a result, change their tactics. By forcing a hostile witness into truncated, frequently interrupted replies, the lawyer accords that person less opportunity to get damaging testimony on the record than he or she would have with the more "fair" narrative response.

The influence of expert witnesses on juries has been barely touched upon by researchers, probably because the gamut of experts is such a broad one. There is some slight indication that doctors may be held in especially high regard by jurors,[140] but that doctors and other experts lose some of their credibility when the jury learns they have been paid by the side that has called them.[141] Judges occasionally call their own expert witnesses, a practice which has jury implications that will be discussed in Chapter Eight.

The Impact of Evidence During Trial.   Our source is Pound, which asked jurors: "Do you recall any particular event in the trial that was most important in making up your mind? If yes, what?" Responding were 291 jurors of whom 158 (54%) could pinpoint such a moment. Of the 170 total responses—a few listed more than one factor—95 (56%) specified evidence elicited from witness testimony (including 16 mentions of "expert witnesses"). Another 31 responses (18%) noted various courtroom exhibits. Thus, 74% of the "most important" element answers named evidentiary factors. Of the remainder, 27 responses (16%) recalled some *manner* of testimony as crucial, and these replies were also frequently evidence-related (i.e., conflicts in testimony, "illogical" testimony). In total, therefore, a highly significant 90% of the crucial trial events recalled was directly evidentiary or demeanor-related, and some of the other responses may have been ("missing evidence" and "missing witnesses" mentioned six times, or 3%). The quality of the lawyers was mentioned eight times (5%) ("excellent lawyer" twice, "poor lawyer" twice, closing speeches three times, and the "way witnesses questioned," once). The judge's charge on the law was specified, perhaps surprisingly, only three times.

These findings give strong credence to the hypothesis that jurors are primarily concerned with evidentiary factors, and that the events of the trial itself (rather than what they hear about the case during voir dire, during opening speeches, and during closing speeches) are the elements crucial to them in reaching a verdict.

Despite what they learn from the evidence, and the vital position they give it in their view of the case, just half the Pound jurors answered "yes" to the question: "After both sides had completely presented their case, did you feel that you had a good idea of what had really happened?" Only 3 jurors (less than 1%) answered "no," while the others "still had questions I wish had been answered."

The discontent that these jurors felt at the close of testimony may have a relationship to missing witnesses. A little more than half the jurors responded "yes" to the question, "Did you wonder why certain people who were mentioned during the trial did not testify?" with a quarter of those holding "it against the side that didn't call certain people to testify who might have had added important information." However, the extent to which the antipathy thus engendered affected verdicts is unclear.

Objections and Inadmissible Evidence.   The impact lawyer objections have on juries is a subject that concerns lawyers.[142] For example, if they are frequently overruled, they worry that either the jurors will assume they are incompetent or that the judge believes the other side should win. Either way, they wonder, how will the jurors react? Will they tend to believe the side whose objections are most often upheld, or else will they perceive the losing side as the underdog, subjected to unfair treatment by the judge? For these and other reasons, the choice between objecting and not objecting can frequently be a close call for the lawyer. He or she doesn't want jurors ever to get the impression that the purpose of the objection is to keep them from learning the facts of the case—even though that might very well be the reason. At the same time, the lawyer knows if an objection is not made, by such an omission he or she may have waived the right to appeal on grounds that the judge's ruling was wrong and prejudiced the verdict.

Pound learned that about 90% of its jurors did *not* think lawyers on either side objected too often. One-third of the remaining 10% thought less of the side that objected too often, suggesting that lawyer worry on that score is not frivolous, since only one negatively responding juror could harm a client's case, especially on a unanimous verdict jury. A related Pound finding is stronger statistically; almost a quarter of its jurors thought that objections were sometimes made to keep important information from them, with plaintiff and defense lawyers equally likely to do so. The use of objections for this perceived purpose, we can assume, was a reason that many jurors believed they didn't get a full view of the evidence, and could possibly indicate a stronger negative reaction to certain objections than was apparent from juror responses to the question about overly-frequent objections. It would be improper, however, to draw the last as a conclusion from the Pound statistics. The most we can say confidently is that jurors overwhelmingly understand and accept the legal purpose of objections as a proper part of the trial process, so that, from Pound, no significant reason emerges for lawyers to change their objection tactics.

The Pound jurors were also asked if their judge seemed to favor one lawyer over another, an opinion they might have gained from the judge's rulings on objections. Almost all the respondents (98%) did *not* get any impression of favoritism, a very strong statistical finding.

Aside from Pound, little substantive information about objections can be gleaned from jury research.[143] One study indicates that when a lawyer objects and the judge rules the statement inadmissible and tells the jury to ignore it, the jury will *not* do so when the admissible evidence is weak and the inadmissible strong and damaging.[144] The impact of inadmissible evidence was also tested in a University of Chicago experiment[145] in which different sets of mock jurors were given variant versions of the same personal injury trial. In one, the defendant testified he had no insurance; in the second, he testified he had insurance and his lawyer didn't object; in the third, he stated he had insurance, his lawyer objected, and the jury was instructed by the judge to ignore the testimony. (In some jurisdictions, mere mention of insurance would lead to a mistrial.[146]) In the trials in which the defendant said he had no insurance, the average award to the plaintiff was $33,000; in those in which he said he had insurance and his lawyer didn't object, $37,000; in the ones in which the defense lawyer objected and the judge instructed the jury to ignore the testimony, the average award was $46,000.[147] Although this study indicates that calling attention to impermissible, harmful testimony through objections can hurt the objecting side, the finding has not been replicated and must be viewed with caution, especially in context with Hastie's mock jurors who frequently warned one another not to discuss certain matters because they had been ruled inadmissible.[148] (As Hastie noted, however, since his subjects knew they were being recorded, they may have been more scrupulous about inadmissible evidence than real jurors would be.[149])

Anecdotal information comes from O'Barr, who happened to serve on several real juries while doing his research; he found that, as with the Hastie jurors, his fellow-members clearly considered it inappropriate to discuss disallowed testimony and made every effort not to do so;[150] other ex-jurors report the same experience.[151] Intent to follow orders, however, does not connote the ability to do so, and it is reasonable to assume, especially in very long trials, that jurors will not always be able to remember, individually or as a group, whether or not a certain piece of testimony was disallowed as a result of objections. Researchers have tackled the recall problem, using mock juries, but the results of their studies are inconclusive.[152]

Videotaped Testimony.   When it is known that a witness will not be available for trial, it has become common practice to videotape that person's deposition; before it is presented to the jury, any statements ruled inadmissible will be excised.[153] The research report card on this limited use of videotaped testimony is favorable. Jurors, it has been found, find it much easier to pay attention to the filmed deposition of the absent witness than to the lawyer reading the deposition into the court record (the only alternative).[154] (For some reason, black-and-white tape seems to be better for this purpose than color.[155]) Several studies also claim that jurors respond better to videotaped testimony than they would to that of a live witness, though other studies question that conclusion,[156] including Pound. More than half the Pound jurors were exposed to videotape testimony in their trials, and when asked to compare it with live testimony, 53.5% preferred live, 28.5% saw no difference, and only 18% preferred videotape.

The practice of videotaping the occasional unavailable witness has given rise to taping entire trials and presenting them to the jury as a movie.[157] An attendant will have to be present to hand the jurors items of physical evidence, but otherwise they see none of the participants in the trial live, not even the judge. The first trial of this type occurred in Ohio in 1971[158] and it and subsequnt ones have been met with an enthusiastic response in some quarters, particularly from certain judges and court administrators. As its advocates point out, the videotaped trial permits the deposing of witnesses at their convenience, rather than requiring them to sit outside the courtroom waiting to be called, sometimes for days on end; and it's a convenience to the lawyers, too, who can tape their opening and closing speeches when they feel like it, just as the judge can tape his or her instructions. Eventually, after all the inadmissible portions have been deleted by the judge, the movie is spliced together. Since judges no longer have to be in the courtroom while the jurors are witnessing the film, they can busy themselves resolving non-trial matters on the docket, thereby presumably reducing the court backlog. Because the movie trial will have no delays, it will be completed much more rapidly than the regular trial, freeing courtrooms for other uses and cutting the backlog that way, too.[159] There are those who find this whole idea appalling.

The critics point out that it violates, at least in spirit, the constitutional guarantee of the right to a public trial and that of a party to be faced by his or her opponents,[160] who might not say quite the same thing when speaking to a videocamera from the comfort and security of their office or home as they would in a public arena, where the person about whom they are talking is right in front of them. People who are being filmed may also act different-ly—more or less convincingly—when they know they are being filmed than when they know they are not. Perhaps more significantly, the trial itself be-comes the creature of the film director whose camera-angle placement determines what the jurors see. The camera might only show the witnesses above the waist, so that revelatory body-language—nervous crossing and recrossing of legs—is eliminated; or, the camera may show *only* the witnesses, so that jurors, unable to see the reactions of the various lawyers and their clients to a piece of testimony, miss still another opportunity to test credibility and demeanor. The depersonalized and isolated circumstance thrust upon the jury by the movie trial, and the absence of the judge as a cohesive authority figure, may also cause the members to take a less serious view of the case than they do when subjected to the immediacy of a live proceeding.[161] Several experiments have been undertaken to determine whether videotaped trials result in different verdicts from live ones; the results have been inconclusive.[162]

Impact of Courtroom Exhibits.   Because jury research has been nearly barren of information on the effect of exhibits on jurors,[163] it was a subject of major interest to Pound. In the questionnaire that jurors answered before leaving the courtroom, 83% said that one or more exhibits (charts, photographs, medical records and the like) helped them make up their minds. When the question was asked differently in the questionnaire to be answered at home, 92% said exhibits were a ''major'' (50%) or ''minor'' (42%) factor in reaching a decision, with the remaining 8% saying they were of no help. (As noted earlier exhibits were named ''most important'' 18% of the time by those who recalled a decisive trial factor.) An exhibit can also make jurors doubt the truthfulness of previous testimony they have heard; 45% of the Pound respondees reported such an experience. Taken together, the Pound study provides very strong evidence to trial lawyers that exhibits typically are of significant importance to juries both in proving one's own case and disproving the opponent's.

Allowing Jurors to Question Witnesses. Ordinarily jurors are not permitted to do so, but we have one experiment in which they were.[164] It was administered by federal court judges who told jurors that if they had questions, they could submit them in writing to the judge who would pose them to the witnesses. The jurors were further informed that some of their questions might not be asked because of legal technicalities or because the judge knew a question was going to be asked later. Allowing jurors to ask questions, it was expected, would alert lawyers to areas of their cases that interested the jurors and which, therefore, they should try to develop. Some lawyers and judges, however, felt that permitting juror questions would tend to disrupt the orderly presentation of evidence and that objections to improper juror questions would not be made for fear of causing resentment on their part.

At the conclusion of the experiment, the judges voted by a two-to-one margin that they found juror questioning helpful in the conduct of a trial; plaintiff lawyers and prosecutors approved the practice unanimously, with most criminal defense attorneys also in favor; a majority of the civil defense lawyers disapproved. Four of every five Pound jurors said they wished they could have questioned one or more witnesses, a further reflection of the belief held by many jurors that they don't hear the entire story. The desire to question can also be taken as an index of the interest that jurors take in their trials and their desire to get at the truth.

Allowing Jurors to Take Notes. Traditionally, jurors have been forbidden to take notes on testimony during the course of a trial; unlike judges, who do take notes, they are supposed to rely on their memories. Those who would uphold the tradition make several arguments: that jurors will be distracted from testimony by trying to jot down highlights of it; that they will make mistakes in what they write; that in the jury room especial weight may be placed on that which is written, perhaps wrongly written, giving the most active note-takers undue weight in the deliberations.

A number of experiments have been undertaken to test these premises. One occurred in the same federal court district that allowed jurors to ask questions. When the test period was over, judges voted in favor of note-taking by a 26 to zero margin, with five not sure. Plaintiff lawyers and prosecutors thought it had worked well by a 10 to three margin, with four not sure. Only defense lawyers, criminal and civil, turned thumbs down, by a 10 to seven margin, one not sure. In only four of the 32 panels employed for the experiment were the jurors themselves polled; they ''enthusiastically'' favored note-taking, according to the authors of the survey.[165]

A study undertaken for the National Center for State Courts involved four juries, a very small sample, as the author notes. Again, the responses were positive.[166] A third study, based on 65 responses from 140 former jurors in the District of Columbia, found that taking notes assisted jurors in recall of the evidence and the judge's instructions; that non-note-takers did not find it distracting to have their fellow jurors do so; and that use of notes in the jury room did not seem to lengthen procedures.[167]

Much more ambitious was a study undertaken by the Philadelphia Bar Association[168] in 1984 and 1985. It developed information from 326 jurors who had served on 39 panels, 30 of them civil, over a 10-month period. Also interviewed were the judges and many of the lawyers involved in the cases. All the trials took place in federal court. Note-taking was always optional, with 70% of the jurors electing to do so.[169]

The results of this study were generally consonant with the three earlier ones. As with those in the New York federal court undertaking, the participating judges found note-taking presented no problems in the conduct of the trial and were, with few exceptions, highly favorable toward it.[170] Reaction from lawyers was more mixed,[171] their principal expressed fear being the traditional one that taking notes would distract attention from what was being said while the writing was going on.[172] If distraction is a problem, it can't be a very significant one since the median number of pages taken per juror was 3.4 in trials that lasted an average of 4.4 days.[173] Most of the notes were taken during presentation of evidence, rarely during speeches by the lawyers.[174] One lawyer in the survey worried that jurors would spend their time in deliberation arguing over whose notes were more accurate[175] but this hardly ever happened;[176] 89% of the respondents, whether they took notes or not, said they had no problems with the accuracy of the information recorded by their peers.[177] Neither did those who didn't take notes find themselves dependent on those who did; only about a third of all jurors said the note-takers led or dominated the deliberations[178] and it may well be that some of the dominant note-takers would have played that role even if note-taking had not been permitted. The note-takers themselves overwhelmingly (89%) said they would do so again, if permitted, the next time they were jurors;[179] three-quarters of them added it gave them an "advantage" in the deliberations.[180] However, when we get to the key question—did the note-taking help them make a decision in the case?—the results were inconclusive. Only 43% thought it did, 39% not; the remainder were uncertain.[181]

Order of Presentation of Evidence.   One early study of persuasiveness determined that the argument presented first to a jury is the one that will have the most effect on it, suggesting that lawyers would be well-advised to lead off with their strongest evidence. Other studies, however, have challenged that conclusion, recommending instead that lawyers should save the best for last since that's the most rememberable, while still other researchers have found that the order in which the arguments are made seems to have no significance.[182]

The Judge's Control of the Jury.   The jury is theoretically the fact-finder of the case that comes before it, but the primary fact-finder is the judge. Judges rule on admissibility of evidence, so in that sense they decide which facts or alleged facts the jurors are allowed to hear. Judges also, as we saw in Chapter One, can be fact-finders in that they can decide that one side has not presented enough evidence to allow the case to go to the jury; and, in multiple-defendant cases, they can direct the jury to find one or more individuals not guilty or not liable. In criminal cases, they can in some instances reverse the jury finding of guilty, and in civil cases decide that the jury's verdict for either side was contrary to the evidence or the law. So they act as fact-finders that way, too. The judge also decides the type of verdict the jury is to render. That can be, and most often is, a so-called *general* verdict (guilty or not guilty, liable or not liable, to the various charges) or it can be a *special* verdict in which the jurors' role is limited to deciding a series of specific questions about the case which are posed by the judge, with the judge then applying the law to the answers.[183]

The judge's overt powers, therefore, are quite considerable in controlling both the content of the trial and the role the jury is to play, if any, in its resolution. But the judge's covert powers may be even more persuasive.[184] Judges are permitted to ask questions of witnesses, and both the questions and the answers to them may strike the jurors as especially significant since the catechism emanates from the neutral arbiter rather than a partisan lawyer. In some places, judges are permitted to comment on the evidence,[185] and can also, by the attitude they express toward one lawyer or the other, one witness or the other, indicate to the jury their opinion of the merits of the case. Opinion need not be expressed by the content of the words the judge utters—judges have to be careful of that, lest they be reversed on prejudice grounds—but more subtly by inflection or by body language (e.g., appearing bored when one side is presenting its case, alert and interested when the other is),[186] little tricks that never appear on the formal court record. The judge can also attempt to influence the jury during the instructions on the law, either advertently through the way the evidence is summarized (occasionally accompanied by the same body language inferences) or simply as a genuine expression of the judge's judicial philosophy. For example, it has been noted that judges in criminal cases who hew to a narrow (i.e., pro-prosecution) definition of reasonable doubt get more convictions than judges who have a wider standard.[187]

Aside from the reasonable-doubt study (and even it is not conclusive, since we do not know how strong the evidence of guilt was in the various cases in the sample), jury research does not tell us how often or to what extent juries are influenced by improper judicial guidance. However, it appears that, although juries almost always seem to have a high regard for their judge,[188] they do not attempt to tailor their verdicts to please him or her. In Pound, only 11% of the jurors said there were discussions of the judge's view of the case during deliberation, and only 9% said they wanted to please the judge with their verdict.

The Judge's Instructions to the Jury. Jurors, the late jurist-author Curtis Bok once observed, are "doused with a kettleful of law, during the charge, that would make a third-year law student blush."[189] His point—according to a panoply of judges, lawyers, and jury researchers—is well-taken.[190]

As the United States Supreme Court put it in 1895 in *Sparf and Hansen v. U.S.*,[191] the charge has the purpose of instructing jurors on the law which they are to "apply . . . to the facts as they find them to be." The charge can be boring and prolix: One lawyer recalled to his horror a judge whose charge lasted for six hours.[192] The judge chooses his or her language primarily with an eye to a later reading by an appeals court[193] which can order a new trial if it determines that the judge failed to instruct with pristine accuracy if not with pristine clarity.[194] Yet, a case can also be reversed, in some jurisdictions, if the judge "has not succeeded in delivering instructions in such a way that they will be understood by the jury," as was stated by the Pennsylvania Supreme Court in *Commonwealth v. Smith*, 1908.[195]

The concern expressed by the Pennsylvania court is manifestly a serious one. Jurors who correctly assess the evidence but then apply the wrong law, or the right law wrongly, can create a technically incorrect verdict (though not necessarily a wrong one on the merits), and, at worst, a serious miscarriage of justice.

Although, following *Sparf*, judges began to put together more regularized instructions on the law than they had before, wording that they hoped could be used in case after case with little or no change, it wasn't until 1938, in California, that the first standardized set of instructions was issued which all judges had to use. By the beginning of the 1980s, 39 states[196] had adopted at least one set of these so-called "pattern" instructions, based on the theory that employment of uniform wording would avoid instances of judicial bias, would lead to equitable treatment of cases by juries, and would make their verdicts more accurate by improving their understanding of the law.[197] It is on this last desideratum that, if the research is to be believed, the practice has frequently failed—in part because the very attempt to write instructions so broadly that they would cover all possible fact situations made them so abstract in their wording that juries have difficulty relating them to the case at hand.[198]

The comprehension problem is one that has long been recognized. In one of the earliest jury studies, Hunter's in 1935, the respondents frequently noted they didn't understand the law they were supposed to apply, while more recent studies in six states have placed juror comprehension of instructions around the 50% level.[199] A 1976 study by Strawn and Buchanan, reported by Elwork, discovered that only 59 of 116 volunteers were able to understand instructions on circumstantial evidence, and that only half understood, from what the judge said, that it was the duty of the state to prove a criminal prosecution beyond a reasonable doubt.[200] A mock jury study in 1971 came up with more encouraging results when it found a 90% comprehension rate for reasonable doubt. However, the majority of those jurors failed to understand "preponderance of the evidence," that slight tipping of the scales which in civil cases is supposed to result in a plaintiff's verdict; the wrong jurors thought that "preponderance" (certainly an unfortunate semantic choice, considering the word's frequent usage to denote dominance) meant that the plaintiff had to show 75% of the evidence as favorable.[201]

Elwork's six-person mock juries didn't fare nearly as well as those of the earlier studies. When asked questions about the judge's instructions in two cases, they were able to answer correctly only 40% and 42% of the time.[202] In still another Elwork test, only one of 34 subjects was able to correctly discern, from the instructions, the difference between attempted murder and assault with a deadly weapon. Elwork further found that jurors who didn't understand instructions were much more likely than those who did to discuss inappropriate subjects—such as the defendant's presumed in-surance—during deliberations.[203]

When Elwork refashioned the misunderstood jury instructions into everyday English, he found that a comprehension rewrite of the attempted murder vs. deadly assault charge improved understanding to 51%, a second rewrite using even simpler language to 80%;[204] for his civil juries, analogous revisions raised the level from 40% to 78%.[205] Other researchers have had similar results.[206] Elwork and his colleagues, for instance, took the following instructions as a basis: ''And, in the course of the instructions or during the trial, if I have said anything that indicates to you how I might feel or how you think I feel with respect to the evidence or some aspect of the evidence in this case, you should disregard my actions or statements and rely upon your own recollections of the evidence.'' They transformed it into: ''Nothing I have said was intended to tell you what I think the evidence shows. You should ignore any feeling that you think I have about the evidence and depend on your own memory and thinking.''[207] Elwork also has produced a list of words to substitute for legal jargon, e.g., ''accusation'' for ''allegation,'' ''lawyer'' for ''counsel,'' ''ask'' for ''solicit,'' ''as part of an agreement'' for ''pursuant to an agreement,'' and so on.[208]

The introduction of simplified language to jury instructions has self-evident merit. However, the murky prose in which the instructions are presently written does serve one purpose; it helps hide the fact that much of the law is open to many interpretations, so that any attempts to make in-structions understandable may serve in many instances to make apparent to the jurors how ambiguous the law supposedly being defined actually is.[209] One can only speculate upon the impact that realization would have on jurors; one study suggests that improved instructions on reasonable doubt may lead to an increase in the number of not-guilty verdicts.[210]

Regardless of whether or not the language should be simplified—and certainly some of it can be without letting any secrets out—many researchers[211] and some judges[212] believe it would be wise to permit the jurors to take a written or videotaped copy of the instructions into the jury room with them. This could be helpful because in the typical pattern of instructions, dependent clauses containing complex information tend to come first and the verb only later, so that the jurors, as listeners, don't receive the directional signal that the verb provides until it is too late. If they could reread the in-structions—videotape would be of less help—that problem, could be solved, at least in part.[213]

A front-end reform has also been proposed. Under the existing courtroom format, almost everywhere jurors learn of the law they are supposed to apply only at the end of the trial. Although they usually are given an orientation lecture by the judge about the trial process before it begins, and a brief introduction to the factual nature of the case ahead,[214] many have suggested,[215] that it might make more sense to explain the applicable law both at the beginning of the case and at its conclusion. Under the present system, jurors are forced to go back in their memories to recall evidence that fits a law that they were unaware of while the trial was going on. Presumably, if they learned about that law from the start, they would recognize evidence relevant to it as the trial progressed; and in fact one of Elwork's experiments discovered that did happen.[216]

It is far from clear, however, that jurors have as much difficulty understanding instructions as this recountal might suggest. Pound found that the overwhelming majority of its respondents believed they understood "most" of what the judge told them about the law, and they might not be wrong. Although Hastie noted[217] that his mock jurors were more likely to make mistakes about the law than about the evidence, he also observed that they frequently corrected one another's mistakes, a phenomenon that Elwork did not discover. (One possible reason: All of Hastie's juries had 12 members while Elwork's only had six, the greater number leading to greater group recall.) Hastie also documented, as Elwork did not, an excellent grasp by the jurors of such theoretical concepts as reasonable inference and presumption of innocence even though they had some difficulty, just as Elwork said, in applying various offense gradations (second degree murder vs. voluntary manslaughter). Then again, these definitions are fact-dependent and jurors are not the only ones who will disagree on those interpretations: so do lawyers and judges. Despite the occasional difficulties Hastie's jurors had in sorting out legal definitions correctly, the errors they made seemed to bear little or no relationship to the legal supportability of their verdicts. That is, his juries that arrived at a legally correct verdict were as likely to have made mistakes on the law as those which came to incorrect conclusions.[218] In total, Hastie's jurors understood enough of the law that they weren't led astray from a meritorious verdict 90% of the time, and in the 10% verdict-error cases the mistakes on the law were not the crucial factor.[219]

Hastie's discovery does not vitiate Elwork's conclusion that simplified wording in instructions would help juries, but it may indicate that the law, despite its frequent ambiguities, is sufficiently reasonable and logical that jurors are capable of separating the general principles from the verbiage and retaining them for a long enough period to apply them to the problem at hand. This is probably why the Chicago Jury Project judges found their juries clearly wrong in their verdicts only 9% of the time,[220] and why Hastie found his juries "exhibiting an impressive display of common sense"[221] when they were grappling with legal meanings.

In addition to instructions, many judges in civil cases provide the jurors with an interrogatory sheet which lists the basic questions they are required to resolve.[222] About 70% of the Pound jurors reported being given such a list, and nearly two-thirds stated that it proved "very helpful" to them during their deliberations.

The Trial Environment.   Pound and one other study[223] found that jurors almost uniformly describe courtroom personnel as polite and helpful. However, courtroom facilities apparently vary a great deal. Half the Pound jurors who heard cases in the Philadelphia Court of Common Pleas described their waiting areas as either crowded, dirty or unpleasant, compared to 99% of the federal jurors who described their surroundings as "comfortable."

The role, if any, that these environmental factors play on verdict-making is unclear, but we might want to keep in mind a letter written by Thomas Jefferson in 1776 in which he noted that one reason the delegates to the Continental Congress came to so quick a decision for independence was their heartfelt desire to get away, as soon as they possibly could, from the swarms of horseflies biting at them in the building that became known as Independence Hall.

Chapter 4

Jury Deliberations

I

During the course of the 1970s, the United States Supreme Court in a series of cases—*Williams v. Florida* (1970);[1] *Johnson v. Louisiana* (1972);[2] *Apodaca v. Oregon* (1972);[3] *Colgrove v. Battin* (1973);[4] and *Ballew v. Georgia* (1978)[5]—removed the unanimity requirement for jury verdicts in civil and criminal cases and reduced the minimum permissible number of jurors from 12 to six.

Although small and non-unanimous juries had been convened in a number of states prior to the Supreme Court decisions, the practice afterward rapidly spread.[6] As a result, within a single jurisdiction, it is today possible to have some juries of 12 persons that must reach a unanimous verdict, others of 12 that don't have to, some of six, some of eight, some of 10, some of the smaller-sized ones requiring unanimous verdicts, some three-quarters agreement, some five-sixths, with the choice in civil cases sometimes left to agreement by the opposing counsel.

The Supreme Court reasoned that the reduction in size would have only a "negligible" impact on the constitutional requirement that juries adequately represent the community from which they are drawn, that it would not significantly change jury verdicts,[7] and that there was no reason to believe that less-than-unanimous verdicts meant that the jurors who formed the required majority would refuse to listen to the opinions of the minority.[8]

Those who approved of the Supreme Court rulings forecast that the introduction of small and non-unanimous juries would mean shorter trials, thereby cutting into backlogs and permitting speedier justice for everyone.[9] The new juries would also mean lowered costs for taxpayers[10] by reducing the amounts spent to pay jurors and courtroom attendants. Moreover, it was predicted that the removal of the unanimous-verdict requirements would mean fewer hung juries, many of which lead to second trials, doubling the public's portion of the trial's cost.

Not all the "pro" arguments, however, were based on developing a more efficient court system. As the advocates have observed, psychological studies show that large groups are likely to form cliques within the whole,[11] with the members of the largest clique dominating the discussion. Because this rarely happens in groups of six, in them and possibly in eight-member juries the discussion would be more widespread and less inhibited than it is in clique-ridden groups of 12, leading to verdicts of a better quality. The non-unanimous jury, it has further been observed, is in keeping, as the unanimous is not, with the American tradition of majority rule.[12]

Critics of the changes see the issues differently. They point out that the Supreme Court's conclusion that majorities would continue to consult with minorities is not only undocumented but contrary both to the results of earlier experiments with non-unanimous juries and to our general knowledge of non-jury group behavior.[13] The small juries have been met with equal trepidation. By their nature, the critics argue, they will be less representative of the community than will be large juries, and since they will have fewer members to recall evidence and the judge's instructions, more mistakes—more wrong verdicts—will result from them than from 12-member panels.

Among the critics, distinctions have sometimes been drawn between civil and criminal cases. Civil suits (save when a government agency is a party) are private affairs, in which the two sides enter the courtroom in a state of theoretical parity, so that perhaps the choice of the composition of the fact-finding forum can rightly be left to their own agreement. However, in criminal cases, the critics note, parity doesn't exist, even in theory; in them, the prosecution enters with all the power of the state behind it, while the defendant, who is usually poor and whose freedom and perhaps life is at stake, has only a (usually) court-appointed lawyer on his side. In that situation, the scales become balanced, at least to some degree, by requiring the state to present a case that is so strong that a body of 12 people will unanimously agree with it. By corollary, when only a majority has to be convinced, eager prosecutors—looking for scalps and promotions—may be tempted to try doubtful cases; when that occurs, quite apart from any injustices that might result, the backlog of untried matters, both criminal and civil, lengthens, thus defeating one of the purposes of the reform.

As might be expected, hardly had the ink been dry on the earliest of the Supreme Court decisions than researchers were busily setting about trying to test the various theories. Some concentrated on the small juries, some on the non-unanimous, others on both.

Monetary Savings Based on Reduced Size.   Juror fees consist of monies paid to and expended on behalf of those who actually serve on a panel, and a lesser per capita amount, but still a substantial aggregate figure, for those who are called but don't serve. By reducing jury size, therefore, we save both on costs for the serving jurors and, since fewer of them will be needed, on the expenditures associated with selecting the venire pool. We will not, however, be able to reduce the pool size proportionate to the jury size, according to a study of the District of Columbia courts; it found that to fill a 12-person panel 27 veniremen, on the average, had to be called, with 21 the number needed to complete a six-person jury.[14]

A much larger expense item, that of courtroom usage, including salaries for personnel, apparently is not affected by the introduction of small juries. The District of Columbia study found that voir dire time remained the same for six-person and 12-person juries, and that the average length of trial also remained unchanged regardless of jury size (7.8 hours).[15] A study of federal courts in New England reached identical conclusions.[16] The Pound study, which incorporated eight- and 12-person juries, unanimous and non-unanimous, found some differences in length of trial based on jury size and verdict requirement, but the principal determinant appears to have been difficulty of case. The average Pound trial, regardless of its jury structure, lasted 3.9 days, while cases that involved medical malpractice or product injury, which are likely to be complicated and to contain voluminous testimony, required 4.9 days. Length of trial also appeared to be closely related to the ultimate dollar-value of the case, with those that resulted in damage awards of $100,000 or more requiring an average of 5.8 days each. The voluminous testimony, the strenuous cross-examination and frequent disputes over evidence admissibility that are common to big-stakes cases help explain their greater duration. (Because juries do not debate their verdicts in a courtroom where large numbers of salaried personnel are on duty but rather in quarters set aside for that purpose, differences in duration of deliberation based on size—which will be discussed below—is an inconsiderable cost factor.)

Quality of Deliberation: Small and Large Unanimous Juries. Probably the most ambitious study concerning the effect of size on verdict was that undertaken by Dr. Alice M. Padawer-Singer, director of Jury Studies, Columbia University, whose findings were published in 1977.[17] For her study, Padawer-Singer used people who had been called for jury duty in Queens County, New York.[18] Eventually, she put together 92 panels, half of which had six members and half with 12.[19] Each jury saw a videotaped reenactment of the same criminal trial, deliberated in regular jury rooms, knew their deliberations were being recorded, and each answered a questionnaire following verdict.[20]

Because the people who served on the Padawer-Singer mock-juries were survivors of a regular voir dire questioning and thus typical of those who serve on real juries in Queens County, she was able to compile pertinent information on the degree of community representativeness likely to be found in six- and 12-person bodies. The result of her study accorded with the assumptions of critics of the Supreme Court: The small juries were markedly less likely to encapsule any kind of community cross section than were the large ones.[21] In terms of racial mix, only 64.3% of Padawer-Singer's six-person juries had a black member, while 84.8% of the 12-person bodies did. Women were also very under-represented in the Padawer-Singer small juries, with 72.7% of them having no female members, and 43.2% of the 12-person juries also entirely male. (The low female representation in both-sized bodies, however, can probably be largely explained by a liberal "domestic duty" exemption for women then in effect in Queens County.[22]) Educational attainment was also much lower on the small juries, with 58.7% having representation from four educational levels compared to 95.7% in the large ones. The very young and very old were also less likely to be present in the small than in the large juries, 4.3% compared to 28.3%.

Pound also examined the community representation issue. In its districts, eight-person juries were in effect in the federal court, eight or 12 in the two state courts. In Pound, no questions were asked about ethnicity. For gender, it found that every one of its juries, regardless of size, had at least one woman, with women, in total, making up 54% of the panels, very close to their percentage of the population. Pound also found no significant differences when it compared educational attainment and the presence of various age groups with jury size.

Taken together, the studies raise the tentative inference that eight-person juries do not substantially differ from 12 on community representativeness, but that six-person ones are seriously lacking in an acceptable cross section. Two studies do not a national picture make, but the results are sufficiently intriguing to suggest further study to determine if the minimum jury size should not, in fact, be eight rather than six.

Group interaction between small and large juries was also different in Padawer-Singer. (Pound had no way of checking this through its post-trial survey method.) Based on the tapings of her juries, Padawer-Singer observed the smaller ones were more polite to one another than were the large ones; frequently they went to lunch together, something that the large ones never did as a single group. Because the small bodies took care not to hurt one another's feelings, head-to-head confrontations, common on the large juries, were rare among them.[23]

Perhaps as a result of all this politeness, but more likely because there were fewer members to make a contribution, Padawer-Singer's small juries did not examine evidence as accurately as did the large ones,[24] nor, according to another study,[25] will small juries recall as much evidence. During deliberations, Padawer-Singer's small juries were also likely to make more inaccurate statements about the case and (quite predictably) exhibited fewer resources of world-knowledge than did the large ones.[26]

Padawer-Singer's small juries, however, showed some strengths not to be found among her large ones. They were more likely to ask the judge for additional instructions,[27] a factor that has been identified[28] as leading to better-informed verdicts. (Pound, however, found no significant differences between large and small juries on questioning the judge, but the sample was small since both groups did so quite rarely.) Several studies also confirm the expectation that participation by members is more likely to be universal in the small than in the large bodies. For example, a 1973 study found that, in its small juries, only two of 48 jurors remained silent throughout deliberations compared to a quarter (24 of 96) who didn't participate, save by voting, in the 12-member panels.[29] Pound also found a tendency toward greater participation by members of small juries. The small group, therefore, although it can't have prospectively as many points of view as the large, or frequently as great a collective recollection of the evidence, may compensate to some degree for these weaknesses by its freer discussion mode.

The effectiveness of jurors who hold a minority view about the proper verdict may also be affected by size of panel, though in some fairly complicated ways, according to several studies. They indicate that a single minority member is less likely to make his or her beliefs known on the large jury than on the small, although, by the very size of the panel, the lone dissident is more likely to find an ally on the large one.[30] However, according to another study, when a dissenting member did speak up on the large jury, that person's participation was more likely to be substantial than on the small one,[31] perhaps because on the small jury that person is inhibited by the politeness factor discerned by Padawer-Singer.

The differences perceived between large and small juries, both in composition and deliberation methods, should in theory lead to differences in verdicts, too. That, however, does not appear to be the case. The mock jury research, which has largely been confined to criminal trials, has discovered few or no significant verdict-variations when panels of various sizes hear the same case.[32] If the mock-studies are producing accurate information (and they may not be), several explanations for the absence of disparity in verdicts suggest themselves: First, the evidence in the criminal cases heard by the mock jurors was so straightforward that virtually all juries, regardless of size, would reach the same result; second, any differences that do exist in composition and discussion-modes are not of a sufficient magnitude to make a difference; third, the weaknesses of each size—i.e., alleged inferior discussion of evidence in the small jury and clique domination in the large—cancel each other out. It is also possible that all three factors could be involved, to one degree or another, in some or all of the experimental trials.

For civil cases, statistical studies on verdicts are available, and by and large they confirm the mock studies for criminal. The jurist-author Lois Forer compiled an analysis of civil jury cases over which she presided and found no important differences in verdict based on size.[33] A 1973 survey of Workmen's Compensation cases[34] agreed with these findings as did a study of a much larger sample of civil cases of all kinds, 391 of them, which found that 58% of the six-member and 57.3% of the 12-member juries returned plaintiff verdicts.[35] A 1969-71 study of state courts in Michigan revealed an equally insignificant differential, showing 52% plaintiff wins in 12-person and 53.8% in six-person juries.[36] (In Michigan, at the time, both types of juries required a five-sixths agreement to reach a verdict in civil cases.[37]) A notable exception to this pattern is to be found in the New England federal court analysis, which turned up a startling 76.9% win rate for plaintiffs from 12-person juries and only 47.5% from those with six members.[38]

In Pound, the opposite occurred. Two-thirds of its eight-person juries produced plaintiff verdicts, while only 44% (seven of 16) of the 12-person ones did. However, all but three of Pound's 12-person jury trials occurred in its suburban court where defense verdicts were more common than elsewhere, suggesting that location of trial may be a verdict factor more important than jury size. (For a more detailed analysis of the impact of location, see *Geography and the Jury* section below.)

When we turn to the amount of money plaintiffs win, our findings on jury size are sparser and apparently contradictory. The New England study learned that 12-person juries gave a median award of $22,050 while the six-person ones were more frugal at $16,950. Another study[39] found the discrepancy much greater, showing 12-person awards at a rate three times higher than six-person. The Michigan study, on the contrary, learned that it was the six-person juries that were more generous, by 10%, than were the 12-member ones.[40]

Comparing the Michigan and New England awards, however, may not be appropriate. In the New England federal courts, lawyers were allowed to choose the jury size, and there is a strong indication[41] that, when that option exists, lawyers will choose 12-member juries when large dollars are at stake—so that the high awards rate from the large juries is predictable.[42] In Michigan, on the contrary, all civil juries had to consist of 12 members in 1969, the first year of the study, and had to consist of six members in 1971, the second year. Therefore, we have no way of sorting out the effect of large-stakes cases by jury size in Michigan as we do in New England.

In Pound, there was virtually no difference in average size of award between its eight- and 12-person juries. Based on these studies, it does not appear that a consistent relationship exists between jury size and award size, save to the extent that lawyers, when permitted to do so, choose large juries for large-dollar cases. However, the studies on this subject are relatively few, the universe of cases quite small, so that large samples might produce different results. It is also possible, even probable, that other factors are more important than jury size in determining award size, and we shall now turn to them.

Quality of Deliberation: Unanimous v. Non-Unanimous Juries. In 1984, Reid Hastie, a psychology professor at the University of Nebraska, along with two colleagues, published a study of unanimous and non-unanimous juries.[43] The mock-method was employed, with each jury having 12 members in order to eliminate variation by size as a factor.

Undertaken in three counties in Massachusetts,[44] Hastie's study, like Padawer-Singer's, used citizens called for jury duty who deliberated in real jury rooms after viewing a videotaped reenactment of a criminal trial. As with Padawer-Singer, Hastie's sample was quite large, 69 juries, one-third of which were required to reach a unanimous verdict, one-third needing 10 of 12 in agreement, one-third eight of 12.[45] Hastie's jurors, however, may not have been as typical of real jurors as Padawer-Singer's since there was only the most cursory voir dire, conducted by the experimenters, not by attorneys or a judge.[46] As with Padawer-Singer's, Hastie's jurors knew their deliberation would be recorded; however, unlike hers, the Hastie jurors were questioned individually about the case before they began deliberations, which could have had a contaminating effect.[47]

Hastie noted a greater tendency on the part of his non-unanimous juries to find the defendant guilty of the most serious charge against him than did those on unanimous-requirement bodies.[48] (The defendant in Hastie's case was charged with homicide, but Hastie made no effort to obtain "death-qualified" mock juries, i.e., ones that would be willing to impose capital punishment under some circumstances. We cannot, therefore, extrapolate from Hastie's juries any information about death-qualified ones.)

Hastie also discovered that his non-unanimous jury members were less likely than those on the unanimous jury to correct one another's errors of fact, a replication of the findings by Padawer-Singer and others for small juries.[49] Since size wasn't a factor in Hastie's study, the reasons for the lower correction rate are unclear. One possibility is that some jurors, realizing their position wasn't going to win and their vote wasn't needed, simply stopped offering corrections. The drop-off rate in participation may also explain, at least in part, the much greater speed with which the non-unanimous juries reached a decision. Those requiring eight of 12 votes took an average of only 75 minutes to decide, the 10-of-12 took 103 minutes, while the 12-of-12 required an average of 138 minutes.[50] Padawer-Singer's small juries, some of which didn't require a unanimous verdict, also deliberated briefly, 77 minutes compared to 154 for the 12-member unanimous and non-unanimous ones.[51] Forer found the same pattern in her civil juries in which, regardless of size, the unanimous ones deliberated for an average of a little more than four hours and the non-unanimous just under two.[52] In the New England study of civil cases, the 12-member average was 3.2 hours compared to 2.5 hours for the six-member.[53]

On the surface, the time differentials seem to confirm what we might expect. Generally, it is easier for a few people to reach a decision than many, easier to reach a majority decision than a unanimous one. From such truisms, however, we cannot conclude that small and non-unanimous juries will, on the average, reach speedier verdicts than the large and unanimous ones, since the nature of the task facing them is also a factor. For example, a six-person jury faced with a complicated case for which it is asked to reach many decisions—e.g., is anyone of several defendants liable? if so, who and for how much?—may take much longer than a 12-person jury hearing a simple case.

Pound tested jury deliberation time in a number of ways. Its eight- and 12-person juries each required a little over three hours on the average to reach a verdict, but that finding is complicated by the fact that 12 of its 21 eight-person juries were required to reach a unanimous verdict and none of its 12-person juries were. The more meaningful figure, therefore, is unanimous vs. non-unanimous regardless of size, and here the Pound findings were more in line with other studies: unanimous requiring 45 minutes longer on the average than non-unanimous (three hours and 43 minutes vs. two hours and 58 minutes). Pound next tested for task factors. Acting on the theory that major injury cases will require more deliberation time (just as they do more trial time) than minor ones, Pound found that "long" deliberations (i.e., any that were longer than the average for unanimous-jury deliberations) led to average awards of $364,949.54, while in short deliberations, any under four hours, the average was $23,128.67. Pound also measured deliberation time based on the judge's assessment of the case's difficulty. The juries generally agreed with the judge's view. For cases the judge thought were easy, the average deliberation time was 2.3 hours, while for those the judge thought were at least of medium difficulty, the average was 4.6 hours. The Pound juries, therefore, provide substantial reason to believe that "difficulty of task" is a much more important factor than either size of jury or verdict requirement in determining length of deliberation.

The expectation that non-unanimous juries will mean fewer hung juries may be a correct one. Although no national statistics are available on hung juries, several studies have found that the unanimity requirement leads to non-verdicts about 5% of the time, non-unanimous 3%, a very considerable 40% reduction in frequency.[54] A Michigan study, however, concluded that in civil cases hung juries are extremely rare, occurring less than 1% of the time regardless of verdict requirement.[55] Though this study has not been replicated elsewhere, the 38 Pound civil juries, both those requiring unanimity and those not, were all able to reach a verdict. To the extent unanimous juries mean more non-verdicts, the loser in civil cases is the plaintiff, since in them a hung jury means the defendant keeps its money just as if it had won. In criminal cases, the personal consequences are less predictable; some defendants will consider themselves lucky to get a hung jury, others won't.

In studying the causes of hung juries, the key factor appears to be the size of the minority. The lone holdout who thwarts—for better or worse—the will of the majority and forces a non-decision in a unanimous-verdict situation is apparently more a figment of lawyer folklore and popular belief than a reality. Studies by psychologists suggest why. They have learned[56] that in any group the single holdout, because of peer pressure to conform, hardly ever maintains his or her position at the end when a unanimous vote is required.[57] However, when at least two people hold a minority position, the possibility of eventual unanimity drastically decreases, even in large groups. Several jury studies confirm the psychological premise. Broeder, in his review of hung juries, never found the holdout group to number less than three;[58] another study of 12-member juries that reached no verdict noted that four was the usual number.[59] Similarly, in each of Hastie's four hung juries, three of which required a unanimous verdict,[60] a multiple-member minority group was present from the outset.[61]

Consequently, if our only goal in rendering justice is to avoid hung juries, the verdict requirement in 12-person juries should probably be no more than eight or nine, with four in six-person juries.

Eliminating the hung jury, were it possible, however, may not always be desirable. Some cases can be too close to call. A judge, faced with that situation, must reach a verdict no matter how grave the doubts he or she may be entertaining, but a jury doesn't have to, and that can be a healthy result in terms of justice, and especially criminal justice. On this point, Kalven and Zeisel found that in fewer than half the hung juries in their study of criminal cases did the presiding judge think that the outcome was an unreasonable one.[62]

Drastic cutbacks in verdict requirement simply to avoid a hung jury could also serve to deter the full discussion of the evidence that is supposed to occur during deliberations. In Padawer-Singer's study, for example, we find that nearly a quarter of her six-person juries *at the outset* had five members in agreement, so that if only a five-sixths verdict were required, there would have been no need among them for any discussion of the evidence.[63]

Jurors' satisfaction with their service, several mock jury studies indicate, apparently is also related to the size of the panel and the verdict requirement. Padawer-Singer discovered the large majority of her jurors, regardless of the type of panel on which they served, preferred the 12-person unanimous.[64] Hastie's non-unanimous jurors frequently complained to him and his associates that their panel wasn't sufficiently "serious," with half those who originally didn't vote for the final verdict still thinking a mistake had been made,[65] whereas the unanimous jurors tended to be highly positive about their experiences.[66] The criticisms about the lack of seriousness, Hastie thought, may rise from the fact that when jurors have to reach a unanimous verdict, ultimately a commitment must be made to it by all of them.[67] In the non-unanimous situation, fragmentation may remain, with the dissidents separated out and likely to perceive what happened as arbitrary and unduly swift, i.e, non-serious. Since popular acceptance of the jury system is formulated, in part, by what former jurors say about it, jurors' satisfaction is not without its importance.

Pound attempted to test these theories among its real juries. As Hastie predicted, the highest percentage of satisfaction with verdict in Pound was among jurors required to render unanimous decisions (93%), although the non-unanimous jurors also expressed a high degree of satisfaction (86%). Pound also asked its respondents whether their fellow jurors took their duties seriously, another index of satisfaction with the process. Again there was a slight difference between unanimous and non-unanimous juries. Among the unanimous, 92% said that all jurors took their duties seriously, 8% "all but a couple of them," and none reported a non-serious jury generally. Among non-unanimous, 85.5% said that everyone took his or her duties seriously, 13.8% saying all but a few did, with only two jurors out of 223 saying that non-seriousness was prevalent.

Just as we hypothesized verdict differences based on jury size, so we should expect that the differences between unanimous and non-unanimous juries will lead to differences in verdict, and that—because of their comparative haste and alleged inferior degree of deliberation—the non-unanimous juries would come more frequently to wrong verdicts.

Hastie tested that premise in his study. The murder trial his jurors watched was one in which four verdicts were possible, according to the judge's instructions: first-degree murder, second-degree murder, voluntary manslaughter, and not guilty by reason of self-defense. The self-defense evidence was largely refuted by the facts, and there was no indication of premeditation, which should, therefore, have ruled out first-degree murder. The verdict reached in the actual trial was second-degree murder;[68] however, three experts consulted for this book agreed that voluntary manslaughter was an equally legally supportable decision to arrive at, and perhaps the more nearly correct one.[69] None of Hastie's unanimous or non-unanimous juries arrived at not guilty. Not counting the hung juries, 60% of all juries reached second-degree, and 31% manslaughter, or a 91% correct rate. The remaining six juries, all of them from among the non-unanimous juries, returned the "wrong" first-degree conviction.[70]

That the incorrect verdicts came from the non-unanimous juries backs the view that they perform relatively poorly, not only in the quality of their deliberations but also in their results. Looked at another way, however, if we count the hung juries as reaching "wrong" verdicts, then 20 of Hastie's 23 unanimous juries or 87% were right, as were 39 of his 46 non-unanimous or 85%. That's hardly a significant statistical difference. But from the defendant's point of view it is, since he had a 0% chance of being wrongly convicted of first-degree murder by the unanimous juries but a 13.3% chance (6 of 45) from the non-unanimous. (The 46th jury among the non-unanimous, it will be recalled, did not reach a verdict.)

Turning to civil non-unanimous vs. unanimous juries, we have only two studies, Pound's and Forer's. In Forer,[71] the unanimous juries returned verdicts for the plaintiff 80% of the time (22 to 6) while only 61% (12 of 22) of her non-unanimous juries did. If we use her statistics as our criterion, therefore, we would have to conclude that non-unanimous civil juries tend to be more pro-defense than the unanimous ones.

But perhaps we cannot. In Pound, the non-unanimous juries were slightly more likely to render plaintiff verdicts than the unanimous, although—just as was true of jury size—in Pound the strong indication is that location of the trial (suburban vs. big city) was a more important factor in determining who won than the verdict requirement. The question of whether verdict-requirement favors plaintiffs or defendants, therefore, remains unsettled.

Both Forer and Pound, however, did discern that requiring a unanimous verdict was likely to lead to lower awards for plaintiffs than in non-unanimous juries for reasons that will be discussed in the *Computing the Award* section below.

When we consider the entire body of research that has been accumulated on jury size and verdict requirement, it is apparent there is no easy or single answer to the question of whether or not the Supreme Court acted wisely in giving its imprimatur to small and non-unanimous juries. Each configuration has its strengths, each its weaknesses, with the six-person jury possibly weaker than the eight; further research on that issue is required. By separating civil from criminal cases, however, we can reach, at the least, some tentative conclusions.

For civil, the Supreme Court decisions do *not* appear to have created substantive unfairnesses that lead to endemic advantages for either the plaintiff or the defendant. Quite possibly, the best manner of determining jury format in these private matters is through agreement by the opposing attorneys, with the judge making the decision when the two sides cannot.

In criminal cases, however, the evidence of inferior deliberation quality by small and (particularly) non-unanimous juries is sufficiently alarming— since a person's freedom is at stake—that prudence dictates return to the 12- person, unanimous jury.

II

Jury Deliberation Methods.   The format of any debate, at least to some degree, controls its content and helps create its result; therefore, anything we can learn about how juries go about structuring their debates is prospectively of significant research importance. On this subject, the mock jury theoretically could provide a learning model, since both its members and those of real juries have been given the same task to perform and must figure out how to go about accomplishing it.

Mock jury studies, however, have almost entirely ignored structure—save occasionally, in vague, inferential ways. Instead, they have concentrated on content where the artificiality of the simulation is most likely to manifest itself, perhaps acutely in a "good behavior" syndrome[72] caused by the subjects' awareness that every word they say is being recorded. Hastie's study is the exception; when analyzing the tapes of his juries, he discerned two distinct structuring methods, although some of his juries adopted elements of both. One he called the *evidence-driven* model, the other the *verdict-driven*.[73] (Exactly why one jury will select one model over another is unclear in Hastie, but presumably someone—perhaps the foreperson— makes the structural suggestion, or else it simply doesn't occur to anyone to do it any other way.)

The labels are descriptive. Evidence-driven juries avoid talking about verdict-preferences until the testimony has been discussed and a series of point-by-point agreements reached about it. Verdict-driven juries, on the contrary, take a verdict-preference poll of the members at the outset, often directly followed by a period in which the jurors offer arguments to support their views. A more generalized discussion of the evidence can then ensue, but during it some jurors are likely to become defensive and feel they have to hold onto the verdict-choice they have already expressed, in that fashion setting up the kind of situation that leads to a hung jury.[74]

Hastie found the evidence-driven juries were more open-minded about accepting new points of view, were more thorough in their analysis of the evidence, less militant in their arguments when they did come to verdict-preferences, and discussed the applicable law more thoroughly than did the verdict-driven juries.[75] Although, no doubt, verdict-driven juries will often reach the same conclusion as the evidence-driven—particularly in relatively simple cases—the virtues of the evidence-driven model remedy, at least in part, the weaknesses that have been discerned in small and non-unanimous juries, and may offer a better means than the non-unanimous to prevent hung juries. Some courts, reaching the same conclusion as Hastie, have placed placards in their jury rooms urging the panel to discuss evidence before taking a vote,[76] and it may be that such a recommendation should become part of the judge's instructions to the jury.

In evidence-driven juries, the balloting functions largely to confirm agreements that have already been reached informally, while in the verdict-driven jury, balloting at the outset, aside from tending to rigidify positions, may also make jurors with non-assertive personalities reluctant to contribute their views in the face of obvious overwhelming opposition. To the extent this occurs, the early ballot does not so much assess the degree of agreement among the members as it prevents open disagreement. The coercion *may* be less prevalent when the ballot taken is secret, rather than open, but we have neither confirmation nor rebuttal for that hypothesis from Pound or other research. We don't even have agreement about how often open and secret ballots are employed. One mock-jury study of criminal cases indicates secret is used about 70% of the time,[77] while Padawer-Singer in her criminal trials discovered a difference based on size, with her six-member juries using secret and open ballots, the 12-member exclusively open ones.[78] No such difference was found among the Pound civil jurors who, in both large and small juries, overwhelmingly used the open raising of hands method.

Whenever the first verdict-vote is taken, and by whatever method, it reveals the degree of division of opinion that exists, if any. In the Chicago project about 30%[79] and in Pound about 18% of all juries were in unanimous agreement from the outset of the verdict deliberation, so presumably little or no further discussion was required among them. However, if the decision in civil was for the plaintiff, there still might be a lengthy debate to determine amount of award; and in criminal, questions about the degree of guilt can also lead to prolonged dispute. Divisions revealed by the balloting, at whatever stage they occur, bring up several questions: How do jurors go about swaying votes? How often do jurors change their minds? How often does the original minority become the majority?

Anapol[80] discovered that a favored method his mock jurors used for changing minds was to divide the panel into groups with several majority-opinion members taking on a minority-opinion member for persuasion, a kind of divide-and-conquer format. Pound, however, found that rarely occurred with real jurors. Among them, the more democratic method of general discussion among all the members was overwhelmingly the mode used.

If studies prior to Pound are correct,[81] in situations where the original vote is less than unanimous, the original majority almost always prevails, with Broeder observing that in only 4% of the Chicago Project juries did the original minority change the view of the majority.[82] (The Chicago Project makes no references to juries that were evenly divided at the outset.)

The Pound results were quite different. Based on a question asked in the survey completed at home, the original majority was overturned in one of every five juries, rather than the one in 25 discerned by the Chicago survey, a startling differential. (The first figure obtained by Pound was 30%, but it had to be adjusted downward to eliminate some contradictory responses.) The Pound phone survey turned up a very similar 18% victory rate for the original minority over the original majority.

Although the Pound findings don't necessarily negate the Chicago ones—the Pound sample is much smaller—from Pound we have a cross-check that wasn't present in Chicago, and that gives added support to the Pound results. The cross-check manifested itself in the frequency with which jurors change their minds during deliberations. Pound asked this question several ways and discovered a 19% to 25% rate, very much in accordance with the total verdict preference changes.

The Pound findings, in terms of both the occasions in which the original majority did not prevail and the frequency with which jurors changed their minds, therefore depict a deliberation process marked by a free and open exchange of views (which is what 98% of the Pound jurors said occurred) in which democracy is very much at work and in which verdicts are not forced by overwhelming pressures laid by an outset majority, as the earlier studies indicated.[83]

The Role of the Foreperson. In a 1984 study, only 36% of the jurors surveyed answered "yes" to the question: "Was the foreperson especially influential during deliberations?"[84] The way the question was worded may have increased the number of negative responses, but the result even so is consonant with two mock jury studies[85] which found no consistent patterns of behavior or influence on the part of forepersons. Pound's results on the foreperson's role were equally inconclusive. A more detailed analysis comes from Hastie. The average forepersons of his juries spoke three times more frequently than other jurors but made fewer statements about their own preferences; in general, they seemed to have performed or attempted to perform the catalyst function that might be expected of them. They were the members who most often introduced legal issues, did the most to generate discussion of the evidence, and were the most likely to summarize what others said.[86] However, in a third of Hastie's 69 juries, despite the leadership position, the foreperson was not the member who spoke most frequently.[87]

The apparent failure of some forepersons to fill the leadership role of their position may rise from the methods of selecting them. In a number of jurisdictions, the judge names the foreperson, and it would be difficult for any judge, no matter how wise, to be able to divine who of six to 12 silent people has natural leadership qualities. Many judges, hoping for the best, simply name Juror Number One, the individual first selected for the panel, as foreperson.

The jurors themselves are in a bit better position to name a leader by having gotten to know each other, at least slightly, during trial recesses. Yet, when they have the opportunity to make the selection, it is far from clear they do it based on the impressions made then. Pound found that general discussion, sometimes incorporating a vote, was the most common method of selection. Research using mock juries has shown a positioning factor frequently at work, with those who happen to sit at the ends of the table in the jury room named foreperson three times more often than would occur by chance.[88] Three relatively early studies (1957, 1968, 1975) determined that men predominantly were chosen for the office, with the most likely candidate a business proprietor who initiated conversations and who was seated at an end position when the selection discussion began.[89] Considering the economic and social advances women have made since the most recent study, we cannot be certain whether that would still be true.

Jury Discussion Content. If Strodtbeck's and Hook's 1961 study can be believed,[90] the shape of the jury table also has an influence on what is discussed and by whom. When the table is rectangular, the study determined, that the end jurors and those in the middle speak the most often. Since they are the ones who have maximum eye-contact with the others, they are able to see when somebody has finished talking so they can jump in. Jurors with executive backgrounds in Strodtbeck and Hook often seized the powerful seats, suggesting they were making use of dominance ploys that they learned from business life. When the table is round, such positional gamesplaying isn't possible, and degree of juror participation is higher.

Regardless of the type of table, regardless of panel size or verdict requirement, juries, according to a number of studies, including Pound,[91] often discuss matters the judge told them to ignore or which were not mentioned in the trial, with insurance apparently the topic most likely to turn up in civil jury debates.[92] (For more on insurance, see *Computing the Award* section below.) According to one study,[93] irrelevant factors, including litigant personalities and social status,[94] are most likely to intrude when the evidence is unclear, a finding analogous to the conclusion reached by a study mentioned earlier, that the more doubtful the case the more likely evidence ruled inadmissible would be entered into the debate. (The results of neither of these studies, however, have been replicated, and Pound had no means of doing so.) A debate, it appears, is what goes on, not a fight. A Goldberg-Walter study found that in only about 10% of the juries it surveyed did members become angry with one another at any point during the deliberations.[95]

Considering our knowledge of group decision-making—from formal studies of it, as well as the common experience of those who participate in such activities—it would be utterly amazing to hear that irrelevancies did not sometimes creep into jury deliberations. What is impressive, based on a consensus view of the research, is how little of it occurs. Studies including Pound virtually uniformly indicate that, contrary to the contentions of irresponsibility raised by Judge Frank and other critics of the system, jury discussions are highly serious,[96] highly relevant,[97] and highly concerned with the facts of the case.[98]

Examples abound. A 1952 study reported jurors' concern about the difficulty of recalling large amounts of evidence in protracted trials, which indicates the seriousness with which they viewed their role; and an earlier study reported the jurors said they found group discussion of the evidence vital in helping them make up their minds,[99] confirming Pound's finding that jurors are frequently uncertain of their outset verdict-preferences. Anapol discovered, just as Hastie did, that discussion of the evidence dominated the activities of mock jurors who, in Anapol, particularly focused their attention on the testimony of expert witnesses, eyewitness testimony, and courtroom exhibits,[100] a finding for which confirmation can be found in Pound. Kalven and Zeisel, in *The American Jury*, concluded that criminal case jurors heavily weighed—and almost always understood—the evidence presented to them.[101] Hastie discovered that evidence discussion took up about 53% of the deliberation time[102] and was of "high quality,"[103] with the key case elements regularly recognized and discussed.[104] His conclusion: As fact-finders, jurors are "remarkably competent."[105]

The Rand study of civil verdicts in Cook County offers supporting statistical evidence. It learned, based on 14,300 cases, that the severity of the plaintiff's injury—the element that would be most likely to sway sympathy toward the plaintiff and away from the facts—bore no relationship to the probability of a plaintiff's verdict.[106] Pound also asked its jurors if seriousness of injury had an effect on their "decision," and contrary to Rand learned that 63% of those whose juries voted for the plaintiff said seriousness was a factor. Pound, however, may not be helpful here since some of the plaintiff verdict jurors may have interpreted "decision" to refer to how they determined the amount they awarded, a point at which seriousness of injury is relevant. Because of the ambiguity of the Pound phrasing, as well as the much larger size of the Rand sample, the Rand result should be considered the more reliable. Another Pound finding was more in accord with the Rand study: Nearly two-thirds of the jurors who voted for the defense reported they felt "sorry" for the plaintiff, presumably because of his or her injuries, but concluded that the law and the facts were against that person.

Jury beliefs about injury, according to lawyer folklore, will harm the plaintiff when jurors decide that the plaintiff has exaggerated the results of the accident or has malingered by not trying to find a job following recovery. Such instances may well occur and have the result that lawyers believe they do (and not necessarily improperly so, since the plaintiff's credibility is a legitimate jury concern). No research on the subject has been uncovered. The Pound juries that considered plaintiff exaggeration or malingering were too few to draw any statistical inferences. It is not permissible from Pound, however, to conclude that juries hardly ever concern themselves with malingering or exaggeration when such evidence manifests itself, since it is possible that the vast majority of the Pound trials simply did not contain situations in which such questions would arise.

In the case of defendants, Pound found that social responsibility guided the thinking of some of the jurors. Fifteen percent of the respondees said that their belief that the "defendant should be taught a lesson" was part of their reason for arriving at a plaintiff's verdict, and 30% hoped their verdict would "prevent other people or companies from doing the same thing as this defendant did." (The jury's role as an arbiter of public conduct will be discussed in Chapter Nine; see also *Computing the Award* section below in this chapter.)

Jurors in their discussions also seem to be concerned with applying the law properly. A very substantial 46% of the Pound jurors said that the law as explained to them by the judge was the most important factor in making their decision. Fifty percent said the evidence; the remainder, the lawyer's closing speeches. (It should be noted, however, that these were the only three choices they were given.)

Geography and the Jury.   Lawyer folklore teaches that rural and suburban jurors tend to be pro-defense in civil cases, while big-city jurors are more likely to be pro-plaintiff. According to this reasoning, the general affluence and conservatism of those who live outside big cities makes them sympathetic toward defendants, especially when they are businesses, while big-city jurors, who are much less well-to-do on the average, are likely to sympathize with the small individual who is taking on the ''system'' (big business, insurance companies) through his or her suit. Except for Pound, no research on the subject has been discovered. (The Chicago Jury Project had a great deal of information available, but apparently never published an analysis.) Since none of the Pound trials took place in a rural area, and since few of the jurors in either the federal or suburban county juries had a rural address, Pound's inquiry had to be restricted to possible differences between suburban and big city jurors. In so doing, it discovered a statistically significant relationship—less than one chance in a thousand that the result could have been achieved by accident—between court location and juror *pre-deliberation* choice of verdict, with the big-city jurors, at that point, leaning heavily toward the plaintiff, and both the suburban and federal juries (most of whose members did not live in a big city) showing pro-defense majorities.

When final verdicts are considered along with pre-deliberation leanings by individual jurors, the portrait becomes somewhat more complex. The big-city jurors eventually found for the plaintiff 70% of the time, as might be expected from the pre-deliberation views, although there were instances in which, despite an initial pro-plaintiff majority, the defense won. The same phenomenon occurred in reverse in federal juries where plaintiffs eventually won 58% of the time, and suburban where a plaintiff's verdict occurred eventually in half the cases.

Pound, therefore, would appear to provide us with a measure of substantiation for the folklore beliefs about suburban and big-city juries, strongly so at the stage before deliberation and much less so but still indicatively (70% plaintiff verdicts in big-city, 50% in suburban) in terms of final outcome.

We cannot, however, conclude from the Pound findings, even were they to be replicated by a national survey, that suburban jurors have pro-defense and big-city jurors pro-plaintiff biases. (Pound discovered no such indications, although its methodology was unlikely to uncover deep-rooted feelings one way or the other.) What we may be seeing, instead, in large part, is a self-fulfilling prophecy at work. For example, insurance companies are likely to be tough on settlements when they have a suburban case because they expect they'll have a favorable jury there and (perhaps more importantly) a greater likelihood than in the big city of a conservative, pro-defense judge presiding. As a consequence, plaintiffs may be forced to trial in weak cases that would have been settled elsewhere, and the juries, recognizing the evidentiary weakness, find for the defendant. Conversely, in big cities plaintiffs may reject settlements because they expect to do better before the pro-plaintiff judge or jury they hope to find there. Again, the juries recognize the merits of the case and find accordingly. If this hypothesis is correct, big-city courts should produce higher plaintiff win ratios, and for larger amounts, because they get stronger plaintiff cases than do the suburban courts.

Trial location decisions can also lead to strong plaintiff cases reaching city courts. For example, if the injured person lives in a suburb and the defendant is a corporation headquartered in a city, the plaintiff's lawyer will probably choose to have the case tried in the city to avoid the presumably more con-servative, pro-defense jurors and judges of the suburbs. Again the prophecy is a self-fulfilling one: A suburban jury might come up with the same verdict as the allegedly more liberal city one, but because the lawyer fears it won't, the case never gets to it. Still another reason big-city jurors might seem more pro-plaintiff than suburban ones is that the most skilled plaintiffs' lawyers—i.e., those who get the best results before a judge or a jury—principally practice in big cities whose residents have easier access to them than do those who live elsewhere.

Thus, suburban jurors (as Pound indicates) may in fact tend to be more pro-defense than big-city ones—with each group reflecting its community values as juries are supposed to—but it also may be that litigant choices, prompted by these perceptions, make them more often true than they would otherwise be.

Though the Pound findings lend themselves to many possible analyses, at the very least they warn us that geographic considerations, which have hitherto been nearly entirely ignored in jury studies, may be a more important verdict-index than either jury size or verdict requirement.

Education.   Jury studies in this area, including Pound's, have not reached any conclusive results, perhaps because none are to be found: A civil litigation has no inherent qualities that should cause bias based solely on educational attainment. Pound discovered its college-educated jurors were more likely to favor defendants than plaintiffs than were those with a high school education or less, but this appeared to be a reflection on economic status: i.e., college-educated people generally have more income and more often hold corporate executive positions than those who don't, leading to the economic conservatism that benefits defendants and their insurance com-panies. (Pound jurors with post-graduate degrees did not show pro-defense inclinations, but the number of them in the sample was quite small.)

Occupation.   Neither from Pound nor other studies can significant substantiation be found for the lawyer folklore beliefs that members of certain occupations are inherently pro-plaintiff or pro-defense, save possibly to the extent that certain occupations lead to high income, causing the "suburban" conservatism to come into play. In terms of participation in jury deliberations, occupation appears to play at most a minor role. One study found that unskilled workers and housewives were the ones least likely to participate in deliberations.[107] In Hastie's juries, there was no discernible pattern in evidence discussion among members of different occupations.[108]

Gender.   The studies regularly report that women jurors are less likely to speak than men. Male participation in Hastie's juries, for example, was 40% higher than female,[109] with women more likely to make irrelevant statements than men.[110] The validity of this information, however, is suspect, since it fails to deal with the possible effects of proportionate representation by sex; i.e.: What is the interaction when women make up the large majority of the jury, when men do, when the division is equal, and so on? Neither do we find studies that compare degree of participation by high-status women vs. low-status men, and all the permutations of that configuration.

In terms of verdict choice by sex, some studies have found women more likely to acquit in criminal cases than men, but others have reached the opposite conclusion.[111] Generally, however, studies agree[112] that men and women display no significant differences in their perception of evidence or their ability to understand the judge's instructions.[113] Pound found no relationship between gender and verdict.

Religion.   Jury research reveals nothing that either affirms or rebuts the lawyer folklore on this subject.

Age.   A British study found that young jurors are more lenient than older ones in criminal cases.[114] Hastie observed that older jurors scored lower than young ones on recall of the case facts and the judge's instructions, with the highest quality contributions coming from those in the 34 to 56 age bracket.[115] Elwork's results, based on comprehension of judge instructions, were in agreement with Hastie.[116] Pound found no relationship between age and likelihood of a plaintiff's or defendant's verdict.

Ethnicity.   We find nothing reliable or even particularly indicative in this area, based on the academic research. One study showed that blacks were more likely to acquit in criminal cases than whites[117] thereby fulfilling the folklore predictions of district attorneys everywhere. (Pound, as noted, asked no questions based on ethnicity.)

Politics.   That a person's political leanings might influence his or her performance as a juror has frequently been a concern of lawyers, but the academic findings are slight[118] and Pound did not ask such questions. Hastie observed some tendency on the part of his conservative jurors to view the judge as favoring the defense, while politically liberal jurors saw the same judge as favoring the prosecution.[119] Such perceptions of judicial bias, however, are rare, according to a Pennsylvania survey of real jurors in which over 98% of the respondents described their judge as "fair and impartial."[120]

Hastie's one consistent finding about the relationship of politics and jury service was a peculiar one: Jurors who were left-wingers and conservatives, he discovered, recalled case facts and legal instructions much better than did liberals or right-wingers.[121] That is something to ponder—but to what purpose is unclear.

Prior Contact With the Justice System.   Our only source is Pound. Among its jurors who had earlier dealings with the justice system in the form of a lawsuit, only 10% reported the experience had been a bad one, no doubt a surprising result to critics of the courts. Perhaps more importantly, in terms of open-mindedness, jurors did not allow their past experiences to determine their verdict preferences. Those who had been defendants voted for plaintiffs 59% of the time, while those who had been plaintiffs voted for defendants

42% of the time, or at almost exactly the same ratio, in both instances, as jurors who had been neither plaintiffs nor defendants.

Previous experience as a juror, according to Hastie[122] and Pound, appears to have no effect on that person's verdict judgment in a subsequent jury.

Psychological Factors.   Studies here are either contradictory, have not been replicated, or could be misleading. For example, two mock studies concluded that juries are psychologically dependent upon the judge and seek to please him or her by their verdict; however, in Hastie's much more sophisticated study, judge-dependency appears only peripherally and then only among some jurors; as noted above, it is nearly absent among the Pound jurors.

Similarly, although a number of studies have found that authoritarian personalities are most punitive, there is little research support for the belief that such people are more likely than others to turn in a guilty verdict in a criminal case. If that is true, then the death-qualified jury, which by its nature consists of people who accept extreme forms of authoritarian punishment, may not be especially conviction-prone, although it will be likely to recommend the death penalty in situations in which a jury composed of less authoritarian types might not. This analysis, however, still lacks conclusive proof in all its aspects. The impact, if any, of authoritarian personalities in civil cases does not appear to have been studied by academic researchers. (Pound had no way of developing psychological profiles among its jurors.)

The difficulty of making assumptions about the psychology of the jury is illustrated by an Ohio study which correlated jurors' views about the causes of crime with the verdicts rendered. It found surprisingly that jurors who believed that crime was caused by environmental factors were *more* likely to arrive at guilty verdicts than those who thought crime was the work of "bad" people.[123]

Bias.   Whether it has its wellspring in psychological or socioeconomic causes, or some combination of both, prejudice whether on the part of jury or judge or lawyer is justice's well-recognized and most formidable enemy. Numerous efforts, as we saw in Chapter Three, have been made to contain its impact or to make its appearance less likely in juries.

Relatively few jury studies,[124] however, have attempted to assess jury bias, quite possibly because the issue is such a subjective one or, as with Pound, the research method prevents it. Most of the evidence we have is negative. For example, neither Padawer-Singer nor Hastie, in their large-scale mock jury studies, report on finding significant examples of it (though that could be due to the nature of the trial they showed to their jurors, or to the good behavior syndrome).

The Rand Corporation undertook the major attempt to assay racial bias in the jury as part of its study of civil cases in Chicago. Its statistics show that over the 20-year period of the study (1959 to 1979), black plaintiffs consistently were less likely to win and black defendants more likely to lose than were white ones, the black-plaintiff win ratio rising only when the defendant was also black.[125] Even when they won, black plaintiffs suing black defendants got 40% less money than did white plaintiffs suing white defendants, with blacks also getting 25% less money than whites for the same type of injury. In cases involving serious injuries, the black average award was $45,000 less than for whites.[126]

Although the differences in results are extreme, the Rand statistics by themselves do not offer proof of racial bias by juries. Rand itself provides one partial explanation based on non-racist reasons when it notes that, in Chicago, a significantly higher percentage of black-plaintiff trials involved automobile collisions than was true among whites. Since auto accident cases are a category in which negligence by the plaintiff is often successfully averred at trial,[127] the result is a relatively low plaintiff win rate, for both blacks and whites, or (when comparative negligence is the criterion) a reduced award. The disparity in award sizes for blacks and whites, however, probably can most frequently be explained by the economic condition of the plaintiff. Blacks, on the whole, earn less money than whites, so that their recoverable wage-loss from an injury will be comparably less. Blacks also are more likely to live in poverty than whites which means they are eligible for Medicaid coverage when they are injured, so that their out-of-pocket medical expenses, a major basis for recovery in an injury suit, will be less, on the average, than for whites.

With these considerations in mind, it becomes clear that, in order to prove racial bias by jurors derived from award differentials, we require comparables, i.e., figures which show that when blacks and whites are of the same income level and incur similar injuries and similar financial losses, blacks still receive less money than whites. The Rand study does not provide that information,[128] nor have any other studies been discovered that deal with this question.

Given the history of race relations in this country, it would, of course, be naive to believe that white jurors are never prejudiced against black litigants or vice versa.[129] In Chicago, the white bias, to the extent it exists, was almost certainly exacerbated during the period of the Rand study by the very low percentage of blacks in the jury pool,[130] the result, as we saw in Chapter Three, of the frequent failure by black citizens to respond to a required questionnaire. Presumably, were more blacks on juries in Chicago, their presence would mitigate the white bias that might exist when they are absent.

The failure to respond to the call to jury duty, in turn, may reflect a sense of alienation that many blacks feel toward the justice system. Rand discovered evidence of this possibility when it learned that blacks generally were less likely to sue than whites, and particularly less likely in cases such as medical malpractice, in which the damage awards can be high. Failure to sue when the grounds are present is, no doubt, frequently the consequence of ignorance brought about by educational deprivation and the social isolation imposed by a ghetto life. In many instances, however, this failure arises from various trepidations more common in members of the underclass (be they black or white) than to members of the middle class. Out of trepidation, an underclass member, who has only the most marginal of work skills and is frequently out of a job, will hesitate, as a middle-class member might not, to bring a legal action against an employer, and may well fear that filing a malpractice claim against a hospital or doctor will cause the "system" to take away his or her welfare and Medicaid benefits. Automobile accident suits are different; they will either be won or lost and carry with them no danger, fancied or real, of economic reprisal.

Even when the decision is made to seek legal help, the underclass member may have difficulty finding a lawyer to take the case, since the prospective plaintiff's poverty minimizes the cash value of the case from which the lawyer earns his or her fee. Still other underclass members may decide to take no action at all, not out of trepidation over consequences but because they aren't familiar with the contingency fee system and assume they'd have to pay a lawyer an hourly rate which they know they can't afford. What the Rand study, therefore, primarily proves is the consequences of being poor and black in America and not the consequences of trial by jury in America.

Multiple Theories for Recovery.   Rand discovered, though no other research has, that the more legal theories advanced by the plaintiff, the greater the likelihood the plaintiff would win.[131] Psychologically, the Rand finding is viable: Give people many reasons for doing what you want them to do, and they are more likely to do it than if you give them only one reason. However, it seems also true that multiple theories advanced for recovery by plaintiffs are most likely to occur in cases in which there are also multiple defendants.[132] For example, if the defendants include both a hospital and a supplier of that hospital's equipment, the plaintiff may wish to show that the equipment was faulty (making the supplier liable) and that the hospital was negligent in not inspecting it (making the hospital liable). In terms of multiple defendants and multiple theories, therefore, the result may be more plaintiff wins, just as Rand says, but not necessarily more defendant losses (e.g., four defendants, four theories, jury accepts one theory against one defendant, result: plaintiff wins but so do three of the four defendants).

Vulnerable Plaintiffs.   A study of 136 cases by Jury Verdict Research, Inc.,[133] found that juries are more likely to find in favor of a plaintiff who was physically or mentally handicapped at the time of the accident than for plaintiffs generally. Sympathy might be involved in handicap-verdicts, but such verdicts may equally likely reflect the jury's belief that such a person is less able to avoid the consequences of an injurious action than the non-handicapped, thereby largely or entirely eliminating contributory or comparative negligence. The very obese plaintiff, on the contrary, was said to have a lower win rate than the average, perhaps because jurors are prejudiced against fat people, but more probably because obesity was a factor in the case as a pre-existing health condition that lessened, in the jurors' eyes, the liability of the defendant. The same study found that plaintiffs with a criminal record were vulnerable to juries, too, not in their likelihood of winning or losing but in that those with criminal records received lower awards than those without them for the same type of injury.

Computing the Award.   When a civil jury has found in favor of the plaintiff, its work has only begun. The members must now decide how to translate the injury into money due the plaintiff. (Exception: In some jurisdictions for some cases, one jury decides the liability issue, and if its verdict is for the plaintiff, a second jury is empaneled to hear the damage evidence and make the award.)

Jurors get little help from their judge on how to go about their damage-award task,[134] though if an interrogatory sheet has been provided, it can help as a guideline. Fundamentally, however, all they are told is that their duty is to make the plaintiff ''whole,'' i.e., restore him or her to the condition that would have existed had the tortious action not taken place. To do this, they are to take into account the plaintiff's *special* damages, such as medical costs and lost income, both existent and those reasonably likely to occur in the future. (Medical expenses, according to Rand, are the best predictor of award size.[135]) If the action is on behalf of a dead person, the special damages reflect the financial loss the death caused the deceased's family, presently and for the future, although in some states a ceiling is placed on the amount that can be awarded.[136] Jurors are also permitted to award *general* damages to cover the plaintiff's pain and suffering, and if they think the defendant's action was outrageous, they may further award exemplary (to make an example of) or, as they are more commonly known, *punitive* damages.

In making their awards, juries have to start somewhere, and several studies strongly suggest[137] that the dollar-figure provided them by the plaintiff's lawyer is usually the basis for their discussion and sometimes its finishing point as well.[138] Pound found that the lawyer's figure was accepted more or less as given only about 32% of the time. However, the Pound figures on this subject may not be useful. Its survey took place in one of the few jurisdictions in which the plaintiff's lawyer is not permitted to name a dollar figure for pain-and-suffering, so that its jurors did not have a dollar-figure available for consideration that most other juries do.

The degree of difficulty that a jury has in reaching agreement on a plaintiff's verdict appears, in some cases, to diminish the amount of money that the plaintiff receives. As was noted earlier in this chapter, the unanimous verdict juries in Forer's study found for the plaintiff more often than did the non-unanimous juries but when (in her judgment) they erred on amount of award, it was usually on the low side, while the non-unanimous juries were more likely to err on the high side.[139]

In theory—a theory which Pound tested—what we are seeing in the Forer figures is the effect of compromise. When a jury has to reach a unanimous verdict in a civil case, three scenarios can develop: first, following discussion everyone agrees on the verdict and if the decision is for the plaintiff, the body then proceeds to the award using the various damage factors discussed in this section; second, following discussion there is no agreement but the majority favors the plaintiff; third, following discussion there is no agreement but the majority favors the defendant. In the second and third scenarios, in order to avoid a hung jury, which no one wants, the majority must find a way to accommodate the views of the minority, with money becoming the basis for the agreement that is finally reached. Hence, when the pro-defense forces are in the majority and cannot convince the minority, they eventually give way by allowing a plaintiff's verdict but only after the plaintiff-minority agrees to a much smaller amount than it would have given. When the opposite situation is true, the plaintiff-majority holds to its verdict and obtains the necessary votes from the defense minority by lowering the amount it wants to give. The result, either way, is more plaintiff verdicts, less money.

In non-unanimous juries, the compromise comes into play only when neither side has enough votes to control the verdict. When the pro-defense forces do, they need pay no attention to a pro-plaintiff minority; when the plaintiff-forces do, they need not lower the amount they want to award in order to get the defense-minority to go along with them. The result is higher awards for plaintiffs.

If this analysis is substantially correct, it means that the unanimous-verdict requirement in civil cases forces compromise contrivances on jurors that they would not otherwise entertain, and may be repelled by. Although this kind of compromise will occur less often in non-unanimous juries, we should expect a fairly high frequency among them even so, dependent on the percentage of agreement required. (Seven of eight required to agree will lead to more compromises of this kind than eight of 12 and so on.)

In the Pound study, all the federal court cases required a unanimous verdict, and in them winning plaintiffs had their awards reduced (though we don't know by how much) 54% of the time in order for the majority to obtain agreement from the minority that favored the defendant. In the suburban courts, which operated on a five-sixths rule (i.e., 10 had to agree when the panel had 12 members, seven when it had eight), such reductions occurred 45% of the time; and in the big-city courts, which also used the five-sixths rule, reductions occurred in one-third of the cases. The generally stronger pro-plaintiff feeling in the big-city court compared to the suburban probably explains the difference in the frequency with which compromise reductions became necessary.

Even when all or almost all the jurors agree that the plaintiff should win, there is sometimes widespread disagreement on amount, and when further discussion fails to produce an agreement, the members may then take all the suggested amounts and average them to reach a result. Pound found this happening about 40% of the time. Elwork also observed the phenomenon among his mock jurors, but noted that it occurred only as a last resort when amounts were far apart and no other form of agreement seemed possible.[140] Kalven reached much the same conclusion, but pointed out that the averaging seemed to emerge as part of the natural flow of the discussion, rather than as a formal process and that may be what typically happened with the Pound jurors.[141] Some critics of the jury system[142] express horror that jurors ever average a verdict, yet judges frequently do the same in settlement conferences, urging the contesting lawyers to "split the difference"—i.e., hit the average between the plaintiff's demand and the defense's offer—in order to conclude the case.

The effect that punitive thinking has upon a jury when computing an award is complex. We know that at least 15% of the responding Pound jurors wanted to teach the defendant a lesson and nearly a third wanted the award to serve as a warning to others, yet in only one Pound jury was a separate punitive damage award made, suggesting that jurors often apply this factor indirectly.

Because of it, they may be more likely to accept the plaintiff's assertion of damages, or they may add the punitive dollars into the pain-and-suffering portion of the award. (The possible impact of hidden punitive awards will be discussed further in Chapter Seven.)

The role that insurance, either the plaintiff's or the defendant's, plays in the jurors' decisions about awards was studied by Pound both through the questionnaire that jurors answered immediately after trial and that which they completed at home. Based on the courtroom questionnaire, we find that 29% of the juries discussed the probability that the plaintiff may have had either medical insurance or workmen's compensation to cover part or all of the injury expenses. However, only four of the jurors answering the question stated that their belief that the plaintiff had insurance affected their verdict in a major way, with 23 more saying the effect was minor.

The home questionnaire produced a different result. It limited its inquiry to juries that made a plaintiff award (unlike the courtroom questionnaire) and asked not whether the responding juror was *personally* affected by the plaintiff's presumed insurance coverage, but whether that person's jury *as a whole* acted on that belief. When the question was phrased that way, there were 123 replies, with 16 (13%) saying their jury lowered the award because they believed the plaintiff had a portion or all of his or her losses covered by medical insurance. Forty percent said the matter was never discussed, and the remainder said the subject came up but was not an award factor. Since for the home questionnaire more jurors responded from some trials than from others, the result cannot be taken to mean that awards were reduced for insurance reasons 13% of the time. Even so, when the answers to both questions are taken together, we can see that award reductions because of jurors' beliefs about plaintiffs' medical insurance apparently occur fairly rarely; that they should happen at all indicates that jurors are often not aware that a plaintiff is ordinarily required to repay his or her medical insurer from any award he or she receives.

Contrary to the belief held in many quarters—see the discussion of "deep-pocket" awards in Chapter Seven—Pound found no evidence that size of award is frequently based on the belief that the defendant has insurance to cover the damages. When asked if they thought the defendant carried insurance, 54% of the Pound jurors said yes (almost always because they knew from personal experience that such a party would be insured), 8% said no, and a very substantial 38% said that insurance never occurred to them. Of the 286 jurors who responded to the defendant insurance question, only nine (3%) said that their belief that the defendant's insurance could cover all or part of the award had an "important" effect on their decision, with 34 more (12%) saying it had a "minor effect" on them. Thus, 85% of the time beliefs about the defendant's insurance played no role in determining award size.

In cases in which there are multiple defendants, the possibility exists that jurors will assess the largest amounts against those they believe have the most insurance. Among the Pound jurors who had to allot liability among several defendants, none said that relative ability to pay was the sole criterion, and only 27% recalled that the subject was discussed even as a minor factor.

In summary, from Pound and other studies we can state with a very high degree of certainty that insurance is frequently discussed in civil jury deliberations, but that it does not appear to have, in most cases, a substantive effect either on verdict or on an amount of award rendered. To the extent either side is harmed by such discussions, it is apparently most frequently the plaintiff, though that conclusion can be stated only tentatively.

In their desire to fulfill their obligation to make the plaintiff whole, some juries, according to Rand[143] (as well as anecdotal evidence), add a sum to the award to cover the interest the plaintiff would have earned on money that was, instead, paid out to cover the cost of the injury. Several studies indicate that jurors also frequently discuss the plaintiff's lawyer's fee.[144] From the jurors' view, such conversation would not be idle, since they have been told by the judge that, if they find for the plaintiff, they must make that person monetarily whole, which cannot happen unless they allow for the lawyer's share. Elwork discovered[145] that between a quarter and a third of his mock juries, therefore, increased the size of the award to accommodate the lawyer's fee. (Both Pound and Elwork discovered that juries are familiar with how the contingency fee works.) Among the real jurors surveyed by Pound, however, only 6% report that this occurred on their jury, a markedly different result from Elwork.

The lawyer's fee can also apparently sometimes be handled by another method. Kalven, in a 1958 study, learned that the members of a high-award faction often successfully make the argument to the low-award faction that the higher amount is necessary to cover the fee,[146] although Kalven also concluded that discussion of the fee, absent other factors, was not sufficient to raise the award.[147] There is no indication of this taking place in the Pound juries, although the question was not specifically asked.

When a negligence trial occurs in a jurisdiction which has a comparative-award rule (as was true in the three courts Pound surveyed), jurors face an additional computing factor. Although comparative statutes vary from state to state, broadly they require that the plaintiff prevail when the defendant is mostly at fault, but with the amount the plaintiff receives reduced by the percentage of his or her own fault. In states which still hold to the contributory negligence doctrine—i.e., the plaintiff loses if at fault to any degree—some juries apparently apply the rule but others don't, adopting the comparative standard on their own. (The history and application by juries of contributory and comparative negligence standards will be discussed further in Chapters Five and Nine.)

III

To this point, we have been principally concerned with the mechanics of jury decision-making; also of importance are the opinions of the process held by those who participate in it, the judges, the lawyers, and the jurors themselves.

The Lawyers.   Of the three groups, the lawyers are least frequently consulted by researchers, even though many of them make it a practice to talk to jurors after a case to learn why they did what they did, and so should be a useful source of knowledge on that score alone.

One of the few studies that did make use of lawyers' discernments about juries focused on medical malpractice trials, which are usually of considerable length and a high degree of legal and factual difficulty. Jurors in these cases were found capable of following the evidence by 94% of the plaintiff lawyers surveyed and 97% of the defense lawyers. The same percentage of defense lawyers and 91% of the plaintiff lawyers agreed the jurors had grasped the legal issues as well.[148] (The jury and the highly technical case is the subject of Chapter Eight.)

The Judges.   Although some jurists, such as Judge Frank, have expressed grave reservations about the jury system and would like to see it abolished or radically overhauled,[149] they appear to be very much in the minority. In 1977, the Association of Trial Lawyers of America polled 6,544 judges across the United States, of whom 3,446 responded with almost 90% favoring retention of the jury system.[150] One respondent wrote: "I think that twelve people can decide factual issues as well as any good judge. Ofttimes, they arrive at a more just result, unplagued by undue consideration of legal niceties we must consider."[151]

They apparently also do their jobs well, if the judges are to be believed. The Kalven and Zeisel judges thought that verdicts by their juries were "without merit" only 9% of the time,[152] with most of the other disagreements rising from reasonable differences in interpretation of the evidence by judge and jury.[153] The 75% agreement between judge and jury on verdict that Kalven and Zeisel discovered is consonant with a number of separate studies which found judges agreeing with jury verdicts from 72% to 90% of the time.[154]

The Jurors.   The University of Chicago Project reported that 48% of all people called for jury duty would have preferred to get out of it—41% among Pound jurors—but that *after* service, 94% declared they wanted to serve again, 3% would be willing, and the remaining 3% not willing.[155] In a 1985 Walter-Goldberg study, jurors were asked if they would be willing to serve "soon again," phrasing that seems likely to develop the maximum number of negative responses; even so, 48% said yes, 29% no, the remaining 23% not certain.[156] A year earlier, a study undertaken in six Pennsylvania courts by the Center for Jury Studies reported that 89% of the jurors it surveyed described their experience as a positive one.[157]

Padawer-Singer discovered that the overwhelming majority of her subjects also endorsed the jury system, and that "almost all were imbued with the importance of the jury . . . once they have sat."[158] If charged with a crime, 89.9% said they would prefer to be tried by a jury, while 78.8% said they would want a jury if involved in a civil case.[159] When asked why they approved of jury trial, the reasons most commonly mentioned by the Padawer-Singer jurors were: It's the "fairest" method of getting justice (29%); the deliberation process was good (13.2%); the cross section of opinion encountered was positive (11.9%); 12 heads are better than one

(9.4%). Among the few criticisms leveled by the Padawer-Singer jurors, the two mentioned most frequently were: Jurors require more education, experience, and knowledge of the law than they have (3.3%) and jurors indulged too much in speculation and valued emotion over facts (2.2%).[160]

The University of Chicago Project questions were somewhat different from Padawer-Singer's but produced similar result: 70% of its juror respondents said they thought jury trial was the best way to try a case, 21% were unsure, with only 9% thinking that bench trials were best.[161] In Pound, 97% of the respondents described the jury as a "good" system for resolving civil disputes. (One complaint that jurors have—and it is expressed regularly—concerns the amount of waiting they are forced to undergo, the waiting to be selected, and the waiting during trial while legal matters are argued out at side-bar or in the judge's chamber.)[162]

IV

What then do we know about the American jury? As the preceding discussion has illustrated, some of the information with which the research provides us is contradictory, is the consequence of studies with substantive structural limitations, or has not been replicated (as is the case with those Pound findings that delved into areas that previous jury studies had not touched upon). The research, for example, is frustratingly anomalous on a matter of great importance to lawyers and their clients, i.e., how to detect the biased venireman in order to keep him or her off the jury. It may be, considering the marvelous complexity of the human soul, that no sound guidelines on that subject can ever be forthcoming.

Some of the research information serves only to confirm what we probably would have assumed to be true had there been no studies. For example, most people serving on criminal juries probably enter with the belief that the state must have some evidence against the defendant or else a prosecution would not have been brought, creating the ingoing pro-prosecution bias we have mentioned. Similarly, Pound's finding that to the meager extent jurors in civil trials had a pre-trial "leaning," it was usually pro-plaintiff would derive from the same reasoning, i.e., the plaintiff must have had some cause for bringing the action. Neither is it especially surprising to learn, as some studies tell us, that forepersons who have strong personalities are more likely to dominate deliberations than those who don't, nor should we be shocked to hear that jurors in different locales bring different community standards to bear upon their case.

Nevertheless, some substantive, consistent, and less intuitively obvious findings can be discerned from the mass of research:

1. Juries overwhelmingly take their duties seriously from the moment they are sworn in until they have reached a verdict.
2. Folklore to the contrary, juries, based on a strong finding from Pound, do not make up their minds about a case following either voir dire or the lawyers' opening speeches. On the contrary, they consistently exhibit open-mindedness, both during the trial and during deliberations.

3.   Juries are evidence-oriented, both during the course of the trial and during deliberations, with the personalities of the participants in the trial and the other subsidiary matters only of minor concern to them. In the average trial, there is good reason to believe they also usually recognize the key elements of the case.

4.   Juries sometimes can be confused by or only partly understand the judge's charge on the law, apparently due principally to the highly-technical, poorly-constructed, and jargon-filled language. However, juries as a group apparently also understand enough of the law that they are able to arrive at legally supportable verdicts in a very large majority of cases.

5.   In terms of deliberation structure, the preferable mode, i.e., to discuss the evidence first and verdict-preferences only later, is the one which juries frequently hit upon.

6.   Jurors in civil cases apparently frequently discuss insurance, and because they often don't fully understand certain aspects of it (such as plaintiffs on occasion being required to reimburse their medical insurers out of their awards), much is left to surmise and mistakes can result. The evidence also strongly suggests that jurors rarely increase the size of an award because they think the defendant has ample insurance to cover it, nor do they ordinarily make awards out of sympathy.

7.   Compromise tactics are frequently used by juries in reaching verdicts and awards, as is typical of any democratic decision-making process.

8.   Juries with a heterogeneous composition appear to be the best safeguard against biased verdicts, and probably usually have the best quality of deliberation due to the richness of points of view expressed.

9.   Those who are most familiar with the jury system—judges, lawyers, and jurors themselves—regard the jury as a highly effective, and perhaps the most effective, means for dispensation of justice.

PART 2

Introduction

As we have seen from Chapters Three and Four, academic studies virtually unanimously give jurors a good report card. Collateral agreement generally comes from those who deal with the jury system the most, the lawyers, the judges, and the jurors themselves when they rate their fellow panelists. Taken together, these views refute the traditional argument that a group of laypeople uninitiated in the ways of the legal system cannot be expected to understand enough of the law or the evidence to come to a sensible verdict, at least in the average case. Their performance, indeed, based on the research, seems almost amazingly good when we consider court procedures and rules on admissibility of evidence that often seem designed to keep the facts away from those who are to judge them.[1] Neither do we find any substantiation for the corollary allegation that, even if they do understand the facts, jurors as a practice will ignore them,[2] not due to any lofty principles, but because, as Frank put it, they go for "the brunette with the soulful eyes."[3]

Assuming the research is correct and that jurors generally do a good job, it does not necessarily follow that the jury system should be retained, or, if it must be, that its usage should not be sharply curtailed. Critics observe weaknesses, inefficiencies, and injustices associated with it that, they believe, have become intolerable in a changing United States with its overburdened legal system.

The critics who hold that the jury presently performs a negative role in society are a varied lot, as are the jury's proponents. The most outspoken critics are casualty insurance companies and those of their customers likely to be hit with large verdicts (e.g., doctors, hospitals, manufacturers). These groups have an understandable desire to limit the amounts juries can award, but they have not expressed any concern about lengthy jury trials slowing the dispensation of justice, and for a good reason: The longer the delay in resolving a case, the longer they keep their money. Plaintiffs and their lawyers, who share in the jury's award, equally understandably have no desire to see limits placed on the amounts they can receive.

When we move beyond these realms of self-interest, we find we cannot predict approval of or opposition to the jury based on ideology or party label. Committed liberals and conservatives, Democrats and Republicans, can be found on both sides. As we observed in the Introduction, Judge Learned Hand, a liberal, had anomalous views about the role the jury should be permitted to play in rendering justice, and Judge Frank, a New Deal Democrat, was perhaps the system's most visible and virulent opponent for many years. Yet his position as leading critic was usurped in more recent years by former Chief Justice Warren Burger, a Republican and a political and economic conservative. Burger's colleague, Byron White, a Democrat, has been one of the staunchest supporters of the jury. So it goes.

It is only when we turn to a critic's philosophy of the good society that we begin to discern who is likely to be an opponent and who an advocate of the jury system. As we will observe more closely in Chapter Eight, people who hold that governance is best left in the hands of those who, because they are the most skilled and the most educated, understand what is good for people, will often view the jury as an intrusion of the ignorant upon the counsels of the wise. Dean Griswold's dismissal of "12 persons brought in from the street," quoted earlier, encapsulates the elitist disdain for the common person and his or her abilities. On the contrary, egalitarians, like Thomas Jefferson and Justice White, favor the jury for the same reasons that make the elitists suspicious of it. They see it as the single portal through which the people can enter to make known their ideas about justice, and that these ideas—quite apart from the merits of individual jury decisions, quite apart from any inconvenience juries may cause in carrying out the day-to-day affairs of our courts—have informed and enriched us, made our democracy safer and better. This can occur, the egalitarians point out, even when the news the juries bring about themselves is negative, as in the South where the exclusion of blacks from juries helped bring the nation's attention to civil rights violations that went well beyond jury composition itself.

On one point the defenders and critics of the jury are in agreement: They recognize that, from Zenger's day onward in this country, juries have raised, advertently and otherwise, significant public policy issues. Occasionally their verdicts uphold our most fundamental ideas about freedom (as in Zenger); at other times, they can affect practices of government or the fortunes of great businesses, creating ripple effects that the critics see as dangerous. In the more narrow legal sense, juries have also raised policy issues by their verdicts, as we shall see later in the discussion of changes they have wrought in our ideas about negligence.

It is the jury's role as policymaker and raiser of policy questions that is the subject of the second half of this book. Because, as we observed earlier, the attacks on the jury have primarily focused on its employment in civil cases,[4] those cases are the ones to which the closest attention will be paid in the chapters that follow. The criminal jury, nevertheless, has also had its critics,[5] and many of the arguments pressed against civil juries are equally applicable to criminal ones. It is not, therefore, unreasonable to assume that, should the constitutional right to jury in civil trials fall, the criminal jury (save possibly for death-penalty cases where judges usually prefer to have jurors make that lifetaking decision) will be next.

Chapters Five and Six address the issue of civil litigation activity in the United States. The jury opponent argument dealt with in these chapters goes something like this: The slow-footed jury system may have been acceptable in an era when court dockets weren't groaning with cases, but it has now outlived its usefulness[6] and become "a luxury we may not be able to afford," as Supreme Court Justice John Paul Stevens has put it.[7]

At the heart of this last argument is the phenomenon known in legal jargon as "hyperlexis,"[8] or more popularly as the "litigation explosion." That such a problem exists has become "axiomatic in both legal and lay circles."[9] It is a "vicious legal spiral"[10] caused, according to former Supreme Court Chief Justice Burger, by the "inherently litigious nature of Americans,"[11] a quality that apparently they long kept under wraps, since, the Chief Justice also said in a 1982 article, their greed has only evinced itself "during this generation."[12] It is marked by an "epidemic of hair-trigger suing"[13] caused by "an abandoned eagerness to hail into court all and sundry"[14] over the "most trivial matters."[15] Its advent has been the subject of countless articles in professional journals with such titles as: "Hyperlexis: Our National Disease";[16] "Court Survival in the Litigation Explosion";[17] and "Litigation-Prone Society: Protection of Professional Life."[18] The press has also taken up the theme: "Everybody is Suing Everybody;"[19] "Legal Pollution";[20] "Too Much Law?";[21] "Why Everybody is Suing Everybody";[22] "On the Evidence, Americans Would Rather Sue than Settle";[23] "California's Colossal Legal Appetite";[24] "Product Liability: The New Morass,"[25] and on and on. At least one author has written a book on the need for non-trial resolutions of disputes, using as a major premise the assumed reality of the litigation explosion.[26]

The key phrase here is "assumed reality." Should we find that no litigation crisis exists or that the jury plays no substantive role in causing court delays during a time of increase in cases, then we have no reason to restrict or eliminate its usage on that ground.

We begin to address the question of "assumption" or "reality" with Chapter Five. It is a background chapter in which our concern is not with juries but rather with the litigation that can bring them into existence, unleashing the powers they have. The chapter describes the history of litigation in America, noting how changes in the society brought about the developments in the law (and the role of lawyers) that set into motion the events of recent years. At the end of that chapter, we will see that good reasons exist to think that the amount of litigation *should* have increased beginning no later than the 1970s, at least in certain legal areas, but that it is far from clear that the reasons should have produced the alleged orgy of litigation that the hyperlexis critics decry.

From Chapter Five, therefore, our question becomes: Did a "crisis" occur which requires draconian measures to bring it under control, including abandonment of or limitation of access to the right to jury trial? It is the purpose of Chapter Six to provide the answer or, as it turns out, the answers.

We next turn to the question of the jury's competence in deciding on monetary awards. If juries habitually make aberrantly high awards, they would create another kind of crisis. According to the arguments of jury critics described in Chapter Seven, this is what happened beginning sometime in the 1970s, leading to several disastrous ill effects which are a matter of public interest. First, the influx of high awards has increased the cost of insurance premiums and thereby the price that consumers pay for products. Secondly, in some instances and most notably in the pharmaceutical field, insurers, fearful of suits and their costs, have withdrawn coverage entirely or made it prohibitively expensive; as a result, manufacturers, not wanting to bear the cost of litigation themselves, remove these products, including beneficial ones, from the market. In Chapter Seven, we will test these premises, looking to find the answer to this question: Are juries (and the members of the public who bring the suits that lead to the jury verdicts) to blame for increases in insurance and lack of insurance availability, or are they the scapegoats in a situation in which the blame resides elsewhere?

Some observers of the justice system have no problem with using juries in simple cases, civil or criminal, but draw the line at so-called complex civil litigation, a term often used as a euphemism for antitrust trials in which huge corporations are a party. The theory is that such matters go beyond the abilities of laypeople to understand or decide rationally. As we shall see in Chapter Eight, the complex case issue, even though it presumably deals with only a tiny number of lawsuits, has resulted in the launching of a substantive attack on our right to jury trial in all civil cases, and could by implication erode the right to a jury in criminal cases as well.

The backdoor attack on the Sixth and Seventh Amendments represented by the complex-case argument leads us to the fear that underlies much of the anti-jury thinking. Because nothing can stop juries from doing what they perceive to be justice in a case, regardless of the applicable law, the opponents see juries as essentially an anarchic force, a challenge to the concept that ours is a society of laws not men. Therefore in Chapter Nine, the final chapter of the book, our subject will be the jury as the purveyor of community (rather than legal) standards of justice, a kind of oversight committee we have managed to establish to monitor our government, our judges, our commerce, ourselves.

Chapter 5

Litigation in America

In one year in the early 1980s, 53 tenants in a single building began lawsuits against one another. Not far away, two neighbors had been suing each other off and on for 30 years in a dispute that began when one of them directed a "dirty look" at the other's dog. Recently, in a large city, a business entered suit against another firm over an unpaid debt of one cent, while in a rural area a brother sued his sister for gathering fruit from a tree he considered his own. Altogether, 227 lawsuits were filed for every 1,000 citizens.[1]

The site of all that suing was not the democratic United States (where everyone presumably has access to the courts) but communist Yugoslavia (where everyone obviously has access to them and apparently almost everyone makes use of them). Based on those statistics, one might say the Yugoslavs are (to borrow Justice Burger's phrase) "an inherently litigious people." They seem to think so themselves. They even have a word for it, *inat*, which, as nearly as it can be translated into English, means "spite."[2]

Compared to the Yugoslavs anyway, the rest of the world adheres to the biblical injunction about turning one's other cheek. An estimate for the United States from the late 1970s was 44 civil cases filed per thousand people, less than one-fifth the Yugoslav rate. In Canada, around the same time, the rate was 46.5, while in Australia it was 62. Near the bottom of the suing ladder in the same study were three European countries, Spain at 3.4 cases per thousand, Italy at 9.6, and the Netherlands at 8.2. Somewhere in the middle are the Belgians who have a litigation rate more than three times that of the non-contentious Dutch whose northern neighbor, the Danes, are nearly as suit-prone as the Americans (41 per thousand).[3]

It may be true, as some analysts of the American "explosion" claim, that the number of lawyers available affects the number of suits that will be filed, but, if so, the statistics from the mid-1970s to the early 1980s offer no proof of that. The United States has about 2.5 times more lawyers than any other country reporting its figures, yet its 2,400 lawyers per million people (at the time of the study) produced only about the same rate of litigation as Canada, which has 890 lawyers for each million. In England, which has a litigation rate only slightly lower than that of the United States—41 cases for each thousand—there are but 606 lawyers per million or one-fourth the availability in the United States. Australia, with its high litigation rate, has about the same percentage of lawyers as Canada, but then again so does Spain, with the lowest rate in the study. The nation with the fewest number of lawyers among the reporting countries was Japan with 91 per million, and at 11.6 cases per thousand it also has one of the lower litigation rates, yet one which is nearly four times that of Spain where lawyers are 10 times more prevalent.[4]

As the absence of a correlation between lawyer availability and court activity begins to suggest, tracing the reasons for a litigation explosion—or a non-explosion, for that matter—could turn out to be a mystifying task. For instance, we might hypothesize, after we eliminate lawyer availability as the crucial factor, that cultural differences probably play the deciding role. Japan, with its fabled tradition of politeness, seems to offer some measure of proof, yet, if that is so, how then do we account for the fact that in Italy, where exquisite good manners are hardly a tradition, the folk sue each other much more rarely than they do in Japan? Turning to Belgium, Holland, and Denmark, we find some cultural similarities and populations with less pronounced differences in wealth and educational attainment than in many other places, yet their litigation rates are startlingly different from one another. Demographically, the United States and Yugoslavia have heterogeneous populations and are in the top ranks of litigiousness, yet the suit-prone Australians (and the even more contentious New Zealanders) have a comparably homogeneous population mix.

Apparently cultural factors don't define likelihood of litigiousness either, so perhaps differences in access to the courts do. That element would seem—much more than politeness—to explain the low rate in Japan where the number of judges has remained at the 1890 level even though the population has more than doubled since then.[5] Unfortunately for that theory, Italy has five times as many judges as Japan and a much lower litigation rate. If access to the courts isn't our answer, then perhaps the laws themselves, the systems of government, might provide a clue. Yet, of the countries in the survey—Yugoslavia was not included—only Spain at the time did not have a democratic form of government, and every nation adhered to either a version of the Roman civil law or the Anglo-American common law, which provide similar legal methods for people to resolve disputes.

Even if we find a key—perhaps in economic growth patterns, in special statutes—to the vast differences in litigation rates, we still won't know, until we do a great deal more research, whether what we see from country to country represents a litigation "explosion." Perhaps when we do that research, we will discover that in Denmark, although the number of cases has been increasing, the number of serious ones has been declining. That could be a significant factor. Serious cases—such as those involving major injuries—can be quite time-consuming for courts, causing delays, while small-claims matters, even in large numbers, can be handled rapidly (just as, on the criminal side, felonies ordinarily take much longer to resolve than do misdemeanors). Therefore, a rise in the number of cases doesn't necessarily create a matching increase in the use of courtrooms and judges.

But, perhaps with a more detailed investigation, something quite different will be revealed. Maybe then we will find that Denmark's litigation rate, despite being higher than Holland's, is presently on a downward curve while Holland's is upward. In that event, it may be Holland, not Denmark, suffering from hyperlexis despite its comparably low rate. Or, alternatively, we may discover that the rate has been on the rise in Denmark during the past 20 years but is still much lower than a century ago.

From this last consideration about Denmark, we come to our first question about the United States: Are we Americans more litigation-prone than we used to be?

I

During the first century or so of the history of the United States, civil cases principally dealt with contract disputes evolving from the buying and selling of land,[6] as might be expected in a vast and capitalistically expanding nation. Although court statistics for the 19th century are fragmentary for many places and nonexistent for others, the figures we have indicate that Americans, during the first half of that century, were hardly shy about going to court when a disagreement occurred.

For instance, thanks to McIntosh's survey[7] we know a great deal about the history of litigation in the St. Louis circuit court from 1820 to 1977. There, in the 1820s, the civil case filing rate was 31.3 per thousand, rose to 38.8 by the 1840s, after which it began a steady descent, reaching a low of 6.9 in the 1890s before beginning a slow but irregular climb to 16.8 per thousand in the 1970s, *still less than half the rate of the mid-19th century*. In Menard County, Illinois, the 1978 rate was less than half that of 1878.[8] Similar lower rates are to be found when appeals court activity in all of Illinois is the base.[9] One answer, therefore, to our initial question—and St. Louis and Illinois are not the only examples[10]—is that there have been times when, and places where, litigiousness was about as common or more so in the United States than it is today.

Tort cases—which involve injury to person or property and which are the kinds of actions that, according to critics, are the principal cause of the "litigation explosion"—were rare occurrences, relative to other forms of litigation, throughout the 19th century. For example, in five counties selected for study by Arthur Young & Company, torts consisted of only 1% of the litigation around the year 1900. By the 1970s, they had risen to 12.4%,[11] a figure that is nearly identical to the 12.5% developed in a 1977 study of 12 states by the National Center for State Courts.[12] While it is unclear if both studies are incorporating the same definitions of tort filings—the Center for State Courts excludes small claims in its tally—the indication is of a steady rise in injury litigation during the course of the 20th century. A number of explanations have been offered. The injury-productive automobile is a 20th-century phenomenon, and during the same period the nation has become ever more urbanized which, as Abel has pointed out, "enormously increased the frequency of interaction among strangers [who] unlike acquaintances or intimates, have less incentive to exercise care not to injure one another inadvertently and find it more difficult to resolve the differences that arise when an injury occurs."[13]

The growth of personal injury *suits* in the 20th century for these and other reasons (which will be discussed later in this chapter) cannot be taken to mean, however, that the frequency of negligent injury *situations* was significantly lower or even lower at all in the 19th century than in the 20th. All the statistics tell us is that tort actions were once less numerous than they now are, not why they were.

The 19th-century injury rate, whether it led to suit or not, was, unlike that of the 20th, principally the product of the industrial revolution. The factory economy that replaced that of the farmer and the cottage-industry artisan was one in which worker safety devices were virtually unknown; large numbers of people, many of them immigrants who could not speak one another's language, worked in situations in which an inability to communicate could, by itself, prove lethal. The principal architect of the enormous business expansionism of the second half of the 19th century was the railroad industry. Its growth was spectacular. In 1860, the United States contained just 30,600 miles of railway track, by 40 years later, more than 200,000;[14] the Pennsylvania Railroad was by the 1870s the largest corporation in the United States and by some estimates the largest in the world. The work that it and its competitors offered could be highly dangerous; among brakemen, the fatality rate approached 100%.[15] Non-employee accidents, typically occurring at crossings, added mightily to the toll.[16]

With railroads as the principal offenders,[17] workplace injuries by the post-Civil War period were mounting into the hundreds of thousands a year.[18] Although they had a legal right to do so, only rarely did workers bring suit against their employers, upon whom they were economically dependent. (John C. Calhoun of South Carolina once congratulated the Northern capitalists on the efficiency of their system, observing that slaveholders had to continue to feed and house their serfs when they became old or injured while the factory owner simply fired his "free" workers when age or misfortune overcame them.[19]) At a time when worker supply—thanks to liberal immigration policies—exceeded demand, only a brave and probably foolhardy worker would dare try to take his boss to court over an injury.

Even so, by the time of the Civil War, tort cases—probably largely those that didn't involve the workplace—were beginning to appear on court dockets, though it wasn't until 1879 that their numbers had increased sufficiently that anyone thought it necessary to publish a textbook on the subject.[20] This first "explosion" in tort cases, minuscule as it was, became possible with the introduction in the 1850s[21] of the contingency fee, whereby a lawyer received a percentage of a plaintiff's winnings, usually half but nothing if he lost. Since most Americans couldn't afford otherwise to hire a lawyer, the contingency system opened the courthouse doors to the injured, although, once they got inside, they found their chances of winning were poor.

Part of their problem came from the very lawyers they now had available to them. Frequently, they were poorly-educated. Throughout most of the 19th century, a person didn't have to pass a bar examination to practice law,[22] and even when testing became commonplace in the 1870s, the standards for licensure were low.[23] Many of the contingency-fee lawyers were also unscrupulous. Suits were often filed for the sole purpose of getting nuisance settlements, with even the strongest cases dropped when the lawyer got a few dollars out of the defendant.[24] Clients of such lawyers were lucky if they saw a penny. When suits were pursued, both sides proved adept at skullduggery. The railroads, for example, hired "accident investigators" whose sole job was to buy up witnesses, or create witnesses where there weren't any, with the plaintiffs (when they could afford it) doing the same, so that many of the cases that got to trial became little more than exercises in wholesale perjury.[25]

But even when the plaintiff's witnesses out-lied the defendant's, the defendant was still likely to win. Judges almost invariably believed that Americanism meant protection of business,[26] and since the defendant almost always was a business in both workplace and non-workplace cases, judicial decisions for the plaintiff at the trial or appeals level was a rarity.[27] In one typical case, the victims of a devastating fire undeniably caused by a railroad's negligence were unable to collect for their lost homes because a judge ruled that to do so would put too heavy a financial burden on the company.[28] Juries, fearful of the economic power of the capitalists, were often reluctant to find for plaintiffs, and if they did so find, it was commonplace for the judge either to reduce or vacate the verdict.[29]

Had all these factors not combined to discourage the "litigiousness" of the 19th-century American, judges did so on their own as they began to alter common-law doctrines to fit the financial interests of businessmen.[30]

From Ethelbert's time until the 19th century, the common law on torts had made the injuring party absolutely liable to the injured.[31] That law had never been fair—it failed to consider that the injured party might be the one at fault—but it wasn't until industrialization took root and injuries sprang from it that the doctrine was discarded, and with a vengeance. Rather than courts instituting the obvious reform, determining awards by the degree of fault of both parties, now defendants won if they could show that the plaintiff caused the injury to *any* degree. *Contributory negligence*, as the new doctrine was called, was in place by the mid-19th century and remains in effect in some states in the 1980s.[32]

A first cousin to contributory negligence was *imputed negligence*, another ingenious 19th-century American common-law theory designed to protect propertied interests from the public. According to it, if a passenger is injured due to the carelessness of a driver, the fault is the passenger's because had the passenger not asked the driver to drive, there would have been no accident. Doubtlessly, a few horse-and-buggy chauffeurs benefited from this reasoning, but its real purpose—which it served admirably—was to prevent railroad passengers from suing when they were injured by a railroad's negligence. Imputed negligence protected businesses against children, too, since any injury caused a child was not the fault of the person who committed it, but rather that of the child's parents who should never have allowed the child to be in a place where he or she could be harmed.[33]

Industrialization not only maimed its victims but also frequently killed them, and that also worried the American judges, not in terms of how to compensate the survivors but how to prevent them from being compensated at all. Seizing on a bizarre British case, the American courts determined that all tort actions died with the victim. That way, the judges reasoned, business wouldn't have the undue burden of paying "pensions" to widows and orphans following their negligent slaying of a husband.[34] As the legal scholar William Prosser dryly noted, the result was that it became "more profitable for the defendant to kill the plaintiff than to scratch him."[35] So patently unfair was this rule that even 19th-century Americans rebelled against it, with every state legislature in the nation eventually passing statutes permitting recovery in wrongful death actions. In many places, however, the lobbying power of the business interests was sufficient to force through low maximums. Those of as little as $10,000 are in effect in a few places more than a century later.[36]

Charities, including charity-operated hospitals, were also exempt from suit, a ban which was expanded by an 1876 decision. In that case, a patient sued Massachusetts General Hospital when one of its interns bungled the setting of a fractured leg. Although Massachusetts General was not a charity-affiliated institution, the court ruled against the plaintiff on the grounds that the hospital was nonprofit which, according to the judge, was synonymous with charity.[37] Since at that time for-profit hospitals were unheard of, the new common law, as long as it remained in effect, meant that no hospital could be sued. Similarly, the doctrine of *sovereign immunity* protected governments from suits against them.

Two other new common law doctrines had as their specific purpose to make it virtually impossible for workers to bring suit against their employers. One was *assumption of risk*. It held that an employee could not recover from the employer in a work-related injury if that person knew the job was dangerous upon accepting it.[38] The landmark case establishing assumption of risk was *Farwell v. Boston & Worcester Railroad* in 1842. The plaintiff, an engineer, had sued the company when his hand was cut off due to the negligence of a switchman; the court held that he did not have the right to sue his employer because he knew such an accident could occur when he was hired—i.e., he assumed the risk—although if he wanted to sue the switchman, he was welcome to do so.[39] (The courts at the time never had any objection to one poor person suing another; it was suing the rich that had to be stopped.)

The same case established another doctrine that proved even more beneficial to employers, the *fellow-servant rule*, which had first surfaced the previous year in a South Carolina case.[40] Contrary to law that had been established both in England and America by late in the 17th century,[41] *Farwell* held that an employer wasn't responsible for employee negligence that caused the injury of a fellow-worker even when assumption of risk wasn't involved. Rather, a worker could win against an employer only if he could show that the employer was *personally* responsible for the injury—conceivable when one worked for an individual, but not for a corporation such as a railroad. As James Dooley pointed out in *1 Modern Law Torts (1977)*: "The rule found ready acceptance in a society committed to industrial expansion at the expense of the working class, and was justified by the American courts on various theories. One such theory was that the negligence of a fellow servant was a risk assumed by the servant as an incident of his employment [and that] the application of the rule would tend to encourage the servant to be more careful . . . and thus reduce the number of accidents."[42]

Even as the courts were implementing these various inequities, in effect forcing the nation's injured millions to be "non-litigious," countervailing forces were beginning to make themselves felt.

The most potent was unionism.[43] Its origins in America go back to colonial days with a strike of bakers in New York City in 1741; in 1799, the Federal Society of Cordwainers (shoemakers), apparently America's first formal union, was in existence and on strike. By 1833, 29 unions had been organized in New York City alone, and these, along with their brethren elsewhere, were making progress in limiting the workday to 10 hours. The depression which struck in the late 1830s—not only in the United States but also worldwide—nearly destroyed the nascent union movement as jobs became scarce, as Irish immigrants who would work for bottom dollar entered the workforce, and as children did, too, in large numbers. By the 1840s, a weaver was earning $4.25 a week, less than the average wage of laborers prior to the Revolution, with children, some as young as 10, working in the mills at a penny an hour for a 14-hour day.[44]

Nevertheless, by the 1850s, at the very time that personal injury suits were first being pursued in countable numbers, unionism again was on the rise; although the history on this is cloudy, it seems likely that there was a connection between the two phenomena. Although there is no evidence the unions encouraged their workers to go to court, the union movement itself represented an awareness by the working class that it had rights to express, demands to make. In that sense, unionism, even in its earliest stages, helped formulate comprehensions of other rights that had always existed but rarely been acted upon, including that of demanding redress for non-workplace grievances.

In the second half of the 19th century, the growth of the union movement was rapid. By the end of the 1850s, the printers' Typographical Union (the first national one) was in existence, along with those of hat finishers, stonecutters, moulders, machinists, and blacksmiths. These unions and others that followed during the post-Civil War period became, after a number of transformations, part of the American Federation of Labor, organized in 1881. By and large, the AF of L represented the skilled, native-American working class. Immigrants and the unskilled found their voice in the much more militant and radical industrial unions which admitted everyone within an industry, from lowest laborer to craftsman, and on an equal basis. By the 1880s the battles between management and labor were always bitter and often bloody; by the 1890s the industrial unions, led by John Mitchell's multiethnic United Mine Workers, were beginning to make substantial organizational inroads.

By then, too, the unionists had begun to gain allies. Muckraking journalists such as Lincoln Steffens, Ida Tarbell and Samuel Hopkins Adams were startling millions of ordinary citizens with their exposes of the unbridled power of a handful of America's richest, their connections with the most venal of politicians, and the exploitation of their workers. Held up to public scrutiny for the first time, for example, were the so-called sweater dens where children, some younger than five, were put to work sewing in tiny rooms in which the roof slanted to no more than four feet above the floor. Similarly, in the 1890s garment district workers, usually immigrants, would be lucky to get wages of $6 a week, out of which they had to pay 50 cents for the use of the electricity for their sewing machines, and 5 cents for a drink of water.[45]

Often it took tragedy to reveal to Americans the terror of the working conditions in their society. In the Triangle Shirtwaist fire of 1911, 145 died due to the gross negligence of the factory owner. Such, however, was the condition of the law at the time that only 23 wrongful death suits were pursued, with an average settlement of $75. As a newspaper account of the time laconically noted, "stricken families are not well equipped to carry on expensive litigation with corporations."[46]

By the time of the Triangle fire, some progress had been made, in other areas, to meet the rising demand for better working conditions. Most of these early efforts had focused on the railroad industry. During the 1890s, the Interstate Commerce Commission—under intense public pressure—had passed a series of safety regulations to which the railroads were expected to comply. If they didn't and an employee was injured, that employee would no longer legally be "deemed . . . to have assumed the risk" and could sue and recover from the railroad.[47] It was an important breakthrough in advancing legal rights (back toward where they had been before the mid-19th century), and it was followed in 1908 by an even more significant event, the passage of the Federal Employers Liability Act (FELA). The employers in question were railroads engaged in interstate commerce, and the act's purpose was to reinstate in full the long-denied rights of their injured workers. The statute removed assumption of risk entirely (which juries were regularly refusing to apply), and even more importantly delegalized the fellow servant rule (which some states had already abolished in their legislatures[48]) and substituted comparative for contributory negligence as the basis for making awards.

The similar Jones Act, to protect maritime workers, followed in 1920. By the early 1920s, most states had also passed workmen's compensation laws—Mississippi would be the last to do so in 1948—which removed proof of negligence as the requirement for payment; instead, the worker had only to prove that his or her injury had occurred in connection with the job. However, unlike employees covered by FELA or the Jones Act, who would be paid in entirety for their injuries, the workmen's compensation acts limited the amount of money per injury and did not allow separate tort actions against an employer to attempt to recover the full amount. Thus, if workmen's compensation laws added to the total of litigation—one still had to prove the injury was work-related—they also made employers liable for but a fraction of the cost of the injuries they caused.[49] The limitations led to the development of a line of insurance which was highly profitable, since the underwriters, unlike those for other types of insurance, knew the statutory maximum they could be required to pay for any injury.

The passage of the two federal statutes and the workmen's compensation laws in the various states had one significant aftereffect. Because the laws finally make workplace injury suits winnable, lawyers with good skills for the first time were attracted to that kind of work. Typically, these lawyers were employed by the unions, which meant they had an income in addition to the contingency fees they could earn from the injury cases. (Probably because of their union connections and the volume of their work, they reduced their contingency charge from the 50% that had been traditional to one-third, which remains the percentage that most contingency lawyers charge today.) As these lawyers began to develop expertise, the amounts of money they were able to get for their clients also increased.[50] Around the same time, the arrival of the automobile attracted other lawyers to personal injury work.

The rise of injury suits in the early 20th century should, theoretically, have added to the burden of the courts. But that didn't happen. Even as the injury cases were becoming common, the number of commercial law, contract, and property cases decreased, probably in part due to the fact that the law in these areas was now more firmly established and land development cases were less frequent as the country neared complete settlement. In the five counties studied by Arthur Young and Company, the total civil filing rate—because of the decrease in non-tort cases—remained unchanged from the beginning of the 20th century to its midpoint (36.8 in 1903 and 36.7 in 1949[51]). The same, roughly, held true in two sample California counties, while in Menard County, Illinois (another frequently studied district), the caseload actually decreased by almost half. In federal courts, the rate increased by about a third during the 50-year period, but still remained small in numbers, going from 0.199 to 0.33 per thousand.[52]

The apparent onslaught of civil suits that arrived with the 1970s, therefore, seemed a startling one. It was as though, after years of litigation somnolence, the American people had taken a Yugoslavian drug and become infected with *inat* overnight. But, assuming one doesn't believe in nostrums, it is necessary to look for other reasons, rational ones, perhaps complex ones that aren't easily reduced to the rhetorical catchphrases of "unparalleled contentiousness" and "hair-trigger suing." We may be able to find them in changes that took place in the American society both immediately prior to and following the magical year of 1970. Some of the demographic factors, which will be discussed first, appear to have had much more impact than others.

II

Population growth.   Between 1970 and 1983, the population of the United States increased from 203.3 to 226.5 million people,[53] or a little more than 1% a year. (Throughout this section, the statistics used are for the most recent relevant year available at the time of the writing in 1986.) The litigation rate during that period varied between 40 and 50 claims per thousand people—our statistics aren't strong enough to be more precise than that—so that we can calculate that population growth should have contributed about a million claims to the litigation "explosion" over 13 years. Such reasoning, however, may be faulty. Although the number of criminal cases that reach courts appears to have a direct relation to population growth,[54] for civil cases that has not usually been true. Between 1950 and 1960, the American population increased by 28 million and by another 24 million between 1960 and 1970,[55] yet in each of those decades, litigation rates showed only a slight upward movement. Therefore, although it is logical to assume that population-increment is a factor in litigation-increment—the more people there are, the more chances someone is going to sue someone—its impact is unknown and is probably less substantive than the numbers would indicate.

Population longevity.   In 1950 the average life expectation at birth in the United States was 68.2 years. Over the next two decades, expectancy inched up to 70.9 years or about 4%. Then, just between 1970 and 1983, a 10% rise took place to 74.7 years.[56] Changes in longevity rates are reflected in the general aging of the population. Thus, in 1950 about 12 million Americans were 65 or older;[57] by 1983, that figure had more than doubled to 27.4 million.[58] Mirroring that trend was Medicare enrollment, which rose from 9.4 to 19.6 million between 1970 and 1983.[59]

The relationship between older people and litigation is a variable one. Since most people over 65 are retired, relatively few workplace injuries take place among them, and because they travel less (to and from work), fewer transportation accidents should result. However, older people are also more prone to serious injuries, especially fractures, than are younger ones and more prone to illness, so that they need large amounts of medical care—and, thanks to Medicare, are more likely to get it than they used to—which, when it fails, could produce malpractice suits. Against these propositions, we have the somber fact that as the number of the very aged in the population increases, so do those who are institutionalized in nursing and boarding homes where they may not have the capacity to assert legal rights even when these rights have been violated.

Because of all these factors, we cannot state with confidence that the aging of the population has *per se* played a discernible role in the number of injury suits filed. It has, however, had one definable incremental effect on civil caseloads. As a population ages, death frequencies increase—from 1,927,000 to 2,014,000 a year in the United States between 1970 and 1983[60]—which means that the number of wills filed for probate (some of which can lead to highly disputatious litigation) is also on the rise.[61]

Knowledge of the Law.   The amount of education received by Americans has been sharply on the rise since the end of the Second World War. In 1950 less than a third of the adult population had completed high school; by 1983, 72% had.[62] That accomplishment, however, may be less impressive than it seems, since, based on test scores, the high school education of the 1980s may not be markedly superior to the eighth grade education of 1950.

More enlightening in terms of educational accomplishment are two sets of figures at the opposite ends of the achievement scale. At the low end, in 1940 13.7% of American adults, about one in seven, had fewer than five years of schooling; by 1970 that figure had dropped to 5.5% and 10 years later fallen by another 40% to 3.4%.[63] At the upper end, in 1940 only 4.6% of all Americans had completed four years of college; by 1970 that had more than doubled to 10.7% and by 1980—in the largest 10-year jump in the nation's history—had risen to 17%, with the figure closing in on 20% by the mid-1980s.[64] Even if one assumes that collegiate standards of education, like those of high schools, are not what they used to be, a college graduate still has to master complex concepts and develop independent learning skills not demanded in the typical high school curriculum.

With few individuals in the population having virtually no schooling and very many a great deal of it, and with half the college education "explosion" occurring since 1970, commensurately more people are knowledgeable of their legal rights and likely to attempt to exercise them when they see themselves as wronged. Even when the college educated have no occasion to take legal action themselves, their growing presence in the population—about five times as many in 1987 as in 1940—means that more people who aren't well-educated now have access to those who are, either within their own families or through acquaintances. Legal knowledge is communicated personally that way; it may not, however, cross ghettoized racial barriers, so that rights-awareness through direct communication may actually decrease when, as happened with blacks in the 1980s,[65] a minority's presence in college-level enrollment begins to decline.

Personal relationships are by no means the only or most significant way of spreading knowledge about the law. Television's very nearly universal reach brings through its entertainment and its news broadcasts vast amounts of legal information to people, including functional illiterates, who might otherwise not be exposed to it or receptive to it. Even though the entertainments may convey inaccurate information about a concept or the news broadcasts distort it (due to brevity), nevertheless the concept itself becomes part of the folk "knowledge." Thus, because of television, vast numbers of people are aware of legal issues and realize they can take action on them. (In that sense, all the shows on television in the 1970s that showed heroic doctors wrongly accused of malpractice by greedy patients and unethical lawyers, may have had as their main consequence the encouragement of malpractice suits.)

Injuries.   Reported injuries—defined by the federal government as "incidents leading to restricted activity and/or medical treatment"—rose from 56 to 68.1 million between 1970 and 1980.[66] That's an impressive increase—about 20%—and would seem to lay the basis for an "explosion" in tort cases.

Such an assumption, however, may not be warranted. By the mid-1970s, 25 states[67] had passed no-fault automobile accident laws which—even though the number of auto accidents increased by about 10% during the decade[68]—probably had a slightly de-escalating effect on the number of tort claims. Much more significantly, automobile insurance rates were marked by large increases, especially in no-fault states, with the result that victims of minor accidents became unwilling to seek legal redress because they feared that by so doing they would invite further hikes in their premiums and even cancellations of their policies.[69]

Another factor which in the past would have increased the number of workplace injuries—and the litigation rising from them—was the rapid expansion of the American labor force, which between 1970 and 1984 grew from 81 million to 107.4 million.[70] However, between 1975 and 1983 the number of occupation-related illnesses and injuries in the private sector *decreased* by about 15%, from 9.1 million to 7.7 million.[71] It would be pleasant to think the downward trend was the result of greater care by both employers and employees, but the more likely reason was the shift from factory and construction work which is highly productive of injury to service jobs which have a two-thirds-lower rate.[72]

The number of disabling work injuries—those most likely to lead to disputes over workmen compensation awards and often to faulty product suits—remained the same through the 1970s (about 2.2 million a year[73]), so that, mathematically, they should have had no impact on the frequency of litigation from decade's beginning to end. Whether they did or not is uncertain; because of the greater awareness of legal rights more people might be litigating even though the number of these injuries did not change.

Even less susceptible to analysis are the 89%[74] of injuries that do not involve workplace accidents. We know that the largest category is home accidents (about 25% of the whole), which are the least likely to lead to tort actions. But that has always been true. About all we can say with any confidence is that the net increase of 12 million injuries, apparently spread generally throughout many categories, *should* have produced some kind of concomitant rise in situations in which there were grounds for suit, but we don't know factually if that occurred.

Changes in the Family and Community.   It has frequently been stated[75] that a primary reason for the litigation "explosion" has been the decline of traditional American institutions. Galanter points out in *Reading the Landscape of Civil Disputes*[76] that the literature of the explosion often has a nostalgic quality to it, with despairing references to a once-upon-a-time when Americans were filled in equal parts with "rugged self-reliance and stoic resignation"[77] and therefore unlikely to go to law over trivial matters. No child would then have thought of suing his or her parents for malpractice, nor a suitor sue his date for standing him up (as apparently has happened). Kline summarized that view when he wrote: "The family, the church, the school, and the neighborhood are losing their authority . . . The schools . . . no longer effectively [discipline the young]; the extended family has ceased to play a decisive role in resolving marital and other family disputes; the churches are no longer the principal places where moral precepts are enforced; and the local communities and neighborhoods no longer constrain anti-social behavior . . . [c]hambers of commerce . . . seem no longer equipped to mediate and settle commercial disputes . . ."[78] Instead, people go to courts which, it is alleged, have gotten into areas beyond their competence,[79] apparently solely because no other agency is available to effect the redress that is sought.

Assertions by the nostalgia buffs are not only not always factually correct—community-based mediation programs have been growing during the "explosion" years—but also fail to consider the heavy price which in days of yore was exacted to bring the now longed-for informal agreements about. For instance, those who yearn for a resurgence of the strong family fail to recall that the family could lay terrible pressures on its members, and especially its female members, to continue in miserable and unfair situations that often subjected them to physical abuse. Similarly, those who bemoan the disintegration of the community in an alienated modern society should remember that the peacekeeping solutions of the community intervenors were all too often those of the powerful upon the powerless,[80] of rich upon poor, men upon women, whites upon blacks, employers upon employees.

Whether or not the dissolution of the traditional family in America has had an indirect influence on any litigation explosion (i.e., because families no longer resolve disputes internally), cannot be measured, but it *has* had a very direct impact on one area of litigation: divorce.

Divorce. If Americans are more contentious than they once were, it may be mostly in their marriages. In 1960, there were 35 divorced persons in the United States for every thousand married ones; by 1970, the rate had risen to 47, a figure that worried those who believed in the sanctity of the family and all its conservative values. They hadn't seen anything yet. Over the next 13 years, the ratio more than doubled over the 1970 level to 114 divorced for every thousand married,[81] more than tripling the 1960 level. Or to put it another way, 708,000 divorces and annulments took place in the United States in 1970 and almost 1,200,000 in 1982.[82]

The resultant burden on the courts did not come so much from the flood of divorces, which ordinarily don't take much court time, but rather, as the University of Wisconsin's Civil Litigation Research Project found, from post-divorce disputes. These cases, typically involving child-custody and property divisions, can not only be acrimonious but also result in a series of subsequent actions, so that a single divorce can be good for years of litigation on various issues.

Changes in the business climate. Kline's assertion that, in the good old days, chambers of commerce and other mercantile associations mediated disputes between businessmen may be accurate, but it is also true that in the good old days (i.e., before 1970) these groups weren't faced with the boom that has occurred since.

The statistics go like this: In 1960, we had nine million businesses in the United States with individual proprietors, increasing only to 9.4 million by 1970, but by 1980 to 12.7 million. Partnerships were at 941,000 in 1960, declined slightly to 936,000 by 1970, but jumped to 1.4 million by 1980. The number of corporations increased from 141,000 to 166,000 between 1960 and 1970, and by 1980 had almost doubled the 1960 figure, reaching 271,000.[83]

As bright a picture as all this burgeoning business must be for believers in the free enterprise system, it is also a development inevitably attended by legal disputes (over taxes, among partners, on contracts with customers, by injured customers, in buy-outs, in corporate take-overs, and so on), each one of which could land in court. We don't know how often that happens, but we do know that businessmen, when things don't go well, are much more likely than other people to call on a lawyer—35% of the time, compared with nonbusinessmen who turn to *any* third party only 3% of the time when they have a possible legal problem.[84]

Bankruptcies.   The downside of any new business is that its high hopes may end in the federal bankruptcy courts. Between 1970 and 1980, the number of business bankruptcies in the United States more than doubled, from 19,103 to 45,857, and then more than doubled again by 1983 to 95,572.[85]

When personal bankruptcies are also included, the figures become even more ominous. In 1950 personal and business bankruptcies totaled 33,392; by 1960, 110,000; by 1970, 194,000; by 1980, 361,000, and by 1983—at the bottom of the Reagan recession—536,000.[86]

Because bankruptcy petitions are not a form of litigation (they can become so if, for example, fraud is alleged), they are not incorporated in the federal civil caseload statistics, so that, in that sense, they are not part of any "explosion." However, the circumstances behind a bankruptcy can be quite prolific of litigation. It is the collection cases and related lawsuits filed against individuals and businesses in *state* courts that generally prompt the bankruptcy petitions in federal court. (The Bankruptcy Reform Act of 1978, which permitted individuals to keep more of their property than they had before,[87] has encouraged personal bankruptcy filings although, according to two studies—one by the Government Accounting Office and the other by the Federal Reserve Bank—by no more than 5 to 6% of all filings.[88]) The startling rise in both personal and business bankruptcies, especially in the 1980s, therefore, strongly suggests an economic climate productive of litigation.

Urbanization.   Between 1970 and 1980, the number of Americans living in cities and their suburbs rose from 149 to 167 million,[89] which, if Abel (see above, page 111) and other observers[90] are correct, should have increased the amount of litigation. That may well be true, but we have no statistical studies to define urbanization as a cause separate from those that have already been discussed.

Impersonality.   As corporations grow larger and fewer and as quality of service and goods may decline, customer frustration may become a source of litigation as it wasn't (or much less so) when relationships between buyer and seller were more direct. We have no studies, however, to back this hypothesis.

III

To this point, we have been concerned primarily with events and shifts in the society that could have spin-off effects upon the litigation rate. The most significant appear to be: more access to knowledge of the law; changes in the business climate; the rise in the divorce rate; and quite possibly population growth, which will be discussed further in Chapter Six in terms of tort cases.

Possibly affecting the amount of litigation even more directly, and more dramatically, than the various demographic factors have been revolutions in technology and in ideas of social justice, which had their origins and development long before the decade of the 1970s but played their most significant legal role during it. These forces, sometimes separately and sometimes in conjunction with one another, have brought about changes in the way the law is interpreted and administered, the quality of lawyer that is available, and have produced new grounds for going to court.

Changes in the Law.   As was observed in Chapter Two, the American justice system is triggered into action principally by forces of choice and chance, so that there is always an unknown amount of law to be defined due to all the cases that could be brought but haven't yet been. As a consequence, the law develops unevenly, spurting ahead in one area in which there is a great deal of interest (as in contract and property cases in 19th-century America) but lagging in others which, for one reason or another, are rarely tested in court.

The courts, however, are not a complete bystander in all this rush and lag. When judges are perceived as speakers for property interests, the un-propertied will see going before judges as unlikely to be fruitful, and when judges interpret the laws to make redress under them nearly impossible, as happened with negligence cases in the 19th century, few people see the point of engaging in a losing battle. The law then appears to be settled and immutable because no one is at hand to push at it.

Visions of the just and orderly society, however, never remain static. Battles for social reform can occur at almost any time, and when they do, they are capable of bringing to the fore issues that may have been ignored previously and those which had earlier been battered down by law and judge but which now are revived as prime means to make the changes demanded legal. Civil rights cases, to use the most famous example, were never entirely absent from the litigation landscape, from the time of the abolitionists onward. But it was not until the 1950s that litigation, most notably over interpretations of the 14th Amendment to the Constitution, began to find its way into court in significant numbers. Often instigated by arrests following street actions, these were cases on which judges began to have to make new decisions or remake old ones. As the pressure mounted, legislative bodies followed with statutes that the courts were then called upon to interpret and enforce when suits testing them were filed.

As the progress of the civil rights movement suggests, organized efforts to change the law are usually marked by a series of highly visible events: the definition of the grievance, the emergence of leaders, the definition of goals, the development of strategy, and a progression of events designed to publicize and fulfill the goals.

Grievances, however, can also emerge in a non-organized way, individually perceived and acted upon. When that happens, since no one is out on the streets demonstrating, the public at first pays little attention to the new phenomenon, and when it is finally noticed, it appears to have arrived without warning, like a terrorist attack. Medical malpractice suits—which were to have a transforming effect on the law—seemed to have that threatening and unwarranted quality when they first reached public consciousness. Although such litigation was hardly unheard of before the Second World War,[91] it was not until the early 1960s that the filing rate began to increase, and then only at a quiet 1 to 2% a year; the pattern radically altered in the late 1960s when upward shifts of 10% annually began,[92] at which point the alarms began to sound. The result was that by 1975 90% of all Americans, according to a Gallup poll, "knew" the nation was suffering from a malpractice "crisis."[93] Analysts from the insurance industry and the medical profession explained the upsurge as part of the same growing public contentiousness[94] that was already allegedly exhibiting itself in other arenas of litigation. To many, the malpractice suits had a particularly despicable quality, occurring as they did at a time when new miracle drugs and miracle surgery were helping people live longer and more healthfully; doctors, it would seem, should be thanked not sued.

Such thinking, which confused scientific advancements with those who applied the advancements, failed to realize that malpractice suits had begun to increase because there'd been an increase in malpractice. That development, paradoxically, had occurred not because doctors were getting worse but because, just as the critics said, medicine was getting better. As it did, a doctor was expected to perform at a higher level. As one example, prior to the Second World War, there was no cure for pneumonia so that when a patient died of it, the doctor could not be held legally responsible. Today, a physician who loses a patient to pneumonia—at least a young patient or one for whom the illness is not a complication on top of a more serious condition—may well have performed negligently. The therapeutic advances also meant that people who once would have succumbed to an illness or accident were now living long enough to suffer new illnesses and accidents which had to be treated, increasing the odds that somewhere along the line they would be exposed to negligent care.

The most likely place for that to happen would be in a hospital, the site of nearly 80% of the medical events that lead to the filing of a malpractice claim.[95] Consequently, the more hospital admissions there are, the more malpractice litigation follows. For 1960, the earliest year for which we have reliable malpractice suit statistics, we find 25 million admissions; in 1980, 38.6 million or an increase of more than 50% in 20 years.[96] An important factor in producing the rising admissions was the new technology itself which frequently required intensive therapies that could not be administered in other than a hospital setting.

Studies on how often hospitalized patients are injured, negligently or otherwise, have produced quite disparate figures. A 1980 study found that 20% of patients received an *iatrogenic*—i.e., treatment-induced—injury during their hospitalization,[97] while a 1981 study of a university hospital discovered a 36% rate.[98] Not all the injuries are trivial either: The fatality rate may be as high as 13%.[99] A much more modest iatrogenic rate of 5% was discerned by an analysis published in 1977 by the California Hospital Association; unlike the other studies, it also attempted to decide how many iatrogenic events were caused by negligence, arriving at one-fifth to one-sixth of the total. Using the low California figures as our base, we can derive a 1960 ballpark figure of 1.2 million treatment-caused injuries, of which theoretically about 200,000 were due to negligence. By the same calculations, in 1980 we would have had roughly 1.9 million iatrogenic injuries in hospitals, with over 300,000 of them negligent. Since a malpractice suit must allege an injury (not merely poor care), every iatrogenic event conceivably could give rise to suit, although in the world of reality only those in which there is at least some evidence of negligence will get past a lawyer's scrutiny. (Since plaintiff lawyers in personal injury suits get paid only if they win, they aren't about to embark on cases that are certain losers, assuming they are minimally competent.[100])

Limiting ourselves, therefore, to those hospital treatment-induced injuries that involve some degree of negligence, it is evident that the number is quite large and has been growing rapidly, from 200,000 to more than 300,000 in 20 years, or seven times that figure if we base our analysis on the 1981 study rather than the 1977 one. Yet, in 1980 only about 36,000 claims were brought based on hospital accidents out of a total of approximately 46,000 malpractice filings, and the figure may have been lower.[101] Apparently, either the American people aren't as litigious toward their hospitals and doctors as they are reputed to be, or they don't know when they have been injured,[102] or some combination of both.

Reliable national figures for the first half of the 1980s are not available, although a Pennsylvania study found no increase in claims frequency during that period.[103] (We have no studies of the number of iatrogenic and negligent injuries that occur in doctors' offices; however, we do know there were more than a billion office visits in 1980—up 10% from 1970[104]—and that only about 9,000 of them (.000009) resulted in a malpractice claim.[105] The remainder occurred in nursing homes and other health-care sites.)

The growth in malpractice suits that began in the 1960s, however, cannot be traced exclusively to a relationship between treatment and injury. Had that happened, the filing *rate* should have remained the same over the 20 years, the numerical increase solely the product of the increase in the amount of care. In other words, based on the 1980 filing rate, in 1960 there should have been about 18,000 hospital-based malpractice claims, but instead there were only about 3,000,[106] or about one-seventh the 1980 frequency.

The public's growing awareness of its right to sue for medical negligence may have prompted part of the increase, but that would hardly explain why a 1 to 2% annual increment in the early 1960s became 10% by the late 1960s. To understand that "explosion," we have to turn to what was happening in the courtrooms.

For most of American history, it was virtually impossible—and still is in a few places—for a plaintiff to obtain the services of an expert physician to testify that another physician had not provided an acceptable standard of care. Without such testimony, a malpractice suit was almost invariably doomed; lawyers knew that and usually rejected them. By the early 1960s, however, a few doctors, outraged when they saw records of medical butchery,[107] risked ostracism by their colleagues and testified. The breaching of the medical wall of silence—with the breach soon widening as plaintiff lawyers began to pay doctors the same hefty fees hitherto available only from the defense—gave plaintiffs victories in cases they should always have won. Malpractice suits began to increase for that basic reason. Of greater long-range legal importance were the new definitions of negligence that judges and juries began to be required to make.

The basic concepts of negligence, despite all the distortions invoked in the 19th century to protect business, were well-established when medical malpractice cases began to arrive. Every judge, for instance, knew or should have known the proper "standard of acceptable care" when it came to a householder who failed to clear a sidewalk of ice and snow; but a judge now had to wonder, facing a first malpractice case, how did the same doctrine apply to a doctor who misdiagnosed an illness that *most* of his or her colleagues would have diagnosed correctly? Did "most" mean 90% of the peers or 51%? Did it further mean that a rural general practitioner should be held to the same standard of care in diagnosis and treatment as the urban, hospital-based specialist? How explain the law to a jury when the judge didn't know the law?

These were thorny problems. As a consequence, cases often were not finally resolved until they had wended their way through a series of appeals courts, and even then a court in one state might rule differently from that in another. As the number of opinions that permitted recovery or left loopholes multiplied, so did the grounds for future litigation.[108] Some of the new cases followed in the footsteps of the pioneering ones, but many others propounded theories that, at the most, had been covered only inferentially until then.

Some decisions from the 1970s provide illustrations of the areas that plaintiffs began to explore successfully. In *Tarasoff*, for example, a student at the University of California killed his fiancee, after telling a campus therapist he intended to do so; neither the young woman nor her family were informed by the university of the danger to her, and the California Supreme Court eventually ruled the school had a legal obligation to warn even though that meant violating traditional doctor-patient confidentiality.[109] Around the same time, courts began to hold doctors liable for failure to diagnose rubella or other conditions that would make a woman likely to give birth to a deformed or retarded child, with the doctor in these "wrongful birth" suits required to pay for the medical bills and support of the child.[110] Failure to explain to patients possible adverse consequences of operations or courses of treatment—the so-called "informed consent" doctrine—brought about a series of decisions, some seemingly contradictory, that have never completely clarified that area[111] for judges, litigants, or jurors.

As these holdings indicate, the elasticity of a legal concept—in this instance, negligence—cannot be known until and if attempts are made to stretch it. To the extent that stretching occurs, new and legitimate grounds for litigation are created, and a crisis becomes evident, which, in fact, is nothing more than a natural progression of the testing and transformation of the law.

Another example of the same principle can be found in the history of product-injury suits that were also difficult to pursue, much less win, until relatively recent years. The problem, again, did not lie in the absence of grounds for suit. A person injured by a product could sue on allegations of negligence or breach of implied warranty, a concept that goes back to Anglo-Saxon days when sellers of cattle had to warrant or swear they were not stolen.[112] Gradually, warranty came to mean that a product is presumed to be safe for its intended purpose and when it has an injury-causing defect, whether caused by negligence or not, the victim can sue. However, the legal requirement of *privity* effectively blocked most suits based on negligence or warranty grounds.[113] Adopted incongruously (but to the benefit of manufacturers) from laws governing sale of merchandise, privity permitted suits only when the injured person was the actual purchaser and then only against the party that sold the product.

To illustrate privity: If A is injured by a product bought from B, he can sue B, but if he gives the product to C, who is injured by it, C can't sue because he wasn't the purchaser. Similarly, if A is injured by a product manufactured by D, he can only sue D if he bought the product directly from D. Consequently, manufacturers could put almost any dangerous product on the market without responsibility, so long as they were careful never to sell it *directly* to a person who might be injured by it. With the law in that condition, we had no product liability litigation explosion; in fact, we had hardly any product liability cases.

A seeming advance for plaintiffs' rights occurred in 1916 when Benjamin Cardozo, later a justice of the United States Supreme Court but then a New York appeals judge, ruled in *MacPherson v. Buick Motor Co.*[114] that privity did *not* apply when the manufacturer could be shown to have been negligent in the production of the injury-causing item. Said Cardozo: "If the nature of a thing is such that it is reasonably certain to place life and limb in peril when negligently made, it is then a thing of danger."

As fine as this ruling may have been in theory, as a practical matter it helped relatively few victims. Given the many steps a product goes through from its raw material stage to the day it is placed on sale, it could be nearly impossible to pinpoint when and how a manufacturer's negligence occurred, even when the investigation itself was not prohibitively expensive for a plaintiff or lawyer to undertake.

Since Cardozo's ruling affirmed the doctrine of privity in warranty cases—i.e., a product-maker still couldn't be sued if it had delivered a defective item, only a *negligently* defective one—manufacturers' principal cloak of protection remained untouched, and matters continued that way for the next 30 years or so. An exception: People injured by contaminated food or drugs were permitted to sue manufacturers, without showing a specific negligent act,[115] on the assumption the item wouldn't have been spoiled absent carelessness. The next major blow against privity was delivered by a jury in *Henningsen v. Bloomfield Motors, Inc.,*[116] which held the manufacturer liable for selling a defective car through a dealer. Then in 1963, in *Greenman v. Yuba Power Products, Inc.,*[117] Judge Robert Traynor extended to dangerous products an ancient Germanic law that had[118] first been applied to animals.[119] Under it, a person who kept an animal commonly known to be dangerous had a legal duty to keep the animal penned. Thus, if lightning struck the corral in which a bull was kept and knocked down a fence and the bull escaped and attacked some picnickers, the owner hadn't been negligent but was still legally responsible for the injuries his dangerous animal inflicted since it wasn't the picnickers' fault they had been attacked. However, had the picnickers entered an enclosure in which they saw a bull grazing and it attacked them, they would then be said to have assumed the risk for their injuries, removing so-called *strict* liability from the bull's owner.

Greenman had done nothing foolish to cause the injury inflicted by the tool he had purchased. Nevertheless, since there was no way of proving there had been some act of negligence in its manufacture, and he could not sue under warranty because he hadn't purchased it directly from Yuba, he seemed doomed—as had millions before him—to suffer the consequences of an injury for which he had not been responsible. Recognizing that the tool was a dangerous bull, Judge Traynor came to his rescue. In applying the concept of strict liability to Yuba, the judge observed that "responsibility [must] be fixed wherever it will most effectively reduce the hazards to life and health inherent in defective products that reach the market. It is evident that the manufacturer can anticipate some hazards and guard against others, as the public cannot. Those who suffer injury from defective products are unprepared to meet its consequences. The cost of an injury and the loss of time or health may be an overwhelming misfortune to the person injured, and a needless one, for the risk can be insured by the manufacturer and distributed among the public as a cost of doing business."

Two years later the American Law Institute adopted Section 402A of the Restatement of Torts Second, removing the privity concept from all product-injury cases, making them what they should have been all along, purely torts, so that now manufacturers, sellers, and various suppliers of products that caused injury during a foreseeable use of them could be held liable. To manufacturers—now required to introduce all manner of safety devices if they didn't want to get sued[120]—it may not have seemed quite the liberating doctrine that it was to the public.

Just as with medical malpractice cases, suits brought against product manufacturers began to explore—and continue to explore—the nuances of the strict liability doctrine. For example, within a few months of the Greenman decision, a court in New York, permitted the survivors of a victim of an airplane crash to sue the manufacturer of the plane under strict liability.[121] Other cases—headline-makers frequently, such as those involving exploding gas tanks in cars and faulty birth control devices—soon followed.

Although these cases descended in a direct line from *Henningsen* and *Greenman* in that they involved injuries from a defective product to individuals going about their private lives, strict liability also was soon to provide a potent dividend for some victims of workplace injuries. Hitherto, they had been circumscribed for compensation by the various state statutes, some of which were quite penurious and few of which allowed full award for a catastrophic injury. Now, if the worker could show that the injury was caused by a defect in equipment or an environmental danger (such as the presence of asbestos[122]), the worker could collect under workmen's compensation *and* bring suit against the manufacturer under strict liability.

To this point, our analysis of the impact that changes in the law have upon litigation is a fairly tidy one. That is, until cases are brought in a certain legal area, judges have no way of responding to the issue; when they do, they define the law and, if it is to prove fruitful in litigation, expand the ways in which it can be applied. That happened not only in medical malpractice and in product liability but also in plaintiffs' antitrust litigation (the way paved by a 1960 case involving a price-fixing conspiracy among electrical manufacturing companies[123]), and even for such apparently mundane matters as divorce and custody cases where, as the number of these matters proliferated, so did the new issues—communal property, the so-called "palimony" suits—each of which required its own definitions and expansions.

When the law responds to new issues, however, it typically does so in a delayed fashion. As Sir Henry Maine observed in 1890: "Social necessities and social opinions are always more or less in advance of Law. We may come indefinitely near to the closing of the gap between them, but it has a perpetual tendency to re-open."[124] Judge Traynor's role in *Greenman* exemplifies Sir Henry's insight. In 1944, Traynor had written a *minority* opinion in an almost identical case for which he received no support from his fellow judges;[125] it took nearly 20 years and the kind of change in the social climate that Maine points out before the California Supreme Court changed its mind and agreed unanimously with Traynor in *Greenman*.

Animating the societal changes to which the courts, and not just California's, were responding was the philosophy and success of the civil rights effort, which in the process spun off ancillary rights (e.g., those of prisoners, those of students, those of women). The issue under challenge in each instance was the traditional belief that courts were primarily protectors of property rights. Now the courts were being asked to liberate themselves from the narrowness of that thinking and to consider the right of the injured individual, whether that injury was caused by discrimination, by a negligent doctor, by an unsafe environment, by price-fixing, or by the rampaging bull of a defective product. They were being asked and they were doing it.

Although the climate that promoted this "rights explosion" had its genesis in the 1950s and 1960s, many of the most important decisions, following some combination of Sir Henry's theorem and the law's delay, did not begin to arrive until the 1970s. This was especially true of the discrimination spin-off cases and those involving medical, environmental, and product injury rights.

The social activism apparent in many judge and jury verdicts of the 1970s led to counteractivism by those who were hurt by the decisions or who believed that they were against the best interests of the nation.[126] By the late 1970s, for example, 25 states had passed statutes which required that medical malpractice plaintiffs submit their cases to mediation or arbitration, and only if it failed were they to be permitted access to trial.[127] Although the usual, ostensible purpose of these reforms—no-fault automobile accident laws led the way in the early 1970s—was to relieve court congestion, the underlying goal[128] was to remove as many cases as possible from juries and judges, lest, either at the trial or appeals level, new liberations of the law would result.

Other non-trial dispute-resolution devices were also adopted in great numbers during the 1970s. One technique that has as its sole announced purpose to reduce backlogs is so-called mandatory court-annexed arbitration. In it, attorneys are hired by court administrators on an as-needed basis to recommend non-binding settlements for civil cases, primarily tort actions, which have a worth within an established ceiling. (In this system, ordinarily, the value of the case is based solely on the amount the plaintiff is demanding.[129]) The eligibility maximum varies widely, from a low of $3,000 in Alaska to $150,000 in several federal court districts,[130] although the median figure is $15,000.[131] By 1985, 16 state courts and 11 federal ones had court-annexed arbitration programs in effect.[132]

The average arbitration lasts about two hours, is held either in a court facility or in the office of one of the arbitrators; present are the litigants and their attorneys, offering their cases in summary with some of the rules of evidence relaxed.[133] Verdicts are usually made immediately after the end of the hearing by the arbitrators—typically three of them[134]—although the litigants may not be informed for some time afterward.

Different arbitration programs have had different degrees of success, but when one is well-administered, the process will lead to rapid hearings, often within three to six months from the filing date[135] rather than the three to six years that might be expected if there were no arbitration. For plaintiffs, especially those in desperate need to replace the money their injuries have cost them, arbitration can be a boon, and for both parties legal expenses will be less than if they went to trial. According to a study undertaken in Pittsburgh, more than 80% of the litigants who went before one of its arbitration panels found their hearings to be conducted in a "fair" manner, and even two-thirds of the losers thought the arbitration was at least "somewhat fair."[136]

Although the arbitrators' verdict is frequently rejected—58% of the time in one federal court in the early 1980s, though as low as 25% elsewhere[137]—such statistics can be misleading. For example, in the 58% rejection district, only 2% of the cases eventually went to trial,[138] suggesting that the arbitrators' decision, even when not accepted, can cause both sides to rethink their positions, leading either to settlement or, in some instances, to a losing plaintiff dropping the matter. We have no way, however, of knowing how often these cases would have settled or been dropped had there been no arbitration, so that we cannot assess how much, if at all, arbitration reduces the backlog.

Although arbitration has the benefits described for plaintiffs, it can properly be seen principally as a defense tool. When a defendant's insurance company rejects an arbitration award to the plaintiff, it is able to hold on to its money and invest it, and can use its rejection to lay pressure on the plaintiff to accept a lower amount than the arbitrators named. Should the side refusing the verdict decide to take the matter to trial, it will be required, in most places, to post bond to cover court costs and perhaps pay the arbitrators' fees,[139] an expense which is of no great moment to an insurance company but could work a great hardship on the plaintiff. (In some jurisdictions, the money will be returned if the party filing for trial fares better there than at the arbitration.[140])

Court-administered conciliation programs are a much older idea than the lawyer-arbitration panels,[141] but they too only began to expand meaningfully in the 1970s. Most commonly they are employed to resolve minor disputes (such as landlord-tenant cases). The mediations may occur in a courthouse with court personnel in charge, but frequently judges simply recommend disputants to existent independent mediation centers of which there are about 200 across the country.[142] These neighborhood centers, which often advertise their services to the public, are typically located in low-income neighborhoods. For example, in 1980 the Atlanta Neighborhood Justice Center primarily served underclass people (average income $6,000), with disputes usually in the $200 range.[143] Lawyers are either barred or discouraged from attending mediation sessions;[144] the mediators are usually neighborhood people or trained social workers.

Although mediation centers primarily exist to resolve civil disputes, occasionally a person who has been arrested for causing a neighborhood disturbance will be referred to a mediator by the district attorney's office, in the expressed hope that mediation will defuse the situation.[145]

The admirers of mediation, whether for civil or criminal matters, see its informal peacemaking role as its greatest virtue. Rather than emphasizing the factors that drive the parties apart, as a trial does, mediation seeks to find common grounds that can lead to a reconciliation between parties. No one necessarily expects the disputants to come out of the parley as friends, but rather that enough areas of mutual self-interest may be discovered so the quarrel can be ended without litigation. Although not legally enforceable, a conciliation agreement is commonly signed and can be morally binding as a court order often is not. (The ordinary first step with a court order is to confer with one's attorney to see if there is some way around it.) Mediation, therefore, is ideally situation-oriented, seeking to solve a problem, not to apportion blame. Trials and court-annexed arbitration, on the contrary, deal with who was right and wrong, very frequently in a narrowly technical way that leaves untouched the festering situation that led to the litigation in the first place. Trial dissatisfaction, often felt by both parties, is especially common in child-custody and other domestic relations matters, with the result that, as one litigation ends, the next is already on its way.

At its best, therefore, mediation can contain or resolve situations which, if left unattended, might spill over into serious legal problems, and it may do so in a way that preserves each party from losing face.

There is, however, another side to the mediation coin. To illustrate it, let us suppose we have a landlord-tenant dispute which has been sent to a mediation program by the court. As is typical, no lawyers are permitted to be present at the session. The tenant, if poor, as is also typical, will almost certainly have had no prior access to a lawyer's advice, but the landlord almost certainly will have, if not for this particular case then from knowledge gained from previous disputes with tenants. As a consequence, the landlord is in the superior position, knows when to hold firm and when not, but the tenant does not and neither does the mediator who takes pride in having no knowledge of the law. In the end we'll assume the mediator resolves the problem through a compromise by which the landlord agrees to make one repair and the tenant another. The landlord goes away happy, knowing that if the case went to trial the tenant wouldn't have to pay for anything. The mediation center is happy because it has scored another "success." The tenant may be happy, too, having avoided the fearsome possibility of going to trial, and may never realize how wrongly he or she was treated.[146]

For a second illustration, we have a man who is arrested on a minor charge, after which the district attorney's office makes a seemingly generous offer: He will be allowed to enter into a mediation program and, if he navigates that successfully, the charges will be dropped. Wishing to avoid a criminal record, the man visits the mediator and agrees to the plan proposed for him. What the man may never know is that the only reason the District Attorney's office made the mediation offer was that it knew it lacked the evidence to convict him of any crime.

In both our exemplars, the mediation process has become an essentially coercive one in which the government is able to control or modify behavior through means that would be impermissible in a courtroom. In each instance, a vulnerable person has entered the process in a non-equitable position and has come out weaker or poorer than if the mediation had not intervened, his position further undermined by his not being permitted legal advice that perhaps would prevent him from signing an unfair agreement.[147]

By succeeding in keeping cases out of the courtroom, mediation programs can also succeed in frustrating the development of the law. This consequence can be particularly ironic when we consider that, like those in Atlanta, most mediation centers profess to benefit the poor and the minorities, almost all of whose significant legal gains have come about as a result of courtroom decisions. Looked at that way, mediation programs, even if that is not their intention, best serve the interests of those who would rather see the poor handled by social workers than represented by rights-seeking lawyers.[148]

Two other means have also been developed to keep certain cases out of the courtroom. They serve the interests of the well-to-do.

The older of the two, rent-a-judge, had its inception in California in the 1970s and has since spread east. The name is descriptive. Rather than wait their turn for trial, parties who can afford to do so pay for the services of a judge to decide their case for them.

In California, though not necessarily elsewhere, there can be a measure of court supervision, in that the parties apply to the court for permission to engage a judge who may be selected by the court. The rented judge's findings are binding, although there is a limited right to appeal if errors in application of the law or a verdict against the evidence can be shown.[149] In other systems, the parties have the right to select their own private judge;[150] in Philadelphia, for example, a group of retired jurists have formed an association to provide the service.

A rent-a-judge "trial" is an abbreviated version of the normal one, has no jury, is held at the convenience of the parties, and usually does not take place in a courtroom.[151] The parties thus gain speed in disposition of their cases and, since the public is not permitted to attend, privacy, making the format particularly attractive to corporations that worry about the possibility of business secrets being revealed, and also for especially unpleasant divorce cases.[152]

Some critics find "rent-a-judge" inherently offensive to American ideas of equal justice, since those who have the money can get their affairs settled in private while all others have to wait in line for their day in a public forum where they have no way of hiding that which they don't want revealed.[153] The counterargument is that most civil cases are resolved privately as it is—occasionally because one party or both fears revelations—so that rent-a-judge doesn't change that. Moreover, those who can't afford to rent a judge are no worse off than they were before—nothing's been taken from them—and indeed, because of the cases that go to the private judge, their own suit may come to fruition sooner than it otherwise would have.[154]

Nevertheless, a public interest can be obstructed by rent-a-judge cases. Because of their *in camera* character—ordinarily not even a transcript is made—corporate or personal misdoings that may be criminal or otherwise endanger the common good can remain hidden as they cannot in open courtrooms where the press reports on what occurs and where jurors and judges can make their displeasure known in a visible and prominent way.

This same objection applies to the mini-trial. Developed by Professor Eric D. Green of the Boston University Law School, the mini-trial is designed primarily for use by corporate litigants to resolve commercial disputes. With the proceeding moderated by a referee or mediator, the trial begins with informal summary presentations by the lawyers, although expert witnesses can be heard and questioned. The idea of the mini-trial is to encourage each side to develop its theory of the case, narrowing the issues in order to remove the legalistic and collateral matters, so that the case ceases to be a lawyers' dispute and returns to being a business problem. Top management representatives will be present who have the power to come to decisions, often with the advice and analysis of the referee.[155] This clearing away of the debris can prove successful. In one case that was in litigation for three years, settlement occurred two days after the mini-trial.[156]

Each alternative dispute resolution device has virtues when it works effectively. Some provide access to at least an approximation of justice for people who could not otherwise afford it; many cut legal costs. And many bring about swift resolutions of matters that hitherto remained for seemingly endless periods in the court system, primarily to the disadvantage of the injured and the poor.

Each, however, also holds the possibility of burying within private colloquies matters which, were they openly aired in courtrooms, might reveal information about problems that people have in common and which require redress.[157] The mediation center, the rent-a-judge, and the mini-trial also move close to creating separate and private justice systems, one for the poor and two for the rich, in what is supposed to be a democratic society.

Changes in the lawyers.   It is not only the people on the streets or the judges on their benches or the litigants themselves who re-form the law. So do the lawyers, and the better they become the more likely old ways will be challenged successfully. For the plaintiffs' bar, progress was slow.

Workmen's compensation laws and related federal statutes enacted during the first several decades of the 20th century attracted for the first time, as we have seen, able and ethical lawyers to the plaintiffs' bar. Many were Jews who entered the field because employment was closed to them by the major defense firms that hired only gentiles. Jews weren't the only ones the firms banned. Lawyers of Italian and Irish background also found scant welcome in the big WASP firms and many of them turned either to negligence or criminal defense work.[158] Not until the 1930s did the anti-Jewish barrier begin to lower and then only in a few places; one of the earliest was a Philadelphia law firm headed by Richardson Dilworth, later that city's mayor. Subsequently, Dilworth's became the first white law firm in the country to hire a black partner in William Coleman, Jr., who was to become President Gerald Ford's secretary of transportation.

The mass production of automobiles had also opened a new and potentially lucrative field for the plaintiffs' bar,[159] but few of the attorneys in this area had the skills[160] or the financial resources to combat the insurance companies with their cadres of doctor-experts who could "prove" that almost any injury had existed prior to the accident that caused it. Delay was another problem they faced. As auto cases crowded court dockets, lawyers who were competent to handle them began to avoid them, not wanting to waste uncompensated hours sitting in a courtroom waiting for a case to be called.[161] Left over were the inexperienced and the connivers.

Although by the late 1920s wholesale bribery of witnesses on both sides of a case had become rare, another practice, that of "ambulance chasing," was commonplace. The 1928 Wasservogel investigation in New York revealed that "runners," who had contacts with the police, would be alerted to an accident, hurry to the scene, and either there or later in the hospital sign the victim to a retainer agreement in which the name of the lawyer was left blank. The retainers would then be sold to the highest attorney bidder. The purchasing lawyers, in turn, would churn the cases they had bought into suits with little or no investigation of their merits; quick settlements were made with insurance companies of $50 to $75 apiece, the amount split fifty-fifty between the lawyer and client.[162] Dozens of cases might be settled in this cynical way in a single sitting with an insurance company representative, who found it well worth the cost to pay small amounts on bad claims in order to save large amounts on the good ones that were being dumped.

In other places, lawyers hired their own runners, and to this day accidents are occasionally faked, followed by spurious medical bills, all under the orchestration of an unscrupulous personal injury lawyer. Definitions of unscrupulosity (whether by lawyer, carpenter, or college professor), however, often depend on who is doing the defining. Thus, even as recently as the 1970s, commissions have been empaneled by gray eminences of the bar to hunt out personal injury ambulance chasers, although somehow no panels have ever investigated ambulance-chasing by partners in the big corporate law firms who use the golf courses of the nation's great country clubs to solicit and sign up their clients. Nor, somehow, have the ethics of insurance companies come under a cloud of calumny when their representatives speed to the bedsides of injured people and hector them into signing releases. Somehow, instead, it is only the plaintiff's lawyer, who at least is trying to get the victim some money, who comes under interdiction.[163]

The contingency fee system that personal injury lawyers employ to generate their income also stigmatized them. The idea that a lawyer should get paid only if he wins apparently had its origin in the later days of the Roman Empire, when the Emperor Justinian castigated such attorneys as having the "morals of a pirate." When the early American tort lawyers resurrected the practice, they found themselves under a similar barrage of criticism. The Supreme Court of Michigan in 1857 declared the contingency fee to be a *malum* (evil) *per se*,[164] and in 1881 the legal scholar Thomas Cooley described the contingency fee lawyers as contemptible individuals who debased the legal profession by working on speculation—rather than on fat fees from corporations—and who created "a feeling of antagonism between aggregated capital on the one side, and the community in general on the other."[165] Even today, the contingency fee is considered unprofessional in England and most other places in the world.[166] As Speiser explains it: "According to [the] traditional theory, lawyers who want to maintain professional standing and detachment should not go into business with their clients."[167]

As self-serving and hypocritical as such reasoning was—it meant that only those people who could afford to pay a "professional" fee were allowed lawyers—it had as its serious purpose to scare the public away from such supposedly unsavory individuals; the whole propaganda effort was also well-awash with anti-Semitism. It worked, too. Even into the post-World War II period, the belief that personal injury lawyers and their contingency fees were somehow unethical continued to keep down the amount of litigation.

Those who mourn the passing of a supposedly non-litigious past in America, therefore, are also mourning the passing of bigotry and the passing of the belief that the poor should not have the same access to justice as do the rich.

The first step by plaintiffs' lawyers to professionalize came about in 1946 with the organization of the National Association of Claimants' Compensation Attorneys (NACCA). In 1960[168], NACCA reformulated itself as the Association of Trial Lawyers of America (ATLA).[169]

ATLA soon began to function as a self-contained bar association primarily for plaintiffs' lawyers and, to a lesser extent, for criminal defense attorneys. Following the lead of the American Bar Association, it published its own magazine and its own law journal. It regularly issued summaries of judicial decisions in relevant cases. It regularly held seminars for attorneys to learn the intricacies of trial practice. But it was not only through its educational mechanisms that ATLA upgraded the performance of plaintiff lawyers. As a national organization with state chapters, it also developed networks by which members got to know which of their colleagues were particularly qualified to handle various kinds of difficult cases. As a result, forwarding of suits, which had always existed to some extent, became highly feasible. The forwarding lawyer typically received a third of any fee the expert earned, with the expert doing almost all the work, although the forwarding lawyer technically remained on the case as cocounsel. Because the forwarding lawyer's earnings came entirely out of the expert's share, the process cost the client nothing and usually meant a much higher award than if the first lawyer had kept the case. The system worked out well for everybody, except defendants.

The result, therefore, of the professionalization of the plaintiffs' bar was that the average lawyer became sufficiently skilled to get good results in routine cases—which hadn't been true, on the average, in the past—and knew how and when to turn the complex matters over to the specialists. The gradual liberalization of discovery rules has also helped attorneys, both in routine and exceptional cases, to obtain information pretrial that had previously been closed to them, thereby measurably aiding their likelihood of winning the case for their clients.

Since the specialists have largely concentrated on major product liability and medical malpractice cases, which can be quite lucrative, they have become able to attract to their firms bright young law school graduates who had previously and exclusively sought employment in the big defense firms. (Some of the most successful of the plaintiff specialists even have their own doctors on staff to evaluate injuries.) The combined development of legal acumen and financial resources to research cases has meant that the plaintiff specialists can combat corporations and hospitals, and their insurance companies, and their high-powered defense firms, on an equal and sometimes superior basis. Had the Triangle Shirtwaist fire occurred today instead of 1911, none of the families of the victims in that massacre of negligence would have had to settle for $75.

The extent, if any, to which the improved quality of the plaintiffs' bar has helped generate litigation in recent years is not readily measurable. Certainly the removal of the stigma of incompetence and unscrupulosity has made prospective clients less loath to seek such lawyers than they were in the past. It is also unlikely that the higher awards achieved have discouraged people from suing. However, save for the impact of the removal of restrictions on lawyer advertising, there seems little evidence to suggest that the reputed litigation crisis has been prompted by lawyers going about fomenting cases—as in the ambulance-chasing days. Not only, as we observed at the beginning of this chapter, is there no apparent correlation between lawyer availability and litigation frequency but also, in the case of the specialists, their problem is not how to find cases but how to make a selection from those offered to them.

Nevertheless, the belief in the ambulance-chaser lives on, with some critics asserting that the rise in malpractice cases in the early to mid-1970s was caused by personal injury lawyers scrounging about for new sources of income after half the states passed no-fault automobile insurance laws.[170] If that is so, the statistics don't show it. In states with no-fault laws, the malpractice rate has been 13% lower than in those that don't have it.[171]

It may even be that the higher standards of performance in the plaintiffs' bar have acted to decrease the amount of litigation.[172] The more lawyers know about the current status of the law, the less likely they are to take on "bad" (i.e., losing) claims on which, since they work on a contingency fee, they get no recompense. The practice of referring complex, high-stakes cases to experts makes rejection even more likely. Not only are these lawyers the most knowledgeable and hence best able to evaluate a case's viability, but they are also likely to refuse even "winnable" cases when their analysis shows them that the amount of time and money that would be required to prepare the case for trial will be greater than the probable award.

The combination of improved legal knowledge and the economic disincentives of the contingency fee system, theoretically should therefore act to de-escalate claims frequency. Partial proof of this hypothesis is found in a study which discovered that 50 to 71% of all malpractice claims brought to any lawyer were rejected, with the refusal rate probably reaching 80% among the specialists.[173]

Nevertheless, even though this portrait of the changes that have occurred in the plaintiffs' bar leads generally to these conclusions, there is some reason to believe (though the present research is primarily confined to one study) that the high road is not taken by everyone. Some plaintiff lawyers apparently bring large numbers of malpractice claims that result either in zero or small-dollar settlements.[174] Such attorneys are either of below-average skills (or they wouldn't so frequently accept cases in which they get no compensation) or else are in the business of filing doubtful claims (and probably not only malpractice ones) on a volume basis for the purpose of obtaining nuisance settlements. In other words, if they file seven losers out of 10 but get $20,000 each on the other three in settlements, their time, as they see it, is adequately compensated for the minimal amount of work they put in.

New grounds for suit.   The litigation spun out from the "rights explosion" did not always have as its purpose to gain money for plaintiffs. Since the 1960s, hundreds of thousands of petitions have been brought by people convicted of crimes who (taking advantage of new laws) have asserted their civil rights were violated somewhere in the process; they are not seeking money but freedom. Dissidents have pursued litigation against the government's use of such hoary protest-control devices as the injunction and the mass disorderly conduct arrest. Still other cases have challenged the government's right to force immunity on protestors in order to jail them when they refuse to testify against their colleagues. Not a few suits have challenged the government's right to build nuclear weapons and other devices of mass destruction. The reinstatement of the death penalty and the legalization of abortion have brought about reams of civil litigation in which people do not seek money but rather moral redress.

Other new grounds for suit prompted by the rights explosion have primarily sought to protect individuals from unjust treatment while in the pursuit of their daily lives. Commonplace have become actions alleging employment discrimination against minorities, women, the handicapped, and older workers.[175] Some have led to sizable verdicts. In one, a saleswoman received a $1.27 million award because she was fired for exhibiting the same aggressive traits that had won promotions for her male colleagues.[176]

A bevy of children's rights cases have led to supposed reforms of the juvenile justice system, and to expansion of children's rights within a parental or custodial relationship, including the right to be free from sexual and physical abuse. Not only individuals but also governments can be held responsible in these cases. To cite one example, Oregon paid $100,000 to settle a suit brought about when a two-year-old received a fractured skull and leg at the hands of a foster-mother hired by the state welfare department.[177]

We have also had litigation which, for better or worse, has tried to make happier the lives of the mentally ill by emptying state hospitals, and which—as in *Romeo*[178]—has extended civil rights to severely retarded individuals who had long been denied them as a matter of course.[179]

Violations of civil rights by the police have also become generally recognized as a cause for suit only since the 1960s. Typically, the claims have involved injury or death resulting from brutality, as in the case of Leroy Shenandoah, a member of the honor guard at President Kennedy's funeral, who was allowed to bleed to death after being shot six times by an officer.[180] In recent years, a series of suits have been brought by women subjected to strip-searches by police. In a Chicago case, a 62-year-old woman who underwent that indignity when arrested on a traffic charge, sued and received a verdict of $50,000; in the same city, a physician whose privacy was similarly violated after she was arrested for a traffic violation received $110,000; in Detroit, still another strip-search case resulted in a $365,000 award.[181] Since strip-searching women for minor offenses had been indulged in by police officers in many districts for decades previous without resulting in litigation, the spate of these suits can probably be laid to the effectiveness of the women's rights movement.

Victims of crimes have also begun to bring suits, not against the perpetrators but against government agencies that were allegedly negligent in preventing the crime. Some examples from the 1980s: In 1983, the town of Ware, Massachusetts, was held liable for $873,679 to cover injuries resulting from an accident that occurred when police failed to stop a drunk driver.[182] Another suit against a municipality resulted in a $3 million verdict after police failed to intervene when a mother requested their assistance to stop her husband from assaulting and mutilating their six-year-old daughter.[183] New York City was held negligent in a $2.5 million verdict when it hired as a park employee a sex deviate who subsequently raped a nine-year-old child.[184] In 1985, a Torrington, Connecticut, woman was awarded $3.2 million by a jury in a case in which police failed to respond to her requests for help when her estranged husband attacked her and left her scarred and partially paralyzed.[185]

Failures in the 911 direct dialing system for police aid have also led to litigation. In one of these cases, a woman who lived in a suburb of Buffalo, New York, heard an intruder in her house and dialed 911; she reached the Buffalo police department which dispatched a car to a street with the same name in Buffalo from where the officers reported there was no crime in progress. Meanwhile, the burglar at the suburban address attacked and murdered the woman who made the call. Prior to the introduction of 911, she would have dialed her local police station which was located just 1,300 feet from her house. Her heirs received a reported settlement of $600,000.[186]

With the exception of the suit involving the hard-driving saleswoman, each of these cases illustrating new ground for litigation had government as the defendant. The theory that government, like an individual, has a legal duty to act non-negligently is itself of relatively recent origin and still another exemplification of the "rights explosion." The doctrine of sovereign immunity, which throughout most of American history had protected nearly every state and most municipalities, as well as the federal government, from suit, has come under increasing attack. By 1980, more than 40 states had abolished or placed limitations on the protection,[187] and by that time most local governments were also permitting themselves to be sued, though often with ceilings on the amount that could be recovered. In 1978, the United States Supreme Court ruled that all municipalities were subject to suit when violations of the civil rights of their citizens were alleged as a result of an "official municipal policy of some nature." In 1986, the Court broadened the ruling to permit suit when damage was alleged as a result of an action by a municipal official even when no official policy is involved.[188]

Under the Federal Tort Claims Act, the United States government can be sued but only for a negligent act by an employee. Similarly, until the post-World War II years, the law throughout almost all the United States held that charitable institutions—and perhaps, based on the 1876 decision, any non-profit organization—could not be sued for negligence. By the end of the 1970s, that form of immunity had been abolished in most states, one way or another; for example, in Maryland the charity couldn't be sued but was required to have insurance and the insurer could be sued.[189]

But it has not been only the civil rights explosion that has set off a kind of chain reaction of new causes for litigation. Technological advances, which can often bring about great benefit, can also cause great harm. The 911 case illustrates that premise. Because of 911, police response time in general has been speeded and doubtless thousands of lives have been saved, but it is also true that the Buffalo woman would almost certainly still be alive if there had been no 911 for her to dial.

Developments in medical technology have similarly benefited countless people. But when one of these gadgets malfunctions, as happened with the pacemaker of an Iowa farmer, his survivors, perhaps understandably unimpressed with that particular medical miracle, sued and received an award of $501,200.[190] We can also assume the United States government had nothing but good motives in mind when it encouraged people to receive inoculations to combat Swine Flu—a novel instance of finding a cure for a disease that didn't exist. But thousands of lawsuits resulted when that particular technological advance crippled some and killed others; one suit alone resulted in a $1.9 million verdict.[191]

Whether nuclear power represents a technological *advance* may be in doubt, but without doubt, had it not been developed, some litigation that has occurred wouldn't have. The atomic bomb tests following World War II led to lawsuits alleging long-term damage due to radioactive fallout.[192] A related case was the famous Silkwood suit involving plutonium contamination. The implementation of nuclear energy for peaceful purposes led to the near meltdown of the reactor at the Three Mile Island plant near Harrisburg, Pennsylvania, in 1978, an incident that gave rise to a series of suits alleging chromosomal damage to nearby residents.[193]

Unlike nuclear energy, seat belts in automobiles have aroused little debate about their benefits, even among those who don't use them. Because they were invented, lives have been saved, yet when they (like pacemakers) are occasionally defective, they also produce litigation.[194] Electric drip coffeemakers, another relatively recent technological innovation, have been purchased in the millions and almost always work just fine; yet, according to one report, in 1982 they caused 2,700 fires in homes, 125 injuries, seven deaths, and more than $8 million in property damage—grinding out, in that fashion, even more litigation.[195]

A new technology can cause litigation not just when it fails but because it succeeds. Smoke detectors, which began to be widely marketed in the 1970s, are a case in point. Landlords' failure to install them has led to several suits after tenants were injured or killed in fires that they might have escaped had the alarm been present. One of these suits resulted in an $11 million verdict.[196] Had smoke detectors not been invented, no smoke detector suits.

New grounds for suit are also supplied by governments—federal, state, and local—in the statutes and ordinances they pass. The question here is not necessarily the value of these laws; many are unquestionably enacted as wise responses to pressing public needs. Manifestly, however, the more laws we have, the more laws that can be broken or allegedly broken, producing increments in either the criminal or civil caseloads, and sometimes both, depending on the circumstances. As one observer has pointed out, a hamburger, from the time it is still part of the steer until it hits the fry pan, could be subject to 41,000 state and federal regulations.[197]

A few more examples from among many. The passage of the Uniform Commercial Code prompted numerous class action suits and other forms of litigation based on questions of interpretation of its provisions.[198] Medicare for the elderly and Medicaid for the indigent, legislated in the mid-1960s, has helped tens of millions of people get much needed health care they could not otherwise have afforded, but alleged evasions and exploitations of these laws by providers and recipients have also led to a host of lawsuits and criminal prosecutions. New regulatory agencies have had similar histories. The Occupational Safety and Health Administration (OSHA), a federally constituted agency, had as its laudable purpose to help protect employees from workplace hazards. Occasionally it may even have succeeded in doing so, but it has also proved enormously productive of litigation, either by the government against businesses or by businesses in appeal of government action. On the local level, beginning around 1980 a series of governments have passed so-called right-to-know laws which require manufacturers using hazardous chemicals and related ingredients to provide public warnings. The legislation may well be socially desirable, but, like OSHA's efforts, it creates new causes for litigation. Federal laws permitting tax shelters have led to both criminal charges and civil suits when these shelters were allegedly used improperly as tax-evasion devices, with private suits charging fraud following in their wake.

Not only new laws but also policy shifts in the interpretations of them—as occurred to some extent with tax shelters—can also create new litigation, occasionally in a quite explosive way, as we shall see in Chapter Six.

Chapter 6

The Litigation "Explosion"

Beginning in the early 1970s, and continuing into the 1980s, the amount of litigation reaching American courts was on the increase. Of that, there is no doubt. All our studies, from the weakest to the most reputable, show it. But was what happened an explosion—one which, as Justice Stevens said, may have made the jury a luxury we can no longer afford—and if it was, how did it occur? In some cases but not others? In some places but not others? or did it occur across the board?

Definitionally, we appear to be in a highly subjective area. One person's explosion could be another's increment. Nevertheless, the two concepts do have certain distinguishing characteristics. Increase carries with it the idea of orderly progression; in it, the litigation-prompting factors described in the previous chapter would manifest themselves in a predictable fashion and consequently (theoretically anyway) become manageable within the framework of the existent justice system, including the right to jury trial. An explosion, however, by its nature is unpredictable, so that its manifestations are unmanageable, absent the introduction of radical reforms to eliminate them, one of which might be eliminating or reducing the number of time-consuming jury trials. Therefore, to prove an explosion in litigation—as contrasted to an increment in it—we must look for evidence of the "unparalleled contentiousness" and "the hair-trigger suing" described by Justice Burger and other critics of the litigation habits of the American people. We are most likely to find it in an aberrantly high increase in personal injury cases, since it is they, with their money damages and the prospect of getting even with somebody, that will presumably have particular appeal to the greedy and contentious personality.

Certain kinds of civil rights actions—for example, those involving disgruntled employees and suits against government officials for insignificant instances of mistreatment—*might* exhibit a contentious (i.e., litigious)

143

personality, but the grounds for bringing these cases are so broad that, unless we examine each individually, we have no way of determining a contentiousness trend. It seems likely, however, that if we do discover a huge increment in personal injury and related tort actions, an increment caused solely by litigiousness, then the same phenomenon is probably at work, at least to some degree, in the civil rights cases. (Domestic relations litigation is a somewhat different matter, and will be discussed separately below.)

If there has been an "assault upon the citadel," to borrow Dean Prosser's phrasing,[1] the nature of it is to be learned from statistics, which brings us to two threshold issues: How reliable is the data available to us? What are the proper inferences that can be drawn from it?

(Currency of data is another problem. Nothing gets out of date quite so rapidly as statistics. For this chapter, which was written in 1986, figures were rarely available after 1983 because of court delays in compiling statistics. However, the period for which statistics were available does coincide with that during which the hue and cry was raised against supposedly greedy litigants forcing the courts into their period of greatest travail. If it should happen there was no crisis when the critics were saying there was a crisis, we have learned a lesson about believing everything we are told. On the contrary, if the statistics do prove a crisis for *that* period, then we should take the necessary steps to prevent its continuance or recurrence.)

I

One statistic which seems to lend credence to the "explosion" theory comes from a national study[2] which shows that, at the beginning of the 1980s, American state courts were admitting to their dockets more than 80 million civil and criminal cases a year. That's a formidable number—one for every three citizens—which indicates, whatever the causes, a prodigious amount of legal activity.

The statistic, however, becomes considerably less impressive when we learn that almost 60 million of the 80-million-plus filings were for minor traffic violations, and that many of the people involved in the cases each year are repeat performers (scofflaws; criminal recidivists; and the same litigants from old cases reappearing in new ones, a condition prevalent in child-custody battles). Knowing that, we might decide to discard the 80 million number as misleading, and go look for others to prove the explosion hypothesis; however, if we tarry with it a bit longer, we find it is not only misleading but also inaccurate.

It is accurate in the sense that it is derived from reports issued by state court administrators, but inaccurate because different states use different counting methods. For example, some states list parking tickets as part of their case filings but others don't.[3] Hence, if states that didn't count parking tickets should have, then the actual number is far higher than 80 million, but 80 million is an inflated figure if parking tickets should never be counted.

The credibility problems of the 80 million don't end there. Because of the way the statistic has been constructed, it can be manipulated to produce misleading yet "true" figures. To show how that can happen, suppose we want to learn the percentage frequency of civil case filings each year. What we come up with depends on how we use the traffic category. Should we decide that parking tickets properly are part of a court's caseload and include in our study only those states that count them, we find that traffic cases now comprise 81% of all listings, criminal and juvenile 9%, civil 10%. Equally logically, however, we might decide a parking ticket simply isn't a "case," and so we limit our compilation to states that don't count them; when we do that, our traffic figure is 61%, civil 18%, criminal and juvenile 21%. Finally, considering all the problems they are giving us, we might decide to sweep *all* traffic figures out of our computations for all states; when we do that, civil becomes slightly more than half the total caseload, criminal and juvenile the remainder. Therefore, depending on what we count (and what we want to prove), we can equally truthfully assert that civil cases make up a tiny minority or the majority of the annual cases filed.

If, however, we don't use case filings as our criterion to learn what is going on in our courts, and instead turn to case dispositions, we have only worsened our dilemma, principally because of a lack of consistent definition, from state to state, of what constitutes a trial. In some states, only cases that result in a verdict are considered trials; elsewhere, the fact that a trial commenced puts it in the trial-disposition column.[4] States in the first group, therefore, appear to have many fewer trials than those in the second, where a case that might end by settlement even before the jury is picked is still considered a trial. Under both methods, there is also a danger of double-counting because some cases are re-tried. The probability of that happening is much greater in states in the second group. In the first group, only completed trials ordered re-tried will be duplicated; in the second group, not only these cases but any matter that was aborted at any stage because of a mistrial, including hung juries, can appear twice in the trial counts. Our statistics don't tell us how often that happens, but it will be recalled from Chapter Four that hung juries alone account for 3 to 5% of all cases.

Dispositions provide us with misleading statistics for other reasons, one of which, present primarily in criminal cases, can skew the figures of court activity that occurs in one state compared to another. To illustrate, let us suppose we have an incident in which two muggers rob two victims, assaulting one and killing the other. Such a case can be counted in any one of three ways depending on the state in which it occurred. In one group of states, each of the two defendants will be charged with three separate crimes (robbery, assault, homicide), and even though there is a single trial, the dispositions will be counted as six cases in the statistics. In the second group, the two defendants face an amalgamated set of charges and the result is counted as two cases. In the third group, the defendants and the charges will be considered as one case.[5] Consequently, states in the first group appear statistically to have more crimes and more court activity than those in the second, the second more than in the third, even though there may be no more crime nor trials in states in one group than in another.

Counting *types* of cases is equally frustrating. For instance, suppose we want to know how many felonies and misdemeanors are prosecuted each year. We can get accurate figures annually on a state-by-state basis; however, when we try to assess a national picture from them, we are stymied when we learn that a felony in one state may be a misdemeanor in another, or that a state has changed its laws, so that what appeared as a felony in its statistics one year has become part of the misdemeanor statistics the next, and vice versa.[6] Similarly, in civil matters some states separate tort cases from other types of lawsuits, but others don't; some count divorces separately from other domestic relations matters (such as adoptions), but others don't,[7] and so on.

Moreover, in both civil and criminal cases, comparables between different years for the same state become distorted if, as sometimes happens, in the interval between one report and the next, the state changes its method of counting and begins to include (or exclude) certain matters.[8]

Backlog statistics are frequently cited to prove both the reality and adverse effects of a litigation explosion. (The theory is that an influx of large numbers of new legal actions makes it impossible for a court to keep up with its caseload, creating harmful delays in the administration of justice.) Unfortunately, our figures there aren't entirely reliable either, since some states have a reporting date which immediately follows a vacation period, during which many cases are filed but few are heard. Such a state, therefore, may be having less trouble disposing of its cases than the statistics indicate, and might actually be doing better than another state which shows a lower backlog solely because of a more favorable reporting date.[9]

Efforts to develop a reasonably accurate portrait of court caseloads and dispositions across the country are also handicapped by irregularities in reporting. Some states submit their statistics in full every year to the National Center for State Courts—our only source for a national picture of state court activity—while others do so one year and not the next, and still others provide fragmentary figures one year, complete the next, and then back to fragmentary.[10]

Recognizing the difficulty of using state court figures, most analyses[11] of the litigation "explosion" have relied on the federal court statistics, and for an apparently good reason. The federal system, year after year, keeps its statistics largely the same way. When a change in categories has to be made the impact is made clear, so that it becomes possible to incorporate it into the previous picture. Federal statistics also are susceptible of long-term study—for some purposes back to the 1790s—whereas those of the state courts only began to be gathered and analyzed for national trends in 1975 with the inauguration of the National Court Statistics Project of the Center for State Courts. Its first survey year, using its present counting system, was 1976.[12]

That the state court statistics are unreliable in many respects and have such a short historical tail does not, however, necessarily mean it is valid to use the federal figures to project a national litigation picture. A quantitative problem in so doing is immediately apparent. In 1984, for example, about 300,000 civil and criminal cases were filed on federal court dockets[13] compared to a projected 27 million for state courts that year (exclusive of traffic violations).[14] Even were we to add to the 1984 federal load approximately 90,000 minor civil and criminal matters that were heard by federal magistrates[15] and the 344,000 bankruptcy petitions filed that year, we still have only 750,000 legal events within the federal justice system, some of which were the same case at different stages. That means the federal workload, at a maximum, represents only about 3% of all criminal and civil cases begun in the United States each year (or less than 1% if we include traffic offenses).

Although the great disparity in numbers of cases within the two systems is troubling, when we consider that reputable polling firms regularly use samples of well under 1% to draw their conclusions, it may be that projections from the reliable federal figures can be used with some confidence to describe national caseload tendencies. That premise is operable, however, only if the two systems hear the same kinds of cases. In many instances, they don't.

The state court civil caseload is an amalgam of dozens of litigation categories, including sizable numbers of small claims, landlord-tenant disputes, divorces, and other domestic relations matters.[16] In federal court, these classifications make up an infinitesimal part of the whole, usually less than one-tenth of 1%. By contrast, almost all federal civil matters come under just three headings: (1) those in which the United States government is either plaintiff or defendant; (2) those involving an interpretation of the United States Constitution or under a federal statute; (3) diversity of jurisdiction cases, which get into federal court when the defendant and plaintiff live in different states. Many product liability suits, for that reason, are heard in federal court since the injury often does not occur in the state where the manufacturer is headquartered.

Criminal caseloads are not comparable either. Although a few violations—bank robbery, for example—can be deemed either a federal or a state offense, many other types of crime will be tried only in one system or the other. The federal government, just to give a few examples, prosecutes mail fraud cases and states don't; states prosecute homicide cases and the federal government (save as a civil rights violation) doesn't; the federal government prosecutes organized crime under the Racketeer Influenced Corrupt Organization statute, which is not available to state prosecutors.

Based on the substantive differences in caseload, the only permissible conclusion is that federal statistics cannot be used to draw inferences about the state courts. Consequently, evidence that might prove the existence of a litigation "explosion" in federal court does not necessarily imply a similar event in the state courts, nor, if there has been an "explosion" in both places, does it follow the reasons are the same. The only possible exception would be in those relatively few categories in which the two systems basically hear the same kinds of cases within the same resolution milieu.

In the sections that follow, therefore, we will deal with the two systems as separate entities, starting with the federal courts, since it is they that have been the focus of the most attention by those who fear that a litigious public is endangering the quality of justice in America.

II

Most of the cases that reach any court system will be dropped somewhere along the line and relatively few will go through trial to a verdict. Consequently, neither trial frequency nor trial verdict statistics—even if they are consistent and accurate as they are for the federal system—give us a sufficient integer for the court's workload. For that we must turn to cases filed, since they, even if dropped almost immediately or never pursued, require some sort of processing, and very many will reach a judge's attention, either to rule on legal motions or for participation in pretrial conferences. It should be noted, however, that case filings provide us only with a numerical gauge of a court's activity, not a time-consumption one. We cannot, therefore, assume that a court with 10,000 filings is "busier" than one with 8,000, since the 8,000-court may have many more cases that require a considerable time-expenditure by court personnel and judges than does the 10,000-court. The time factor is particularly evident when we compare federal with state courts. The federal bench entertains a much higher percentage of cases of legal complexity[17] than does the state bench where, for instance, the average business collection case is not only simple legally but also usually requires less than five minutes of a judge's time. Since, however, no one at the federal or state level keeps an ongoing record of the pretrial time expenditure, cases filed is our only documented gauge of total court activity and provides us with sets of comparables that are useful for a number of purposes.

In the United States District Courts (i.e., those of original jurisdiction, not appeals courts), the civil case filing statistics between 1960 and 1984 (the last year for which complete figures were available at deadline for this book) were: 1960: 59,284; 1970: 87,321; 1980: 168,789; 1984: 261,485.[18] (Preliminary statistics for 1985 indicate the civil case filing figure will be about 275,000, a relatively modest 5% increase.[19])

As these numbers show, federal court original civil docket entries more than quadrupled in 24 years, and very nearly doubled between 1970 and 1980 alone. Moreover, if the rate of escalation that occurred between 1980 and 1984 continues at the same pace, 1990 will see almost 400,000 filings or more than double the 1980 figure. It is, however, far from certain this will occur. As the chart on p. 149 shows, when we trace case-filing history year-by-year rather than employ the convenient decade guideposts (1960, 1970, 1980) plus 1984, very considerable fluctuations in filing rates become evident. For example: If, as we have been told, the United States was in the midst of a litigation explosion in the late 1970s, why, in 1977, was there such a sharp percentage drop? Similarly, the spectacular increment for 1982 and 1983 is followed by a notable leveling off in 1984 and apparently in 1985, leaving us with the unanswerable question of whether 1982 and 1983 predict 1990 or whether 1984 and 1985 do. (The 1990 question is unanswerable,[20] but there are reasons, as we shall see, that help explain some of the shift.)

The number of civil case filings, in any event, has risen rapidly—arguably, explosively so—in federal court, but the trend is different for criminal cases. Never a major part of the federal docket, criminal cases decreased in frequency from about 40,000 in 1970 to 34,700 in 1983, the last year for which figures are available.[21] (Preliminary figures show, however, by 1985 they were again on the increase.[22])

Appeal cases in federal court have followed the same track as the civil filings: They doubled between 1970 and 1980, from 11,662 to 23,200 (of which 15,000 were civil appeals[23]), and rose another 8,500 by 1984.[24]

Percentage Change In Civil Filings (1960-1984)

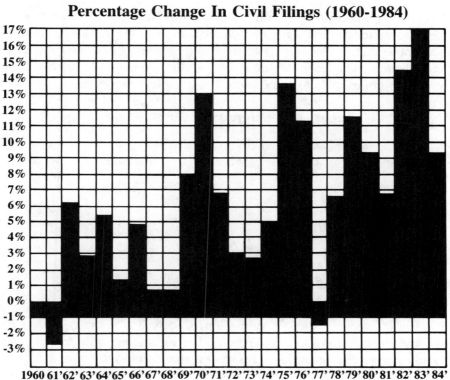

Although the increase in federal civil entries has been the figure most commonly cited to assert the reality of the litigation explosion, as a gross number it tells us little since it does not reveal where the cases are coming from. Should we discover that the principal increments have occurred in categories exclusively involving private parties—i.e., not directly related to shifts in government policies and changes in regulatory statutes—then we have significant evidence of unprompted litigiousness. (In other words, when government action forces people into a courtroom, either because they are being sued by the government or are responding to a government action against them—as a business proprietor might when fined by OSHA—the result is litigation, not litigiousness.) Although, for the reasons given earlier, we cannot assume that evidence of litigiousness developed from private-party cases in federal court proves the same pattern is at work in state court, it may be an indicator when we limit our analysis to private cases of the kind that appear in both systems.

Private cases brought in federal court include those of diversity of jurisdiction and those proceeding under federal statute. Contract and tort cases make up the overwhelming majority of those in the diversity category and generally don't differ in kind from those to be found in the state courts. Federal statute litigation, on the contrary, while it contains some matters similar to state court filings, also includes suits alleging violations of United States civil rights acts, federal antitrust laws, and patent disputes which don't reach state courts. (State courts hear cases involving their own civil rights statutes, frequently with issues identical to the federal; however, administrative bodies—e.g., human rights commissions—resolve many of these cases at the state and local levels, so that the ones that eventually reach state court trial may not be analogous to federal where such intervening bodies do not operate as mediators.) The federal cases in the diversity category, therefore, are the ones truly comparable to some cases that get into state courts.

Table One: Diversity of Jurisdiction[25]

Year	Total Cases	Diversity Cases	Increase	% of Total
1970	87,321	22,854	—	26.5%
1980	168,789	39,315	16,521	23%
1984	261,485	56,856	17,481	22%
1970-84	517,595	119,085	34,002	23%

As Table One shows, diversity cases as a percentage slightly decreased between 1970 and 1984, and the number of them rose by 250% compared to 300% for all cases. In terms of category, increments in diversity cases occurred generally rather evenly across the board, with the most substantial rise that of products cases.[26] Although a 1% decrease occurred in diversity cases in 1984 over 1983,[27] the otherwise very substantive upward numerical trend could be interpreted as evidence of a growth in private-party litigiousness.

Before we assume that is so, or dare to extrapolate the federal experience to the state level, another factor has to be taken into consideration, one which proves again the danger of taking any statistics at their face value. Diversity cases, as it happens, don't have to be heard in federal court; when both parties agree, they can be tried in the state court of their choice. Hence, the apparent growth in diversity cases that we see in the federal court statistics may be prompted, at least in part, by a growing preference on the part of disputants to use federal courts over state. That preference apparently exists and is based on the widespread belief[28] by lawyers that the quality of the federal bench has been and continues to be superior to that found on the state level. For that reason alone, a lawyer will be likely to opt for federal trial in a diversity situation, especially when the lawyer has a good case of some degree of legal complexity. But that's not the only reason. Cases also come to trial more quickly, on the whole, in federal than in state court, so that rises in state court backlogs also encourage going into federal when the opportunity occurs.[29] Because of these choice factors, we cannot properly say that the federal statistics, by themselves, serve as proof of any national trend toward litigiousness.

Table Two: Federal Question[30]

Year	Total Cases	Fed. Question Cases	Increase	% of Total
1970	87,321	34,846	—	40%
1980	168,789	64,928	30,082	38%
1984	261,485	92,062	27,134	35%

Cases brought under federal statutes have advanced substantially in numbers since 1970, though, as with diversity, their share of the caseload has declined (40% to 35%). Suits involving violations of civil rights acts make up a substantial part of the federal question category. They are of two kinds: First are those involving the general public (discrimination on race, sex, age, etc.), and second, petitions entered by prisoners alleging such violations sometime during the incarceration process that began with arrest.

Cases in the public group roughly doubled between 1970 and 1980; though they remained steady at the 12-13,000 level between 1976 and 1980,[31] they had jumped to almost 21,000 in 1984.[32] About 90% of the general public cases are between private parties, with the federal government as plaintiff or defendant in the remainder.[33] Altogether, the general public civil rights cases have steadily made up about 20% of all federal question cases between 1970 and 1984. Considering the 1980 to 1984 period alone, they accounted for about 10% of the total federal caseload increment. As noted earlier, some of these cases could be brought by contentious personalities, but we have no statistical way of knowing that.

Table Three: Prisoner Petitions[34]

Year	All Civil Filings	Petitions	% of Total
1960	59,284	2,177	3%
1970	87,321	15,977	18%
1980	168,789	23,287	14%
1984	261,485	31,107	11%

Prisoner petitions illustrate the impact of judicial activism in establishing protections of the rights of individuals charged with crimes. The category barely existed in 1960, and—although we do not have a breakdown for that year—almost certainly consisted almost exclusively of such ancient writs as those for habeas corpus, mandamus, and motions to vacate sentences. By 1970, the new civil rights allegations were making up about 45% of the prisoner petitions and, in total, accounted for half the growth in the total federal civil caseload between 1960 and 1970. In 1980, civil rights violation allegations were the basis of 60% of all prisoner petitions, and just slightly more than that by 1984 (18,856 of 31,107).[35] Prisoner civil rights cases, thus, increased by 5,800 between 1980 and 1984 and caused 6% of the growth of the total federal caseload during that period. Civil rights suits filed by prisoners do not fit the ordinary definition of litigiousness as an effort by one party to obtain money from another.

Table Four: U.S. Government as Plaintiff[36]

Year	Total Cases	U.S. Plaintiff	Increase	% of Total
1970	87,321	13,310	—	15%
1980	168,789	39,810	26,500	24%
1984	261,485	64,815	25,004	25%

The United States government can become a plaintiff in civil suits for many reasons, but most commonly when it is carrying out a policy mandated by the President or the Congress.[37]

One such policy decision was reached in the late 1970s, when the government began serious attempts to recover defaulted student loans and alleged overpayments to veterans. At the beginning of the decade, these suits barely existed, and as recently as 1975 there were fewer than 700 of them. By 1980, the number had grown to 15,588.[38] The 1980 figure, thus, represented nearly 19% of the total increase of 81,648 civil cases between 1970 and 1980. During the early 1980s, the category rose at an even more rapid pace, with 45,925 collection cases in 1984 or 70%[39] of all suits in which the government was the plaintiff, compared to 40% four years earlier and 5% in 1970. If there's any litigiousness in these cases, it is on the part of the federal government.

New policies affect the litigation rate not only when the government is the plaintiff but also when it is the defendant:

Table Five: U.S. Government as Defendant[40]

Year	Total Cases	U.S. Defendant	Increase	% of Total
1970	87,321	19,037	—	21%
1980	168,789	23,818	4,781	14%
1984	261,485	47,053	23,235	18%

As Table Four shows, cases involving the government as a defendant were already a significant part of the caseload when the federal litigation "explosion" began. Some of the suits were brought by people who had been injured on or by government property, such as a mail truck, but the majority, throughout the 1970s, were disputes concerning Social Security payments. In 1970, about 1,700 of them were filed; the figure rose to a high of 10,300 in 1975 and declined to 9,000 at the decade's end,[41] meaning they accounted for roughly 10% of the increase in the federal litigation rate during the 1970s.

In the early 1980s, the Reagan administration began cutting off Social Security Disability and Supplemental Income payments to individuals allegedly not eligible under the new standards that were adopted. The cutoffs resulted, in 1984, in 28,689 suits to restore benefits—or better than 30% of the increase in litigation of all kinds for that year over 1980.[42] Such actions do not meet the usual definition of litigiousness.

Still another classification that added substantially (5%) to the growth rate of federal cases between 1980 and 1984 was suits rising from bankruptcy petitions. Too few to be counted as a category in 1980, 4,500 of them were filed in 1984.[43]

To summarize: 54% of the growth of the federal caseload between 1970 and 1980 occurred in just two types of cases, civil rights actions (approximately 16%) and government as plaintiff and defendant (approximately 38%). All other cases accounted for 37,000 filings over the 10 years, or about one extra case every six weeks per judge per year. (Since many cases never get beyond the filing stage, the real increment is less than that.) Between 1980 and 1984, we see a marked change in the composition of the growth rate. During that period, cases in which the government was plaintiff or defendant alone accounted for 54% of the increment; when two other categories, civil rights and bankruptcy-based litigation, are added we have reached 75% of the growth.

We can, therefore, conclude that the so-called litigation "explosion" of 300% in case filings in federal court between 1970 and 1984 principally represented cases in which the government was a party or cases (such as most civil rights matters, including prisoner petitions) that directly rose from the passsage of citizen-protection legislation. A rise in private cases, diversity and other, is steadily evident—roughly 3.5% per year over 14 years—but is a minor factor in the increase, apparently legitimately prompted by the combination of factors described in Chapter Five. It does not offer proof of any sudden explosion of contentiousness or hair-trigger suing.

III

Regardless of the nature of the prompting factors, whenever case filings begin to multiply, they can cause corrosive effects throughout an entire justice system. The front-end clogging, eventually leading to a backlog rise, is the most apparent consequence, and it shows up in the federal court statistics where, between 1970 and 1980, the number of untried cases that were three years old or older almost doubled, from 90,932 to 175,798.[44] (That may not be quite as bad as it sounds, however; many of these are cases that have been abandoned by the plaintiff without the court being notified.)

Although an inundation of entries, by itself, creates delay, it is its by-product, the growth in the number of trials, that does the most mischief, or so it has been argued. Because of the increase in trials, judge and courtroom availability become constrained, meaning that large numbers of trial-ready cases have to take their place in line, and they begin to age. This, in itself, can have an adverse impact on the quality of justice. For example, the older a matter becomes, the more likely that witnesses' memories will fade or crucial evidence be lost, so that the chances for a proper verdict diminish.

As dockets swell, administrators lay pressure on judges to try to settle as many civil cases as they can, with the judges then laying their pressure on the litigants. As settlement activities take up more and more of a judge's time, his or her main job—to preside in the courtroom—becomes less important, and a judge may begin to feel the need to rush through a trial simply to get back to the activities which are supposed to prevent trial. The effectiveness of all this scurrying about is open to question. Two studies[45] found that judge interventions were no more likely to settle a case than when the two sides were permitted to negotiate privately. This is not to say that judge-guided settlements may not be more fair to both parties than private negotiations in which one side is stronger in legal talent and financial resources than the other. The issue here, rather, is that the mandatory pretrial settlement conference designed to reduce delays may actually cause them, and will certainly do so when it fails.[46]

The simplest solution to all these case management problems is to add to the number of judges, and the federal court system did just that during the 1970s when the number of authorized judges rose from 401 to 515[47] and again in 1984 to 600.[48] If a crisis in entries persists, as it did in the federal courts, this solution can pose a heavy burden on the taxpayer, not only in salaries for new judges and their staffs but also in the building of new quarters to accommodate them. (A 1981 study of a California county concluded that the net cost of adding a single judge was in excess of $117,000.[49])

This worst-case scenario—i.e., ever more cases requiring ever more judges housed in ever more buildings—which has been vividly promulgated by Justice Burger and other analysts, would seem to call for reforms limiting access to the right to trial by judge or jury. As we saw in Chapter Five, court-annexed arbitration and various forms of mediation have been adopted as trial-diversion tactics in many systems. In federal court, to relieve some of the caseload burden, diversity of jurisdiction cases could be transferred either partially or in their entirety to state courts,[50] thereby adding to *their* costs of operation.[51]

The most radical proposal, but one which is highly favored in some quarters, especially as a way of relieving the federal court burden, is to abolish civil jury trials on the grounds that their great length compared to bench trials makes them the single greatest cause of delay in bringing cases to resolution.[52]

The doomsday reasoning of the reformers seems self-evidently correct: An explosion in civil filings will lead to an explosion in trials and then the relatively slow-moving jury trials will exacerbate the delays, leading to ever-lengthening backlogs until the courts finally drown in an ocean of litigation. Nevertheless, there is no harm in looking at the statistics.

Table Six: Civil Trials (Jury & Bench)[53]

Year	Cases Filed	No. of Trials	% of Filings
1970	87,321	9,449	11%
1980	168,789	13,191	8%
1983	241,800	14,689	6%

From Table Six, we learn that the worst-case projection does not hold true in a linear fashion for civil cases in federal court. Rather, the more cases filed, the *lower* the percentage that go to trial. One reason may be that cases are being settled with greater frequency, but the likely dominant factor is the incursion we have observed of large numbers of legal matters—such as prisoner petitions—that aren't susceptible of trial.

Nevertheless, though the number is much lower than projected, we do have an increase in trials, an average of a little more than 400 a year throughout the entire federal court system over a 13-year period. Or, to put it in percentages, a 300% growth in civil cases between 1970 and 1983 led to only about a 55% increment in trials.

Table Seven: Criminal Trials (Juries & Bench)[54]

Year	No. Cases Filed	No. of Trials	% of Filings
1970	39,959	6,583	17%
1980	41,020	6,634	16%
1983	34,681	6,656	22%

When we compare Table Six with Seven, we see that, using the 1983 figures, criminal matters made up only about 19% of the federal caseload yet resulted in 40% of all trials. Criminal cases thus were much more likely to go to trial than civil, 20 of every hundred compared to seven of every hundred. The greater frequency of criminal trials explains why they, although they make up only 12% of the total caseload, account for a third of the appeals court cases. Therefore, if criminal cases were to begin to "explode," as have civil, any gains that might be made by limiting civil trials would quickly be swallowed up by the growth of the criminal ones.

Whether that would ever happen on a large scale is problematical. As is apparent from the statistics, the federal courts have been unaffected by the crime wave of the 1970s, largely because most of those offenses have been street crimes which rarely involve breaches of federal law. As one example: State courts get millions of cases annually that are directly or indirectly the product of drug use and sales, whereas federal courts get only a relative handful of drug cases of any kind, typically prosecutions of major distributors who have crossed state lines to sell to the local distributors who sell to the street. A mere 2% annual increase in arrests by federal agents would more than double the number of criminal trials in 20 years. (Preliminary figures for 1985 indicated a 10% increase.[55])

Table Eight: Trials Per Judge[56]

Year	Total Trials	No. Authorized Judges*	Trials per Judge
1970	16,032	401	40
1980	19,825	516	38
1982	21,417	515	41

* Not including senior judges; not including 1984 increment of 85 which had been only partially implemented at time of writing of this book.[57]

As Table Eight points out, the number of trials heard by a federal judge remained about the same between 1970 and 1982, despite the total trial increase. This was accomplished entirely by increasing the number of judges; had that number remained at the 1970 level, each judge would have had 10 more trials—or, at an average length of three days per trial[58]—about one month's additional trial work per year. Nevertheless, the increase was made, and the consequence is that the number of trials has not affected the judges' workload. What has affected it—and makes the trial work more burdensome—is the simultaneous rise in the number of legal matters that don't lead to trials. This workload, it would seem, based on our previous analysis, has been caused largely by actions of the federal government, not private cases.

Table Nine: Jury Trials[59]

Year	# of Civil Trials	# of Civil Jury Trials	% of Civil Trials	# of Criminal Trials	# of Criminal Jury Trials	% of Criminal Trials
1970	9,447	3,331	35%	6,583	4,226	64%
1980	13,191	3,937	30%	6,634	3,418	52%
1983	14,689	4,977	34%	6,656	3,653	55%

Table Ten: Jury Trials as % of Whole[60]

Year	Total No. Trials	Total No. Jury Trials	Jury as % of All Trials
1970	16,032	7,557	47%
1980	19,825	7,355	37%
1983	21,345	8,630	40%

From Tables Nine and Ten, we observe that, during the litigation "explosion" decade of 1970 to 1980, both the number and the percentage of jury trials actually decreased. The rise between 1980 and 1983 was substantial in numbers but insignificant as a percentage increase and still well below the 1970 percentage level. The period was also marked by a reduction in jury trial caseloads. In 1970, when there were 401 authorized judges, the average was 19 jury trials per judge, criminal and civil; in 1983, with 515 judges, the caseload was 16 per judge.

As these statistics make clear, the *frequency* with which juries are used has not escalated in proportion to the total growth in cases, in trials, or in the number of judges available; but that, as we have been told, is not the problem with them. It's their length. Get rid of them and their slow-footed ways, and we free up the courtrooms, free up the judges, make it possible to cut into the backlog.

But do we?

By eliminating juries, we eliminate voir dire, saving anywhere from a half-hour to several weeks of pretrial time. (The longer period, as we have seen in Chapter Three, will occur only in lawyer-conducted voir dire for which the judge need not be present, so that his or her time is not appreciably used.) Evidence introduction procedures are also simpler in bench than jury trials, so we should save time that way, too. However, to make a meaningful comparison, we must consider that every trial is going to require a certain amount of time and that the more complex the issues and the greater the number of witnesses, the longer the trial becomes, whether tried by judge or jury. Therefore, to estimate how much trial time we would save by eliminating juries, we first have to learn the impact of the time-lengthening factors that are common to all trials. Though there is no certain way of doing that, federal court statistics on jury and bench trials provide some help.

For them, we turn to the detailed, decade-ending federal report of 1980 which showed that three of every four trials, criminal and civil, required three days or less to complete, an indication that these matters did not involve especially complex issues, huge numbers of witnesses, or lengthy arguments on the law. Among the "short" trials, 80% of the bench trials came in under three days, but so did 60% of the jury trials.[61] It would appear, therefore, that a speedy jury trial is hardly a rarity even when compared with bench trials.

Protracted trials which, we can assume, usually involve more complex issues than the short ones, are defined by the federal courts as those lasting four days or more. The cutoff point is arbitrary and not very enlightening, since one four-day trial might mean 16 hours of actual trial time, another 32 hours, and so on. However, since the "day" figure is the only one we have, we are forced to use it, and, according to it, protracted trials have been growing both in frequency and length, probably primarily due to the gradual introduction in recent years of various legal safeguards.[62] In 1972, our earliest year for this figure,[63] 13.8% of bench trials lasted four days or more, as did 22.8% of jury trials. By 1980, 20.3% of the bench trials were protracted, as were 39.4% of the jury trials. However, criminal jury trials, the continuance of which is not under attack by reformers, are the ones much the most likely to be protracted, probably because juries are almost always demanded when the charges are very serious. (A single organized-crime conspiracy case can take months.) In 1980, 90% of all criminal trials that required four or more days to complete were jury, compared to 60% of the civil ones.[64] When we turn to the most lengthy trials, those of 20 days or more, the differences become even sharper. In criminal, 95% of 20-days-plus trials were jury, while in civil only 53% were.[65] Of the eight longest civil cases (two months or more), five were non-jury, including the top two of 199 and 159 days.[66]

From these statistics, we can probably conclude that, in civil cases anyway, the most important factor in predicting length of trial is the complexity of the case, and the voluminousness of its testimony, not whether it is tried by judge or jury.

The length of a case, however, cannot only be counted in the number of courtroom days it requires. From a workload point of view, the major indicator[67] is the length of time it remains in the system. For example, a case that requires 10 days to try might be much less lengthy than one which requires only three days, if the three-day case involved numerous time-consuming motions and other legal actions *prior* to the time it reached trial.

Although by no means infallible, a useful indicator of the *work* a case requires on the way to resolution is its age when it reaches trial. Using this as our criterion, we find that, in 1980, the median time required in federal court to handle a case from beginning through trial was 15 months for bench trials and also 15 months for jury trials.[68] (In England, where civil juries are forbidden in injury cases, the average case of that kind requires three years to come to trial.[69])

It would appear, therefore, that the availability of juries does not contribute in an appreciable way to the delay in the administration of justice in the federal courts.

But perhaps jury trials are too costly. Beyond doubt, they are more expensive than bench trials of the same length. Jurors must be paid fees; room and board must be provided in the rare instances in which jurors are sequestered; salaries must be paid to the personnel who supervise jurors and those who maintain the jury lists.

In 1984, the total budget for the federal courts was $875,104,000, of which payments to jurors and jury commissioners was about $44 million or 5% of the total.[70] That comes to a little less than 20 cents per citizen per year to retain the right to trial by jury in the federal system. (By comparison, we spend about 40 cents per citizen for federal probation officers.[71])

Juries sometimes lead to savings in both cost and time, although there is no ready way to measure the amount. During the course of a civil trial heard by a jury, the judge is permitted—indeed, is usually expected—to hold sessions with the lawyers in chambers in an effort to bring about a settlement; such off-the-record discussions are not permissible when the judge is the sole fact finder.[72] The result is that a case that might have taken weeks of court time and expense as a bench trial is resolved in a couple of days because a jury has been empaneled. Since a settlement ends a case, as a judge or jury verdict often does not, the number of cases reaching the appeals courts is also reduced. (We are not even considering here the cases that settle at the pretrial stage, because one side or the other fears what a jury would do.)

Moreover, if we had no jury system, we might have to adopt a more costly substitute for it. Most countries that don't permit juries have found it necessary to employ one version or another of the multiple-judge system—one of the judges may be a layperson knowledgeable in the subject of the case—with three or more judges typically hearing a single case.[73] Because to some extent juries in the United States are used for the same purpose as multiple-judges in other countries, Americans pay for far fewer judges—who get paid a lot more than jurors—than do citizens of such nations as France, Italy, Sweden, and West Germany.[74]

In summary, the case-filing increment in the federal courts during the 1970s and early 1980s did not result in any significant expansion in the use of juries and had no effect on the trial caseload of judges. Jury trials, in terms of courtroom days, often take longer than do bench trials, but when the issue is the length of time a case is in the system, jury and non-jury matters have the same duration, with half or more of the lengthiest trials non-jury. Juries are a minor factor in the total expense of operating the federal court system and may represent a savings.

IV

Tables Eleven and Twelve (pp. 159, 161) depict portions of the state court caseload from 1976 to 1983. The footnotes to Table Eleven, originally

published by the National Center for State Courts,[75] document a number of
the reliability problems mentioned at the beginning of this chapter.

Even with these drawbacks in mind, it is apparent when we compare the
criminal and civil statistics that the two legal systems follow divergent tracks
in state court, just as they do in federal. For example, in Oregon an 11%
decrease in civil litigation was accompanied by a 21% increase in criminal
prosecutions, while in Hawaii the opposite happened, an increase in civil of
51% occurring simultaneously with a decrease of 24% in criminal.
However, the general trend for both during the 1978-83 period was upward,
with 33 of 40 jurisdictions that provided reports for both years showing an
increase in civil and 32 of 36 in criminal. In total, prosecutions in state courts
during the five-year period were up about 4% a year nationally in contrast to
the decrease in federal court criminal cases during the same period.

Table Twelve, covering 1976 and 1980 as well as 1978 and 1983, provides
the more complete picture of patterns in civil cases. (For it, unlike in Table
Eleven, all figures have been rounded to the nearest hundred; 1978 statistics
for New Mexico and Ohio, and 1983 ones for South Dakota, which were not
available when Table Eleven was compiled, have been included in Table
Twelve.) In the discussion that follows, we will first consider the 1976-83
period, then 1980 to 1983 alone, and finally the preliminary results of a National Center study for 1981 and 1984 that are not depicted in either Tables
Eleven or Twelve.

Table Eleven:
Percentage Change in Civil and Criminal Filings
in Courts of General and Limited Jurisdiction, 1978-83

	Civil			Criminal		
	CY 1978 or FY 1977/78	CY 1983 or FY 1982/83	% Change	CY 1978 or FY 1977/78	CY 1983 or FY 1982/83	% Change
Alabama	206,523	210,626	2%	121,391	136,986	13%
Alaska	23,901	30,065	26%	24,688	30,697	24%
Arizona	118,630[a]	152,186	28%	(b)	(b)	
Arkansas	89,404 [c]	114,282[d]	28%	130,978[c]	141,737	8%
California	1,391,856	1,637,247	18%	794,679	961,769	21%
Colorado	141,251	194,727[c]	38%	54,482[e]	56,396[e]	4%
Connecticut	207,361	199,912	-4%	91,122	116,633	28%
Delaware	40,015[f]	52,975	32%	53,449[f]	74,312[g]	39%
District of Columbia	159,682	133,377[h]	-16%	22,126	31,846	44%
Florida	477,563	565,367	18%	330,035	486,361	47%
Georgia	258,390	297,488[i]	15%	293,969[j]	383,157[j]	30%
Hawaii	33,656	50,902	51%	40,400	30,687	-24%
Idaho	48,172	54,209	13%	29,219	40,965	40%
Illinois	689,701[k]	590,790	-14%	517,975	640,239	24%
Indiana						
Iowa	143,817	143,007	-1%	(b)	(b)	
Kansas	92,076	115,426	25%	25,211	23,371	-7%
Kentucky	165,994	183,970	11%	203,860	221,832	9%
Louisiana	202,575	256,660	27%	348,405[j]	471,528[j]	35%

	Civil			Criminal		
	CY 1978 or FY 1977/78	CY 1983 or FY 1982/83	% Change	CY 1978 or FY 1977/78	CY 1983 or FY 1982/83	% Change
Maine	48,536	58,563	21%	(b)	(b)	
Maryland	472,980	610,718	29%	137,325	159,508	16%
Massachusetts	295,117	397,564[l]	35%	209,001	216,680[l]	4%
Michigan[b]						
Minnesota[b]						
Mississippi						
Missouri[b]						
Montana	25,055	25,072	0%	2,842	2,933	3%
Nebraska	70,947	75,551	6%	168,530[j]	171,698[l]	2%
Nevada						
New Hampshire	65,351[f]	84,959	30%	41,282[f]	79,487	93%
New Jersey	465,682	575,283[m]	24%	376,250	447,419[n]	19%
New Mexico[b]						
New York	723,113[fo]	1,217,035[o]	68%	544,411[f]	717,907	32%
North Carolina	335,341	401,457	20%	413,679	472,104	14%
North Dakota	21,666	29,979	38%	18,719	19,236	3%
Ohio						
Oklahoma	181,020	223,289	23%	59,348	67,890	14%
Oregon	139,608	124,920	-11%	118,660	143,374	21%
Pennsylvania	419,375	403,641[p]	-4%	558,733	548,600[q]	-2%
Puerto Rico	140,460	152,732	9%	76,579	66,035	-14%
Rhode Island	41,125	42,601	4%	34,638[j]	42,967[i]	24%
South Carolina	72,169[f]	89,137[r]	25%	30,308	36,646	21%
South Dakota[b]						
Tennessee[b]						
Texas	566,956	665,175	17%	1,099,822	1,480,519	35%
Utah	63,230[s]	104,136[t]	65%	51,314[s]	103,956[u]	103%
Vermont	22,336	28,046	26%	19,299	19,749	2%
Virginia	528,486	732,290	39%	338,923	445,898	32%
Washington	176,425	204,677	16%	139,273	160,939	16%
West Virginia[b]						
Wisconsin	188,406	196,348[v]	4%	62,592	101,287[w]	62%
Wyoming[b]						

a = No data were reported for six Justice of the Peace Courts and five Municipal Courts.
b = Data were submitted but could not be used in this table because of problems with comparability.
c = Data are incomplete. No reports were received from approximately 50 cities.
d = The civil caseload does not include paternity cases.
e = Does not include post-judgment actions.
f = The number of cases disposed of is used as an estimate for the number of cases filed in some of the courts included.
g = Criminal caseload includes all juvenile cases and Court of Common Pleas traffic cases.
h = The apparent reduction in the civil caseload is attributable to a decline of 34% (11,059) in small claims cases and 20% (21,988) in landlord/tenant cases.
i = The civil caseload for the Probate Court (25,277 cases) was removed from the 1983 figure to make it comparable with 1978.
j = Criminal caseload includes some traffic cases. In Louisiana, however, no traffic cases are included from the courts of limited jurisdiction.
k = Includes 75,166 personal property tax cases no longer filed after 1980.
l = Excludes caseloads of the Superior Court and Boston Municipal Court to make the figure comparable with 1978.
m = Excludes 679 Surrogates Court cases to make the figures comparable with 1978.
n = Excludes 14,772 domestic violence cases to make the figures comparable with 1978.

o = Civil caseload in New York includes juvenile cases.
p = Tort figures are 97% complete for Courts of Common Pleas.
q = Felony figures are 98% complete for Courts of Common Pleas. Excludes 29,900 cases for Pittsburgh Magistrates Court to make the figures comparable with 1978.
r = Excludes 15,307 Probate Court cases to make the figure comparable with 1978.
s = Does not include 20 of the 181 justices of the peace.
t = 80% of the total increase in civil filings is accounted for by the increase in filings in the City Court, which was replaced by the Circuit Court on July 1, 1978.
u = 86% of the total increase in criminal filings can be accounted for by the increase in the Justice Court, which handles only misdemeanors and preliminary hearings.
v = Excludes 97,565 uncontested small claims cases to make the figure comparable with 1978.
w = 11,858 traffic misdemeanors and 41,303 uncontested ordinance violation cases were removed from the 1983 figures to make them comparable with 1978.

Table Twelve: Civil Cases, State Courts[76]

Total Civil Filings	1976	1978	1980	1983
Alabama	n/a	206,500	222,000	210,600
Alaska	19,700	23,900	24,600	30,000
Arizona	92,400	118,600	146,000	152,700
Arkansas	76,100	89,400	104,500	114,300
California	1,268,000	1,392,000	1,591,000	1,637,000
Colorado	151,400	141,300	182,700	194,700
Connecticut	217,100	207,400	208,000	200,000
Delaware	35,300	40,000	46,900	53,000
District of Columbia	170,000	159,700	146,700	133,400
Florida	465,400	477,600	504,500	565,400
Georgia	174,600	258,400	269,300	297,500
Hawaii	29,700	33,700	38,400	50,900
Idaho	40,200	48,200	53,200	54,200
Illinois	633,200	689,700	723,200	590,800
Indiana	n/a	n/a	n/a	n/a
Iowa	125,400	143,800	195,000	143,000
Kansas	80,600	92,000	17,000	115,400
Kentucky	122,300	166,000	183,100	184,000
Louisiana	160,400	202,600	242,900	256,700
Maine	44,500	48,500	58,200	58,600
Maryland	395,000	473,000	545,000	610,000
Massachusetts	418,000	295,100	494,000	397,600
Michigan	n/a	n/a	n/a	n/a
Minnesota	146,900	n/a	186,700	n/a
Mississippi	n/a	n/a	n/a	n/a
Missouri	n/a	n/a	n/a	n/a
Montana	18,700	25,100	27,300	25,100
Nebraska	61,000	71,000	84,600	76,000
Nevada	n/a	n/a	n/a	n/a
New Hampshire	56,800	65,400	70,600	85,000
New Jersey	420,700	465,700	514,400	575,300
New Mexico	47,500	54,800	64,000	n/a
New York	686,000	723,100	700,000	1,217,000
North Carolina	235,600	335,300	373,000	401,500
North Dakota	15,000	21,700	25,300	30,000
Ohio	573,700	615,200	661,600	n/a
Oklahoma	160,600	181,000	198,900	223,300
Oregon	117,800	137,700	154,500	124,900
Pennsylvania	399,000	419,300	544,000	403,600
Puerto Rico	125,200	140,500	155,800	152,700

Total Civil Filings	1976	1978	1980	1983
Rhode Island	40,800	41,100	43,700	42,600
South Carolina	171,400	71,200	n/a	89,100
South Dakota	n/a	n/a	39,500	38,600
Tennessee	n/a	n/a	n/a	n/a
Texas	n/a	567,000	n/a	665,100
Utah	49,700	63,200	86,200	104,100
Vermont	24,100	22,300	24,300	28,000
Virginia	465,000	528,500	715,000	732,300
Washington	162,000	176,400	231,000	204,700
West Virginia	n/a	n/a	n/a	n/a
Wisconsin	208,300	188,400	219,000	196,300
Wyoming	n/a	n/a	n/a	n/a

n/a - not available does not necessarily mean there are no figures for these states, but rather that they are not complete or did not use reporting methods comparable to other years. For an explanation of New York figures, see below.

For the longest interval, 1976 to 1983, 32 states plus the District of Columbia and Puerto Rico are represented. They produced a growth in case filings from 7,721,800 to 9,789,700, or 21% for the seven years. For 1978 and 1983, the 40 systems reporting depict an increase from 9,533,100 to 11,426,800, or 19.7%.

Consistent patterns, state by state, even when we account for differences in reporting techniques and omissions of statistics, are difficult to decipher, and may, according to one analysis, be prompted frequently by purely local and temporary conditions.[77] Only six of the 34 systems that reported both 1976 and 1983 figures are close to the national average (California, Florida, Nebraska, Texas, Washington, Puerto Rico). For 1978 and 1983, four are (again California and Florida, plus Maine and North Carolina). Well above the national average in the 1976 to 1983 group were: Arizona, Delaware, Georgia, Hawaii, Louisiana, Maryland, New Hampshire, New York, North Dakota, Utah, and Virginia. Decreasing litigation jurisdictions for the same period were: Connecticut, Illinois, Massachusetts, South Carolina, Wisconsin, and the District of Columbia. (The District of Columbia decline, however, is less substantial than it appears; in 1976, landlord-tenant cases were included in its statistics but not in 1983; had they still been incorporated, the 1983 figure would have been 22,000 cases higher or a net drop of 15,000 rather than the 36,600 the table indicates.[78])

Geography seems to play no role in litigation activity. Some of the regional findings, in fact, are markedly incongruous. New Hampshirites, for example, are apparently decidedly more litigious than either their Vermont neighbors or fellow New Englanders in Massachusetts and Connecticut. In the mid-Atlantic states, Pennsylvanians are shown as less likely to go to court than New Yorkers. In the south, Georgians are more prone to do so than South Carolinians, and so on.

Even within an individual state, we see remarkable shifts in civil case frequency. Filings in Pennsylvania rose from 399,000 in 1976 to 544,000 in 1980, but by 1983 were back to the 1976 level. Iowa jumped by about 60%

between 1976 and 1980, yet by 1983 had returned to the 1978 level. Both Wisconsin, and even more spectacularly Massachusetts, seem to change their litigation spots every year.

One obvious explanation for changes in civil case filings would be accompanying shifts in population. Statistical confirmation for that premise, however, is in short supply. For example, it is true that New Hampshire's population grew by about 20% between 1976 and 1983, but that, at best, offers only a partial explanation for its 50% increase in filings. Maryland and Virginia had sharp rises and South Carolina a sharp drop in filings, yet each had about the same population-increase percentage during the 1976-83 period. Nationally, the litigation rate rose at about double the population growth, but the exceptions, state by state, are so numerous that the 1976 to 1983 findings do not provide meaningful statistical relationships between population change and litigation rates. (However, see also discussion of the 1981 to 1984 study below.)

Other factors probably had a more substantial effect during the 1976 to 1983 period. Changes in statutes may encourage or (more rarely) discourage litigation. Court decisions, especially at the appeals level, can have the same result. For example, it seems quite possible that part of the decline in filings in Pennsylvania between 1980 and 1983 was due to clarifications by the courts of the state's no-fault law which had the effect of removing a number of grounds for litigation.[79] Similarly, changes in economic conditions, leading to more or fewer bad debt cases, could have significant if temporary impact in one state—or a portion of it—and not in another.[80]

Because there are so many variables in developing the litigation picture for any state, as well as for individual jurisdictions within a state, we cannot attempt an analysis of local and regional differences in case filings, much less dispositions of them. Nationally, however, despite the absence of reports from some states and incomplete figures from others, the case filing sample is sufficiently large and sufficiently accurate[81] for each of the years depicted in Table Twelve that we may make meaningful trending extrapolations from the totals—that is, we can after one major correction is made. It relates to New York. Table Twelve shows its civil case filings remaining steady between 1976 and 1980, though with a slight increase in 1978. Then, between 1980 and 1983, New York apparently suffered an astounding increase of 70% in litigation, a statistic that has been used to prove the inherent, albeit suddenly expressed, litigiousness of the American people (at least in New York). But it never occurred.

An interview with a New York court official[82] revealed that matters handled by family and surrogate courts were not included in the New York statistics *until* 1983. These omitted filings averaged 300,000 and later 400,000 a year. Consequently, the correct figure for New York for 1976 should have been roughly a million cases, not the 686,000 that were released. When the New York statistics are changed to account for the cases omitted in earlier years, we find that the real increase has been about 2% a year between 1976 and 1983.

Once we make the New York adjustment, and allowing for the other discrepancies, we can conclude with a high degree of confidence that the average annual growth rate in civil case filings in state courts between 1976 and 1983 ranged from slightly over 3% a year to an upper limit of just under 4%.

The contrast with federal court is a striking one. There, between 1976 and 1983 civil filings rose from 130,597 to 241,842, and from 138,597 to 241,842 between 1978 and 1983, i.e., a 12% to 16% increment per year depending on which starting year is used.

It appears, therefore, that federal court litigation has been moving upward annually at a pace about four times that of the state courts.

It further appears, when we confine ourselves to the first five years of the 1980s, that state court civil activity was increasing at a rate of less than 1% a year, with marked decreases occurring in a sizable number of jurisdictions.

To document these conclusions, we have two sets of figures, each from the National Center for State Courts but each using different base years and different reporting sources. The first is Table Twelve, which incorporates all types of civil case filings, and provides comparables between 1980 and 1983. For those years, we have 36 states plus the District of Columbia and Puerto Rico reporting, with 14 of these sources (37%) showing decreases in filing—compared to just three for those reporting both 1976 and 1983 figures—and total filings rising from 10,644,300 in 1980 to only 10,878,100 in 1983, or about seven-tenths of 1% per year. In contrast, the federal court filings for the same years rose nearly 10% per year (168,879 to 214,842).

The second set of figures, published in 1986, compares 1978 with 1981 and 1984.[83] Called the Preliminary Report, it uses a smaller sample—a maximum of 25 states and not always with each jurisdiction in each state—and confines itself to tort, contract, real property, and small claims cases. Using that base, the National Center discovered that small claims cases, which had been increasing by an average of 6% a year between 1978 and 1981, decreased by an average of of 2% a year betwen 1981 and 1984. Decreases were also observed in real property, contract, and tort cases when considered as an entity (a total of 14% increase between 1978 and 1981 and a decrease of 4% between 1981 and 1984). When tort cases were separated out, the Center found they had increased by 9% between 1978 and 1984 and 7% between 1981 and 1984. The increments in tort cases were much in line with population growth, i.e., the total 9% gain took place during a period in which the nation's population grew by 8%, with the largest growth in tort cases occurring in the three states (Alaska, California, and Hawaii) which had also had the largest gains in population.[84]

A very large category of civil activity, domestic relations cases, was not analyzed in the Preliminary Report nor do we have figures for 1983. Therefore, to study the domestic relations impact, we only have available 1976 and 1980 figures derived from the National Center's annual reports for those two years.[85] Those studies show that these cases rose from 633 to 807 per 100,000 during that four-year span—by comparison, tort cases during the same period averaged about 255 per 100,000[86]—or, in total number of cases, a jump of about 30%. Thus, between 1976 and 1980, domestic relations matters contributed about 2.5 times as many cases as the total average annual increase (roughly 7.5% to 3%). Considering the leveling-off process in civil case filings between 1980 and 1984, we can probably assume that domestic relations cases also declined but that, even so, they were responsible for the major share of the small total increase that occurred. While it is undoubtedly true that the parties in many domestic relations disputes are contentious, these cases are not of the "hair-trigger suing" variety that is normally defined by the word "litigiousness." However, if we equate litigiousness with acrimony, then if we have had a litigation explosion of any kind in state courts, it is the domestic relations arena, and only there, that we find it.

Case filings, however, only give us an index of the type of litigation entering a court's docket. Like the different federal court districts, one state may have fewer docket entries than another, yet the state with fewer entries but more serious and active cases may have more difficulty managing its caseload than a state that has more case filings. It is also true that civil cases do not exist in a vacuum; a state which has a modest increment or even a decrease in civil cases might have problems keeping current with them if, at the same time, its criminal case docket was rapidly growing. The human element cannot be ignored either. Some court administrators will be more creative and efficient in managing caseloads than others, some judges much harder working than others.

One sign that such conjectures are not mere hypothesizing can be found in those states which by 1985 had adopted arbitration programs to relieve their civil caseloads. Of the 16 of them, 11 reported figures for 1978 and 1983, and had an average filing rate increase of 15.5% for the five years, or about the national average. Of nine states which in 1985 were thinking of beginning arbitration programs, statistics for all of them between 1978 and 1983 show an average increase of 13.8%, or below the national average. Of the remaining 26 which, according to their officials, were not considering arbitration because the "demand on judicial resources did not warrant the use of alternative dispute resolution programs,"[87] statistics are available for 20, and they show a 23.7% increase for the five years. In other words, the states employing arbitration or considering it, based on the caseload statistics, had the least need for it, and those which had rejected the idea, appeared to have the most. From these figures, it is apparent we are entering into highly hazardous areas when we attempt to use raw numbers as proof of the existence or non-existence of a supposed problem.

We should, however, have one index—fluctuations in backlogs—for determining if substantial caseload management problems exist nationally at the state court level. If they are high, then we can assume that the cases that continue through the system are forcing substantial delays in the administration of justice that may make reforms—including limitation of the right to jury—necessary. However, because of the problems with the reliability of the backlog statistics (i.e., cases filed vs. dispositions) described earlier, they do not offer us much help, nor would they even if complete figures were available, which they are not from the vast majority of states. Therefore, we are required to turn to appeals court backlogs for which our figures have a high degree of reliability. Our most recent year is 1983, with 39 states plus the District of Columbia and Puerto Rico reporting.[88] In these jurisdictions, a total of 148,342 appeals were filed and 144,830 were disposed, an average backlog of 85 cases per court. Of the 41 systems, 16 decreased their appeals backlogs between 1982 and 1983. Well over half the total backlog of 3,512 cases came from New York, with 1,634, and South Carolina, with 931. When these two exceptionally slow-moving states are removed, the backlog average becomes 25 cases per appeals court. While zero would be the desideratum, 25 hardly constitutes a crisis.

Based on our best—though incomplete—information from all our sources, we can conclude that by the mid-1980s, state courts, as a whole, were not or should not (given adequate management techniques) be facing substantive problems in handling their civil caseloads, though the rises in criminal cases could, at places, be an exacerbating factor.[89]

V

Because of the definitional variations from state to state of what constitutes a trial, we lack for the state courts the accurate figures that are available from the uniform federal system. Nevertheless, based on the statistics that can be culled with some degree of reliability, we will consider in this section the role that bench and jury trials play in the state court system.

Turning to criminal cases first, we find our resource material, though quite soft, indicates that about 10 to 11% of all prosecutions begun lead to trial, bench or jury—about half the federal court frequency.[90] Civil figures are somewhat more reliable at the state level, and depict a much greater number of cases as at least reaching the point at which trial begins, about a third of the total,[91] than at the federal level, with its 10% figure. (The principal reason for the lower federal percentage is the presence there of many matters—e.g., statutory petitions—that aren't ordinarily susceptible of trial resolution; by contrast, few state litigation categories *can't* lead to trial.) We have an indication, based on several studies, that the percentage of civil cases going through a *completed* trial is on the decline in both systems due to an increase in the frequency of in-trial settlements.[92]

The importance of the jury trial in state courts can be measured in a number of ways, with the choice of method largely depending on what the person doing the measuring plans to show. If the goal is to indicate that the civil jury is so insignificant to the judicial process that it would not be missed if eliminated, then we can claim that only 1% of all civil cases are resolved by jury. If, on the other hand, the goal is to show that the jury is an important part of the state court system, then the measurer will come up with an equally reputable 17%.

To obtain the 1%, we would use *all* civil filings, including those that get no farther than entry before they are settled, those that are dismissed, and those that rarely, if ever, could lead to a jury trial, a category that includes estate matters and other equity cases.[93]

The more realistic 17% use of juries is derived when we consider only case filings that are likely to go to bench or jury trial: misdemeanors and felonies in criminal, and many of the tort and contract disputes in civil. Although it is exceedingly unusual for a misdemeanor case to result in a jury trial (less than 1% of the time), about 63% of all felony prosecutions in state court, based on 1976 and 1978 figures, are decided by a jury,[94] not much different from the 57% in the federal courts between 1970 and 1982 (see Table Nine). The civil jury in state court, however, is empaneled at a much lower frequency than in federal, about 4%[95] compared to 32% of all trials in federal. The ultimate 17% is derived by dividing all trials—felony, misdemeanor, civil—into the number of jury trials.

The apparent percentage difference in use of juries in civil trials in the two systems, however, is misleading, again due to the differences in docket classifications: The state courts have many essentially non-jury groupings (such as domestic relations cases) that are absent or nearly entirely absent in the federal lists. For comparables in jury usage, therefore, we require case categories that are heard in both systems. Torts provide the best example.

Fragmentary evidence from the state court statistics suggests that torts (largely personal injury suits) that go to trial—i.e., a trial at least begins—are held before a jury more than half the time.[96] If that is so, considering the rarity of jury use otherwise, tort cases probably make up the large majority of state-court civil jury trials. The federal statistics on this point are not, for once, illuminating since they don't specify jury trial by type of case. However, based on internal evidence—i.e., comparing frequency of jury trial and deleting categories in which trial of any case either never or rarely happens—the federal pattern is probably not significantly different from the state. We can, therefore, probably conclude that tort cases produce more civil jury trials than all other categories combined.

Because of all the statistical pitfalls, projections of the actual numbers of annual jury trials in state courts cannot be given with confidence. However, based on several analyses[97] and using the most conservative figures derived from them, we can estimate somewhere between 100,000 to 125,000 criminal jury trials in state courts in 1985, and 45,000 to 75,000 civil jury trials.

As a taxpayer item, state court jury trials by 1980 were costing about $6 a year per citizen compared to $3 for bench trials.[98] The jury cost figures include use of courtroom facilities beyond that required for a bench trial, and the salaries of the people who administer the jury system. Juror fees alone are an inconsiderable part of the total; for example, in Pennsylvania they come to about 50 cents per citizen annually.[99]

An argument can be made that the cost figure, in part, represents an unfair assessment against juries; were juries not permitted, the courtrooms would still have overhead expenses, and since most jury administrative personnel are patronage appointees in state courts, it may be naive to assume their jobs would disappear if juries did. Looked at another way, as a percentage of total judicial expenditures, costs for state court juries are around the same 5% as in the federal courts,[100] or about one-tenth of 1% of state operating budgets.[101]

VI

To summarize the findings of this chapter:

In the federal court system, a case explosion occurred; it began around 1970 and showed some (but perhaps only temporary) signs of slackening by the mid-1980s. Tort cases accounted for about one-fifth of the increment; some are those which could have been filed in state court but landed in federal because of the desire of lawyers to make use of the perceived superiority of the federal bench. The overwhelming majority of the case growth, however, was caused by congressional action in the civil rights area and (most notably beginning in the 1980s) by changes in federal policy that initiated legal actions in which the government was either plaintiff or defendant. Evidence of a sudden outbreak of litigiousness as a significant causative factor is not to be found.

In state courts, between 1976 and 1983, litigation increased at about one-quarter the federal rate, accompanied by indications of a leveling off close to a 0% growth rate between 1980 and 1984. State courts, however, unlike federal, incurred about a 4% growth rate annually in criminal cases which apparently had varying effects on the manageability of their dockets. The civil case increment between 1976 and 1983 is apparently attributable primarily to the rise in the divorce rate leading to a very substantial increase in domestic relations cases, though there may be a leveling off in the 1980s. Tort suits do not appear to have increased their presence on the state court dockets to a degree that should cause a management problem. There is no ascertainable evidence at the state level of a litigation explosion, as defined at the beginning of this chapter, nor do we see any proof of growing public contentiousness other than perhaps in the marital problem area.

The availability of the jury does not lengthen the time a case stays in the court system, and—based on federal statistics, which should also hold true in state court—the jury apparently is ordinarily a lesser factor than the evidentiary and legal nature of the case in determining the length of trial. Cost of juries to the public is inconsiderable, and in civil cases juries may represent a net savings in taxpayer dollars due to the settlements their presence induces.

Chapter 7
Juries and Mega-Verdicts

In England, juries were abolished in personal injury cases in part because jurors allegedly had proven themselves incapable of making reasonable cash assessments of damages.[1] By this was meant they awarded too much money, not too little. American juries, according to one frequently quoted study, suffer from the same proclivity, on the average awarding twice as much money as do judges.[2]

When these supposedly over-generous awards become very large—a million dollars is the magic figure—newspapers often publish stories about them, presumably encouraging those with minor or non-existent injuries to enter suit in hope of winning a similar "jackpot"[3] or mega-verdict. The effect of all this jury largesse, we are told, is inflationary, harmful to the solvency of insurers and defendants, an injustice which cries out for the adoption of the British system or some variation thereof.

I

The thesis that juries are more generous than judges is one of such long standing that it seems almost an article of faith in the legal community and among the public. Documentation for it, however, is scant and ambiguous.

A case in point is the study that supposedly shows juries are twice as generous as judges. On investigation, it turns out to be a report on average awards by juries and judges in personal injury suits in New York City over a 10-month period in the 1950s, a narrow and very old statistical base from which to draw any conclusions. But even in its own time and for its own place, the study had no probative value because of a critical omission: It didn't tell how many of the trials, judge or jury, involved serious injuries and how many minor ones. Since, as the authors of the study themselves point out, a jury is typically waived when the dollar stakes are small and demanded when they are large, it follows that jury awards, on the average, should be higher than judge awards, perhaps even more than twice as high. It is conceivable, therefore, that if we had the relevant information, we would discover that the judges in New York were relatively more generous in their small cases than the juries were in their large ones, so that the study might actually prove the opposite of its popularized conclusion.

A much more reliable method, prospectively anyway, to learn if juries are more generous than judges is to obtain judges' views of jury verdicts. One way to do that is to search court records to find the percentage of cases in which the trial judge reversed the verdict or reduced the award. Sometimes, however, a trial judge's reversal will itself be reversed by an appeals court, so we also have to find out how often that happened, but when we do, we still don't have an accurate figure, since there are also occasions when the trial judge lets the jury's award stand and an appeals court reverses it, or else a higher appeals court reverses the action of a lower one so that we have to find those figures, too. Should we navigate our way successfully through all these reversal shoals, our prize, even so, may not prove worth the seeking, because all we have really learned is how often jury awards are ultimately reversed after various judges get done quarreling with each other about them. What we still don't know is how often a trial judge forced a *posttrial settlement* to his or her liking by merely threatening to overturn the award; nor do we know—and this should be the largest category—how often a judge disagreed with an award but not to the extent that he or she thought anything should be done about it. A case in point is Judge Forer's study of civil juries described in Chapter Four; she was unhappy about some of the awards in her cases but overturned none of them.

The only study that is illuminating in depicting the total universe of disagreement between judges and juries is one published by Kalven in which the cooperating judges stated that they would have given lower awards than their juries in about 52% of the cases; would have given the same amount 10% of the time; and would have given a higher award 38% of the time.[4]

Kalven's findings appear to confirm the English experience. For, if juries overcompensate more than half the time and undercompensate nearly 40% of the time—i.e., they are wrong on 90% of their money decisions—their ability to assess damages must be called seriously into question, even if they usually reach the correct verdict on liability.

Frequency of disagreement, however, is only one consideration; degree of difference is another. For that we have Broeder's study, based on Kalven's statistics, which revealed that when judges believed jury awards were too high, the area of dispute was about 10%.[5] Therefore, if a jury awarded $2 million, the judge would have awarded $1.8 million. In actual money, that's a substantial difference, but if we define the mega-verdict as a million dollars or more, the judge's award would have been a mega-verdict, too. Broeder did not ask judges—or, if he did, he didn't publish the results—by how much they thought juries undercompensated; but assuming that would also be around 10%, we appear to be delving into distinctions that can be described as reasonable differences of opinion.

We could feel more comfortable with that conclusion were there parity between the frequency of overcompensation and undercompensation. However, if Kalven is correct—and we have no reason to doubt the accuracy of his findings or his research method—juries are more likely to overcompensate than undercompensate, according to judges. Consequently, even if the dollar differential on the average is statistically insignificant, the cumulative effect of plus-dollar awards in a single year could be substantial. For example, using Kalven's percentages, if we had 10,000 cases in which juries awarded $100,000, the total overcompensation in them would be $14 million.

Our question, therefore, is whether the $14 million actually does represent an overcompensation. We can only conclude that it does if we can prove that judges are more accurate as assessors of damages than juries are. For, if they are not, or if there is no reliable way to find out if they are, then studies like Broeder's and Kalven's are, in fact, nothing more than a catalog of differences in opinion, no one of which should be taken more seriously than the next.

In evaluating the differing abilities of judges and juries, the judge's superior knowledge of the law is not an especially significant factor when it comes to figuring dollars. It is true that juries may sometimes consider elements they shouldn't—insurance, lawyers' fees—but it is far from clear that judges invariably ignore them either. In any event, the laws governing awarding damages are deliberately vague, leaving judges and juries theoretically on basically equal footing in determining them. More pertinent are the differences in the decision-making process. The jury's act is a consensual one, which means that even if the large majority of the members reach the "correct" award, they may be forced to accept an improperly high or low figure in order to get agreement from the remaining members. The judge has no such need since his or her decision is unsullied by compromise. The judge also has experience, that the jury lacks. In the days when the judge was a practicing lawyer, he or she would have learned at least something about how to evaluate the dollar-worth of a case; and since ascending to the bench he or she has probably presided over dozens, perhaps hundreds, of trials which aren't all that different from one another, and has learned from them. The judge, therefore, has a considerable professional store of case-worth measuring tools while the amateur jurors have none. Based on these reasons, we seem to be on sound theoretical grounds if we agree that judges, in general, should know what they are talking about when they say a jury's verdict was too high or too low.

However, when we turn from the world of theory to the world of reality, we find we have a problem in making that assumption unreservedly. In the real world, lawyers consider many factors in deciding whether to ask for a jury or a bench trial, but the one that is almost invariably present—and may be the most common final determinant[6]—is the lawyer's opinion of the judge assigned to hear the case. Thus, if the judge is believed to be pro-defense, the plaintiff's lawyer asks for a jury; if pro-plaintiff, the defense does. Whenever it is the judge's presumed bias that is the deciding factor—and it is often more than a presumption, for word gets around in the real world and lawyers know which judges favor defendants and which plaintiffs—then we must call into question all assumptions about juror generosity or lack of it.

To illustrate the distorting effect the judge's view can have, let us consider a case in which the judge has a pro-defense bias and consequently the plaintiff asks for a jury—which awards $2 million. When asked by a researcher, the judge doesn't disagree on the question of liability but says (based on Broeder's 10% differential) $1.8 million would have been an accurate award. Now, assume the case had been assigned to a pro-plaintiff judge and the defense asks for a jury—which awards $2 million. When asked, the pro-plaintiff judge doesn't disagree on liability but says the award should have been $2.2 million. The same case has been heard, the same award made, yet one jury is perceived as over-generous and the other as over-frugal, with a $400,000 disagreement between the two judges.

Therefore, when Kalven—who made no effort to learn how many of his cases became jury trials because of who the judge was—found that juries are much more often "generous-wrong" than "frugal-wrong," all he may have discovered was that we have that many more pro-defense than pro-plaintiff judges.

What then can we say about the "generous" jury? To this point, we seem able to reach only two valid conclusions. First, juries are more often perceived as overly-generous than overly-frugal by judges, but that view, to some unknown degree, is the product of the judges' own pro-defense or pro-plaintiff leanings. Secondly, many cases get to jury not because juries are believed to be biased on money matters but—quite to the contrary—because judges are.

An illuminating coda to our analysis comes from a 1983 Rand Corporation study of settlement practices by insurance companies. It discovered that when claims adjusters within a firm—which meant each was applying the same corporate guidelines—were given the same hypothetical case, they reached widely varying amounts on its dollar-value.[7] If those who earn their living by being correct on such matters can't agree with one another, it may be that our only proper conclusion is that translating injury into dollars is an exercise of such subjectivity that to attempt to evaluate one result as right and another as wrong is both futile and misleading.

II

Even though we have no responsible criteria to apply to prove that juries, on the whole, are either too generous or not generous enough, it may be that they are guilty, in certain cases, of another accusation made against them. According to this indictment, juries regularly make unseemly large awards against those who, the jurors think, have nearly unlimited money to pay for the damage they have inflicted. Such defendants are said to have "deep pockets."[8] Included in this group would be large corporations, governments, and, in general, all individuals, businesses, and institutions which, the jurors know from their life experiences, are likely to carry large amounts of insurance. To give one example, suppose there are two gasoline stations, one owned by an oil company, the other by an individual proprietor; under the deep-pocket premise, if identical injuries occur at the two places, the oil company will be hit for the higher verdict.

The deep-pocket concept is an attractive one psychologically. Even though Pound found no evidence it exists, the theory *sounds* like something average people would do when they serve on a jury—let the big guy pay through the nose for what he did to the little guy. It is a belief that is very much part of lawyer folklore. Those who hold this view assert that the size of settlements demanded by plaintiff lawyers and agreed to by those of the defendant in deep-pocket cases often proceed from a higher dollar demand point than they would if juries were not in the picture.

However, it is far from clear, the extent to which, or the consistency with which, lawyers rely on jury verdicts to create standards for settlements. Some lawyers make use of companies that provide reports of jury verdicts (the basis of the Rand study), but others don't; some may go by rumor, some by hunch, some by their own previous experiences or those of their colleagues. Relationships between plaintiff and defense lawyers, between plaintiff lawyers and claims adjusters, between defense lawyers and their insurance company employers, all play a role. Fox example, a defense firm that feels it is in danger of losing its contract with an insurance company client may proceed much differently on claims-settlement during that period than when it is confident of its relationship. As another example, a plaintiff lawyer who has a reputation for willingness to take cases to trial and a winning record when he or she does will often be able to command a higher settlement price than a lawyer who has a reputation of settling everything.

All of this doesn't even take into consideration the varying settlement practices by insurance companies themselves. As we have already seen, different claims adjusters will evaluate similar cases differently. Some insurance companies seem more settlement-prone than others, and the same company may be "tough" on settlements in one part of the country, not in another, tough at one time and not at another, tough on some types of claims and not on others. An insurance company's customers can also affect the size and frequency of settlements, since the company cannot resolve a case prior to trial without the customer's agreement. It's a big complex world out there, filled with clashing policies and motivations, and to state as a fact that high jury awards create high settlements is not to state the full truth.

The Rand Corporation's statistical studies of San Francisco and Chicago jury verdicts use, at times, confusing terms: in particular, the distinction made between "business" and "corporate" defendants is frequently blurred. However, Rand seems to be concluding that business defendants (or, at least, corporate ones) pay more than do individuals—2.5 to 4.0 times as much—when the injuries are "severe."[9] However, it should be emphasized that the Rand studies cannot be considered authoritative in a national sense. As the Pound findings strongly suggest and as lawyer folklore would have it, once we move away from big cities like Chicago and San Francisco, plaintiffs win less frequently and award sizes are lower. (See Geography and the Jury section, Chapter Four.) Moreover, the substantial variations that the Rand research discovered in award patterns between its two cities,[10] and even within the same city from time to time,[11] make any generalizations questionable, probably largely because there are so many factors that go into determining which cases eventually go to trial and which do not. It should also be borne in mind that the Rand statistics have no contextual meaning; they do not tell us if the "very high" awards were or were not similar to settlements or bench trial awards in the same kinds of cases during the same period.

Nevertheless, it may be that the Rand statistics do prove, contrary to Pound, that jurors dig into deep pockets. Before we assume that they do, however, we must consider the possibility that in an unknowable number of the Rand cases other factors may have been at work. To illustrate, assume we have two cases in which the injuries were of the same degree of seriousness, same medical bills, same loss of income, and so on, yet for one, an automobile collision, a jury awards $40,000 while in the other, which occurred in a department store, a jury awards $100,000. On the face of it, the department store appears to have been treated as a "deep-pocket" defendant. However, that may not be what happened. In the auto case, the jury may have been acting on its real-world knowledge that drivers in its state were required to carry $50,000 worth of insurance and, not wanting to delve into the defendant's private pocket, decided not to go beyond the insurance limit. Moreover, let us further assume, the jurors decided the plaintiff was 20% at fault and reduced the award by that amount, leaving the $40,000. In the department store case, on the contrary, jurors, who would have no real-world knowledge of the amount of insurance such a defendant carries, decided $100,000 was the proper verdict, and since they didn't see the plaintiff as having any fault, let it go at that.

As these two examples suggest, before we make any assumptions about the prevalence of deep-pocket awards, we have to know (a) whether the jury was acting on its beliefs about the pool of money available; and (b) whether it decided to reduce the award because of the plaintiff's degree of culpability, a step that is often taken informally and not stated in the award-verdict presented to the court.[12] The Rand study doesn't tell us how often either element was present for the very good reason that it had no way of finding out, case by case, and neither do we.

Therefore, although we have evidence that juries—to a statistically significant degree—make higher awards against certain classes of defendants than others, we cannot, from that knowledge, conclude that the deep-pocket awards are invariably or even frequently *improperly* high, since it is equally possible that the low awards to which they are compared are improperly low due to jury perception in them of a defendant's shallow pocket. The gap between deep-pocket and shallow-pocket awards in cases involving similar circumstances can widen when the jury considers the defendant's conduct particularly egregious. In such instances, the jury may indirectly incorporate punitive damages, perhaps as part of the pain-and-suffering portion of the award, against a deep-pocket defendant, an addition it will deem pointless when the case involves a shallow-pocket. Documentation on this point comes from the Pound study, with its indication that jurors—without making a separate punitive damage finding—sometimes add to an award against a defendant, their purpose to chastise or warn about improper conduct, not to promiscuously pick some insurance company's pocket.

The appearance, but not the reality, of a deep-pocket award can also occur in at least one other situation. It will be recalled from Chapter Four that the Chicago Project found that 30% of all jurors are unanimous in their view of liability at the outset of deliberation. In those originally unanimous bodies, there is no need for compromise as in split juries, where a pro-plaintiff majority may agree to a lower award than it would prefer in order to get the pro-defense minority to go along with it. Based on these decision-making dynamics, let us suppose we have two cases involving identical damages, the first involving a deep-pocket defendant and the other a shallow-pocket one. In the deep-pocket case, as it happens, the jurors are in immediate agreement on liability, but in the shallow-pocket they are not. The result is a higher award in the deep-pocket case than in the shallow, a resolution not caused by consideration of pockets, deep or shallow, but rather from the jury's need to compromise in order to reach any verdict at all.

The question to be resolved about jury awards is not whether they are higher or lower than the judges would want them to be (that is essentially irrelevant) or whether deep-pocket awards will be comparably higher than shallow-pocket ones (they often will be) or even whether juries sometimes make clearly improper awards (they do, but so do some judges as the appeals court records attest), but rather whether the jury system generally produces consistent awards. In other words, do juries, given the same sets of circumstances, generally arrive at about the same award results or are their findings wildly divergent from one another? If the latter is the case, then we have rather strong evidence that juries act capriciously in awarding money, so that results which judges and lawyers would perceive as reasonable are a matter of luck. If that is so, the very large sample of 14,300 cases analyzed by Rand should tell the tale.

But that's not what Rand found.

Over the 20 years of its study, it discovered that most awards didn't vary in terms of constant dollars,[13] with the median award in 1979 ($8,000 in constant dollars) actually a trifle less in Chicago than it was in 1960.[14] As Rand concluded, in part: "[The study] provides reassurance about the stability and sensibility (*sic*) of our system of jury trials,"[15] suggesting that perhaps Federal Court Judge Charles Wyzanski was right in 1952 when he noted that the common people who live and work in the everyday world are better able to estimate losses suffered than a judge who is less in the mainstream of society, and hence will do so more consistently.[16]

Rand's negative finding—no pattern of capriciousness—does not, however, give us guidance to the rare situations in which a jury goes badly off in its award, either high or low (e.g., $1 million for a broken ankle; $100,000 for quadriplegia). We have some evidence[17] that juries may more frequently err on the conservative side in major-injury cases than on the exorbitant. That pattern was observed by National Association of Insurance Commissioners (NAIC) in a mid-1970s study of malpractice case awards which found that plaintiffs with the most severe documented injuries and expenses were the most likely to be undercompensated[18] by judge, jury, and by settlement. The same study and others have also found that over-compensation is most likely when injuries and their costs are minor, but this phenomenon is probably largely caused by insurance companies making settlements in doubtful cases to avoid litigation costs.

When a capricious award does occur, various protocols exist by which it can be remedied. As we have already seen, when a judge finds a jury's award excessively high, it can be reversed. An alternative choice open to the judge is the remittitur, which means that if the plaintiff agrees to accept a lower amount, and the defense also agrees, the case ends with the acceptance of the reduced award. If not, the judge orders a new trial on the damage amount only. In a few states, the opposite—called an additor—is also permitted when the judge feels the award was improperly low; the process that is followed is the same as with the remittitur.

Such judicial balancing actions are often unnecessary. Competent lawyers on both sides know when an award by a jury was either excessively high or low, and also know the dissatisfied side may pursue the matter through lengthy and expensive appeals with an end result neither side can foretell with certainty. As a result, settlement negotiations are reopened. The excessively high or low verdict may have an impact on the discussions—after all, it might eventually be allowed to stand—but compromise is almost certain. For example, assume a case in which the jury awards $1 million, but which the plaintiff's lawyer had valued at $500,000 tops and on which the defense pretrial offer was $100,000; further, assume the plaintiffs, pretrial, would have been willing to settle for $300,000. The jury's high verdict *might* drive the compromise figure up to $350,000 or $400,000 or it might have no effect at all. In the case of the excessively low verdict, even when additor is not present, the defense may volunteer some upward compromise offer in order to prevent an appeal of the verdict on other grounds which could lead to a new trial and a more reasonable verdict from its jury.

In the real world, therefore, the fate of any jury verdict is an uncertain one, and the aberrant verdict hardly ever stands as given.[19] To know this, however, does not answer a seemingly perplexing question raised by Rand and others: Why did mega-verdicts by juries escalate so rapidly beginning sometime in the 1970s?

Rand found that, despite the consistency of jury verdicts in average-size cases, toward the end of the study period another consistency had developed at the upper end, one which appeared with such regularity it could not be explained as an aberration or capriciousness by an occasional incompetent jury (or possibly an incompetent judge or incompetent lawyer on one side or the other, who led the jury astray). In Chicago, Rand discovered, the size of the highest 10% of all awards doubled during the 20-year period, even after accounting for dollar-devaluation.[20] Conditions that had always produced high awards were leading to ever higher ones. Those for "large income loss" (Rand's term) increased by 20%; for wrongful death, 30%; for medical malpractice, 20%; for product liability, 20%, with the latter cases also escalating in number from 3% of the total in the 1960s to 8% in the 1970s.[21] By the 1970s, 1.5% of all cases were contributing 40% of the dollars awarded.[22] The size of verdicts involving catastrophically injured plaintiffs,

Rand observed, "became unstable, leading repeatedly to unprecedented awards."[23]

The phenomenon discerned by Rand in Chicago and San Francisco is part of a national trend. The first million-dollar award in the United States occurred in 1962; in 1970, there were seven; in 1980, 134; and in 1983—the last year for which figures are available—360.[24]

Before attempting to assess the causes of the rapid rise in the mega-awards, and the jury's responsibility for them, if any, it may be useful to consider more specifically the *types* of situations that are likely to lead to mega-awards. The cases that follow were all decided in the 1980s, the award granted by a jury unless otherwise stated:

$1.4 million:	Plaintiff suffered a stroke following the use of an oral contraceptive.[25]
$9.3 million:	Death caused by burns when a Ford Mustang exploded following a rear-end collision.[26]
$4.075 million:	Two children died when the fuel tank exploded in a 1980 GM Chevette; children were trapped inside when the rear doors jammed on impact.[27]
$1.1 million:	Toxic shock syndrome injury.[28]
$1.9 million:	A judge's verdict in compensation for paralyzing Guillain-Barré syndrome suffered as result of receiving Swine Flu vaccine.[29]
$2.4 million:	A judge's verdict in another Swine Flu case.[30]
$3.1 million:	Based on fraud of a 68-year-old man by an insurance agent.[31]
$2.6 million:	Settlement shared among four plaintiffs exposed to the hazardous chemical, Dioxin.[32]
$15 million:	Quadriplegia suffered by a 36-year-old man when the Kansas City Hyatt Regency Hotel skywalk collapsed on him.[33]
$6 million:	Principally punitive damages in the wrongful death of an 81-year-old woman caused by use of Oraflex, a treatment for arthritis.[34]
$2.6 million:	A settlement involving 10 plaintiffs exposed to nuclear radiation in Nevada.[35]
$6.8 million:	Including punitive damages in a Dalkon Shield, intrauterine device, case.[36]
$2.25 million:	Near fatal injuries suffered when an antenna struck a power line.[37]
$1.2 million:	Settlement in a case involving brain damage, spastic quadriplegia, and cerebral palsy suffered by a child during birth.[38]
$3.373 million:	To a 19-year-old woman who suffered permanent brain damage when a tube was improperly removed during an operation.[39]
$6.1 million:	Settlement in a case in which a 3 1/2-year-old boy suffered brain damage when his meningitis went undiagnosed.[40]

$1.15 million:	Settlement in a case in which a 17-year-old boy was killed when a power line fell on him while he was riding a bicycle.[41]
$15 million:	To a 43-year-old receptionist who had to have both legs amputated and suffered a fractured spine while boarding a train which began to move.[42]
$1.1 million:	Compensatory and punitive damages for an investor who was defrauded by his partner.[43]
$3.0 million:	Against a school board for negligence in permitting circumstances that led to the rape of a 13-year-old girl.[44]
$4.4 milion:	Settlement of a case in which a mechanic suffered brain damage and partial blindness when a boom truck crashed into a boiler room.[45]
$3.2 million:	Settlement for brain damage and other physical injuries suffered by 37 schoolchildren exposed to atmospheric lead emitted by a smelter.[46]
$1.5 million:	Settlement in a Jones Act (maritime law) case involving injury suffered by a workman during an underwater explosion.[47]
$12.2 million:	Against a burglar alarm company for negligent design, installation, and monitoring of its system, resulting in an $8 million theft from a customer's property.[48]
$4 million:	To a 26-year-old woman who suffered brain damage when struck by a hit-and-run driver.[49]
$1.2 million:	Settlement for brain damage suffered by a two-year-old boy who nearly drowned in an apartment swimming pool, the gate to which was left open while repairs were being done.[50]
$2.4 million:	Including punitive damages to a 32-year-old design engineer who had to have an arm amputated and suffered other severe injuries when struck by a car operated by a drunk driver; co-defendant was the taproom that apparently permitted the driver to drink all day.[51]

Finally, although it wasn't a million-dollar verdict, but to show such things can still happen, in Kansas in 1983 a 64-year-old woman was hanging clothes in her backyard when she was attacked by a bull, and received multiple injuries. A jury awarded her $800,000.[52]

From these cases, chosen at random from 13 issues of the *ATLA Law Reporter*—a monthly recountal of the ghastly things in life that can overtake people—we see that not only juries hand out what Rand calls "blockbuster" awards, but also judges sometimes, and that many of these awards are the consequences of private settlement. Personal injury suits lead the way, but business fraud claims also frequently result in mega-verdicts, with one category of business fraud claims—the antitrust case—producing most of the very largest, probably because winning plaintiffs in these cases receive treble damages under the provisions of the Clayton Act. Although antitrust was not presented in the ATLA sampling, we can provide one example, in a 1985 case, where five major record companies settled a class action antitrust suit for a total of $17.1 million.[53]

In several of the ATLA cases, we see that the size of the verdict was, or may have been, prompted by jurors' outrage at the conduct of the defendants. We find punitive damages as part of the award in the Dalkon Shield case, the Oraflex case, the investor case, the insurance case, and the drunk driver case. (It may have also appeared, tucked away in the pain and suffering or mental anguish damages, in several of the other cases, such as the $4 million total award in the hit-and-run case and the $3 million levied against the school board for hiring a rapist.)

Perhaps most importantly, the ATLA case summaries make clear that the vast majority of the plaintiffs in mega-dollar injury awards were either survivors of those who died from their accidents or people so severely and permanently incapacitated from them that death might be preferable. A few years earlier, the NAIC study of malpractice claims found the same pattern at work; *every* case that it studied that reached a million-dollar verdict or settlement had been described by the defending insurance company—not the plaintiff—as involving a ''grave'' injury, a term defined as incorporating such conditions as ''quadriplegia, severe brain damage, lifelong care or fatal prognosis.'' Moreover, the average severity of injury for awards in excess of $100,000 but less than $1 million was depicted by the insurers as ''major,'' including ''paraplegia, blindness, loss of two limbs, and [lesser] brain damage.''[54] Those are tough ways for anyone to get a ''jackpot'' verdict.

Rand found the same thing. It described the cases that led to its so-called ''blockbuster'' verdicts as involving ''catastrophically injured'' victims.[55] Indeed, despite its frequently expressed concerns about the effect of a perceived deep-pocket as a cause of overly-generous awards, Rand found that *the prime predictor about the size of award was not the identity of the defendant but the severity of the injury*,[56] an absolutely proper jury concern. (Disabling injuries, for example, resulted in awards 46% higher than for similar accidents in which there was no long-term or permanent damage.[57]) And who were those who were most severely harmed? According to Rand, typically they were the victims of workplace injury, medical malpractice, and faulty products.[58] In other words, deep-pocket defendants—supposed victims of misguided jury sentiment that yields grandiose awards—were precisely those who caused most of the worst damage which led to the most pain and suffering, the highest medical expenses, and the greatest losses of income.

When all this evidence is taken together, it is apparent that we must look elsewhere than to supposed misguided jury generosity—save in the occasional case—to explain the sudden rise in mega-verdicts during the second half of the 1970s.

Changes in the cost of living provide one reason. If we use 1976 as our first year for the late 1970s, we find that between it and 1983 (the last year for which figures are available), the purchasing price of the dollar declined by about 40%.[59] Consequently, a plaintiff who could have been made whole by a $600,000 award in 1976 required $1 million to have the same result achieved by 1983. Therefore, in order to see if there were more million-dollar awards in 1983 than in 1976, *in terms of dollar-value*, we need the number of $600,000 awards in 1976 as our true comparison, not the number of million-dollar awards then, and those figures aren't available. The same would be true for any other years we select.

Inflation in medical expenses has been extraordinary during the same period. Between 1976 and 1982—throughout this discussion, the most recent year for which figures are available is used—average hospital care went from $152 to $327 a day; from 1976 to 1983 hospital room rentals rose from $83 to $195 a day;[60] from 1976 to 1984 the cost of prescription drugs also more than doubled as did that of physician services.[61] The cost of medical care for the *average* patient, therefore, increased by more than 100% within less than a decade.

But mega-verdict plaintiffs aren't average. Their typically grave injuries frequently require protracted and heroic intervention of the most costly kind just to keep them alive. Although we have no statistical sources available for these upper-end medical charges, it is reasonable to suppose (if for no other reason than that the services of specialists are a great deal more expensive than those of general practitioners) that mega-verdict plaintiffs will have medical bills far higher than the norm.

The Rand study offers a partial confirmation of this assumption. It found that medical expenses for catastrophic cases in Chicago between 1975 and 1979 averaged $23,000, compared to $3,000 for "very serious" injuries.[62] The Rand figures do *not* include future medical costs,[63] a major omission since they are not only a pertinent aspect of the jury's award consideration but are also particularly likely in catastrophic injuries to be a continuing and increasingly expensive part of the plaintiff's future.[64]

Inflationary factors, however, do not completely account for either the growth in size or frequency of the mega-dollar verdicts. Part of the remaining difference can be attributed to the improvement in the quality of the representation offered by the plaintiffs bar. Cases susceptible of mega-verdicts typically involve the best of these lawyers. Because they do their homework, sometimes thousands of hours of it for them and their staffs, they are remarkably well-prepared—just as are the defense lawyers, because the best defense lawyers usually come into action in these cases, too—so that the jury is led through the evidence in the most illuminating way possible. The better the jury understands the monetary impact of a catastrophic injury, the more likely it is to give a large award (assuming it decides for the plaintiff), especially if the circumstances also suggest outrageous conduct by one or more of the defendants.

The discrepancy between the size of deep-pocket awards and those assessed against individuals may also indicate a change in perception by juries of differing standards of care to which certain defendants should be held. Adept plaintiff lawyers may in part be educating juries to this perception, but it could also reflect a growing belief on the part of the public that governments, businesses, doctors, and hospitals are in a better position to take steps to prevent injury than are most individuals, and when they fail to do so, their conduct in that sense is outrageous and must be duly compensated.[65]

Assuming that such an evolution in jury thinking has come about, it is well within the proper boundaries of jury functioning—juries are expected to reflect the community's views of proper conduct—and even in a legal sense is appropriate, since the law recognizes that different individuals under the same circumstances are not always to be held to the same standard of care in avoiding injury to others. (See also Chapter Nine.) If juries, in fact, are generally developing higher standards of care for certain classes of defendants, then it can be argued that they are not making excessively high awards at present but, rather, were making unduly low ones in the past.[66]

A factor that does not seem to be present in mega-awards is pro-plaintiff juror bias, although some corporate defendants think it is present.[67] Pound found no evidence of that; neither did Rand. The latter study learned that malpractice and product liability plaintiffs in Chicago won only about 40% of the time before juries compared to 52% for all plaintiffs, with San Francisco malpractice plaintiffs also winning about 40% of the time and product plaintiffs 54%, compared to 59% plaintiff wins overall.[68] These win-loss figures should not be taken beyond what they say about juries in these types of cases. It must be remembered that the great majority of injury cases, large and small, are "won" by plaintiffs at settlement—in the sense that they get some money—with the settlement "win" percentage probably higher than the norm in catastrophe suits, because of the reluctance of defendant-insurers to allow jurors to take a look at such grievously injured people. By the same reasoning, that would mean that cases the insurers *don't* settle may be legally or factually doubtful for the plaintiff,[69] so that the low plaintiff-win percentage in them derives from the jurors' comprehension of the weaknesses, which overrides any natural sympathy they feel for the plaintiff due to the extensiveness of the injury.

We would appear, therefore, to have five reasons to explain the apparently sudden rise in mega-verdicts, none of which has anything to do with jury competence *per se*. First, as was discussed in Chapter Five, changes in the law have made it possible for people injured by malpractice and defective products to get to court with a reasonable chance of winning; hence, there are more mega-cases pursued in these categories than there were in the past. Second, we appear to have an actual increase in the number of mega-cases, principally brought about by technological advances which can cause catastrophic injuries when they go awry or—as in the $ll-million smoke alarm case—create new grounds for suit because technology is available and not used. Third, better lawyers for plaintiffs have meant better results for them. Fourth, the cost of injury has grown spectacularly, particularly in catastrophic events, many of whose victims would have died in earlier years, but now, thanks to new advances in care, can be kept alive, brain-damaged or paralyzed or both, indefinitely and expensively. Fifth, although the evidence is less strong on this point, jurors may be holding some defendants to a higher standard of care than in the pre-1970s era.

III

To this point, we have been considering mega-awards solely in terms of individual cases. Much more costly in aggregate damages paid is the *mega-*

category as distinguished from the *mega-case*. To illustrate, the two largest verdicts in our selection of mega-cases taken from the *ATLA Law Reporter* were each for $15 million, a considerable sum certainly. But $15 million is less than a tenth of the $180 million settlement reached in the *mega-category* litigation brought against the manufacturer of Agent Orange by Viet Nam War veterans who had been exposed to it. As the Agent Orange case suggests, a mega-category is defined as any large number of suits—ranging from the hundreds to the thousands—brought about by the same cause, in which no single case need reach the mega level but the total amount of money at stake does. Although occasionally a mega-category can rise from the consequences of a natural disaster such as a fire, the alleged causative factor is usually a product. Occasionally, the at-risk population lives or works within a limited geographic area (e.g., those exposed to Agent Orange or to atmospheric testing of the atom bomb following World War II), but most often, probably, the exposure to the harmful product is widespread (e.g., asbestos).

Legally, efforts will be made to adjudicate a mega-category as an entity. Because the injuries involved tend to have similar causes and symptoms—even though one injured party may be more grievously affected than another—trying each one individually is perceived as being not only enormously time-consuming for everyone involved (thousands of victims waiting in line for years for their day in court) but also repetitious, since the similarities will usually lead to similar results. (The mega-category, in this sense, must be distinguished from those categories of cases, such as medical malpractice, in which there is a significant amount of legal activity involving large amounts of money in total but in which each case is different legally and factually.)

One way to bring a mega-category to a resolution is through the class action, the path taken by the plaintiffs in the Agent Orange litigation. By doing so, those who take part in the joint venture agree to slice into equal pieces the single large money-pie that will result if the suit is successful. Attorneys' fees come off the top, the largest share going to the lead counsel. Participation in a class action suit can be mandatory or voluntary. When voluntary, a person who decides not to join the suit or later opts out of it can sue separately, but as a practical matter that can be a difficult and expensive course to pursue. (The class action is almost invariably employed in private antitrust cases, but they are beyond the scope of this discussion since, although they involve mega-dollars, the number of plaintiffs can be very few.)

In a mega-category injury case, the class action can be productive for plaintiffs but the principal advantages lie with the defense. Should it win, all its problems are solved, since even those who didn't join the action are likely to be deterred from following their suits due to the verdict. But even should the defense lose, at least it knows how large a pool of money it must find to liquidate its exposure, something it can't ascertain for many years if the cases are being tried individually. The defense also benefits from the fact that jurors in a class action trial don't have an individual plaintiff sitting across from them. Rather than being able to consider the human tragedy that overtook that person, they are asked to visualize the condition of hundreds or thousands of faceless ones and may, as a consequence, reach an inappropriately low award.

An alternative is the test-case method. As an approach to coming to grips with mega-category litigation, it is more protracted than the class action (at least theoretically) but more discriminating and equitable. In it, certain typical cases representing sub-groups of the large group are tried just as though they were individual suits. Therefore, the jury in these trials, unlike in the class action, actually sees the victim and is better able to grasp the dimensions of the injury, which makes appropriate verdicts more likely. The verdicts in the test cases then act as benchmarks for settlement of other cases within each subgroup. Not all cases will be settled as a result, but even those that aren't become amenable to more expeditious trials since the legal issues adjudicated in the test cases apply to the subsequent ones and cannot be reargued.

In other instances, faced with a batch of mega-category cases, a court administration may institute mandatory arbitration, although either side, if dissatisfied with the arbitrator's decision, can then demand trial. As a settlement device in mega-category litigation, arbitration appears to have a mixed record.[70]

The largest mega-category of litigation in American history, by the mid-1980s, was that involving injuries caused by exposure to asbestos. Within 10 years of the time the first suits were filed in the early 1970s, asbestos exposure had generated $1.006 *billion* in claims and expenses; by the year 2010, according to one source, asbestos contamination will cause somewhere between 74,000 and 250,000 deaths over and above those already attributed to it.[71] Each of these fatalities and related medical conditions that might not prove lethal is also likely to lead to suit, adding billions of dollars more in damage payments and legal costs.[72]

The huge financial outlays prompted by mega-verdicts, whether they are derived from a category like asbestos or from differentiated suits aimed at some crucial service such as medical care, can lead to economic and societal dislocations. These consequences have caused critics, most of them self-interested but not necessarily wrong for that reason, to urge reforms of the tort system to bring the number of suits and their costs under control. Basically, the thrust of these reforms is to limit the right to trial and to limit the freedom of juries to reach adequate awards based on the damage evidence before them.

One frequently cited example of the dire public effects presumably brought about by mega-verdicts, is the plight of Johns-Manville, the principal asbestos manufacturer. In reaction to the spectacular losses it was facing, the company filed for bankruptcy. Though that action, by itself, doesn't mean a company intends to go out of business or will, when bankruptcy does result, it creates economic ripples that can be especially severe when the departing company, such as Johns-Manville, was a significant corporate presence. In such a situation, the company's suppliers and retailers can be swept into insolvency as part of the fallout. Governments no longer receive taxes from the company or its employees, but instead are in the position of paying out tax money in the form of unemployment benefits.

The laid-off workers themselves, because they have less money to spend, can't afford to patronize the businesses in their communities as they once did; those businesses, therefore, have less money to put in the banks and the banks less money to loan to other businesses or to ordinary citizens.

But that is not all. Mega-litigation itself presents an added burden to taxpayers who have to pay for the courtroom time that the mega-category cases create. (For example, so numerous and apparently endless are the asbestos cases that, in some jurisdictions, judges and courtrooms have been assigned to hear them on a permanent basis.)

But that is still not all. When the danger of the product is identified, based on the suits brought against its manufacturer, insurance rates rise which are passed on to the public. In the case of asbestos, companies that were hired to remove asbestos insulation from workplaces and schools found it difficult to obtain insurance at affordable rates, allegedly because underwriters were fearful that the very act of eliminating the hazard would cause more hazard and more suits.[73] Unwilling to proceed without coverage, companies either turned down the work so that the danger remained, or else taxpayers were forced to come up with new monies to pay for the insurance.

Approaching the dollar magnitude of the asbestos cases has been the projected aggregate cost of the Dalkon Shield litigation brought against A.H. Robins, a manufacturer of pharmaceuticals and therapeutic devices. Between 1974 and 1984, Robins was hit with 12,100 claims from women asserting they had been harmed by the Shield, an intrauterine device that has caused pelvic diseases, spontaneous abortions, and difficult pregnancies. By June 1985, the company revealed, it had already paid out $378.3 million[74] to settle more than 9,000 of these claims—an average of $42,000 each—and had set aside $615 million to handle those still unresolved or expected to be filed.[75]

Around the same time that Robins was describing to the press its Dalkon Shield problems, one of its competitors, Dow Chemicals, announced it was withdrawing a pharmaceutical called Bendectin from the market. Designed to control morning nausea during pregnancy, Bendectin had been sold for nearly 30 years before a rash of suits broke out alleging it caused birth defects. In stopping manufacture of the drug, Dow was not admitting the merit of the charges; rather, it said, it was forced to take the step when insurance premiums on the product reached $10 million on a $12 million annual sales volume.[76] (This is an amazing figure; ordinarily product insurance is based on 2 to 3% of sales.[77])

Even as Bendectin became unavailable, two other pharmaceutical houses, Wyeth and Connaught, were telling the press they were ceasing production of anti-pertussin, the vaccine to prevent whooping cough. Although the vaccine accomplishes what it is supposed to do, in rare instances it also allegedly precipitates brain damage in children, leading to suits which, Connaught was quoted as saying, have made it impossible to continue to obtain insurance for the product.[78]

If that is, and continues to be, a correct statement of the problem faced by the two anti-pertussin manufacturers—a subject to which we will return later in this chapter—then a significant social policy issue is raised by jury verdicts and settlements in those cases. Unlike the Dalkon Shield and Bendectin, the whooping cough vaccine is a specific disease preventive. Therefore, it can be argued that, even if the suits it has produced have merit, the injuries occur so rarely that they should not be allowed to drive from the market a product that otherwise has proven itself to be of great value for millions of children.

To keep such a product on the market, we can guarantee the manufacturers that they will not be liable for any legal actions brought against them, hence relieving their need for the costly insurance. There is nothing new in taking such a step. At the time of the non-existent Swine Flu epidemic, Congress passed legislation that immunized its vaccine manufacturers from suit and required injured parties to name the United States as defendant. Before taking such a step on behalf of Connaught and Wyeth, however, we should be aware that, by so doing, we will open the way for other manufacturers to seek protection under the same umbrella; given their lobbying abilities, such a possibility should not be lightly discounted. The consequence could be that, instead of safeguarding the rare product in the exceptional circumstance, we could find ourselves paying directly for tens of thousands of suits, to say nothing of the salaries of all the new government lawyers who would have to be hired to defend them. Looked at from a slightly different perspective, our "public interest" category could be construed as encouraging corporate blackmail, by which a manufacturer threatens the removal of any valuable pharmaceutical until the public caves in and grants it freedom from liability, thereby maximizing its profits at taxpayer expense.

The Dalkon Shield presents a different public policy consideration. On the surface, it is difficult to be sympathetic toward A.H. Robins. It manufactured a product which by the company's own admission—it began to withdraw it from the market in 1974—caused harm to thousands of trusting users. One might say Robins deserves to have to pay out the billion dollars, or whatever the final figure will be. But once one is done with feeling virtuous about such sentiments, issues remain that, some would say, are more important than any critiques of Robins' negligence. In an immediate sense, the issues appear to be the same as for Johns-Manville and asbestos, i.e., the prospect of immediate and manifold economic dislocations should litigation force such a major company out of the marketplace. (In August of 1985, Robins filed for protection from its creditors under Chapter Eleven of the Bankruptcy Code; the company, at that time, announced that it did not expect to have to go out of business.[79]) In one important way, however, the Robins and Johns-Manville situations are not alike. The latter produced *a* product which proved dangerous; the former produced many products of which *one* proved dangerous. Consequently, were Robins to cease operations, its socially valuable products could be temporarily or permanently lost to consumers along with the bad one. Alternatively, even if Robins (or any company facing such problems) continued in business, the cost of litigation against the one product might force up the price of the remaining products, thus hurting the public, and—even more harmfully in the long run—possibly causing the company to cut back on experimentation that would have led to the development of new lifesaving therapeutic items.

The same argument, by extension, can be made concerning medical malpractice suits. In the mid-1970s, increases in malpractice insurance rates, allegedly prompted by the influx of suits and resultant high jury verdicts, caused doctors in several sections of the country to go on strike, threatening medical care availability. There's no reason to think that cannot happen again. It did briefly in 1987. Quality of care can also be threatened, or so it has been said, when doctors can no longer look at their patients as people they want to help but rather must see them as potential enemies who will sue should the least thing go wrong. If that is the doctor's concern, he or she has good cause to feel that way, according to the American Medical Association, which asserts that the frequency of malpractice claims rose from five for every 100 doctors in the mid-1970s to 16 for every 100 in the mid-1980s.[80] During the same period, the size of the average malpractice award (jury and other) skyrocketed from $350,000, according to an insurance industry estimate,[81] to $850,000, by the AMA's calculations, and $962,258, according to Jury Verdict Research, Inc.,[82] with the resultant rising insurance rates leading to higher fees for patients. The fear of suits and high awards has also forced doctors, says the AMA, to increasingly practice "defensive" medicine (i.e., ordering unnecessary and frequently expensive tests, solely to have a track record of diligent care when the lawyers come). The defensive medicine cost to the public, estimated as low as a $1 billion in 1975,[83] reached a gargantuan $14 to 15 billion in 1984,[84] the AMA asserts.

But perhaps our policy concerns should not be limited only to health providers, since large verdicts against governments can also be construed as against the public interest. For example, in southeastern Pennsylvania, the government-operated transportation system was hit with $18 million in injury-verdicts—$9 million in one jury case alone—during the first three months of 1985. This helped to bring about, according to a company official, a rise in the fare from $.85 to $1.25, which principally affected low-income citizens, since they are the most frequent users of mass transit.

Based on all these ominous signs, we might decide, as the tort reformers would have us do, that the public's interest isn't sufficiently served by merely protecting a handful of products or services. Instead, maybe we should act firmly and across-the-board to cut into all socially threatening suits and reduce the cost of the biggest ones. To achieve this, the reform menu proferred is a large one.

One entree, especially attractive to some reformers, would be to substantially limit the right to trial by jury, thereby, or so the theory goes, reducing the number of jackpot awards which, in turn, establish the basis for settlement negotiations in similar cases afterward. As these advocates tirelessly point out, the abolition of the jury in injury cases has had that effect in England where awards are markedly lower than in the United States. It is also true—though the reformers usually neglect to mention this—that in England national health insurance is available which covers all or most of an injured party's medical expenses, thereby removing or considerably lessening what is typically the highest cost factor in American awards, whether made by jury, judge, or settlement. (Although national health insurance presumably would have the same effect on damages in the United States, we need not tarry with that thought since the likelihood of its enactment here is remote at best.)

As enchanting a prospect as it is to the reformers, outright abolition of the jury right is rarely overtly proposed by them because of constitutional problems, though some feel it might be possible—in the protected-category cases—to allow juries to continue to assess liability while the supposedly more parsimonious judges determine damages. (It should be noted that defense attorneys in mega-dollar cases ordinarily do not favor abolishment of the jury, recognizing, as their principals sometimes do not, the dangers of submitting their case to a judge who might be pro-plaintiff.) Another proposal which would succeed in abrogating the right to trial, jury or bench, is to require protected-category cases to undergo binding arbitration. (There need not be a legislative enactment, in some instances, to bring this about. For example, patients on the eve of surgery could be required to sign waivers stating they agree to abide by an arbitrator's decision should their operations maim them.) Mandatory, but not binding, arbitration is the less radical of the jury avoidance schemes, and has been adopted, as we have seen, by various courts to handle mega-category cases and has been made a statutory requirement in some states, principally in regard to medical malpractice suits. Although neither mandatory arbitration nor mediation directly violate the jury right, they may when the law requires the losing party to post heavy indemnity bonds before being permitted a trial, as occurs in Massachusetts.[85]

Should efforts to remove or limit the right to jury in the protected-category cases fail, we might then want to accept the AMA's long-cherished goal of placing caps on awards,[86] which would not only lower the cost to insurers of the most catastrophic injuries but also, through the maximums they establish, tend to suppress awards for less-serious injuries.[87]

Or we could adopt another AMA proposal to place a limit on the money that can be paid for pain and suffering and eliminate punitive awards, no matter how despicable the defendant's conduct. Although opponents of the jury system have published a considerable literature charging that punitive awards in prodigious amounts have become routine, a 1986 preliminary report on a study by the American Bar Foundation[88] strongly suggests this isn't so. The analysis, which covered 30 jurisdictions in 10 states, including large cities and rural areas, found that punitive damages were generally awarded in less than 10% of all cases, that they cluster about fraud and other willful misconduct suits (not medical malpractice or products liability), and were especially infrequent in large cities, although the amount of award in such places tended to be higher than elsewhere, with the median punitive awards between $14,000 and $25,000, except in Los Angeles and San Diego where they were much higher. In the study, there is an implicit indication that case-dependent factors (quite properly) lead to variations from place to place, which would mean that if the study were done again five years later, the places which were indicating an upsurge in punitive awards, both in size and frequency, might shift. To place limits on punitive awards may be, like Swine Flu, a case of finding a cure for a disease that doesn't exist.

When we further consider that safeguards already exist in the judicial process to substantially reduce or eradicate improper punitive awards, reforms designed to limit or eliminate them from the judicial process are not only unnecessary but would thwart the desirable social purpose of punitive damages, which is to discourage egregious conduct both by the defendant in the case at hand and by those who might otherwise be tempted toward the same line of improper conduct in the future. (That punitive awards should go to the state rather than the victim of the outrageous conduct, as has been suggested, is itself so outrageous a remedy that it does not require serious attention.)

In the few places in which award-limitations have been enacted, they have, as might be expected, led to reductions in trial awards (by about 30%) and settlement sizes (by about 25%).[89] However, they have not led to reductions in insurance rates; on the contrary, by the mid-1980s, as discussed below, in those states as well as others, insurance rates were sharply on the rise.

Apparently, therefore, we must do more than we already have to please the insurance companies. As a financial incentive to insurance companies, we could enact statutes that forbid lump-sum payments to plaintiffs, replacing them with periodic installments, in that fashion allowing the insurers to hold on to their money longer and invest it rather than letting the victims get it and invest it. We might also consider forbidding plaintiff demands for specific sums as award-guidelines for jurors. Insurer losses for all mega-award cases could further be reduced by instructing jurors to deduct from them any amounts the plaintiff collected from collateral sources such as Workmen's Compensation.[90] To protect government and some hospitals, we can reinstate sovereign and charitable immunity,[91] and we could require losers in a suit to pay the winner's legal costs[92], which wouldn't hurt insurance companies, who could afford that when it happened, but would certainly deter people of average or lower income from suing lest they find themselves facing thousands of dollars in expenses if they lose. The Federal Rules of Civil Procedure[93] provide a model that some have suggested should be followed in state courts; under its terms, if a defendant's offer to settle is rejected by the plaintiff and the plaintiff subsequently receives a lesser sum, the plaintiff then has to pay the defendant the difference between the two amounts. (In federal court, however, this idea reportedly has not worked out very well; it has encouraged defendants to make absurdly low offers, since they have everything to gain and nothing to lose by so doing; when these offers are rejected, settlement becomes less likely and trial more likely.[94])

Another frequently advocated panacea is to apply to the protected categories some species of no-fault law. This is the philosophy behind workmen's compensation and which became statute in 25 states between 1971 and 1976 in automobile accident cases.[95] Theoretically, no-fault deters litigation because it sets a statutory maximum payment in enumerated categories of injury regardless of cause, thereby effectively eliminating pain-and-suffering payments, punitive damages, and other high cost items, and theoretically (very theoretically, as it turned out, in the case of automobile no-fault) reducing insurance premiums. Such schemes, however, have had a history that should give their proponents pause. The limits placed on compensation for workplace injuries have made victims look for other sources of money to make them whole, a significant reason behind suits against manufacturers of the products involved in the injury. Similarly, the automobile laws, by limiting or removing payment from the at-fault driver, have led some victims—successfully—to sue the auto manufacturer.[96] Applied to products liability and medical malpractice, the no-fault philosophy might well prove disastrous. It could mean that *everyone* who suffered an injury from a product could now collect, since negligence would no longer ever be an issue, while in medical injury, all victims of iatrogenic mishaps would have grounds for collection even though, as the concept has it, no one was at fault.

For those most avid to protect corporate America, probably the best solution is the simplest one: Delegalize contingency fees. That way, no poor person and very few middle-class people would sue anyone since they would not be able to hire a lawyer at $150 an hour.[97] Only the rich would be left to sue the rich. (A halfway-house proposal, designed to discourage lawyers from accepting protected category cases, is to penalize them when they do by reducing the percentage rate of their contingency fee. Since the mid-1970s, 32 states have passed such laws.[98])

It will be noted that none of these reforms considers the possibility that the best way to reduce the number of mega-dollar verdicts is for doctors and hospitals to offer better care, for governments to train their employees against negligence, and for manufacturers to market safer products. Apparently, the public is to direct its anger at the injured people, not those who cause the injury.

If we were to think in terms of protecting the victims—present and future— then we might want to consider a 1983 study of malpractice claims by Florida's insurance commissioner. It found that, between 1975 and 1982, seven-tenths of 1% of Florida physicians accounted for 24% of the claims for which payment was made,[99] with a single doctor accounting for 31 paid claims during the late 1970s. At the time of the study, this doctor was still practicing medicine and had never been disciplined by the state's licensure board.[100] A similar study of 8,000 Los Angeles-area physicians revealed that 0.6% of them accounted for 10% of all claims and 30% of all payments.[101] In Kansas, a survey of 700 claims revealed that less than 1% of all doctors prompted 16% of the claims.[102] Research in Pennsylvania discovered that 1% of that state's doctors were responsible for 25% of all payments made;[103] the same study demonstrated that if only 10 hospitals across the state improved their performance to average standards, the claims rate against hospitals would fall by 20%.[104] These figures, if replicated nationally, indicate that a very substantial part of the malpractice problem could be solved by rooting out habitually malpracticing physicians and improving risk-management in hospitals.[105]

The same approach might well be efficacious if applied to regular offenders in the industrial and governmental sector as well. Considering, however, the entrenched powers of bureaucracies and the lobbying might of the medical profession and industry, it may be whimsical to suppose any such efforts could be enacted, much less carried out. It is always easier to kill the messenger than listen to the message.

What all these legal reform proposals have in common, aside from the fact that they are to be applied only to members of the public and not to those who harm them,[106] is their oppressiveness in seeking to protect a threatened economic interest by abrogating common law and Constitutional rights.[107] Variously, the reforms would limit or destroy our right to trial by jury, our right to be made whole for our injuries, our right to (affordable) legal counsel. Before adopting any of them, simple prudence dictates that we should first make sure we are actually facing the problems that make these radical excisions of our freedom of action supposedly necessary.

IV

We have good reason to be cautious. As we saw in Chapter Six, the much-heralded ''litigation crisis'' which has also led to demands to limit our access to our courts and juries is largely fictitious. It actually represents, at the most, an annual 3 to 4% increase in state court filings over eight years, the large majority of the growth emanating not from ''hair-trigger suing'' leading to jury trials but from domestic relations matters, small claims, and collection cases which don't lead to jury trials. In response to the calls for immediate action against mega-verdicts—crisis rhetoric always demands immediate action—we should demand satisfactory answers to two questions: Is what we are told true? If it is true, will it continue to be true?

Considering the second question first, from neither the historical study in Chapter Five nor the statistical one in Chapter Six does a pattern emerge that suggests any ineluctable upward march in litigation. Rather, fluctuations appear to be the norm, principally brought on by extrinsic factors—e.g., a worsening economy leads to more indebtedness, leads to more collection cases—including, at the federal level, the impact of changes in government policies. Should the extrinsic situations change, so will the litigation rates.

Therefore, even if we had grounds to describe the events that began in the 1970s as a litigation ''explosion,'' have no rational or experiential basis for supposing that it would continue.[108]

More specifically, turning to the mega-type cases, and focusing on malpractice first, it will be recalled that a direct relationship exists between rate of hospitalization and frequency of suit. That being so, any predictions about the future frequency of malpractice litigation are, to some considerable extent, hospital-admission based. That is, if hospital admissions continue to increase through the remainder of the 20th century, as they did in the 1970s and before, we would then have reason to expect that the number of malpractice suits will continue upward, too. However, that is not an assumption we can properly make. On the contrary, since the early 1980s,[109] hospital admissions have been on a downward trend that seems likely to become more pronounced as time goes on. There are a number of reasons for the reversal. One has to do with physician availability and hospital usage. By the 1980s, reversing a condition that had existed for decades before, the United States began to have an oversupply of doctors,[110] leading to increased competition among them for patients. According to several studies,[111] physicians will meet the challenge by keeping directly under their care many patients they formerly would have ordered hospitalized, thus maximizing their income from such patients. Doctors who have joined together in the increasingly common and medically-sophisticated group practices and medical corporations will be in a particularly strong position to do this.[112] (Physicians, in fact, seem to be compensating nicely even if depopulating hospitals are not. In 1984, physicians' income rose 7.8% while cost of living rose 4% with incorporated group practices faring best.[113])

Perhaps even more significant as an anti-hospitalization force are Health Maintenance Organizations (HMOs). Long shunted to the suburbs of the medical metropolis, the HMOs' sudden emergence in the 1980s can be attributed to their sponsorship by businesses[114] which see them, because of their emphasis on preventive-care programs, as a proven means[115] of cutting down on employee time lost due to illness or hospitalization. Emerging even more rapidly have been the proprietary hospital chains such as Humana and Hospital Corporation of America,[116] which could deter malpractice frequency out of enlightened self-interest. Unlike the traditional medical institutions dominated by physician-management,[117] the commercial chains are hard-bitten, bottom-line oriented and for that reason, if no other, constantly scrutinize their staff doctors. They have no old-boy compunctions about getting rid of those who make mistakes "if only [to avoid] corporate liability for malpractice."[118] Then there's the high cost of medical care itself and the resultant cutbacks by the government in taxpayer-supported programs such as Medicaid[119] and Medicare; the less treatment offered, the less chance of malpractice suits. Should blue-collar employment continue to decline in America, which seems almost certain, so will the number of workplace injuries, thus reducing the need for surgery, a significant factor since about half of all hospital malpractice suits rise from operating-room mishaps.[120]

Just as the decline in blue-collar employment should deter malpractice suits, so should it reduce product-injury actions. A person is much less likely to be injured by a faulty tool when employed in an office than in a factory or—bitter as this may be—when not employed at all. More importantly, the mega-dollar verdicts have succeeded in removing some dangerous products from the market, cutting off those lines of litigation, and have made[121] (or should make) manufacturers more careful about their production processes. Something like that occurred in the late 1960s and early 1970s when a large number of malpractice suits were brought asserting that scissors, sponges and other items had been left in patients' bodies during operations. The suits forced hospitals to introduce implement counts, with the result that allegations on those grounds have nearly disappeared. Looked at that way, the tort system with its jury trials has served its purpose admirably: Its verdicts alert possible defendants to practices they should eliminate or improve, leading them simultaneously to avoid grounds for suit and better serve the members of the public with whom they deal.

As the introduction of the implement counts also points up, it is often a much better idea to solve a problem than to write legislation to control it. The answer to the whooping cough vaccine dilemma, therefore, is not to pass statutes to protect manufacturers from suit, since that does nothing to protect the children who might be injured, nor to take if off the market, since that harms the vast majority who aren't endangered by it, but, rather, to find ways to identify those who are allergic. This can probably be accomplished, at least to some substantial degree, even under the present state of medical knowledge. It appears that among those most at risk are newborns with central nervous system disorders,[122] and further inquiry might well define other indicia that will suggest which children should not be given the vaccine. (It's better to expose them to whooping cough than to brain damage.) It is also possible that a safer vaccine can be offered. An attorney[123] familiar with these cases reports that an earlier manufacturer, using a formula different from the current one, produced a product apparently free of adverse effects.

Those who would protect manufacturers from the harm they do may also be wrong when, in one of their doomsday scenarios, they claim that the high cost of verdicts will raise prices and cut back on research. Perhaps so, but it is at least as likely that a corporation that has lost market share because of lack of faith in its products, brought on by the publicity of verdicts against it, will decide to become more competitive, not less, on prices, and engage in more new-product research, not less, to regain or improve on its former profitability.

As this analysis of the future of mega-award verdicts suggests, today's realities can always be overtaken by tomorrow's, and those who face problems often can find ways to resolve them that do not affect the legal rights of others.

But what of today's reality? Have we—to return to our first question—been told the truth about the blockbuster jury-verdict crisis by those who promulgate it? To what extent is what we have been told verifiable?

Earlier, we noted how the American Medical Association, as part of its campaign to have limitations placed on malpractice awards, announced that 16 claims were filed for every 100 doctors in 1984, as against five in the mid-1970s. However, when we go back to 1976, we learn the AMA *then* was saying there were not five but 14 claims for every 100 doctors.[124] We might wonder in which year, if either, to believe the AMA.

The AMA's further contention that the average award in a malpractice suit was $850,000 in 1984 also raises questions of credibility. The alleged $350,000 average award for the mid-1970s, offered by an insurance industry spokesman, turned out to be quite different from that uncovered by the National Association of Insurance Commissioners for the same period. Using insurance companies' own statistics nationwide, it found the actual award average was $26,786,[125] not $350,000, while the insurance industry's own rate-making body, the Insurance Services Organization, put the average at $44,951.[126] It is difficult to believe that the average could have increased by more than $800,000 in less than 10 years.

When we turn to the even higher $962,000 average reported by Jury Verdict Research, we find it is based on only 238 cases nationwide for 1982; that same year, the Insurance Information Institute, which is hardly likely to deal in low figures, said that the average award in 60 malpractice cases in California was $257,222, so that the average award in the rest of the nation must have been positively enormous, if any of these figures can be believed at all. Average awards, in any event, are a poor criterion to use, since a handful of cases involving huge amounts—the highest reported in 1982 was $29 million—will skew the average into virtual meaninglessness. A much more reputable figure is the *median* or mid-point verdict, and for that, from the Jury Verdict Research partial sampling, the figure was $200,000 in 1982;[127] and even that is probably high. Jury Verdict's "research" principally consists of news clippings about jury awards and correspondence from attorneys about their cases. Modest awards are not likely to be reported either way.

Another study undertaken in 1982 by the magazine *Medico-Economics for Surgeons* suggests we have good reason to be skeptical of all these statistics. "Judging by newspaper headlines," the article noted, "you'd think most malpractice plaintiffs walk away with huge payments. But our survey doesn't bear that out." The magazine found, instead, that the median settlement before trial was $9,050; during trial, $13,350. Of the 819 physicians responding to the questionnaire who had been sued at least once, only 28 of them (or, rather, their insurers) were ever faced with a trial verdict or settlement of $100,000 or more.[128]

We might also want to be careful of accepting the AMA's $14 to $15 billion figure for the annual cost of "defensive" medicine. The term itself is undefinable, since one doctor's defensive medicine will be another's normal standard of care.[129] Looked at this way, if medical malpractice suits have forced normally careless physicians to engage in testing that the prudent ones have always done, the awards may well have served a highly beneficial public purpose.[130] But even if we take the AMA at its word and assume that purely *unnecessary* testing is now rampant—in itself a curious admission for the medical profession to make—we have no reason, other than the AMA's unsubstantiated assertion, to think that the uncalled-for testing is done primarily or even ordinarily to build a track record as a defense in a malpractice suit. We *might* think so, if all this unnecessary testing were done free of charge, but it isn't. The patients pay and the doctors and the hospital profit—by deliberately engaging in medical procedures[131] they know to be unnecessary (or even wrong) to the tune of $14 to $15 billion a year. If there is a scandal to be found here, it may not be emanating from malpractice suits or jury verdicts.

Claims by insurers that sudden onsets of malpractice and product liability cases have caused them huge losses (and hence forced them to raise rates) have also not, on past occasions, been borne out by the facts. In 1976, at a time when the casualty insurance industry was first waving the flag of warning about a product liability "explosion," the Insurance Information Institute estimated there would be one million such suits filed that year, a figure that appeared in insurance industry advertising.[132] The actual number of suits, the same source later admitted, was between 60,000 and 70,000.[133]

Predicted future losses had played a role a few years earlier when the malpractice underwriter for doctors in New York, Employers of Wausau, told that state's insurance commissioner that they estimated losses of $36 million for the year in claims incurred but not yet reported to them. Based in part on this assertion, the company received a large rate increase; the following year, the $36 million had been halved to $18 million, with only $6 million accounted for by shifts to claims paid and reserves for future payments. The whereabouts of the other $12 million that helped bring about the rate increase for doctors remained a mystery.[134] Another insurer, Argonaut, in 1975 received a 200% rate increase on malpractice premiums in Pennsylvania, again largely based on amounts they asserted they'd have to pay out on future claims. During that year, according to a study by an independent actuary of 139 consecutive closed claims, Argonaut had overestimated the amount of their losses in 137 of them, a total of nearly a million dollars, and also had overestimated legal expenses by three times the amount actually paid.[135]

Around the same time in California, Travelers Insurance, allegedly also facing huge future losses in malpractice underwriting, had received a compensating rate increase. Subsequently, the Southern California Physicians Council demanded rebates for its members, alleging that Travelers, far from losing money on these predicted losses, had made "enormous profits." In 1981, the suit was settled, with Travelers returning $50 million to the Council.[136]

By then, however, the insurance companies had accomplished a number of their goals. By threatening to stop writing policies on high-risk lines, they frightened state legislatures into passing laws that reduced both plaintiff rights and insurance company risks. In malpractice during the mid-1970s, for example, every state in the union adopted reform legislation designed to limit the right to sue or to put a ceiling on the amount that any insurance company could lose on an individual case, forcing doctors and hospitals to pay the excess out of their own pockets through assessments paid to so-called catastrophe funds. Meanwhile, supine or ignorant state insurance commissions continued to give huge rate increases virtually on demand, even though, according to one conservative estimate, the casualty insurers between 1970 and 1976 netted over $1 billion in *underwriting* profits alone on malpractice,[137] despite their repeated assertions they were losing hundreds of millions annually.

By the late 1970s, the casualty insurers were telling new tales of woe about their latest deficits. The 1979 publicized "loss" figure was $985 million, a figure that, it turned out, included $629 million paid out in dividends to stockholders, and that omitted the $4.3 *billion* in profits on investment earnings.[138] A survey of the 100 leading casualty insurers for that year revealed that they took in $1.2 billion in product liability premiums, paid out $971 million in actual losses plus reserves for future losses, some of which (based on history) would never occur. The 25% net on that single line of underwriting was for an industry that claims to gear its rates to achieve a 5% profit margin.[139] Still another study found that malpractice insurers, between 1978 and 1983, earned $300 million more in interest investments on their loss reserves alone than they paid out from them.[140]

Despite the supposed horrendous losses of 1979, by 1980 a calm had descended over the casualty industry. Rates stabilized, even were reduced in some of the high-risk lines, including product liability.[141] In 1983, however, the industry announced it was now paying out $1.12 for every $1 in premium it was taking in, leading to an underwriting loss of $11 billion; this, however, was nicely compensated for by interest earnings that led to a net gain of $9 billion.[142] By 1985, matters had gotten much worse, according to industry statistics, which showed a loss (including underwriting and interest earnings) of $5.5 billion,[143] although a subsequent retraction admitted a $1.7 billion profit.[144] The actual profit may have been at least $7.6 billion.[145]

Despite their poor-mouthing, the insurers had never been doing better. Between 1974 and 1983, the total net gain for the industry was approximately $72 billion.[146] (They kept most of it, too; during that period, they paid just $1.2 billion in federal income taxes or 2% of their net gain.)[147] Others seemed to think they were in a healthy condition, too. Between 1980 and 1985, the casualty companies handily outperformed the Dow-Jones average stock earning (194% to 84%[148]). In 1985, also, the casualty industry's consolidated balance sheet assets rose about $49 billion, to approximately $313 billion; the increase alone was more than their total assets as an industry just 20 years earlier.[149] Since assets don't necessarily portray bottom-line profitability, a more meaningful statistic is a shift in net worth surplus, which rose from $63.8 billion to $76.9 billion or by about 20% in 1985 alone.[150]

The insurance availability crisis that became headline news in 1985, therefore, occurred at a time when the industry was enjoying unparalleled prosperity. It further occurred at a time when litigation frequency was stabilizing or perhaps declining nationally. (The insurers didn't have to rely on state court statistics to tell them that; their own trending was showing the same pattern.[151]) It is true it also occurred at a time when very large jury verdicts were becoming more frequent; however, that development was well-established by the beginning of the 1980s, when rates were holding steady or declining, and insurers were willing and even eager to underwrite risks in the lines that were producing those verdicts.

In view of these conditions, insurers' demands in the mid-1980s for extraordinary rate increases[152] and their decision to stop underwriting entirely in some lines appear to have been prompted primarily by the desire to seize an opportunity for both immediate and long-range greater profits.

In running its business, an insurance company has two ways of making money. It can "win" as a salesman of policies sold at a profit—i.e., the money coming in the front door is greater than that leaving the back through claims paid—or as an investment banker of the money while it is still in the house. In the optimum situation, presumably, both winning activities are desirable. However, when there are opportunities for quick, high-yield investments, an insurance company will often price its policies at rates it knows are not profitable solely to beat the competition[153] and get the maximum amount of money coming through the front door. (This apparently happened in the early 1980s in medical malpractice underwritings and in product liability as well.)

As long as the investment situation remains bullish, the system works for the insurers, and the premium-holders benefit by the lower prices. That was a situation which had prevailed from about the early 1960s until the mid-1970s as the stock market, in which the casualty companies were heavy investors, continued on its seemingly permanent rise. Then, in 1974, the Dow-Jones average, which had topped the magic 1,000 mark for the first time in 1972, skidded to 607. The insurers' stock market losses for that year reached an estimated $3.3 billion. Although insurance industry spokespersons assured Congress that their subsequent demands for huge rate increases in medical malpractice had nothing to do with their stock market losses—only Argonaut admitted the connection—the fact remains that on the heels of the one event came the other.[154]

By the mid-1980s, in eerie recall of the events of 10 years earlier, the prime interest rate dropped drastically from 20% in 1980 to 9.5% in 1985.[155] A decline in average interest earnings, however, did not have the direct and precipitous effect on the casualty insurers that the stock market crash had, and may in some instances have permitted short-term capital gains. By 1986, too, the insurers had the vast majority of their investment portfolio—about 83% of it[156]—in bonds, both long and short term, in which the purchase interest rate would not fluctuate with any change in the prime rate.

Nevertheless, the decline in the prime interest rate meant that the time was not opportune for the insurers to generate underwriting business at competitive rates for investment purposes. Rather, the bounty they were enjoying permitted them the luxury of being able to reject any line of underwriting that projected any kind of risk, unless it was also a very large dollar-yield field, which malpractice and day-care centers—another field in which it was next to impossible to get insurance—were not. Even in the high-yield field of auto insurance some draconian limitations were temporarily set. In effect, the casualty insurers had gotten into the coupon-clipping business and out of the risk business.

At least they were, until the next turn of the economic wheel, when bonds and securities could again be bought at better rates. The hiatus period, however, could be put to a good use beyond coupon-clipping. If the insurance companies could convince their customers as well as the public and their legislators that their reason for tightening insurance availability was not greed but rather a supposed crisis of litigiousness and overly generous jury verdicts, then they could revive the panic atmosphere that had proven so useful in the 1970s in forcing governments to limit the right to sue and limit awards.

When the investment picture improved, the backdoor gains made by any restrictive changes in the law would remain in place, further adding to the insurers' profits. By inventing a crisis and then withdrawing their services, the insurers had created the best of all possible worlds for themselves at the expense of their customers, and at the expense of the public's right to take their grievances to court.

It may be, in getting the answers to our questions, we will decide that it is not "greedy" litigants or "generous" juries that are in need of reform.

(A note: As this book reached deadline, the casualty insurance industry announced its results for 1986: an $11 billion profit. Congress's Government Accounting Office said more than $19 billion. The crisis seems to have served the insurers well.)

Chapter 8
The Paper Building

"[T]he circumstances that constitute cases proper for courts of equity are in many instances so . . . intricate that they are incompatible with the genius of trials by jury. They require often such long, deliberate, and critical investigation as would be impracticable to men called from their occupations, and obliged to decide before they were permitted to return to them. The simplicity and expedition which form the distinguishing character of [the jury] mode of trial require that the matter to be decided should be reduced to some single and obvious point; while the litigations usual in chancery frequently comprehend a long train of minute and independent particulars.

". . . [T]he attempt to extend the jurisdiction of the courts of law to matters of equity will . . . tend gradually to change the nature of the courts of law and to undermine the trial by jury, by introducing questions too complicated for a decision in that mode."

—*Alexander Hamilton*, The Federalist, No. 83.

I

In the early 1970s, one of the great American go-go stocks was that of U.S. Financial (USF),[1] "a high-flying real estate development company which," as a federal judge later put it, "began losing altitude in 1972 and finally crashed in 1973."[2] The crash exploded in many directions. Bankruptcy cases were filed; criminal charges were leveled; the Securities and Exchange Commission investigated; and a welter of civil damage claims were pursued, the defendants including brokerage and accountancy firms that allegedly had attested to the soundness of the USF offerings.[3]

By the time the principal consolidated lawsuits reached the pretrial stage in the United States District Court for Southern California in 1977,[4] the paperwork had reached a total of 150,000 pages in depositions and more than five million documents, which, if placed one on top of the other, would reach as high as a three-story house.[5] The trial, it was expected, would require two years.[6] But before the trial could even commence a question had to be decided: Should the matter be tried by a jury, as the plaintiffs preferred, or by the judge acting as a court in equity, as a few of the defendants[7] demanded?

The Seventh Amendment to the United States Constitution seemed to provide an unequivocal answer to that question. It permitted a jury trial for any lawsuit in which damages of more than $20 were at issue; the demands in USF were in the millions. However, the presiding judge in the USF case, Howard B. Turrentine, didn't see it that way when he issued his opinion in June 1977.[8] Noting the complicated, "often boring"[9] nature of the testimony, Turrentine pointed out that "an unusually long trial may make extraordinary demands upon a jury," so that its members could not "function effectively."[10] Based on this reasoning, Turrentine ruled that "the legal and factual issues were of such complexity as to be beyond the practical abilities and limitations of a jury."[11] That meant there was "no adequate remedy at law,"[12] and the case had to be tried in equity, i.e., no jury. Alexander Hamilton's argument had won in California in 1977. Or so it seemed.

While the USF case continued to stew away—the losers had appealed Turrentine's decision—at the opposite end of the country, in the Eastern District of Pennsylvania, another federal court judge, Edward R. Becker, was confronting the same problem in the Japanese Electronics Anti-Trust litigation[13] in which, in part, Japanese manufacturers were accused of predatory practices in the United States.[14] Facing Becker were 100,000 pages of depositions, more than 20 million documents, and a trial that was likely to take a year.[15] Again, the plaintiffs wanted a jury trial; the Japanese defendants said it should be forbidden on complexity grounds. (The Japanese, considering the allegations made against them, may also have wanted to avoid American jurors.)[16] Becker, going through much of the same case lore as had Turrentine, but in more detail,[17] could find no grounds for a complexity exception; if the plaintiffs wanted a jury in a case involving damages, they should have one, Becker declared, just as the Seventh Amendment said they could. Hamilton had lost on the east coast. Or so it seemed.

Matters were about to take an ironic turn. In December 1979, the United States Court of Appeals for the Ninth Circuit rejected Hamilton, reversed Turrentine,[18] and embraced Becker's reasoning.[19] Seven months later, in July 1980, the Third Circuit Court of Appeals, sitting in Philadelphia where the Constitution was written, embraced Hamilton, in part rejected Becker, and accepted Turrentine's conclusion.[20] Hamilton was no longer welcome on the west coast, but he could resume residency in the east.

Or could he? The conflicting opinions in the two cases, as well as similar disagreements in a handful of others during the same period,[21] stirred up a controversy that quickly developed a veritable cottage industry of law journal articles, with this pile of legal paper soon threatening itself to reach the height of a one-story building.[22]

The complexity issue, everyone presumed, would eventually have to be decided by the United States Supreme Court; however, at the time of the writing of this book, no test case was yet before it.[23] The Court had refused to accept an appeal of the Ninth Circuit's ruling in the USF case,[24] and subsequent legal maneuvering in Japanese Electronics apparently made the jury issue moot there.[25] Should some similar case eventually be accepted—and the Supreme Court doesn't have to take on any issue it wishes to avoid—it is far from certain how the voting would go. As long as Chief Justice Burger remained on the scene, the proponents of the complexity-exception to jury trial appeared to have one vote they could count on,[26] but other justices, including the influential Byron White,[27] have shown themselves to be firm believers in the jury system.

Among litigants in complex cases like USF and Japanese Electronics—complex if only because of the vast amount of paperwork they have generated—typically it is the defendants who oppose and the plaintiffs who favor the jury trial. The defense's antagonism toward the jury is based on several considerations. First, if the defense is a technical one, the defendants may legitimately fear that jurors will be less able to understand it than will a judge. Second, if their actions have been of the kind that lay people might consider unethical, they may fear resultant juror wrath. Third, since in these cases the defendant almost invariably has big dollars at stake, the jury may also be feared because of its supposed habit of digging into defendants' deep pockets.

The defense thinking, however, is often not quite that simplistic. Litigation that is likely to contain highly complicated fact and legal issues, such as antitrust, is almost invariably tried in federal court where judges, because of both their legal and social backgrounds tend to be sympathetic toward—or, at a minimum, not antagonistic to—the capitalist expansionism that is often at the heart of the allegations against the defense (e.g., conspiracies in restraint of trade). But even if the judge assigned the case doesn't have such a bias, he or she may still be preferred over a jury because a judge, unlike a jury, is required to ignore reprehensible conduct as long as it is legal. For the same reasons that defendants oppose the jury, the plaintiffs want them. (This is not to say that all defendants and all plaintiffs in such matters reach the same conclusions; in the USF case, for example, most of the defendants were content to let the matter be tried by a jury.)

Once we move beyond the natural self-interest of antagonists in litigation, it becomes apparent that the complexity-exception argument is somewhat different from the criticisms of the jury discussed in previous chapters. Unlike in those criticisms, no one is saying (at least overtly) that juries should *generally* be forbidden on grounds of competence or over-generosity, but rather that they should be removed only in certain especially difficult cases. Indeed, the complexity-exception advocates frequently argue, implicitly or explicitly,[28] that *most* of the time the jury is a capable dispute-resolution device. The cases in which it is not, the advocates observe, are not only few in number—about 5% of all civil suits, according to one estimate[29]—but also reassuringly narrow in legal scope, being almost entirely confined to private antitrust suits[30] and other intricate financial matters, as in USF. It has been urged that by removing such rare and rarefied legal issues from jury consideration, we are, far from attacking the jury system, instead protecting its credibility by not requiring lay people to try to decide matters beyond their intellectual capacities. And at the same time we are relieving prospective jurors of the burden of giving a year or more[31] of their lives to resolving the legal problems of corporate America.

When we scratch the complexity-exception proposition a bit deeper, however, we see that it is concerned not so much either with the competency of jurors or their convenience as it is with imposing an elitist view upon the egalitarian premises of American democracy. For, when we declare that juries are not able to handle certain types of difficult cases, we are assuming the existence of a meritocracy that *is* capable or else there would be no point in raising the issue at all.

The expert agency for that purpose might be an administrative body, as Justice Burger has suggested,[32] or a jury from which average people are eliminated and replaced by those with specialized knowledge of the subject of the suit (as occasionally happened, it will be recalled from Chapter One, in the Middle Ages). Or, the superior agency could be judges who, it has to be assumed from the argument, are better able to understand a complex subject and its applicable law[33] than a jury of laypeople.

Whatever particular elite is chosen, if there is to be a complexity-exception to the Seventh Amendment, someone has to decide when it comes into effect. To attempt to do so by legislative fiat raises constitutional questions of intrusion on the judiciary, so that the likely mode would be—as in the USF and Japanese Electronics cases—to allow the trial judge to make the original ruling, subject to appeal.

Once that formulation is in effect, it could be said, we have applied a scalpel to the Bill of Rights. No longer, in a lawsuit, can we as plaintiffs or defendants require that our case be tried by a jury of our peers. If the judge who hears our petition is, like Becker, of an egalitarian persuasion, we will probably get our jury, even though our case is to some degree or another complex. But if the judge is of an elitist turn of mind, we may well have to submit our cause to his or her wisdom, whether or not we think—based on that judge's past record—that he or she is likely to be fair to our pleadings. Either way, we no longer have the *right* we used to have (even if 99% of the time juries are still given on request), but, in its place, only a privilege that need not ever be extended.

Those who hold to the complexity-exception position do not agree with this analysis. They point out that since there never has been an unlimited right to jury trial in civil cases, their view entails no abrogation but, rather, properly defines the situations in which the jury trial is permissible. In taking that stance, they rely upon a two-pronged legal argument. One derives from the powers of equity, exemplified by Turrentine's opinion in the USF case. The second rises from the conflict that can exist, as the advocates see it, between the Seventh and Fifth Amendment portions of the Bill of Rights.

The equity argument has the longest history, going back to the days when the toadying commission appointed by King James the First held that the chancery courts were superior to those of common pleas, and had the right to remove from common pleas any matter chancery found them incapable of handling. Though chancery has long vanished in both England and the United States, its functions meshed into a unified system, the idea behind it remains. Many judges[34] have held that certain difficult cases, especially those demanding an accounting of assets, are properly disposed of by the equity mode even though they might contain lawsuit elements. As Turrentine noted in USF, "complicated accounting problems are not generally amenable to jury resolution."[35] Turrentine's rather gingerly-made statement was dramatically expanded by the defendants in Japanese Electronics who asserted that "[a]t the time the Seventh Amendment was ratified . . . litigations involving complex facts or sophisticated business transactions were tried before a Court and not a jury."[36]

That statement raises the thesis that complicated matters aren't merely "generally" unamenable to jury trial but that they have never been so amenable, since a complexity-exception existed at the time the Seventh Amendment was adopted. The amendment has repeatedly been held to mean that whatever was considered a common-law case in 1791, the year of its adoption, remains one now, and that by analogy, causes for civil actions that have arisen since that time (such as antitrust and trademark infringement cases) are also jury-susceptible when they have the classic common law indices, i.e., a demand for money damages or associated assertions of legal rights (as in discrimination suits).[37] The complexity-exception caveat doesn't deny that general premise but adds that, since American law is based on British law and British law prior to 1791 permitted chancery to remove complicated and sophisticated business matters (especially accounting cases) from jury purview, the complexity-exception has constitutional standing.

To document their position,[38] the advocates have uncovered two English trials prior to 1791 in which judges took cases from juries specifically on the grounds that the evidence would be too difficult for jurors to understand. The principal case, *Towneley v. Clench* (1603), occurred when the battles between chancery and common pleas were at their peak, with the judge who denied the right to jury a leading opponent of Coke who supported the jury.[39] The Towneley case, therefore, was a pawn in a political battle and would seem, for that reason, to have little precedential merit. Moreover, neither it nor the second case, *Blad v. Bamfield* (1674)[40]—a very unusual one involving international treaties—were considered legally significant in their own time, leading some opponents of the complexity-exception theory to conclude that framers of the Seventh Amendment wouldn't have known about either of them and hence were acting on the assumption that no complexity-exception existed in 1791.[41]

Their reasoning does not lack surface persuasiveness; people cannot be held to have intended that which they know not of. To say this, however, does not mean that the authors of the Seventh Amendment would not have agreed to the complexity-exception restriction had they been aware of it. The complexity-exception, therefore, probably does have constitutional standing if the following can be proved: First, by 1791 British law had established that civil cases could be removed from jury trial solely on the basis of difficulty; second, the Seventh Amendment was intended to adopt *all* aspects of the British law concerning when a case was suitable for equity and when for jury trial. The complexity-exception thesis, however, *probably* falls if American and British law differed on equity by 1791, indicating that the Americans had no intention of adopting the British system in every respect. And the argument *clearly* falls if the authors of the Seventh Amendment were aware of the complexity issue and rejected it.

Since we have no definitive statements by anyone involved in the writing of the Seventh Amendment to tell us precisely how it was to be interpreted, we must turn to the history of the period to see if we can find answers. By way of context, we know from the Declaration of Independence that one reason the Revolution was fought was to preserve the right to jury trial, a right which the British government had abrogated when it removed unpopular prosecutions under the Stamp and Navigation Acts to the equitable courts of chancery and admiralty. The judges of these courts were widely perceived in America as creatures of the Crown: Appointed by the prime minister, they were expected to do his bidding. In these courts no voice of the people could be heard as in Common Pleas where, although the judges were appointed the same way, the jury was present as an independent countervailing force.

The framers of the Constitution reflected this fear of oppressive control of the courts when they established the judiciary as independent of both Congress and the President. Although the enactment proves that not all British judicial practices were to be considered sacrosanct in the United States, it does not, by itself, indicate any quarrel with the British rules governing which cases had to be tried under equity. That basic British equity principles were accepted in the United States, we know, if from no other source, then from the Seventh Amendment itself which, by limiting jury trial to law cases, granted all others to equitable jurisdiction just as in England.

Our question at this point, therefore, is whether or not American laws governing equity prior to 1791 differed from the British in any way.

A glance back through colonial statutes turns up one such early departure. It occurred in Pennsylvania where, in 1711, the legislature passed a statute ordering that when a case had both equitable and common-law elements, the latter could be tried by jury,[42] a position which could not have been more directly contradictory to British equity law, and which provided a precedential ground for the United States Supreme Court's decision in the Beacon case (see Chapter One) nearly 250 years later.

When we turn to the period immediately following the Revolution, we find no universal reliance on British law; on the contrary, in some states cases were being tried by juries that would have been considered equitable matters in England.[43] Moreover, following the passage of the Constitution, the congressional debate over the Judicial Act of 1789 focused on means of limiting not expanding equitable jurisdiction.[44] The underlying issue was laid out by Alexander Hamilton in the passage quoted at the beginning of this chapter where he bewails the fact that "intricate" civil cases, which he thought properly belonged before a judge, were now being tried by juries that, in his view, should be limited to deciding cases in which the litigation was over a "single and obvious point" of law. In other words, it was the complexity—the "intricacy"—of the case that determined whether it should be tried by judge or jury, just as today's complexity exceptionists would have it.

Based on this history, the learned disquisitions about the presumed impact of the Blad and Towneley cases become an exercise in obfuscation. It doesn't matter whether Jefferson—the principal author of the Seventh Amendment—or Hamilton or anybody else had ever heard about them. They already knew about the complexity argument as it related to equity and the jury; it was raging all about them, and had been stated by Jefferson's opponent, Hamilton, with a precision that has rarely since been matched. The only issue that remains, therefore, is what did they decide to do about it? The Seventh Amendment wording provides the answer. Had its adoption been made possible only by Jefferson giving way to Hamilton and the Federalists on the controversial complexity issue, that compromise would logically be found in the Amendment. But no such reference exists. Rather, the Seventh Amendment language can be read as a specific rejection of Hamilton's proposal that intricate civil cases be transferred to equity, since it specifically states that only minor common law suits (worth $20 or less) are to be removed from jury purview.

Thus, from the historic evidence we can conclude that the pro-jury forces knew about the complexity argument, opposed it, and prevailed in their opposition. We have a bit of negative evidence to support that conclusion, too. During the years immediately following adoption of the Seventh Amendment, many cases were argued in which the issue was whether the trial should be in equity or at common law; in none of these cases did the side arguing for equity claim that the case belonged there because it was too complex for a jury,[45] an indication that during the period contemporary to its passage the Seventh Amendment was acknowledged as saying what it meant and meaning what it said.

Under the Seventh Amendment, therefore, a civil case is either common law or equitable based on the relief being sought: The forum has nothing to do with the nature of the evidence, complex or simple.[46] If the relief is money (more than $20) then the case is jury-triable; if the relief is to force a party to do something it doesn't want to do—such as uphold a contract—then the case goes into equity.

That sounds straightforward enough and the United States Supreme Court has so ruled,[47] as did the California Appeals Court when it overturned Turrentine. (The Third Circuit Court of Appeals also upheld the section of Becker's opinion in which he rejected the argument that accounting evidence brought a case, per se, into equity.[48])

Courts, nevertheless, have constantly worried about the appropriateness of trying accounting issues before a jury, and seem to have sought ways to encourage, or force, litigants not to do so. In an 1887 case, a court ruled that "[t]he complicated nature of the accounts between the parties constitutes itself a sufficient ground for going into equity."[49] Other cases have used similar language,[50] but they also have held that, regardless of how sensible it would be to try the case in equity, if the *plaintiff* in a damage-accounting case wanted a jury, then the plaintiff could have one, though apparently a defendant on demand could not.[51] The reverse of that proposition was that should a plaintiff want to try the case in equity and the defendant want a jury trial, the plaintiff's desire prevailed *if* the plaintiff could convince the judge that the "accounts between the parties [were of such a] complicated nature" that only a court sitting in equity could decide them.[52]

The accounting argument, by itself, therefore, appears to present substantial legal problems to those who advance it as a reason for forbidding juries in damage cases. But what of the other equity argument that Turrentine upheld? He stated, as we have seen, that the accounting elements and the other complicating evidentiary factors in USF, along with the projected length of the trial, meant that no jury would be bright enough or patient enough to understand the case; hence, there was no adequate way to try it before a jury; hence, into equity it went. Those who hold to that belief have taken heart from a single footnote to a 1970 U.S. Supreme Court decision, *Ross v. Bernhard*.[53] This case, in which the directors of the Lehman Brothers brokerage firm were the defendants,[54] involved complicated accounting evidence and a demand for money (i.e., return of allegedly illicit profits[55]). The Supreme Court ruled that trial by jury should be permitted. But there was also the footnote which read: "As our cases indicate, the 'legal' nature of an issue is determined by considering, first, the pre-merger custom [i.e., of chancery and common pleas] with reference to such questions; second, the remedy sought; and third, *the practical abilities and limitations of juries*,"[56] (italics added). This was the wording picked up by Turrentine for his decision.

Those who seek a complexity-exception have seized on the seven italicized words as proof that the Supreme Court perceives the Seventh Amendment as they do.[57] At least four judges have held that the footnote has "Constitutional dimensions" and have refused jury demands based on it.[58] (Of the nearly ceiling-high stack of law journal pages referred to earlier, perhaps half consist of articles gleefully seizing on the footnote, tugging it this way and that, to force it into the desired shape.)

But is that what the Supreme Court meant? Common sense—which, unfortunately, is not always a safe criterion to use when scholars are observing the number of angels dangling from the head of a legal pin—would seem to dictate not. To begin with, the decision in *Ross* actually *extended* the right to jury trial in cases in which previously it had been thought equity applied,[59] and it seems weird that in such a situation the Supreme Court would take away in a footnote that which it had granted in the body of the decision.[60] It also is passing strange that the Supreme Court, in any decision, would cavalierly rescind a portion of the United States Constitution as the third of three criteria relegated to footnote status.[61] Moreover, on at least five occasions since *Ross*, the Supreme Court has considered the Seventh Amendment—though not precisely on the complexity-exception issue—and has never made further reference to the "practical abilities and limitations of juries,"[62] even when, as in *Rogers v. Loether*,[63] the lower court did.

We probably can conclude, therefore, that no matter how much the complexity-exception advocates would like the *Ross* footnote to read their way, the Supreme Court did not grant them their wish.

But what then does the footnote mean? In context, it relates to the distinctions to be drawn between law and equity cases, apparently in the narrow sense of the secondary suits that were the subject of *Ross*,[64] but beyond that, according to the California Appeals Court in USF, its meaning is "unclear."[65] Becker found perhaps the most persuasive answer. He believed the Court was simply referring to federal administrative hearings in which juries aren't present and to those accounting cases in which equity may be *elected* when the plaintiff—who can choose the forum—is concerned about the "practical . . . limitations" of jurors.[66]

The equity argument, persuasive or not, is one with enormous appeal to elitists; it has a nostalgic quality, reminding them of the good old days in England when the Courts of Chancery, appointed by the resident despot,[67] reigned wisely over the mere courts of law in which juries could intrude with their folk wisdom. If juries must be, then let them be limited, as Hamilton would have it, to "some single and obvious point," i.e., the run-of-the-mill criminal case in which affairs of great moment to great people are not to be decided. For the great affairs, only the judge or some other learned tribunal is to be trusted.

The second argument against using juries in complex cases derives from the due process clause of the Fifth Amendment which guarantees the right to a fair trial. (Similar wording occurs in the Fourteenth Amendment.) When the jurors lack the capacity to understand the case, fair trial, say the complexity-exception advocates, becomes impossible and the Fifth Amendment, thereby, is violated.[68] Judge Turrentine agreed with this proposition in USF,[69] and the Third Circuit Court of Appeals adopted it as a matter of legal principle when it returned the Japanese Electronics matter to Becker to determine if, in fact, the case was too complex for a jury. Said the Third Circuit's opinion: "We conclude that due process precludes trial by jury when a jury is unable to perform this task with a reasonable understanding of the evidence and the legal rules."[70] Thus, when the Fifth and Seventh Amendments cross paths, the Seventh must give way to the Fifth.

Nothing could seem more reasonable.[71] Certainly the purpose of justice is to provide justice, and if a jury—no matter how willing, how fair-minded, how representative a cross section of the public it may be—simply can't comprehend what is going on, the goal of justice is thwarted; verdicts are based on ignorance or miscomprehension, and if they are correct, it is only by chance.

The due process argument, however, may not be as reasonable as it sounds, and can create greater difficulties than that which it claims to solve. As a reform, what it seeks to do is substitute *prospective* justice[72] for the *retrospective* system already in place. Under existent law, only reversals of improper verdicts are permitted, a retrospective act; a jury's right to make a decision cannot be withheld beforehand because the judge thinks it probably doesn't understand the evidence. To put it another way, the due process argument imposes prior restraint on the right to jury by assuming that lay people will not be able to comprehend fact issues that have yet to be debated or assess witnesses who have yet to be questioned.

Even if we have no problem with prospective justice in this formulation—and it is a concept that American jurisprudence has never treated kindly, although authoritarian nations have long been fond of it[73]—the due process argument slips other kinds of inequities into place. For one, juries, unlike judges, are free to reject a law they think will work an injustice in the case before them; therefore, by forbidding juries in so-called complex cases, judges are denying the litigants in them a form of relief that remains otherwise available. (For a further discussion of jury justice, see Chapter Nine.)

A question of equal treatment under the law is also raised when we have two cases of equal degrees of complexity, and in the one the judge (based on his or her intuition) permits a jury, while in the other the judge doesn't. We have then to ask: If the judge's decision provided due process in the one case, how could the opposite decision have provided it in the other? And must we not further ask: If due process dictates removal of prospectively incompetent juries from a complex case, should we not conduct a similar anticipatory test in order to remove incompetent judges from them?[74]

But that is not all. Whichever way the decision goes on permitting the jury in the complex case, the side that thinks it was unfairly treated will—as we have seen from the USF and Japanese Electronics suits—appeal the decision. A case that is already protracted, because of the time it took to get all the documents together, is then even further delayed, perhaps by years, and where then is due process—in terms of the right to a speedy trial?

Still other problems loom by having judges determine when a case is too difficult for a jury to understand it. Although the treatises on complex cases—possibly out of an excess of delicacy—assiduously ignore it, empowering judges to decide when a jury should not be permitted opens the way for corruption. A litigant that fears what a jury will do, but that previously had to put up with the prospect, can now avoid it— if able to find a willing open hand. Although *known* cases of judicial corruption happily are rare, the proposed reform could encourage the practice—it is easier to buy one judge than 12 lay people—and is unwise on that score alone.

It is also possible that a few judges will seize on the "complexity-exception" argument in order to maintain under their control cases that contain economic or political issues of concern to them, and which they do not want to leave to a non-ideological jury to decide. Taking that argument one step further in a slightly different direction, we have to ask ourselves which is preferable: a confused jury in a complex case which gives, in effect, a toss of the coin verdict (50% certainty that it will be right) or a biased judge who decides it according to his or her political predilections or ambitions?[75]

Finally, a more subtle but no less important question of appropriate forum in complex cases arises when we consider the different qualities that judges and juries bring to the deliberative process. For the purposes of this argument, we will assume that all judges are individuals of the highest moral rectitude and possessors of splendid judicial abilities and that all juries consist of individuals of similar honesty but without knowledge of the law. Our hypothetical ideal judge brings to the complex case (as he or she does to all others) a cache of knowledge from cases that judge has heard or from the judge's knowledge of decisions on similar cases reached by other judges. The case, therefore, is not novel to the judge as it will be to the jury. Bearing that in mind, the litigants may decide—as is their right—that the previous experience, coupled with the judge's temperament and ability, makes that judge the proper person to try the case.

However, there is also a universe of cases, both in simple and complex matters, in which one party or the other—probably most often the plaintiff—will wish to have the matter tried by the jury precisely because it, unlike the judge, comes to the case new, unjaded, with no preconceptions. Thus, to the jury, its case in all its elements, possibly including outrageous but technically legal conduct by one party or the other, has no foreshadowing. Though there are no statistics on this point, based on writings by lawyers, there is no doubt the "freshness" of the jury is one factor they will consider in deciding whether or not to ask for a jury trial. Since the right to ask for a jury on that basis is at present unquestioned in cases of simple or moderate difficulty, both in the civil and criminal courts, to remove the right of jury in cases deemed complex deprives those litigants of an important right that others continue to possess. And where is due process then?

Not all those who worry about the ability of the average juror to understand a complex case believe such cases should be turned over to the exclusive jurisdiction of judges. Their preferred mode for deciding such matters is to have them heard by specially qualified jurors,[76] "of figure and fortune," as they were sometimes called in England,[77] who would either serve in the normal fashion or as some sort of administrative body in a courtroom setting.[78] Such "blue-ribbon" panels[79] have been permitted from time to time[80] in state courts,[81] although the United States Rules of Civil Procedure forbids them at present in federal court where litigants are guaranteed random selection of jurors with literacy the only educational test.[82]

Assuming the random selection problem can be licked, we are then faced with determining appropriate standards for our blue-ribboners. In a complex patent case, for example, we may want our jury to consist only of inventors. In a case involving corporations, we may want corporate executives because only they understand the business. However, if we do that, we again have a due process problem. An inventor who thinks a valuable idea has been stolen will argue a fair trial is impossible from a panel consisting of other inventors who may earn all or most of their living from the kind of corporation that is being sued. Similarly, those who see themselves as the victims of sharp business practices are hardly likely to agree they will get due process from a special jury consisting of business executives, some of whom are successful because of their sharp practices. A related suggestion—the "introductory" jury of experts to determine if a violation has occurred, and if they say there has, a lay jury to determine damages[83]—suffers from the same drawback.

If such narrowly qualified jurors present an insurmountable fairness problem, then possibly we can work out a more generalized test to find people competent to hear complex cases. But what qualifications shall we look for? A certain minimal IQ? a prodigious memory? A minimal education level,[84] be it BA, M.A., or PhD? And might we not want a *few* jurors who have at least *some* working knowledge of the technical subject of the suit, for instance, computers?[85]

As these questions suggest, there are criteria problems; however, since we Americans are, as Lincoln Steffens once said, an inventive people, let us assume we can develop a formula that will unfailingly produce jurors who meet the standards that we have established. Thereby, we have corraled the brightest and the best individuals, but does that mean we have also corraled the best and brightest jurors? Perhaps not.[86] From Chapter Three, it will be recalled that jury studies indicate that homogeneous panels—those of like backgrounds and abilities—may be less adept at reaching reasonable verdicts than are the heterogeneous ones. The latter bring to the decision-making process a rich mix of points of view, of life experiences, and are more likely than the homogeneous jury to recognize and offset one another's biases. Pretesting jurors for capacity to understand complex evidence also fails to take into consideration that one of the prime duties of every juror, in simple cases or hard, is to assess the demeanor and credibility of witnesses; there is no way to pretest for this ability.

Still another way to get better qualified jurors for complex cases, it has been suggested[87] is to pay them more money, up to $1,000 a week.[88] By doing this, our better-educated and more successful people will supposedly have no basis for seeking exemptions from jury service based on financial hardship. Whether this would happen is far from certain; for many such people, it is not the pay that jurors get that is the relevant consideration, but rather their fear that while they are away from the office on jury duty some rival will get a jump on them. What does seem certain is that such a reform would attract the poor and unsuccessful to jury duty in record numbers, with the "truly needy," as they have sometimes been referred to, probably clamoring in the streets to express their good citizenship by serving on complex-case panels. A more conservative means of making it sometimes possible to attract better-educated and more successful people to jury duty in complex cases, would be to require their employers to pay their salaries while serving. Many companies already voluntarily do this[89] when any employee is called for jury duty, and—in terms of obtaining representativeness on the venire—it is a practice much to be encouraged, regardless of whether the case is complex or simple, civil or criminal.

In discussing these alternatives, we have been ignoring the underlying premise of the complexity-exception argument, namely, that the average person lacks the ability to understand complex cases, while judges, as the Third Circuit Court of Appeals declared in Japanese Electronics,[90] can understand them because of their superior intelligence.

When we turn to the literature on the comparable abilities of juries and judges, we find that, contrary to the Third Circuit's view, a significant number of students of the jury system, including judges, have concluded that not only are judges not necessarily better triers of fact in complex cases but that jurors are at least as capable and perhaps more so.[91] Kalven and Zeisel discovered in their studies that juries performed at the same high level in cases that judges thought were "difficult to understand" as they did in simpler ones.[92] Since Kalven and Zeisel, however, were dealing only with criminal cases, which aren't the concern of the complexity-exception advocates, more pertinent perhaps is the comment of the judge in a civil case of such inordinate difficulty that it required 14 months to try. He discovered its jury was able to understand the evidence, evaluate the exhibits, and follow the law even though the members were largely housewives, clerks, unemployed and retired people, only two of whom had attended college,[93] suggesting that the common people may be more intelligent than the uncommon people give them credit for being.

Of the same mind was Judge John J. Gibbons who, in his dissent to the Third Circuit ruling in Japanese Electronics, observed that he could not conceive of a case that would be comprehensible to a judge that would be too difficult for a jury.[94] Judge J. Blaine Anderson, the author of the opinion that overturned Turrentine in the USF case, expanded on the thought: ''Although judges are lawyers,'' he wrote, ''they generally do not have any more training or understanding of computer technology or economics than the average juror. Whether a case involves computer technology, aircraft design, or accounting, attorneys must still educate the uninitiated about the matter presented in their case. While we express great confidence in the abilities of judges, no one has yet demonstrated how one judge can be a superior fact-finder to the knowledge and experience that citizen jurors bring to bear on a case. We do not accept the underlying premise of the appellee's argument, 'that a single judge is brighter than the jurors collectively functioning together.'''[95]

Hamilton's enemy, Thomas Jefferson, put the same thought more pithily when he said the ''common sense of twelve honest men gives a still better chance of just decision'' than any other trial method yet devised.[96]

Becker, who was subsequently elevated to the bench that overruled him (leading one to wonder what the result would have been if the Japanese Electronics matter had been argued a few years later), agrees with Jefferson. ''Our view,'' he has written, ''is that a jury, applying the collective wisdom, judgment and common sense to the facts of a case . . . is brighter, more astute, and more perceptive than a single judge, even in a complex and technical case; at the least it is not less so.''[97] A complementary comment from a different perspective comes from Harold Kohn, perhaps the nation's premier trial lawyer in antitrust litigation,[98] who says that it has been his experience that juror ''biases blend so that they end with fewer prejudices about the case than the lawyers or the judge who wants to keep to his point of view and may become biased for that reason.''[99]

The equal or superior quality of performance by jurors compared to judges in many complex matters, as noted by Becker and others, may arise, in part, from the probability that evidence in a complex case will be presented more understandably before a jury than at a bench trial. As a federal court judge in Texas, Patrick Higginbotham, has noted: ''Both the 'technical' and the 'big' case arguments overlook an enormously valuable contribution made by the presence of a jury. The process of distilling complex materials into a comprehensible form operates less effectively in bench trials than in jury trials. Although the rules of evidence purport to discipline an advocate's presentation, they are generally only loosely followed in bench trials, on the assumption that the trial judge will consider only admissible evidence. I have found that as counsel drop their evidentiary antennae they also tend to lose their sensitivity to questions of relevance; correspondingly, the marshaling of proof so essential to clarity suffers. Trial to a jury imposes a fierce discipline on the advocates. The virtue of forcing counsel to organize a complex mass of information into a form understandable to the uninitiated is that counsel ultimately must understand the issues and evidence in the case well enough to teach. If counsel cannot comprehensibly present their case to lay persons, is it likely that counsel do, in fact, understand the case? One need only view how trials of complicated matters are conducted by able counsel to appreciate the powerful contribution that the presence of a jury makes to clarity of argumentation. The jury's presence not only encourages the clear presentation of facts during a trial, but the process of drafting the [judge's] charge also contributes to the clarification of the controlling legal issues. When properly designed and freed of obscure 'legalese,' the charge enhances understanding by the court and counsel, as well as by the jury."[100] A federal court judge in Illinois came to much the same conclusion when he observed that before lawyers start complaining that their cases are too difficult for a jury to understand, they should first consider whether the real problem is not their own inferior abilities in presenting their arguments to juries.[101]

Perhaps not always. A case can occur which is so complicated that neither a judge nor a jury (or, for that matter, the contesting lawyers and their clients) can understand it. In that event, the judge's supposed superior intelligence is of no moment, and the jury remains the preferable forum, since, even though it will be as bewildered as everyone else, by permitting it we are upholding the Seventh Amendment's implicit purpose of bringing the community's sense of fairness into play; for that reason, its guess may be better than the judge's[102] and could not be worse. The occasional case of this kind—incomprehensible to any rational person under existent law—may be inappropriate to adjudication and should be placed before a legislative body[103] where rationality has never been a necessary criterion for solving anything.

A practical reason also exists for continuing to permit juries in complex cases. Because lawyers consider jurors more unpredictable than judges, whenever one side demands a jury, the chances immediately improve that the parties on both sides will move to settle the case.[104] Consequently, as we noted in Chapter Six, by forbidding juries, we may only succeed in adding to the number of lengthy and difficult trials on the court docket, a particular problem in federal court, where most of these matters are filed and which is already overburdened with cases.

II

Despite the urgency with which they present their various arguments for a complexity-exception to the Seventh Amendment, the advocates are hard put to find examples of complex cases that juries couldn't handle quite well.

Only one case has regularly been cited to prove jury incapacity. Called *ILC Peripherals v. IBM*,[105] it was heard in California in 1978. For it, both sides admitted that the evidence was complex, and the trial, after a five-month duration, ended in a hung jury. Afterward, the judge questioned each member of the jury lengthily, leading him to conclude that the case was too difficult for any jury to understand. He then issued a directed verdict for IBM and ordered that, if the matter were to be retried, it would have to be in equity. In support of his position, the judge quoted the foreman of the jury as saying, "If you could find a jury that's both a computer technician, a lawyer, an economist, knows all about that stuff, yes, I think you could have a qualified juror, but we don't know anything about that."[106] But when we turn to the transcript,[107] we find another juror, not quoted by the judge in his opinion, who says: "Yes, I feel that a jury definitely can decide a case like this. I think that we were very close and it's really tragic that we didn't . . ."[108] The jury, in fact, contrary to the judge's view of the case, had stood nine to two in favor of ILC.[109] In general, the jurors felt they had no trouble understanding the facts;[110] their problem, rather, was with the judge's instructions, which some found confusing.[111] The case, therefore, that is supposed to prove jury incompetency in complex cases may only demonstrate the problems created by overly complex instructions on the law in such cases.

The single significant research study designed to assay the abilities of juries in complicated cases was published in 1981 by the Federal Judicial Center of the United States Supreme Court. The direction of the research was "guided," the authors say, by concerns expressed by then Chief Justice Burger in an August 1979 speech to the conference of State Chief Justices. In that address, Burger asserted that "the masses of complicated technical information adduced [in complex trials], combined with the often difficult legal issues involved, strain the abilities of the juries to find the facts competently." Echoing Hamilton he also expressed his worry "about the fairness of requiring citizens to serve for extended durations" as jurors.[112]

Turrentine, as we have seen, also raised the duration issue, just as have others who purportedly worry about people losing income or career advancement due to lengthy jury duty. For example, the Third Circuit Court of Appeals in *Japanese Electronics* observed that the "long time periods required for most complex cases are especially disabling for a jury."[113] Exactly what constitutes a "long time" is as subjective a definition as "complex" itself, but the fact is that hardly any cases, complex or not, last anywhere close to the year projected for Japanese Electronics. In 1980, the most recent year for which figures are available, the longest civil jury trial in federal court was 132 days and the second longest 94.[114] Altogether, only 53, or 1.3%, of all civil jury cases that year lasted 20 days or more.[115]

The duration argument, therefore, appears to be one in which the extraordinary rare case is treated as the norm, since that is the only way any "evidence" can be created to support it. Using such evidence, the jury's opponents can piously urge its abandonment on purely humanitarian grounds. A Maine judge goes even further; he would abolish the jury on the basis that it is a violation of people's civil rights to ask them to serve on one.[116] Either way, the jury is to be destroyed for the sake of the jurors.

We can predict the conclusions that the Federal Judicial Center was expected to reach on both the complexity and hardship issues when we learn that it was to submit its report to the Subcommittee on Possible Alternatives to Jury Trials in Protracted Cases, the creature of a mandate by the Chief Justice and the Judicial Conference of the United States "to consider possible alternatives to lay jurors as fact finders in lengthy, complex trials."[117] If the advocates of the complexity-exception were ever to find documentation for their beliefs, no more likely source can be imagined than the research that followed by the Federal Judicial Center.

Right from the outset, however, the Center had a problem, the same one that advocates of the exception rule always try to avoid facing, namely: When is a case complex? "The terms *protraction* and *complexity* have multiple, ambiguous meanings as applied to civil trials," the Center's authors admitted with an organizational sigh.[118] (If a problem can't be defined, how research it?) In fact, in a section entitled "Definitions of Protraction and Complexity," no definition is ultimately even attempted by the Judicial Center for complexity,[119] though an arbitrary one is assigned to protracted, i.e., any case which requires more than 19 days or more than 100 hours of trial time. The inference from the section is that a relationship exists between difficulty and length of trial, but that is not necessarily so. Voluminous testimony will lengthen a trial and could complicate the issues, but it could also, in the end, simplify them. Other cases become lengthy, not because they are complex but because of the time taken to argue admissibility of evidence.

Recognizing the problems, the Center's investigators interviewed judges and lawyers who had participated in the 17 protracted trials that had been selected for study, seven of which were decided by a jury. (Considering the purpose of the subcommittee and the report, the jury sample is astonishingly small.) The interviewees were asked if their cases contained complex issues. On that, in five of the seven jury trials, disagreement was widespread,[120] with plaintiff lawyers most likely to say the matter wasn't complex, and defense lawyers and judges saying that it was.

Although, as a result of these interviews, the complexity definition remained as elusive as ever,[121] not all was lost. The research had produced by its own definition long trials and those which, if only by a majority vote, had difficult evidence problems. Consequently, it seemed possible to show, for this small number of cases anyway, that at least some of the time it was difficult to find jurors willing to serve in such lengthy proceedings and that those who were selected sometimes couldn't understand them. Since the Chief Justice identified these as the two prime areas for investigation, one would expect that the major portion of the report would be devoted to them.

That did not happen.

The research on the juror hardship issue rated but a single brief mention within a paragraph as a sub-subject of an entirely different topic.[122] This remarkable tucking-away may perhaps be explained by the fact that the findings were the opposite of what the study was supposed to prove. Instead of learning it was difficult to get jurors to serve on panels for what they were told would be lengthy cases, the investigators found that "the voir dire examinations and challenges were always accomplished rapidly, that is, within a day or two."[123] The efficiency was achieved even though several judges, without further inquiry, excused any jurors who said the service would be difficult for them. The ease with which it was possible to obtain jurors for protracted and complex cases may be explained by Kohn's observation[124] that, for many people, serving on a jury of this kind is an exciting and challenging experience, something new in their lives, and, therefore, something they want to do, Burger's beliefs to the contrary.

As embarrassing as the hardship data were to the Burger cause, they were not central to it. Competency was. That was really why the study had been undertaken, to help prove there was a need "to consider . . . alternatives to lay jurors . . . in lengthy, complex trials."

The study, however, does not devote a single one of its 39 sections, much less one of its 11 chapters, to the competency issue. Rather, in 96 pages just three sentences deal with that aspect of its research. The probable reason: Once again, the data derived were directly contrary to what the investigators were supposed to find.

The first reference occurs on page ix of the Executive Summary where we read: "Judges and lawyers were uniformly complimentary of the diligence of the juries. With slightly less consensus, they also affirmed the validity of the juries' deliberative processes." The first sentence has no qualitative meaning—diligence and competence aren't necessarily related—while the second is a little masterpiece of bureaucratese. It is not until we get to Chapter Four, "The Difficulty of the Legal Issues," that we get our second reference: "Almost without exception, respondents who acknowledged the existence of difficult issues in their jury trials also mentioned explicitly that *the jury had made the correct decision or that the jury had no difficulty applying the legal standards to the facts*."[125] (Italics added.) From that, the discussion goes on to a different point, never to return to the prime purpose of the study.

III

That juries apparently have "valid" "deliberative processes" even in complex cases does not mean that their jobs couldn't be made easier for them, and the likelihood of reasonable verdicts further increased.

A number of ideas have been offered—and many have been implemented by judges—with that goal in mind.

As judges know, the best time to begin to simplify is before there is a jury, and the best place to begin is with the paper mountain. Neither the most brilliant of juries nor the most awesomely talented of judges can be expected to understand, much less retain, all the information contained in millions of documents, a feature in both the USF and Japanese Electronics suits. If it were necessary to do so, if each piece of paper were part of a mosaic and failure to grasp one item made it impossible to understand the meaning of all others, and if each piece of paper itself were open to multiple nuances of interpretation of the most intricate financial or technical nature, no fact finder could reach the right decision other than by luck.

Fortunately for the sanity of all concerned, the paper mountains that accumulate in cases like USF and Japanese Electronics invariably contain huge chunks of material that are, at best, peripheral to the key issues of the suit. Much of the paper is engendered by depositions of claimants and cross-claimants, prime and secondary defendants, the depositions themselves frequently accompanied by appendices in the form of supporting documents. The depositions of key players, in turn, suggest to the information-gathering lawyers the names of others who could be questioned, and they, in turn, still others, so that eventually the most minor of spear-carriers might find himself or herself undergoing weeks of pretrial grilling. Although a rationale can no doubt be offered for each deposition by the lawyer who orders it, the resultant "waves of discovery"[126] seem primarily engaged in by major corporate defendants that have been sued by an individual or a small company; defendants in these circumstances expect that the cost of all the pretrial accumulation of paper will eventually force the plaintiff to drop the case because it has become financially impossible to pursue it any longer.[127] Strategy, therefore, and not any pursuit of the truth, can create the slag that makes up much of the mountain.

Lawyers' own financial self-interest can also be involved. The defense attorneys are billing their clients each time they look at the case, and the longer they look, the more they make at rates that can range between $200 and $600 an hour. The plaintiff attorneys would seem to have no motive to protract pretrial discovery, since they get paid only if they win and then as a percentage of the award, not by the hours they put in. However, piling up paper can also serve their purpose when, as will happen in certain types of complex litigation, and as is the rule in certain courts, the percentage they receive is determined by the judge, who will often go by the number of hours the plaintiff lawyer submits, whether all those hours were necessary or not.[128]

The wise judge knows how cases are built and does something about it by riding close herd during the pretrial stage. A number of judges are quite skilled in this art, which may involve selective lawyer head-knocking or—as occasionally is done—sidestepping the lawyers and bringing into conference the chief executives of the corporations involved in the suits. Such meetings not only help the judge understand the issues of the case better but have been known to result in settlements.[129]

Simplification can be brought about in many ways. By learning the issues that aren't disputed or which can be defined and by encouraging stipulations to them, the judge cuts off one wasteful area of deposition-hunting as well as later lengthy trial testimony. For example, in an antitrust case, the economic nature of the market in question could be agreed upon by the parties, although whether the defense violated it remains a jury issue.[130] The wise judge is also alert to the various counterclaims which often do more to confuse the case than any other single factor, as they did in USF.[131] When the judge has spied out this problem he or she can sever the cross claims from the principal trial,[132] letting them be tried later if the verdict in the principal case has not made the secondary issues moot. The federal Manual for Complex Litigation puts it this way: "[T]here are no inherently protracted cases, only cases that are unnecessarily protracted by inefficient procedures and management."[133]

Even when the paper slag has been swept away, many cases, as they reach trial, still retain complex legal and fact issues, with even the undisputed facts open to varying interpretations. This doesn't mean, however, that the end of simplification has been reached.

At this point, a judge may be able to obtain agreement among the parties as to which of the remaining issues are key to the case. If so, it may then become possible to present the evidence on each issue as a unit, with the jury retiring and rendering its verdict on it. In this way, lesser and later issues may be eliminated, since the core verdicts make it unnecessary to try them.[134] As a result, what had seemed in prospect a case of enormous complexity has become relatively straightforward.[135]

Other virtues have been perceived for the issue-by-issue approach. Theoretically, as each verdict is rendered, the contesting lawyers obtain a sense of the factors the jury considers important in the case and are better able to organize the material that comes next. Thus, the case is further simplified, the evidence more effectively presented, the trial shortened. The technique also acts as a device to warn the judge when there may be a problem with the jury. Should the jury's verdict on an issue, for example, be completely contrary to undisputed evidence that has been presented, the judge can then reverse the verdict on that point,[136] most likely causing a mistrial. Should that be necessary, it is better it occur early than after weeks or months of trial, when years of appeals would be virtually inevitable.[137]

Issue-by-issue verdicts, however, mean that in many cases the jury never has the opportunity to hear the evidence in its totality. Thus, if the plaintiff fails to prevail on issue number one, it may never be able to present issue number two which, if the jury heard it, might make it reflect further on issue one. In that sense, the issue-by-issue approach is essentially a pro-defense device, since it need win only once to win the entire case.[138] Under a proposal by the legal scholar Lempert, the jury would still retire to reach issue verdicts, but the verdicts would be considered tentative rather than final, with the jury, at the trial's conclusion, allowed to reverse any early verdict which it has decided on the basis of later evidence to be improper.[139] In this fashion, all the virtues of the issue-by-issue approach are maintained and the pro-defense inequity is removed.

Other methods have also been employed to make the jurors' task easier, and a reasonable verdict more likely. Often, a neutral lawyer is appointed as a master to provide the jury with simple language interpretations of the facts.[140] The master's report, which is admissible as evidence,[141] carries with it, however, the danger of confusing rather than easing the jurors' task, since it provides them with still one more block of information that they have to consider on top of everything they are hearing from the judge, from the lawyers, and from the witnesses.[142] Questions have also been raised about the competency and qualifications of some of those who are appointed as masters.[143]

To further help jurors in antitrust or other complex commercial litigation, a judge will occasionally appoint an expert witness to tell them about standard practices in the business in question. This sounds like a fine idea. From the testimony, the jury can learn what should have taken place and compare that with what did take place. There's a problem, however. Most businesses are dominated by a single corporation, so that the people knowledgeable in the field have almost invariably been trained by or influenced by that corporation's procedures, and either accept them or oppose them. A judge's expert witness who is neutral in appearance but not in reality can improperly influence the outcome of the trial,[144] since a jury is likely to give great credence to that person's testimony.

Some of the suggestions that have been offered to improve the conduct of ordinary cases may be particularly appropriate for complicated ones. Permitting jurors to take notes, according to several studies,[145] may be especially beneficial. Further, although there is considerably less unanimity about this proposition, it might occasionally be wise to allow jurors to ask questions.[146]

One observer thinks this procedure would be especially helpful to jurors when they need clarification of highly technical information offered by an expert witness.[147]

Offering the jurors instruction on the law at the beginning of the trial as well as at its end has already been widely adopted in protracted cases in federal court,[148] and several analysts have urged that, in very lengthy cases, jurors should be given instructions regularly or daily.[149]

The danger of this reform is that it can lead the judge to over-direct jurors toward certain kinds of evidence that he or she considers relevant and away from testimony that the jurors otherwise might have found meaningful, an improper impingement on the jury's independent fact-finding mission.[150]

Regardless of how they feel about early instructions, judges in complex cases will usually give the jurors a copy of the final instructions to take into the deliberation room with them,[151] and some think that a videotape of the speech would be even more useful,[152] so that jurors gain the benefit of the judge's inflections to help them understand the language. Although this variation may have some merit, if the judge is verbose or fond of intellectually deadening syntax, subjecting jurors to a repeat performance by videotape could at times come under the heading of cruel and unusual punishment. Adoption of simplified wording for the instructions might be of greater benefit,[153] and of greater benefit still a requirement that judges take lessons in writing expository prose.

It has also been proposed that at the end of each day's session, the jury be given a transcript of the proceedings which, presumably, out of an excess of zeal, they'll read before they go to bed that night.[154] Another helpful idea is to permit lawyers to summarize—very briefly—their view of the material covered during that day, or perhaps subject-by-subject.[155] The jury's understanding might further benefit if, prior to the testimony of a witness who is going to delve into highly technical areas, the lawyer explains in simple language the ground that is going to be covered.[156]

Not all technical evidence, however, is relevant; some of it is introduced for the sole purpose of confusing the jury,[157] and the wise judge will always be on the alert for such excursions into obfuscation. In federal court, where almost all these cases are heard, judges have a weapon, too, in the form of Rule 403 of the Federal Rules of Evidence,[158] which allows them to put a stop to such ploys. Some judges, federal and state, attempt to reduce the amount of irrelevant evidence by the simple expediency of limiting the number of hours each side has to present its case,[159] although in so doing unfairness could result when one side may legitimately require more time than the other.[160] Quite apart from discouraging introduction of deliberately misleading testimony, the time limit has the considerable benefit of encouraging more forthright and understandable presentations of the evidence and relieves the jury of the tedium, which can itself be confusing, of hearing the lawyers involved luxuriate in making the same point over and over again, an all too common occurrence when no one has a stopwatch on them. There's a practical reason for all this redundancy: Lawyers who charge by the hour churn added profits for themselves and their firms to the extent they can get away with arguing minor points of the law and introducing deliberately lengthy and repetitious testimony.[161]

At least two scholars[162] think jurors should be given training sessions on how to understand complex cases, with the foreperson offered special instructions for conducting deliberations. In the hands of an intrusive or manipulative judge, the training could become indoctrination. However, should such sessions be limited purely to organization of the deliberations[163]—e.g., evidence first, verdict preferences later—probably no harm would be done and possibly some good.

One other reform might be worth some consideration. In altogether too many courts, executives and members of learned professions are too readily excused from jury duty. If we are really concerned about the ability of jurors to understand complex issues, routinely exempting that segment of the community hardly seems a helpful practice.

IV

The complexity-exception argument, fraught though it is with legal weaknesses and an inability to prove the existence of the problem it alleges, nevertheless has strategic significance to those who mistrust the civil jury system. From Hamilton through to Burger, they have been prevented from having their way due to the high esteem in which most Americans hold their right to jury trial. Because of that regard, to attempt to repeal the Seventh Amendment, using constitutionally-approved means that would call attention to what was being done, has always seemed doomed to failure.

The complexity argument provides a means to accomplish covertly what cannot be done overtly. The very failure of the argument to define itself then becomes its greatest strength, since, if we don't know what complexity is, it can be almost anything. Thus, Turrentine perceives "boring" testimony as a factor of complexity, while other judges will have their own "nebulous criteria," as Sperlich has observed.[164] Much of the "complexity" is, in fact, promoted by lawyers who busy themselves manufacturing complexity issues where none exist solely because they're afraid of what will happen if a jury gets a look at what their client has done.[165]

The result, Judge Anderson declared in the USF opinion, is that "[o]nce we open the door, it would be difficult to keep it partially open."[166] Of the same thought is Judge Gibbons who has warned that should trial judges be given the power to refuse the right to jury, very few appeals courts would overturn them when they did so, nor would the upper courts be likely to reverse a decision in a case if denial of a jury were the only grounds for doing so.[167] The Seventh Amendment is then destroyed, by erosion and not repeal.

At the heart of the complexity-exception argument—and, if successful with civil, it could be applied to criminal cases, too, on due process grounds[168]—resides a dread of lay people doing justice as they see it. However, the justice rendered by juries, in cases complex and simple, has made unique and lasting contributions to our society. They are the subject of our final chapter.

Chapter 9
Jury Justice

"Law and Justice," the legal scholar John H. Wigmore once wrote,[1] "are from time to time inevitably in conflict. That is because law is a general rule (even the stated exceptions are general exceptions); while justice is the fairness of this precise case under *all* its circumstances."

When the law and justice diverge, "everyone," Wigmore says, "knows [it] . . . But the trouble is that the Law cannot concede it: Law—the rule—must be enforced—the exact terms of the rule, justice or no justice." The judge, because sworn to uphold the law, must "apply [it] as he finds it alike for all." In fact, Wigmore goes on, "the whole basis of our general confidence in the judge rests on our experience that we can rely on him for the law as it is. But, this being so, the repeated instances of hardship and injustice that are bound to occur in the judge's ruling will in the long run injure the same public confidence in justice, and bring odium on the law. We want justice, and we think we are going to get it through 'the law,' and when we do not, we blame 'the law.'"

"Now this," Wigmore adds, "is where the jury comes in."

I

The jury, for example, "comes in" in these two hypothetical cases: In the first, we have Mr. Jones who subjects his neighbor Mr. Brown and his family to a campaign of vicious verbal harassment, as a result of which Brown, in frustration, finally punches Jones who has Brown arrested. In the second, Mrs. Smith buys a set of living room furniture for which, by the terms of her agreement, she must continue making payments or else lose her home; when the furniture begins to fall apart within a month of purchase, Mrs. Smith stops paying and the furniture company sues her.

The essence of the law is found in these two cases—violence is to be proscribed, the sanctity of contracts upheld—and a judge, as Wigmore points out, would have to find against both defendants. Juries, however, from *Bushel's Case* onward, have had the right to ignore the law when they think it will create an injustice, and we will assume that in our two cases, their verdicts favor Mr. Brown and Mrs. Smith. In that event, the juries will have acted in a way that Wigmore would applaud. They have seen it as wrong that Brown go to jail for punching Jones who was the instigator, and they have found it equally wrong that Smith lose her house over furniture that fell apart within a month of purchase.

When a jury, as in Brown and Smith, deliberately does not apply the law the judge has said is governing, it is often described as having engaged in an act of "jury nullification."[2] Despite its routine usage in law-journal prose, the phrase is both inaccurate and improperly pejorative. Its origin can be found in the discredited doctrine adopted in South Carolina in 1832 which held that sections of the United States Constitution contrary to those of state law did not have to be obeyed. As a legal concept, nullification, therefore, is hierarchical in intent: A set of superior laws voids and replaces inferior ones, although the inferior laws that have not been replaced by superior ones remain in effect. Juries do not do substituting of that kind; they do not declare one law inferior to another, nor can they void a law. In the courts only judges can void a law by declaring it unconstitutional.

Even if we were to distort the meaning of "nullification" to cover only those instances in which a jury rejects a law in order to reach what it sees as an equitable result, the term is still an inadequate one. In many cases, probably the large majority of them, the judge gives the jury descriptions of a number of laws which can be applied depending on what the jurors find the facts to be. When that occurs, a jury doesn't have to reject *the* law to make its feelings known but rather can select *a* law that most nearly fits its sense of right and wrong in the case.

The law selected may not have been the one the judge would have preferred, may not technically fit the evidence, but the jury has rejected a law only in the narrow sense that it has chosen another; the one it has rejected remains in effect.

As an alternative to nullification, *conscience verdict* occasionally turns up in legal writing and is preferable because it, at least, contains the idea of ethical concern as the basis of such a decision. Better is *jury justice,* since it incorporates not only the Wigmorean "conscience" situation but also the role that juries play in creating concepts of permissible and impermissible conduct in our society.

In the discussion of jury justice that follows, the focus will first be on its basis in the law, the conditions in which it is likely to be invoked, and the reason it is viewed with fear and loathing in certain quarters. We will then turn to jury justice as an instrument of the people to invoke changes in public policy and private conduct.

II

The jury's right to refuse to apply a law[3] has been perceived as the main reason for its existence. Supreme Court Justice Byron White took that view in his opinion in *Duncan v. Louisiana*: "Providing an accused with the right to be tried by a jury of his peers gave him an inestimable safeguard," White pointed out, "against the corrupt or overzealous prosecutor and against the compliant, biased or eccentric judge . . . Fear of unchecked power . . . found expression in the criminal law in this insistence upon community participation in the determination of guilt or innocence. The deep commitment of the Nation to the right of jury trial . . . as a defense against arbitrary law enforcement qualifies for protection under the Due Process Clause of the Fourteenth Amendment, and must therefore be respected by the States."[4]

Closely coupled with the jury's watchdog role is its recognized right to be merciful. As the United States Ninth Circuit Court of Appeals put it in a 1979 case: "The jury has always exercised the pardoning power, *notwithstanding the law*, which is their actual prerogative."[5] (Italics added.)

As firmly established as is their right to reject the law, for whatever reason, most people who have served on juries will probably be surprised to learn they can do so. Here, for example, is what California jurors are told at the end of a trial about the limitations of their powers, in wording quite similar to that used in other states: "Ladies and Gentlemen of the Jury," the California judge says, "[i]t becomes my duty as judge to instruct you concerning the law applicable to this case, and *it is your duty as jurors to follow the law as I shall state it to you* . . . The law forbids you to be governed by mere sentiment, conjecture, sympathy, passion, public opinion or public feelings. Both the people and the defendant have a right to demand . . . that you will . . . consider and weigh the evidence and *apply the law* of the case . . ."[6] (Italics added.)

Which leads us to a nice question: How can a right exist when the people who hold the right are told that it doesn't exist?

The answer, to the extent there is an answer, was several hundred years in the making. Justice Vaughan's decision in *Bushel's Case* had been a body blow to the judges, who had assumed they had the power to force juries to obey the law and to throw into jail for contempt those who refused to come up with the verdict that was wanted. Following *Bushel*, judges still instructed on the law and (as we saw in the Zenger case) sometimes continued to tell juries the verdicts they were supposed to reach; however, by the mid-18th century, in both England and the American colonies it was generally conceded[7] that juries were the ultimate determiners of the law in every trial, just as they were of its facts.

However, even then, not everyone perceived the jury's right to interpret the law as unlimited. John Adams, for example, writing in the early 1770s, assumed that juries should follow the judge's explanation of the law, except in cases involving "fundamental principles" of liberty, in which it was not only the juror's "right, but his duty . . . to find the verdict according to his own best understanding, judgment, and conscience, *though in direct opposition to the direction of the court*."[8] (Italics added.)

Twenty-seven years later, when Adams, by then less dedicated to freedom, was President of the United States and had succeeded in enacting the Alien and Sedition Laws, even that repressive legislation specifically stated "the jury who shall try the cause shall have a right to determine the law and the fact . . . as in other cases."[9] When the juries refused to convict, the statutes became unenforceable.

A law passed in 1820 turned out to be the vehicle for reasserting judicial power over the jury.[10] This statute made it a capital offense for an American citizen to "seize any negro or mulatto" with the intent of selling him or her into servitude. In 1835, in a Massachusetts case, the defendant was a sailor who had served on a ship that picked up blacks who were already slaves in Africa and were later sold in the United States. Presiding over the trial was Joseph Story, a member of the United States Supreme Court. (In those days, Supreme Court justices occasionally sat as trial judges.) Story was worried that the jury, in antislavery Massachusetts, would sentence the defendant to be hanged, even though, as Story interpreted the law, it was not intended to cover a person, such as a sailor, who had neither originally enslaved the victims nor had anything directly to do with their sale.[11] To prevent the possible miscarriage of justice, Story told the jury: ". . . I hold it the most sacred constitutional right of every party accused of a crime, that the jury should respond as to the fact, and the court as to the law. It is the duty of the court to instruct the jury as to the law; and it is the duty of the jury to follow the law, as it is laid down by the court."[12] They did.

Slavery was also involved in the next major decision on the subject, in 1851. By then, Congress had passed the Fugitive Slave Act, requiring return of captured runaways to their owners. Throughout the North, the law was regularly defied and prosecutions were brought against those who aided the fugitives. Just as regularly, juries refused to convict. In the 1851 case, which also occurred in Massachusetts,[13] another Supreme Court justice, Benjamin R. Curtis, sitting as a trial judge, took umbrage when the defense attorney told the jurors that they "were rightfully the judges of the law as well as the fact." Interrupting the lawyer, Curtis informed the jurors they were not permitted to decide the law, since that would mean they could even overturn Supreme Court decisions which Congress in 1802 had declared were to be considered final.[14]

Well into the second half of the 19th century, the legal weight of the judge's instructions remained unclear, as increasingly were the instructions themselves, which by then were written almost exclusively for the purpose of withstanding appeals court scrutiny, not to enlighten jurors.[15] Finally, in 1895, Story and Curtis were upheld by the United States Supreme Court in *Sparf and Hansen v. U.S.*,[16] mentioned in Chapter Three as the case that led the way to the practice of rote instructions to juries such as the California one, quoted above. In *Sparf*, the Court declared that since jurors "cannot be allowed to increase the penalties or create laws on their own, they cannot be allowed to reduce such penalties or nullify the law."[17]

Since *Sparf* is the law and has never been overruled, and *Duncan* and similar rulings upholding conscience verdicts are also the law and have never been overturned either, our judges, it would appear, must do some fine intellectual juggling to keep these two opposing concepts from smashing into one another. They have proven capable of doing just that.

Two 1972 cases provide examples. In *U.S. v. Simpson*,[18] the defendant had destroyed draft board files as a protest against the Vietnam War, and his attorney asked the judge to instruct the jurors that they could acquit him, regardless of whether he violated the law, if they decided he shouldn't be punished. The judge refused. When the case got to the Court of Appeals, the panel gracefully noted "how well our society's interests have been served by acquittals resulting from application by the jurors of their collective conscience and sense of justice,"[19] giving the Penn and Zenger cases as examples. After giving that obeisance, the court went on to say that the judge was right in not giving the requested instruction *because jurors already knew they could return a conscience verdict without an instruction*. The second case, *U.S. v. Dougherty*,[20] which had similar facts, reached the District of Columbia Federal Appeals Court where the majority decision described how the "pages of history shine on instances of the jury's exercise of its prerogative to disregard uncontradicted evidence and instructions of the judge"[21] and mentioned Zenger and the Fugitive Slave Act cases as its two examples. The majority opinion, however, then went on to note that the "way the jury operates may be radically altered if there is an alteration in the way it is told to operate."[22] So much for prerogatives. In the annals of judicial hypocrisy, the Simpson and Dougherty cases provide their own shining examples.[23]

In 1973, something quite different occurred. This was another Vietnam War protest case, known formally as *U.S. v. Anderson, et al*,[24] and on the front pages of newspapers as the Camden 28 trial.

There was no doubt the defendants had violated the law. They were caught while destroying records at the Camden, New Jersey, selective service office, encouraged to do so by a government informant, with the FBI secretly supplying the tools to help them commit the act.[25] The federal district judge, Clarkson S. Fisher, allowed the defendants to make statements about their motives, but he also warned the jurors they did not have the right to "nullify" the law. David Kairys, the defendants' lead counsel—they also represented themselves—succeeded in convincing Fisher he was wrong. As a result, Fisher informed the jurors in his charge on the law that they should ignore his earlier comment that they could not give a conscience verdict, adding that "if you find that the overreaching participation by Government agents or informers in the activities as you have heard them here was so fundamentally unfair to be offensive to the basic standards of decency, and shocking to the universal sense of justice, then you may acquit . . ."[26] which is what the jury did.[27]

Those who oppose the concept of jury justice and would seek to curtail it by hiding from jurors their right to practice it, perceive it as a form of anarchy[28] taking place in the very courtrooms where the law is supposed to be supreme, at the hands of the very people selected to administer it. Ours is, after all, or so say these critics, a government of laws not men,[29] and nothing is more likely to create disrespect of the law than to allow jurors to flaunt it.[30] That being so, any injustices that may result from juries blindly obeying the law are an acceptable price for society—including, presumably, the victims of the injustices—to pay.[31]

Those who uphold the supremacy of the law, therefore, do not think it is hypocritical or illegal of judges to tell jurors they are to apply only the law and to ignore their consciences.[32] Neither do those who worry about anarchy find it useful, in developing their thesis, to point out that district attorneys flout the law each time they refuse to prosecute a case in which they have sufficient evidence to convict. Nor, in making their points about juror law-lessness, do they mention that it is an equally acceptable and, indeed, an in-stitutionally encouraged practice, to settle civil cases even though they may involve violations of the criminal as well as the civil law. The legal anarchy argument, rather, is reserved only for that single occasion when lay people are provided their opportunity to evaluate the law.[33] Whether it is meritorious or not, the jury-anarchy position has at its core the same elitism—law as sacrament to be administered exclusively by an endowed priesthood—that pervades the complexity-exception philosophy described in Chapter Eight.

If we find the laws-not-men reasoning less than persuasive, what then of the arguments of those who hold that ours is a society of laws-*and*-men? They say the women and men of juries serve society by adding "common sense,"[34] by moving "where the equities are,"[35] thereby invoking "the conscience of the community"[36] to enforce widely-held views of right and wrong upon the cold proscriptions of the law.

All these phrases have a nice ring to them, but by their subjective nature, each is undefinable and not necessarily benign.[37] What, for example, do we say of the "common sense" in the south that blacks were inferior to whites, and which saw to it that only the white "conscience of the community" was present on its juries? Toward what equities were Hitler and the compliant masses of German people moving when millions of Jews were slaughtered? What, after all, is oppression but the justice of those who have the power to impose it?

From the lessons of history, we thus have cause to worry about the con-science of any community and reason to be cynical about the likelihood of it displaying common sense, or invariably sensing where equities are.

Based on this reasoning, our conundrum is apparently of no mean proportions. For if a law is unjust or will create injustice when applied to a particular case, then the jury's right to reach a conscience verdict can protect us from it. But if we permit that right, and even encourage its expression by explaining it to a jury, we may be allowing into our courts forces that can be as dark with the danger of a lynch mob as those bright with justice.

To test the various premises of the jury-justice debate, we need the answers, if they are to be found, to some questions: First, how often do juries refuse to apply the law or choose the one that meets their moral views rather than that which most nearly fits the evidence? Secondly, when are they most likely to do so? Thirdly, what have been the legal consequences when they do?

Theoretically, we should expect that jurors would rarely refuse to apply the law as given to them, even if they weren't told they had to. Most people agree with most laws, and they don't stop just because they have become jurors.[38] There is good reason this should be so. The overwhelming number of our laws are designed to protect persons and their property from the misconduct of others; for these situations, society after society, including quite disparate ones, have worked out remarkably similar rules, suggesting that basic con-cepts of fair and unfair dealings in personal relationships hold a substantial measure of universal acknowledgment. When applied to particular events, defined as either civil or criminal, these ideas become our *consensus* laws, accepted and acceptable, but occasionally capable of creating an injustice in a specific case. Contrasted to them is imposed or authoritarian law, to which there has been no popular assent. The distinguishing characteristic of imposed law is that its purpose is to carry out an ideological or economic goal that an empowered class feels to be in its interest. The imposition can be accomplished by statute, as with the Fugitive Slave Act, or it can occur by means of judicial reinterpretations of the common law to serve a felt need, as when injured workers in the 19th century were virtually excluded from redress for the sake of industrial expansionism.

Although imposed law can be designedly oppressive (e.g., Hitler's race laws), at other times the empowered class seeks to rectify inequities either out of benevolent intent or as a means of defusing a threat to the domestic tranquillity (e.g., the various civil rights laws of the 1960s). Because, for good reasons or ill, an imposed law seeks to serve a beneficiary class (in a repressive regime very often the government itself), it has the capacity to create animosities and controversy (as did the civil rights laws), whereas consensual law by its nature does not. (When consensual law causes controversy, it is due to a perception of failure to carry out its goals—for example, complaints about ''leniency'' in punishing criminals—not from any philosophical disagreement about the goal itself.) Imposed doctrines, therefore, might be considered the cutting edge of the law; they have the capacity for doing great harm or great good and are typically perceived that way. Consensual law, on the contrary, is both beyond and beneath ideology, the bedrock of regulation designed to make ordinary commerce between ourselves and others reliable and predictable.

Just as there are two types of law, so, therefore, do we have two types of jury rejectionism, the one applied to a consensual law gone astray in a particular case, and the other to the imposed law the jurors consider bad of itself or at least in some part of itself.

Due to jury room secrecy, we have no authoritative way of knowing how often juries react negatively to either kind of law, or, when they do, how often they take action on their feelings. Were we privy to the jurors' debate, we might find that what appears to be rejectionism is nothing more than a misinterpretation of the evidence or a failure to understand the law as it was explained by the judge. (When a verdict contrary to the law is the product of institutionalized racism in the selection of the jury pool, the result is not a form of jury ''justice'' but the product of intentional systemic injustice.[39])

Interviews with jurors after an apparent conscience verdict could confirm its occurrence; jurors, however, may be reluctant to say so and give other reasons for their action, fearing they will get in trouble with the judge should their disobedience of his or her direct order become known. Mock jury studies have proven of little help in ascertaining the frequency of the conscience verdict. They reveal only a few instances in which the subjects even talked about a law being unfair, but the rarity of such events could be due to the artificial nature of the experiment, or, more likely, to the nature of the case they were given to decide. (Our research discovered no instances in which mock jurors were given a case that had ideological implications or involved a consensual statute the application of which might cause an injustice.)

The only significant effort to study the frequency of conscience verdicts was that undertaken by the Chicago Jury Study Project. The judges who answered the questionnaires, it will be recalled, agreed with their juries' verdicts in civil and criminal cases about three-quarters of the time, so that, for starters, there could not have been more than a 25% conscience verdict rate. The study was able to hone in a little closer than that when it discerned that the judges found jury verdicts without legal merit only 9% of the time,[40] a result which, according to the reporting judges, occurred most often when the members were asked to apply ''unpopular''[41] laws. These conclusions, however, must be treated with caution, in part because they deal only with criminal cases—none were offered, on this score, for civil—and in part because of the methodological problems with the study that were described in the Introduction above. Assuming, even so, that the study's results were accurate, we still haven't progressed very far, since they don't tell us how often the jurors knew that they had the prerogative to deliver a conscience verdict. If, as the Simpson opinion assumes, 100% knew and only 5% acted, then we are looking at one phenomenon; but if only 9% knew and 5% acted, then we are looking at another.

The probability is that the figure is nearer 9% than 100%. Pound's phone survey came up with 8%. The reason: When jurors are told they *must* do something by the only person in the courtroom they assume is always telling them the truth—the judge—the probability is that, under this judicial compulsion, they are not very likely to remember John Peter Zenger or similar lessons in freedom they may have learned in their history classes.[42] As one example, in 1968, following another of the war protester cases, several jurors told author Jessica Mitford they would have acquitted the defendants (including Dr. Benjamin Spock) until they were told by the judge what the law was and that they had to apply it.[43]

If deliberate misinformation fed to juries about their right to deliver conscience verdicts inhibits the practice to some substantial degree, we might wonder what happens when they are given accurate information. To try to find that answer, we can look to Maryland and Indiana, the only two states which, in their constitutions, specifically state that juries have the right to determine the law as well as the facts in criminal cases.[44] In Maryland, for instance, the jury is told by the judge that ''. . . whatever I tell you about the law, while it is intended to be helpful to you in reaching a just and proper verdict in the case, it is not binding upon you . . .''[45] Such an instruction should lead, if the jury justice opponents are correct, to a rash of verdicts in which the juries take the law into their own hands and either acquit groundlessly or convict improperly, creating their own laws as they go along. Yet this seems not to have occurred,[46] and ample safeguards exist to see that it doesn't. The judge, in these two states as elsewhere, has the right to decide on admissibility of evidence[47] and can order a directed verdict of acquittal if the prosecution hasn't met its burden of proof; in Maryland, should the jury misapply the law in the judge's view, a guilty verdict will be set aside and a new trial ordered. A 1975 survey of Maryland judges revealed that only 8 of the 44 responding opposed the jury-as-law-interpreter instruction; most thought it should be retained, at least in part because its impact had been so marginal,[48] as we should expect from our analysis of consensual law.

In Indiana, the State Supreme Court has repeatedly held that the jury's right to "decide" the law in a specific case does not mean it has "declared" any law unconstitutional, or that it is defining the meaning of a crime for future cases.[49] In neither state, moreover, need we fear that a jury given a law-interpretation instruction will move a case to a *higher* degree of wrongdoing than the maximum allowed by the law, since, should a jury attempt to do so, its verdict would simply be reversed.[50] We are not considering here the situation in which a jury, perhaps motivated by racial bias or hatred of the crime, finds the highest degree of guilt *legally* permitted, even though the evidence may not merit that; appeal courts exist to rectify that kind of error and—sometimes—they do.

At this point in our discussion, we can reach several conclusions about conscience verdicts, in civil or criminal cases, as an aspect of jury justice. First, because jurors have the right to disregard a law when they think it will work an injustice, the fact that they do so rarely (even when they are told they can) gives the law a popular imprimatur that it would not otherwise have. Secondly, as Justice White points out, jurors foster the legitimacy of the legal system by acting within it to root out official oppression, as they did in the Zenger and Camden 28 cases. Finally, the jury directly serves the law's purpose, in the Wigmorean sense, through its pardoning power, forgiving the sinner without condoning the sin. The English jurist, Mr. Justice Chalmers, rounded out Wigmore's argument when he wrote: ". . . there is an old saying that hard cases make bad law . . . The Judge is anxious to do justice to the particular parties before him. To meet a particular hard case"—such as Mrs. Smith's affair with the avaricious furniture company outlined above—"he is tempted to qualify or engraft an exception upon a sound general principle." Should he do so, Chalmers went on, the result may be that his opinion will distort the meaning of the good law and cause it to create inequities when the opinion is applied to later cases. "But hard cases," Chalmers observed, "tried with a jury do not make bad law, for they make no law at all . . . The legal principle is kept intact while the jury do justice to the particular case by not applying it."[51] In other words, both judges and the law are lucky they have jurors to get them off the hook on the "hard" case.

But juries can do much more than that.

Although they cannot by themselves either make or unmake a law, they are the people's only direct representative within the justice system, and they act through their verdicts as popular reviewers of the law and the social policy issues which the law codifies. Their review decisions can set into motion events that change the law and set boundaries upon permissible conduct.

It need not be a single jury that brings about the transformation; very often, it requires dozens or hundreds of juries dealing with the same issue, perhaps over a period of many years. The accrual effect that multiple juries can have is exemplified by the history of negligence law in the United States. During the 19th century, the refusal of jurors, in case after case, to apply the notorious fellow-servant rule[52] was the major reason leading to its abandonment.[53]

Contributory negligence doctrines, over the years, have similarly and frequently met with juror disapproval.[54] Apparently jurors' sense of fairness told them, despite what judges told them, that since it was wrong to hold a defendant fully liable when the plaintiff was partly at fault, so was it equally wrong to exonerate the defendant—as contributory negligence would have it—when the fault was principally his or hers. In his attack on the jury system in 1949, Frank singled out the refusal of juries to apply contributory negligence as proof of their lawlessness and a sound reason to abolish them.[55] However, the juries apparently are going to have their way. By 1983, contributory negligence had been replaced in 38 states by the comparative rule that reflects traditional juror thinking.[56]

Nevertheless, sometimes a single jury will have a direct impact on law and policy. Its verdict may render a law inoperable, not because the law has been voided by the verdict but because those in power perceive that future prosecutions under it will probably reach the same result (the effect of Zenger on seditious libel). In other instances, it is not directly the verdict but an issue that rises from it that changes the law (as with Bushel's appeal over his incarceration following the Penn trial). At still other times, a single jury will point out such an egregious unfairness in the law that it can no longer be ignored.

That was what happened in *Henningsen v. Bloomfield Motors Inc.*, the 1960 New Jersey case mentioned in Chapter Five. Mr. Henningsen had purchased an automobile and signed the typical privity warranty of the period, which expressly stated that the manufacturer and dealer would be liable only to the buyer for any injuries caused by defects in the car. As it turned out, the car had a faulty steering mechanism which led to a collision while Mrs. Henningsen was driving. When she sued to recover damages for her injury, the defendants pulled out their warranty with Mr. Henningsen's signature to prove they could be held accountable only for injuries to him. The jury disagreed. It ruled, in effect, that such warranties were against public policy, and an appeals court confirmed their interpretation when it upheld the verdict.[57] The jury's action, a clear refutation of the existent law, established the principle that occupants of automobiles now take for granted, namely, that anyone who is in lawful occupancy of a car, be it driver or passenger, has a right to sue the manufacturer when the vehicle malfunctions. Again the jury didn't "make" law—it took the appeals court to do that—but if the jury hadn't acted as it did, the appeals court would not have been confronted by the jury's opinion of what public policy should be, a judgment of popular concern to which the appeals court had to give, and by its ruling did give, great weight.

A jury need not challenge an imposed doctrine—as privity in warranty was—to have a catalytic effect on social conduct. The civil jury has played the dominant role in performing that function since it, unlike the criminal, has an opportunity to observe and assess the processes by which businesses, professions, institutions, and governmental agencies carry out their activities.

The hypothetical case involving Mrs. Smith and the furniture company depicts the civil jury's potential to effect change at its broadest. On the surface, both her civil and Brown's criminal cases appear alike in that their juries rejected a consensual law because it would have worked an injustice. The Brown verdict, indeed, can be viewed as the ideal Wigmore/Chalmers configuration in that the verdict had no consequence beyond itself; it did not suggest that it is all right ordinarily for people to go around punching each other, and no one would read it that way. In Smith, however, the jury was giving a policy signal. It was not challenging the principles of contract law but rather saying that a contract *of the type* that Mrs. Smith signed was unconscionable, and that would be exactly how the furniture company would interpret the verdict. Because of it, the company had a powerful incentive to change the way it worded its contracts, not because it wanted to but because it would realize that once the jury's verdict became generally known in the local legal community, all future trials of cases involving these collection methods would be by jury and have the same likely result. But the effects would probably not end with that one company. Other businesses that had been writing similar contracts would now realize they could no longer get away with them either, and would change their policies. If they didn't, it is quite possible that legislators, learning of the problem through the Smith verdict, would pass a law forbidding contracts of the kind she signed.

The ripple effects of the Smith verdict are not merely hypothetical, as can be discerned in a number of the randomly-chosen civil cases outlined briefly in Chapter Seven. In the Ford Mustang and GM Chevette cases described there, the juries by their awards ($9.3 million and $4.075 million) were not only compensating the plaintiffs but also sending a clear—and deliberately expensive—signal to automobile manufacturers that the public demands cars that are safe to drive. The manufacturers of the exploding Ford Pinto learned the same lesson from a jury. Similarly, in the award to the 60-year-old man ($1.3 million), a jury was not telling just one insurance company but all of them that certain sales practices will not be tolerated by the public when it enters a jury box.

In the numerous cases involving pharmaceutical manufacturers, jurors are telling companies that profits at the expense of customers' well-being are not to be countenanced. Concern for public safety was also apparently behind the huge verdict by an outraged jury in the smoke-alarm case in Philadelphia described in Chapter Five; its $11-million missive reached the city council which passed an ordinance requiring owners of all single and multifamily units in the city to install such devices.[58] Because of a verdict of another civil jury, this one in New York, inflammable cotton flannelette is no longer used as a fabric in children's nightwear.

The role of the jury as policy-changer can also be seen in medical malpractice verdicts which have forced hospitals and doctors to adopt reforms to assure better care for patients. Hospitals, to use just one example, have introduced implement counts following operations, have adopted better methods of communicating test results from their pathology laboratories to their operating rooms, have installed safety devices that make in-hospital accidents, such as falls from beds, more unlikely—all because of jury verdicts.

Civil juries can also act to oppose bigotry and violence. In February 1987, a jury in Alabama found the United Klans of America (KKK) liable for the lynching of a 19-year-old boy and awarded his mother $7 million.[59]

In complex commercial litigation, juries have often sat for months listening as the secrets of business practices are revealed to them. They don't always like what they hear. A Texas jury in 1985 didn't. It assessed $10.53 *billion* in damages against Texaco, Inc., for improperly interfering with a binding merger between Pennzoil Company and Getty Oil, a verdict subsequently upheld by the judge as not excessive. Said the foreman of that jury: "We wanted to send a message to corporate America that they can't get away with this type of action and not be punished."[60]

IV

At the beginning of this book, we referred to the late Justice William O. Douglas's description of the jury as the only agency of government that has no ambition. Unlike others who earn their living from participation in governance and seek advancement in it, jurors' sole purpose is to do their job and then get on with their lives. Most of them are, according to Pound's study, willing to serve. They see jury duty as part of their service as citizens, and afterward they are almost always glad they served. At the least, they have added a new and unusual experience to their lives; at best, they go away fulfilled, sensing that they have helped see justice done.

Sometimes they are wrong in that feeling. Juries can make terrible mistakes in their verdicts. The innocent have been sentenced to death by juries.[61] Litigants have won and wrongly lost large amounts of money because of juror error. (As we have seen, jurors are not always responsible for their bad verdicts. Such can be caused by instructions on the law from the judge that are virtually impossible to understand; by a poor presentation by the lawyer for the side that should have won; by the admission of perjured or deliberately misleading testimony by one side which the other side failed entirely to rebut.)

Since making mistakes is possible in any human enterprise, the relevant question about erroneous jury decisions becomes: Can the mistakes be caught and rectified? In theory, anyway, they can be. In Chapter Seven, we observed that the American justice system has developed a panoply of safeguards to prevent error persisting beyond the verdict. The only mistake that cannot be rectified occurs when a jury (or a judge) finds a person not guilty of a crime that person actually committed; the only way to avoid that is to convict everyone accused without a trial. On the civil side, the system has developed particularly strong brakes to prevent excessively high awards from being paid; however, in many jurisdictions the plaintiff who receives an unduly low award is less protected, and we might recommend that the additor become as universally applied a rule as the remititur.

We also have good reason to believe that juries are, on the whole, remarkably adept as triers of fact. Virtually every study of them, regardless of research method, has reached that conclusion as have, by and large—as we saw in the Introduction and Chapter Four—the professionals who preside over or try jury cases. The capabilities of jurors—perhaps not as individuals but as a group—even appear to extend to cases of the greatest complexity. Critics who think otherwise have not been able to find a single research document or a single case that convincingly backs their view; indeed, the one study that was undertaken to prove that juries *can't* understand complex litigation, the Federal Judicial Center research mentioned in Chapter Eight, found, despite itself, that jurors *could* understand. The burden of proof is on the critics, too; it is they who want to rescind part of the United States Constitution.

Based on the information developed in this book, therefore, we have reason to believe that the jury, as a fact-finding body, generally performs with a substantial degree of competence. Moreover, the civil jury (and this allegation has only been made against the civil jury) does not appear to significantly slow the dispensation of justice, and may speed it, since the prospect of a jury trial causes many litigants to settle their cases, thereby decreasing the backlog. (See Chapter Six.)

Even were we to assume that alternative methods (bench trials, arbitration, mediation) would produce equal or even superior verdicts—and we have no evidentiary basis for thinking that; on the contrary, each alternative produces its own problems—the societal role the jury plays, both in giving popular consent to our laws and as the barking dog against injustice, gives it an importance that transcends the merits, real and imagined, of any replacements for it.

When Justice White wrote of the watchdog function, he was referring to criminal cases where trial by jury is not, at least not yet, under serious attack. The civil jury, on which the attack is both serious and multifaceted, performs, as we have seen in this chapter, a guardian role against oppression that may be even more important. It helps protect us against those who threaten our health and our safety; it sets standards of responsibility and fair-dealing by government and business. Were there no other reasons for maintaining the civil jury's existence, these would be ample.

There is one reason more.

We have given much of our democracy away, sometimes willingly and sometimes not, sometimes out of apparent necessity and sometimes out of convenience, and because we have, we often feel alienated from our representatives whose agendas we may neither understand nor know, helpless in the hands of the bureaucracies we have substituted for our own actions in a society too complex for us to govern, powerless in the hands of great corporations whose profits we hope will benefit us but whose decisions we know we cannot control. But in one place we still have a direct voice and can be heard, and that is through our juries. Because of them, we are still direct participants in our democracy. They have met Thomas Jefferson's expectations of them.

NOTES

INTRODUCTION

1. Alan Scheflin and Jon Van Dyke, "Jury Nullification," *Law & Contemporary Politics*, Vol. 43, No. 4 (1980), p. 113, quoting William O. Douglas, *We the Judges* (1956), p. 389.
2. William V. Luneberg and Mark A. Nordenberg, "Specially Qualified Juries and Expert Nonjury Tribunals," *Virginia Law Review*, Vol. 667 (1981), p. 888, quoting C. Joiner, *Civil Justice and the Law* (1962); Larry Pressler, "Right to Jury Trial," *Trial Magazine*, Vol. 19, No. 9 (1983); Wallace D. Loh, *Social Research in the Judicial Process*, New York: Russell Sage Foundation (1984), p. 42.
3. Harry Kalven, Jr. and Hans Zeisel, *The American Jury*, Chicago: University of Chicago Press (1971), p. 5, quoting 1962-3 Harvard Law School Dean's Report, pp. 5-6. (Hereafter referred to as *American Jury*.)
4. Gordon Bermant et al, *Protracted Civil Trials*, Washington, D.C.: Federal Judicial Center (1981), p. 1; Warren Burger, "Is Our Jury System Working?" *Reader's Digest*, Feb. 1981.
5. *Duncan v. Louisiana*, 391 U.S. 145 (1968).
6. Harris G. Mirkin, "Judicial Review, Jury Review and Right of Revolution Against Despotism," *Polity*, Vol 6. No. 1 (Fall 1973), p. 36; though not always for civil cases, see Edward J. Devitt, "Should Jury Trial be Required in Civil Cases?," *Journal of Air Law & Commerce*, 495, No. 47 (1982), p. 513.
7. Richard B. Morris, *Fair Trial*, New York: Alfred A. Knopf (1953), p. 94.
8. Loh, op. cit., p. 429.
9. Jerome Frank, *Courts on Trial*, Princeton: Princeton University Press (1949), pp. 108-45.
10. *Duncan v. Louisiana*, op. cit., pp. 156-7; Luneberg, op. cit., p. 924.
11. Patrick Devlin, "Equity, Due Process and the Seventh Amendment," *Michigan Law Review*, Vol. 81 (1983), pp. 1571-1638.
12. Devitt, op. cit., p. 507.
13. G. Thomas Munsterman and Janice T. Munsterman, "A Survey of Jurors in Selected Pennsylvania Counties," Williamsburg: Center for Jury Studies, National Center for State Courts (1983), p. 12.

234 THE JURY IN AMERICA

14. Dale W. Broeder, "University of Chicago Jury Project," *Nebraska Law Review*, Vol. 38 (1958), p. 751.
15. *Trial Magazine*, Vol. 20, No. 1 (1984), p. 25.
16. Georgia F. DuPre and Charles F. Myers, "The Jury Sums Up: A Bibliography," *Litigation*, Vol. 7, No. 1 (1980). During the course of writing this book, three such articles appeared in the author's hometown press, one by syndicated columnist Mary McGrory on her favorable experiences as a juror, the other two, also pro-jury, in Philadelphia weeklies; see *Chestnut Hill Local*, June 13, 1985, and *Welcomat*, January 23, 1985.
17. The only direct reference was found in William M. O'Barr, *Linguistic Evidence*, New York: Academic Press (1982), p. 103, and then only because O'Barr coincidentally was called for jury duty while working on his book.
18. Frank, op. cit., pp. 114-15.
19. Loh, op. cit., p. 460.
20. The fascination lies in the fact that juries, unlike other groups, are always given the same task to perform within a formalized structure and similar environments; juries, therefore, theoretically anyway, provide the opportunity to study interactions among people in a milieu in which variables are relatively few.
21. Loh, op. cit., p. 355.
22. *American Jury*, op. cit., pp. 541 ff.
23. The original edition was published by Little, Brown & Company. The 1971 University of Chicago reprint with a new introduction was consulted for this book.
24. If there ever was any doubt about the privacy of jury deliberations, it was settled during the course of the University of Chicago Jury Study Project's research. As part of its program, and with the agreement of judges and counsel but not the jurors, actual deliberations were recorded in five civil cases in the federal district court in Wichita, Kansas. When knowledge of the recordings became public, it led to a public censure of the Project by the Attorney General of the United States, a hearing by a subcommittee of the Senate Judiciary Committee, and passage of statutes in more than 30 states forbidding tapping of juries. See Preface to first edition of *The American Jury*, op. cit., pp. xiv-xv. In 1986, portions of an actual jury deliberation, along with excerpts from the trial, were broadcast on television as part of the *Frontline* documentary series. The film, produced by Stephen J. Herzberg, was made possible by the cooperation of the parties involved, including the jurors. Although the program offered a unique opportunity to observe jurors deliberating (and doing it quite seriously and well), its value is limited by the fact that only about 40 minutes of the deliberations, which lasted more than two hours, were broadcast; it is also possible, though by no means certain, that the content and quality of the deliberations may have been affected by the jurors' awareness that they were being filmed for a program that would be seen by a national audience.

25. *American Jury*, Preface to Second Edition, pp. v-vii.
26. Ibid., p. 35.
27. Ibid., p. 63.
28. Ibid., pp. 46-47.
29. *Duncan v. Louisiana*, op. cit., p. 156; *Williams v. Florida*, 399 U.S. 78, p. 100.
30. John Guinther, "Courtroom Caper Papers," *Philadelphia Magazine*, August 1978.
31. John Guinther, "Better Make a Federal Case of It," *Philadelphia Magazine*, December 1973.
32. *American Jury*, op. cit., pp. 58, 63.
33. Ibid., p. 39.
34. Ibid., pp. 430-3.
35. Jacob D. Fuchsberg, "Court in Session," *New York Times Magazine*, March 1, 1964, p. 2.
36. Reid Hastie, Steven D. Penrod, Nancy Pennington, *Inside the Jury*, Cambridge: Harvard University Press (1983), p. 40.
37. Ibid., p. 39.
38. Malthon M. Anapol, "Behind Locked Doors," *The Barrister*, Vol. 4, No. 4 (1973).
39. Ibid., pp. 2, 9.
40. Ibid., p. 9.
41. Ibid., pp. 9, 11.
42. Broeder, op. cit., p. 753.
43. Amiram Elwork and Bruce Sales, "Jury Instructions," Chapter 11 of *Psychology of Evidence and Courtroom Procedure*, Beverly Hills: Sage (1984), pp. 280-97.
44. Anapol, passim; James H. Davis et al, "The Empirical Study of Decision Processes in Juries," Ch. 26 of June Louin Tapp and Felice J. Levine, *Law, Justice and the Individual in Society*, New York: Holt, Rinehart, Winston (1977), p. 342; Howard S. Erlanger, "Jury Research in America," *Law & Society Review*, Vol. 4, No. 3 (1970), p. 353.
45. Davis, ibid., p. 349; author's interview with Amiram Elwork, 1985.
46. Alice M. Padawer-Singer, "Justice or Judgments?" *American Jury System*, Washington, D.C.: Roscoe Pound Foundation (1977), p. 51.
47. Hastie, op. cit., p. 43.
48. Ibid.
49. Ibid.
50. Davis, op. cit., pp. 327, 333; Joan B. Kessler, "The Social Psychology of Jury Deliberations," Ch. 3 of *The Jury System in America*, Rita James Simon, ed., Beverly Hills: Sage Publications (1975), p. 333; Loh, op. cit., p. 461.
51. Anapol, op. cit., p. 9.
52. Bettyruth Walter-Goldberg, *Jury Summation as Speech Genre*, paper presented at Sociolinguistic Forum 5, University of Liverpool, Sept. 1984, p. 12. In the big-city court system under study, it was rare for a jury to have more than one to two persons who had even a partial

college education, much less were college students. Pound phone survey found only 4% of jurors, regardless of educational attainment, are between 18 and 24.

53. Anapol, loc. cit.
54. Michael Zander, "The Jury in England: Decline and Fall?" *American Jury System*, op. cit., pp. 39-41.
55. Donald Vinson, "Shadow Juries," *Trial Magazine*, Vol. 19, No. 9 (1983), p. 78.
56. Thomas D. Lambros, *Summary Jury Trial & Other Alternative Methods of Dispute Resolution*, Washington, D.C.: Report to the Judicial Conference of the United States (1984), p. i.
57. Ibid., pp. 23-4; Appendix.
58. Ibid., pp. i-ii.
59. Ibid., pp. 3-6.
60. *Report on the First 4 Years*, Santa Monica: Rand Corporation, Institute for Civil Justice (1984), p. 11 (hereafter referred to as *First Four Years*); Mark A. Peterson, *Civil Jury Verdicts in Cook County*, Santa Monica: Rand Corp., Institute for Civil Justice (1984), pp. viii-ix (hereafter referred to as Peterson, *Cook County*). Rand's Institute for Civil Justice has also published other booklets on the Chicago and San Francisco studies which cover the same material footnoted here; they will be annotated individually below.
61. *First Four Years*, op. cit., p. 18.
62. To get at such information would have required an examination of all civil court dockets over a 20-year period. In Chicago, information about jury verdicts was readily at hand through *Cook County Jury Verdict Reporter*, see Peterson/*Cook*, op. cit., p. v.
63. Broeder, op. cit., pp. 747 ff., for a description of the University of Chicago Project efforts in this direction; Walter-Goldberg, op. cit., p. 10 ff., though the study was limited to jurors' views of closing speeches; Munsterman, op. cit., conducted surveys of more than 2,000 jurors but they were not asked about their deliberation processes, pp. 7-13.
64. Broeder, op. cit., pp. 755-56.
65. Ibid., p. 747.
66. In the Pound survey only one juror failed to fill out the in-court questionnaires.
67. Michael J. Saks and Reid Hastie, *Social Psychology in Court*, New York: Van Nostrand Reinhold Co. (1978), pp. 167 ff.

CHAPTER 1

1. Frank, op. cit., pp. 378-9.
2. Hans Zeisel, "The American Jury," in *American Jury System*, op. cit., p. 93.
3. Sir Frederick Pollock and Frederic William Maitland, *The History of English Law*, Cambridge: Cambridge University Press (1895), Vol. 1,

p. 14. Although Pollock's name appears as first author, the work is principally that of Maitland and hereafter will be referred to as *Maitland*. Since each of the two volumes begins with page one, the page references, as necessary, will be distinguished as Maitland 1 or Maitland 2.

4. Maitland 1, p. 16.
5. Ibid., pp. 6-7.
6. Ibid., p. 143.
7. Ibid., p. 27.
8. Ibid., p. 46; Maitland 2, pp. 450-51.
9. Charles Rembar, *Law of the Land*, New York: Simon & Schuster (1980), p. 69.
10. Maitland 2, op. cit., p. 578.
11. Ibid., p. 580.
12. Maitland 1, op. cit., pp. 55-6.
13. Ibid.
14. Ibid., p. 54.
15. Maitland 2, op. cit., p. 471.
16. There were 90 rules in total. Some other examples: No. 4: "If a freeman steal from the king, let him pay 9-fold." No. 10: "If a man lie with the king's maid, let him pay a bot [fine] of L. Shillings." No. 22: "If a man slay another at an open grave, let him pay XX Shillings." See *Ancient Laws and Institutes of England*, London: Commissioners of Public Records of the Kingdom (1840), pp. 2-3.
17. Maitland 1, op. cit., pp. 33, 47.
18. Ibid., pp. 37, 46-7; Rembar, op. cit., p. 98.
19. Maitland 1, op. cit., p. 58.
20. Ibid., p. 482.
21. Loc. cit.; Maitland 2, op. cit., p. 449.
22. Maitland 1, op. cit., p. 478.
23. Ibid.
24. Ibid.
25. *Book of Dooms*, No. 49, in *Ancient Laws*, op. cit., pp. 62 ff.
26. Maitland 1, op. cit., pp. 42-43.
27. Ibid., p. 43.
28. Maitland 2, op. cit., p. 520.
29. Maitland 1, op. cit., pp. 32-33.
30. Ibid., p. 43.
31. Ibid., pp. 634-35.
32. Maitland 2, op. cit., pp. 461-62.
33. Rembar, op. cit., p. 103.
34. Maitland 1, op. cit., p. 52.
35. Maitland 2, op. cit., p. 599.
36. Rembar, op. cit., p. 107.
37. Maitland 2, op. cit., p. 601.
38. Maitland 1, op. cit., p. 39.
39. Maitland 2, op. cit., p. 601.
40. Maitland 1, op. cit., pp. 39, 74.

41. Maitland 2, op. cit., p. 634.
42. Rembar, op. cit., pp. 108-09.
43. O'Barr, op. cit., p. 10.
44. Maitland 1, op. cit., p. 77.
45. Ibid., p. 66.
46. Ibid., pp. 40-1.
47. Ibid., p. 143.
48. *Williams v. Florida*, op. cit., p. 1901.
49. Maitland 1, op. cit., pp. 142-43.
50. W.C. Holdsworth, *History of English Law*, London: Methuen & Co. (1922), Vol. 1, p. 312; Frank, op. cit., p. 108; Maitland 1, p. 140.
51. Ibid., p. 141.
52. Loc. cit.
53. Rembar, op. cit., pp. 117-18.
54. Holdsworth, op. cit., p. 313.
55. Maitland 2, op. cit., p. 642.
56. Maitland 1, op. cit., pp. 40, 114.
57. Rembar, op. cit., p. 73.
58. Winston Churchill, *History of the English-Speaking People*, New York: Dodd, Mead & Co. (1956), Vol. 1, p. 212.
59. Maitland 2, op. cit., p. 189 ff.; Maitland 1, op. cit., pp. 126-8.
60. Ibid., p. 177.
61. The failure was not complete. On a key issue, making clerical appointments when a vacancy occurs, Henry was able to retain that right, despite Becket's and, after his death, Rome's efforts to gain it. The Crown thus held an important patronage weapon over the clergy's head; several hundred years later, this so-called "advowson" right would become the basis of antipapal statutes. See also Maitland 1, op. cit., pp. 125-6.
62. Churchill, op. cit., pp. 216-17.
63. Maitland 1, op. cit., pp. 44-45.
64. It could be profitable for the king too. Fines payable to the king, we learn from the Domesday book, were in place for most crimes that broke "the Peace." For example, he who broke into a city by night had to pay 100 shillings; rape was worth eight shillings, four pence, as was adultery, though in that case both parties had to pay. For a more complete list see Maitland 2, op. cit., pp. 456-57.
65. Ibid., pp. 463-4; Churchill, op. cit., p. 216.
66. Maitland 1, op. cit., p. 203.
67. Rembar, op. cit., p. 143.
68. Churchill, op. cit., pp. 219-20.
69. Maitland 1, op. cit., p. 224.
70. Ibid., pp. 176-7.
71. Ibid., p. 136.
72. Ibid., p. 615; Holdsworth, loc. cit.
73. Maitland 1, op. cit., p. 60.
74. Ibid., p. 145; Holdsworth, loc. cit.; Rembar, op. cit., p. 176.
75. Maitland 1, op. cit., p. 147.

76. Rembar, op. cit., pp. 112-13.
77. Maitland 2, op. cit., p. 636.
78. Ibid., p. 595.
79. Ibid., pp. 625, 628.
80. Morris S. Arnold, *Select Cases from the King's Court, 1307-1399*, London: Selden Society (1985), Vol. 1, p. xxxi; however, by the 13th century at the latest, juries would sometimes ask the judge to rule on the law when they realized they lacked the knowledge to do so, ibid., p. xxi. The judge's greatest power lay in his rulings on pretrial pleadings which determined, often quite narrowly, the legal issue which the jury was to decide; there was rarely more than one; ibid., pp. xxiv, xxix.
81. Loh, op. cit., p. 354.
82. Holdsworth, op. cit., p. 318.
83. Maitland 2, op. cit., p. 654.
84. *Duncan v. Louisiana*, op. cit., p. 1631.
85. Rembar, op. cit., p. 163; Maitland 2, op. cit., p. 626.
86. Maitland 1, op. cit., pp. 146-7; Rembar, op. cit., p. 183.
87. Maitland 1, op. cit., pp. 56-57.
88. Maitland 2, op. cit., pp. 8-9, 38, 41; Morris S. Arnold, op. cit., pp. ix-x.
89. Ibid., p. 519.
90. Ibid., p. 537.
91. Ibid., pp. 534-6.
92. Rembar, op. cit., p. 184.
93. Maitland 1, op. cit., p. 203.
94. Maitland 2, op. cit., p. 621.
95. Loh, loc. cit.
96. Maitland 2, op. cit., p. 652.
97. Ibid., p. 643.
98. Holdsworth, op. cit., p. 335.
99. Maitland 2, op. cit., p. 643.
100. Loh, loc. cit.
101. Holdsworth, op. cit., p. 324.
102. Maitland 2, op. cit., pp. 621-56.
103. Holdsworth, op. cit., p. 322.
104. Ibid., p. 325; Maitland 2, op. cit., p. 621.
105. Although this isn't quite clear, apparently, at least by the time of Henry III, there could be two trials, one by the jury of the hundreds and, if they found the defendant guilty, then by the jury of the four townships. Agreement of both was needed for a verdict. See Maitland 2, op. cit., p. 647; see also, Holdsworth, op. cit., p. 322.
106. Ibid., p. 327.
107. Maitland 1, op. cit., p. 652.
108. Rembar, op. cit., p. 167; Holdsworth, loc. cit.
109. Ibid.
110. Maitland 2, op. cit., pp. 649-50. It is also conceivable that the double jury practice, where and as long as it was invoked, may have, through

disagreements between the two bodies, added to the number of not guilty verdicts, but that is only speculation.

111. Holdsworth, loc. cit.; Arnold, op. cit., pp. xiv, xviii, xxvii, indicating that the law by then was making not guilty verdicts technically more difficult to arrive at, and also suggesting that guilty verdicts may have been less numerous than records indicate, since not guilty verdicts were often not entered on the rolls. It should also be kept in mind that during this period "guilty" and "not guilty" verdicts were applied to many cases we would now consider civil.

112. Joseph M. Hassett, "A Jury's Pre-Trial Knowledge in Historical Perspective," *Law and Contemporary Problems*, Vol. 43, No. 4 (1980), p. 158.

113. J. Irving Kaufman, "Verdict on Juries," *New York Times Magazine*, April 1, 1984, p. 47; Maitland 2, op. cit., pp. 542, 655.

114. *De Audibus Legae Angliae*, quoted in Hassett, loc. cit.

115. Lois G. Forer, "The Split Verdict: An Empirical Study of Civil Jury Cases," ms., p. 12.

116. Maitland 2, op. cit., p. 631.

117. Ibid., p. 632.

118. Ibid., p. 641.

119. Maitland 1, op. cit., pp. 443-44.

120. Ibid., p. 203.

121. Churchill, op. cit., pp. 219-20.

122. Hassett, op. cit., p. 157.

123. Rembar, op. cit., pp. 346-47; Luneberg, op. cit., p. 902.

124. Maitland 2, op. cit., p. 656.

125. Frank, op. cit., p. 109; Rembar, op. cit, pp. 348-49.

126. Hassett, op. cit., p. 158, quoting Sir Edward Coke.

127. Ibid., pp. 158-59.

128. Holdsworth, op. cit., pp. 319, 336; an instance of jurors as gatherers of evidence occurs as late as 1735 in America where that right or duty is mentioned in connection with the Zenger case; see Arnold, op. cit., p. xv.

129. Hassett, op. cit., pp. 162-63, quoting *U.S. v. Burr*, 25 F Cas (CCD Va. 1807).

130. *Williams v. Florida*, op. cit., p. 1899.

131. *Apodaca et al v. Oregon*, 406 U.S. 404 (1972), p. 1631.

132. Maitland 1, op. cit., p. 58.

133. *Williams v. Florida*, op. cit., p. 1901 quoting Proffat, *Trial by Jury* (1877).

134. Rembar, op. cit., p. 161.

135. *Williams v. Florida*, op. cit., p. 1900.

136. Churchill, op. cit., p. 252.

137. Rembar, op. cit., p. 168; Maitland 1, op. cit., p. 173.

138. Ibid.

139. American Council of Learned Studies, *The Great Charter*, New York: Pantheon Books (1965), p. 26.

140. Ibid., p. 25.

141. Maitland 1, op. cit., pp. 198-99.
142. Rembar, op. cit., pp. 198-99.
143. Ibid., p. 201.
144. Maitland 1, op. cit., p. 189.
145. Ibid., pp. 211-17.
146. Rembar, op. cit., pp. 274, 280.
147. Maitland 1, op. cit., p. 41.
148. Ibid., pp. 183-84.
149. Rembar, op. cit., p. 292.
150. James W. Moore *et al, Moore's Federal Practice*, New York: Matthew Bender (1984), Vol. 5, 38-10.
151. Rembar, op. cit., p. 299.
152. Frank, op. cit., p. 109.
153. Devlin, op. cit., pp. 1572-73.
154. There were two Conventicle Acts, the first in 1664, re-passed in 1670. The quotation is from the 1670 statute. See Paul L. High and Roger Fries, editors, *Crown and Parliament in Tudor-Stuart England*, New York: G.P. Putnam's Sons (1959), p. 271.
155. Catherine Owens Peare, *William Penn*, Philadelphia: J.B. Lippincott (1957), p. 107.
156. Ibid., p. 112.
157. Ibid., p. 113.
158. *The People's Antient & Just Liberties Asserted in the Trial of William Penn & William Mead* (also published as *A Suitable Proposal for Every Free-Born Englishman*), London: 1670. A London 1774 edition was used here; the narrative of the trial and all quotations are based on this contemporaneous report and transcript. But see also *The Tryal of William Penn and William Mead for Causing a Tumult* (London: 1719) for a slightly different version of the testimony.
159. Livingston Rutherford, *John Peter Zenger*, New York: Peter Smith (1941), for the events of Zenger's life and the events leading to the trial; the transcript of the trial, which Zenger published in 1735, is included in this book.
160. Ibid., pp. 35-6.
161. Morris, op. cit., p. ix.
162. Rutherford, op. cit., p. 57.
163. Morris, op. cit., p. 91 quoting Gouverneur Morris.
164. "That trial by jury is the inherent and invaluable right of every British subject in these colonies."
165. *Duncan v. Louisiana*, op. cit., p. 1447.
166. *Federalist Papers* No. 83; Patrick V. Higginbotham, "Continuing the Dialogue: Civil Juries and the Allocation of Judicial Powers," *Texas Law Review* Vol. 56: 47 (1977), p. 49 quoting Henderson, "Background of the Seventh Amendment," *Harvard Law Review* Vol. 289, pp. 291-5; Loh, op. cit., p. 464 re *Parsons v. Bedford* 28 U.S. (3 Pet.) 433 (1830).
167. Devitt, op. cit., p. 512, quoting Wolfram, "The Constitutional History of the Seventh Amendment," 57 *Minnesota Law Review* 639 (1973).

168. Rembar, op. cit., p. 381, re *Aregesinger v. Hamlin* (1972); National Center for State Courts, *Business of State Trial Courts*, Williamsburg: National Center for State Courts (1983) (hereafter *Business of State Trial Courts*), re *Baldwin v. New York*, 399 U.S. (1970); Marjorie S. Schultz, "Jury Redefined: Review of Burger Court Decisions," *Law & Contemporary Problems*, op. cit., p. 11.

169. Robert C. Johnston, "Jury Subornation Through Judicial Control," *Law & Contemporary Problems*, op. cit., p. 41.

170. Ibid., pp. 35-36, 38-39.

171. Lawrence M. Friedman, *History of American Law*, New York: Touchstone (1973), pp. 343-46.

172. Audrey Chin and Mark Peterson, *Fairness in Civil Jury Trials*, Santa Monica: Rand Institute for Civil Justice (1985).

173. Morris S. Arnold, "Historical Inquiry Into the Right to Trial by Jury in Complex Civil Litigation," 128 *University of Pennsylvania Law Review* 986 (1980), p. 829.

174. Devitt, op. cit., p. 494.

175. 359 U.S. 500 (1959).

176. Devitt, op. cit., p. 495.

177. Johnston, op. cit., pp. 27-28; Devitt, op. cit., pp. 495-96.

178. Scheflin, op. cit., p. 71.

179. Rembar, op. cit., p. 366.

180. *American Jury*, op. cit., p. 311.

181. Higginbotham, op. cit., p. 51.

182. Ibid., p. 60; Montgomery Kersten, "Preserving the Right to Jury Trial in Complex Civil Cases," *Stanford Law Review*, Vol. 32: 99 (1979), p. 51.

183. Higginbotham, op. cit., p. 51.

184. Ibid., p. 52.

185. Ibid.

186. Zander, op. cit., pp. 29-30.

187. Francis and Frank Hanna, "The Defence of the Jury," *AUEW Journal*, February 1986.

188. Higginbotham, op. cit., p. 53.

189. *Duncan v. Louisiana*, op. cit., pp. 451-52; see also Chapter Nine for more complete discussion of implications.

190. Schultz, op. cit., p. 9.

191. Ibid., p. 10.

192. Ibid., p. 12; Luneberg, op. cit., p. 971.

193. Ibid., pp. 963, 965; 430 U.S., p. 450.

194. Scheflin, op. cit., p. 72.

CHAPTER 2

1. But perhaps not always. See *Gregg v. Georgia*, 428 U.S. 153 (1976), in which the U.S. Supreme Court, in a case interpreting the Georgia

death penalty statute, wrote: "If a jury refused to convict even though the evidence supported the charge, its verdict would have to be reversed and a verdict of guilty entered or a new trial ordered since the discretionary act of jury nullification would not be permitted." The broader application of this interpretation is not clear. Quoted in Benton L. Becker, "Jury Nullification: Can a Jury Be Trusted?" *Trial Magazine*, Vol. 16, No. 10 (1980), p. 42.

2. U.S. Department of Justice, *Report to the Nation on Crime and Justice*, Washington, D.C. (1983), p. 7. Projections based on 1981 statistics. (Hereafter, referred to as *Report to the Nation*.)
3. U.S. Department of Justice, *Criminal Victimization, 1983*, Washington, D.C. (1984), p. 3. The figures do not seem to have changed much over the years: 37% was also the figure for the nation's five largest cities in 1972 (see U.S. Department of Justice, *Crime in the Nation's Five Largest Cities*, p. 28).
4. *Report to the Nation*, op. cit., p. 25; U.S. Department of Justice, *Criminal Victimization in the United States, 1982*, Washington, D.C. (1984), p. 18.
5. *Report to the Nation*, op. cit., p. 52.
6. John Guinther, "Child's Garden of Horrors," *Philadelphia Magazine*, April 1974.
7. *Report to the Nation*, op. cit., p. 31.
8. Lois Forer, *Money and Justice*, New York: W.W. Norton & Co. (1984), pp. 134 ff.
9. *Business of State Trial Courts*, op. cit., p. 37.
10. *Report to the Nation*, op. cit., p. 55.
11. *Business of State Trial Courts*, loc. cit.; Robert T. Roper and Victor E. Flango, "Trials Before Judges and Juries," *Justice System Journal*, Vol. 8, No. 2 (1983), p. 191.
12. *Report to the Nation*, loc. cit.
13. Hastie, op. cit., p. 1.
14. *Report to the Nation*, op. cit., p. 64.
15. *Business of State Trial Courts*, op. cit., p. 38.
16. Roper, op. cit., p. 189; *Statistical Abstract of the United States 1984*, Washington, D.C.: U.S. Department of Commerce, p. 189. (Hereafter, *Statistical Abstract 1984*); *Annual Report of the Director of the Administrative Office of the United States Courts*, Washington, D.C. (1980), p. 404. (Hereafter, *Federal Court Statistics 1980*.)
17. Ibid., p. 140.
18. *Business of State Trial Courts*, op. cit., p. 28.
19. *Federal Court Statistics* 1980, op. cit., p. 462.
20. *Business of State Trial Courts*, loc. cit.
21. No accurate national figures are available, but 15% female arrests is a figure often given. Women account for 10% of violent-crime arrests, and 21% of property-crime arrests, and 20% of all juvenile arrests. *Report to the Nation*, op. cit., p. 35.
22. Roper, op. cit., p. 191.
23. *American Jury*, op. cit., p. 265.

24. Roper, op. cit., p. 197.
25. For felony cases, based on estimates provided by the Common Pleas Court of Philadelphia. Lengths of bench trials will vary somewhat by jurisdiction, depending on prosecutorial policies on plea bargaining. When they are liberal, there will be few bench trials, but those that are tried this way will be seriously contested and more lengthy; when plea bargaining policies are astringent, defendants often go to trial, not in hopes they will be found innocent but in expectation they will provide enough mitigating evidence that the judge will find them guilty only of lesser charges, the same outcome they would have received from a plea bargain.
26. David M. Trubek *et al*, "The Costs of Ordinary Litigation," *UCLA Law Review*, Vol. 31, No. 1 (1983), p. 87.
27. Ibid., pp. 72, 75. The UCLA Law Review article is a summary by Trubek *et al* of their *Civil Litigation Research Project: Final Report*, March 1983, University of Wisconsin Law School, in three volumes.
28. Ibid., p. 86.
29. Ibid.
30. Chin, *Fairness in Civil Jury Trials*, op. cit., p. 2.
31. Ibid.
32. Zeisel, op. cit., p. 66. For a discussion of the meaning of these statistics, see Chapter Six.
33. Maitland 2, op. cit., p. 627.
34. Loh, op. cit., p. 427; *American Jury*, op. cit., p. 7.
35. Ibid.; Higginbotham, op. cit., pp. 59-60, quoting Judge J. Irving Kaufman.
36. David Kairys *et al*, "Jury Representativeness," *California Law Review*, Vol. 65, No. 4 (1977), p. 782.
37. *American Jury System*, op. cit., pp. 97-99.
38. Ibid., p. 99.

CHAPTER 3

1. *Strauder v. W. Virginia*, 100 U.S. 303 (1880), quoted in Loh, op. cit., p. 360.
2. Ibid., p. 363.
3. *Barrow v. State*, 235 Ga. 635, 221 S.E.2d 446 (1975), pretrial transcript, p. 158, quoted in Courtney Mullin, "The Jury System in Death Penalty Cases," *Law and Contemporary Problems*, Vol. 43, No. 4 (1980), p. 145.
4. Kaufman, op. cit., p. 47; Luneberg, op. cit., p. 909.
5. Kairys, *Jury Representativeness*, p. 812; Loh, op. cit., p. 359.
6. Erlanger, op. cit., p. 364.
7. Saks, op. cit., p. 50.
8. Luneberg, op. cit., pp. 929-31.

9. Ibid., pp. 903 ff; *Haas et al v. United Technologies Corp.*, brief filed U.S. Supreme Court, October Term, 1982, p. 9.
10. Zeisel, *American Jury System*, op. cit., pp. 74-75.
11. *ATLA Law Reporter*, Vol. 27, No. 7 (1984), pp. 313-14.
12. Kairys, op. cit., pp. 777, 805, 807-08.
13. Ibid., pp. 807-08.
14. Ibid., p. 805; Mullin, loc. cit.; for Hispanics, see *Hernandez v. Texas*, 347 U.S. 475 (1954), in which a murder conviction was reversed because of discrimination against Mexican-Americans in jury selection, quoted in Luneberg, op. cit., p. 928.
15. Kairys, op. cit., pp. 777-80.
16. Kairys, op. cit., p. 823.
17. Zeisel, *American Jury System*, op. cit., p. 72.
18. 28 USC 1869j (Supp. 1980); Nathalie M. Walker-Dittman, "Right to Trial by Jury in Complex Civil Litigation," *Tulane Law Review*, Vol. 55: 491 (1981), p. 511.
19. Ibid.
20. *Report to the Nation*, op. cit., p. 67.
21. Loh, op. cit., p. 388.
22. Hassett, op. cit., pp. 156, 167. Citation for case is *United States v. Haldeman*, 559 F.2d 31 (D.C. Cir. Ct. 1976), *cert. denied*, 431 U.S. 93 (1977).
23. Kairys, op. cit., pp. 777-78.
24. *Swain v. Alabama*, 380 U.S. 202, quoted in Gordon Bermant and John Shapard, *The Voir Dire Examination, Juror Challenges, and Adversary Advocacy*, Washington, D.C.: Federal Judicial Center, reprinted from *The Trial Process*, Bruce Dennis Sales, edit., Plenum Publ. Co., 1981, p. 74. (Hereafter referred to as *Voir Dire Examination*.) Loh, op. cit., p. 356. The opinion, loc. cit., points out that "token inclusion" of minorities is forbidden in the venire as is "total exclusion" throughout the state, but it raised no problem with the fact that, in this case, the number of blacks on the venire were so few that the prosecutor could get rid of all of them by peremptory challenges. The defendant, a black man, was sentenced to death after being convicted of rape.
25. Loh., op. cit., pp. 356-60.
26. *Smith v. Texas*, 311 U.S. 138 (1940), quoted in Luneberg, op. cit., pp. 916-17.
27. *Taylor v. Louisiana*, 419 U.S. 522 (1975). The issue the appellant raised was the absence of women from the venire in his trial.
28. *Thiel v. Southern Pacific*, 328 U.S. 217 (1946).
29. *Duren v. Missouri*, 439 U.S. 357 (1959), quoted in Mark A. Nordenberg and William V. Luneberg, "Decisionmaking in Complex Federal Civil Cases," *Judicature*, Vol. 65, Nos. 8-9 (1982), pp. 424-25.
30. *Batson v. Kentucky*, Supreme Court No. 84-6263. (Ruling was in May 1986.)

31. *Glasser v. United States*, 315 U.S. 60 (1941), quoted in Luneberg, op. cit., pp. 917-18.
32. Loc. cit.
33. Luneberg, op. cit., p. 921.
34. Ibid., pp. 936-37, quoting *Duren*, loc. cit.
35. *Voir Dire Examination*, op. cit., p. 76, for a partial list of cases in which the issue has been raised.
36. Zeisel, "American Jury," op. cit., pp. 90-91.
37. Ibid; *Dallas Morning News*, March 12, 1986.
38. Mullin, op. cit., p. 147.
39. *American Jury*, op. cit., pp. 340-41.
40. Ron Bloomberg in a letter of complaint to the Judicial Inquiry and Review Board of Pennsylvania, January 13, 1971.
41. *Voir Dire Examination*, op. cit., p. 77, quoting A. Ginger, *Jury Selection in Criminal Trials*, Tiburon: Law Press (1977), 1977 Supp.
42. Loh, op. cit., p. 387, quoting R. W. Balch *et al*, "The Socialization of Jurors," *Journal of Criminal Justice*, Vol. 4 (1976), pp. 271-83.
43. Ibid., quoting Dale W. Broeder, "The Voir Dire Examination," *Southern California Law Review*, Vol. 38 (1965), pp. 503-28; Amiram Elwork *et al*, "The Trial: A Research Review," Chapter One of *The Trial Process*, Bruce Dennis Sales, edit., New York: Plenum Press (1981), p. 17; Padawer-Singer, op. cit., p. 59.
44. Broeder, *Chicago Jury Project*, op. cit., p. 756. The question was asked but no record has been discovered of the findings ever being published.
45. *Voir Dire Examination*, op. cit., p. 92.
46. The number varies from jurisdiction to jurisdiction and by type of case. Loh, op. cit., p. 388.
47. *Voir Dire Examination*, op. cit., pp. 93-98.
48. 55%, according to Ibid., p. 94.
49. *Report of the Committee on Juries of the Judicial Council of the Second Circuit*, New York (1984), p. 33 (hereafter referred to as *Second Circuit*).
50. *Voir Dire Examination*, op. cit., pp. 79, 81.
51. Ibid., p. 81.
52. Ibid., p. 87.
53. Kaufman, op. cit., p. 48.
54. Padawer-Singer, loc. cit., quoting W. Levit *et al*, "Expediting Voir Dire," *Southern California Law Review*, Vol. 44 (1971).
55. Second Circuit, op. cit., p. 20.
56. Elwork, *The Trial*, op. cit., p. 18; Donald P. Lay, "Can Our Jury System Survive?," *Trial Magazine*, Vol. 19, No. 9 (1983), pp. 53-54.
57. Ibid., p. 54; Elwork, *The Trial*, op. cit., p. 18.
58. Ibid.
59. Peter Perlman, "Jury Selection in the Products Case," *Trial Magazine*, Vol. 18, No. 11 (1982), p. 61.
60. Second Circuit, op. cit., p. 31.

61. Herald P. Fahringer, "In the Valley of the Blind: A Primer on Jury Selection in a Criminal Case," *Law and Contemporary Problems*, Vol. 43, No. 4 (1980), pp. 117-18, in part quoting J. Murray and J. Eckman, *Follow-up Study of Jury Selection*, paper presented at annual meeting of American Psychological Association (1974) which reported that a number of jurors in a politically controversial case gave different answers, when interviewed privately after the trial, from their responses at voir dire.
62. Ibid., p. 130.
63. Interview, Clark DeLeon.
64. Fahringer, op. cit., p. 117. The author should know whereof he speaks; he is a practicing attorney and Fellow of the American College of Trial Lawyers.
65. Joseph Kelner, "Jury Selection: The Prejudice Syndrome," *Trial Magazine*, Vol. 19, No. 7 (1983), p. 48.
66. Hastie, op. cit., p. 123.
67. Kelner, loc. cit.
68. Ibid.
69. Fahringer, op. cit., p. 119.
70. Ibid., p. 135.
71. Kelner, op. cit., p. 49.
72. Ibid., p. 50; Fahringer, loc. cit.
73. Davis, op. cit., p. 334, quoting Simon (1967).
74. Hastie, op. cit., p. 123.
75. Fahringer, op. cit., p. 119.
76. *Dallas Morning News*, loc cit.
77. Margaret Covington, "State-of-the-Art in Jury Selection Techniques," *Trial Magazine*, Vol. 19, No. 9 (1983), p. 86; Fahringer, op. cit., p. 133.
78. Covington, loc. cit.
79. Elwork, *The Trial*, op. cit., p. 19.
80. Hastie, loc. cit. Although others disagree, ibid., p. 122.
81. Covington, loc. cit.
82. Elwork, *The Trial*, op. cit., p. 21.
83. Fahringer, op. cit., p. 132.
84. Ibid., p. 127.
85. Ibid., pp. 121-22.
86. Hastie, op. cit., pp. 123 ff.
87. Covington, op. cit., pp. 84-87.
88. Loh, op. cit., p. 399.
89. Correspondence to author.
90. Bermant, op. cit., p. 47.
91. Undertaken at national convention, Association of Trial Lawyers, 1985.
92. Whether such an allegation would have legal merit is questionable but defending oneself against such a charge could be time-consuming and expensive.

93. Fahringer, op. cit., p. 116; Loh, op. cit., p. 357.

94. E.g., Donald J. Goldberg, a prominent criminal defense lawyer; Harold Kohn, plaintiffs' antitrust attorney; interviews.

95. Zeisel, *American Jury System*, op. cit., pp. 78 ff.

96. Ibid., p. 81.

97. Ibid., p. 83.

98. Ibid., p. 82.

99. Ibid., p. 79.

100. Loh, op. cit., quoting Broeder, *Voir Dire Examination*, op. cit., p. 505.

101. Loh, op. cit., p. 397.

102. Ibid., p. 402; Saks, op. cit., p. 65; Elwork, *The Trial*, pp. 19-20. Each source cites a number of studies that reach contradictory conclusions.

103. Saks, op. cit., pp. 63-64.

104. Hastie, op. cit., p. 127.

105. Loh, loc. cit., quoting S. Penrod, "A Study of Attorney and 'Scientific' Jury Selection Models," Harvard University (1979), unpublished doctoral thesis.

106. Ibid., p. 403.

107. Ibid.; to the extent biases play a role, they appear to be of a subtle and complex nature and co-exist with other motives that may be more objective; see Hastie, op. cit., pp. 171-74. No studies were discovered reporting evidence of overt prejudice during deliberations.

108. Covington, op. cit., p. 86.

109. Hastie, op. cit., pp. 9, 136; Davis, op. cit., p. 332, implying significance of heterogeneity; interview, Harold Kohn; Richard O. Lempert, "*Uncovering 'Non-Discernible' Differences: Empirical Research and the Jury Size Cases*," *Michigan Law Review*, Vol. 73 (1975), pp. 44-45.

110. O'Barr, op. cit., pp. 32 ff., 62 ff.

111. Ibid., p. 32

112. Ibid., p. 63, quoting F. Lee Bailey and Henry D. Rothblatt, *Successful Techniques for Criminal Trials*, Rochester: Lawyers Cooperative Publishing Co. (1971), pp. 190-91.

113. Ibid., p. 35.

114. Moira Dunworth interview, *Commonwealth v. Chestnut*, CP #8304-1249-52 (1983).

115. David S. Shrager, *Opening Statement on Behalf of Plaintiff*, Washington, D.C.: Roscoe Pound Foundation (undated), p. 1.

116. Ibid.

117. Donald F. Vinson, "How to Persuade Jurors," *ABA Law Journal*, October 1985, p. 73.

118. Ibid., p. 75.

119. Bettyruth Walter-Goldberg, *Jury Summation as Speech Genre*. Presented to the faculties of the University of Pennsylvania in Partial Fulfillment of the Requirements for the Degree of Doctor of Philosophy (1985), p. 49. (To distinguish this paper from same

author's identically titled speech, *supra* note 52, Chapter One, hereafter it will be referred to as Walter-Goldberg dissertation.)

120. Anapol, op. cit., p. 10.
121. Walter-Goldberg dissertation, op. cit., p. 2.
122. Ibid., p. 246.
123. Walter-Goldberg, *Jury Summation as . . .* , op. cit., pp. 20-21.
124. Walter-Goldberg dissertation, loc. cit.
125. *American Jury*, op. cit., p. 114.
126. Hastie, op. cit., p. 230.
127. *American Jury*, op. cit., pp. 200 ff.; Elwork, *The Trial*, op. cit., pp. 25-26.
128. Saks, op. cit., pp. 156-57. Some of the studies quoted indicate that because of all the variables involved, it is difficult to specify the "attractiveness" factor with confidence.
129. O'Barr, *Linguistic Evidence*, op. cit.
130. Ibid., p. 59.
131. Who apparently had trouble mimicking the real witnesses, loc. cit.
132. Ibid., pp. 61-75.
133. William O'Barr and John M. Conley, "When a Juror Watches a Lawyer," *Barrister*, Vol. 13, No. 3 (1976), p. 9.
134. O'Barr, op. cit., pp. 70-71.
135. Ibid., pp. 74 ff.
136. Ibid., p. 125.
137. Ibid., p. 82.
138. O'Barr and Conley, op. cit., p. 11.
139. Ibid.; O'Barr, op. cit., pp. 79-81.
140. Anapol, op. cit., p. 11.
141. Ibid., p. 9.
142. O'Barr, op. cit., p. 103, quoting Robert E. Keeton, *Trial Tactics and Methods*, Boston: Little Brown (2nd Edit., 1973), p. 167.
143. Elwork, *The Trial*, op. cit., p. 36. Elwork found only two studies that dealt with the subject, and he notes they produced "mixed results."
144. Davis, op. cit., p. 337, citing S. Sue *et al*, "Effects of Inadmissible Evidence on the Decisions of Simulated Jurors," *Journal of Applied Psychology*, Vol. 3 (1973), pp. 345-53.
145. Broeder, *Chicago Jury Project*, op. cit., p. 754.
146. Philip D. Calderone, "Advertising the Economics of High Jury Awards," *Washington and Lee Law Review*, Vol. XXXVII (1980), p. 185.
147. Broder, loc. cit.
148. Hastie, op. cit., p. 87.
149. Ibid.
150. O'Barr, op. cit., p. 103.
151. Author's interviews.
152. Loh, op. cit., p. 515, quoting two studies that reached different conclusions on issue of whether jurors could disregard instruction to ignore defendant's prior convictions.
153. Ibid., p. 502.

154. Peter Perlman, "Town v. Country," *Trial Magazine*, Vol. 19, No. 9 (1983), p. 71.

155. Elwork, *The Trial*, op. cit., p. 47.

156. Ibid., p. 48; Loh, op. cit., p. 507.

157. Ibid., pp. 501-08; Elwork, *The Trial*, op. cit., pp. 45-48.

158. Loh, op. cit., p. 501.

159. Ibid., p. 503.

160. Elwork, *The Trial*, op. cit., pp. 45-46.

161. Loh, op. cit., p. 507.

162. Ibid.

163. The subject was mentioned, and then only in passing, in only two of the more than 100 articles and books presenting studies of the jury that the author consulted. Quite possibly, considering the size of the litera- ture, some articles may have been missed on the subject, but none were noted in the general survey literature.

164. Second Circuit, op. cit., pp. 51 ff.

165. Ibid., p. 70.

166. Bettyruth Walter-Goldberg, *Note-Taking by Jurors in the Federal Courts*, Philadelphia: Philadelphia Bar Association (1985), p. 2 (hereafter referred to as Walter-Goldberg, *Note-Taking*) quoting Victor E. Flango, "Would Jurors Do a Better Job if They Could Take Notes?" *Judicature*, Vol. 63, No. 9 (1980), pp. 436-43.

167. Ibid., quoting Hon. Henry F. Greene, *Memorandum to Attorneys*, May 1982.

168. Ibid., passim.

169. Ibid., pp. 3-5.

170. Ibid., pp. 22-24.

171. Ibid., pp. 24-26.

172. Ibid., pp. 25-26.

173. Ibid., p. 26.

174. Ibid., p. 15.

175. Ibid., p. 26.

176. Ibid.

177. Ibid., p. 13.

178. Ibid. The figure was 36%.

179. Ibid., p. 11.

180. Ibid., p. 15.

181. Ibid.

182. Loh, op. cit., pp. 488-89, 491-92; Davis, op. cit., pp. 338-39; Saks, op. cit., pp. 105-07.

183. Johnston, op. cit., pp. 28-29.

184. *American Jury*, op. cit., p. 322, re leading juries toward the verdict the judge wants.

185. Johnston, op. cit., p. 24.

186. Morris, op. cit., p. xiv.

187. Davis, op. cit., p. 347.

188. Munsterman, op. cit., pp. 2, 12. 98% thought the judge conducted the trial in a fair and impartial manner.

189. Frank, op. cit., p. 117.
190. Elwork, *The Trial*, op. cit., pp. 34-36; O'Barr, op. cit., pp. 17-18.
191. Elwork, *Jury Instructions*, op. cit., pp. 280-81, quoting *Sparf and Hansen v. United States*, 156 U.S. 52 (1895), p. 102.
192. Author interview.
193. Friedman, op. cit., p. 347; Rembar, op. cit., p. 356; O'Barr, op. cit., p. 23.
194. Loh, op. cit., p. 538; Frank, loc. cit.
195. Elwork, *Jury Instructions*, op. cit., p. 281; *Commonwealth v. Smith*, 221 Pa. 552, 70 A 850 (1908), p. 553.
196. Amiram Elwork *et al*, "Toward Understandable Jury Instructions," *Judicature*, Vol. 65, Nos. 8-9 (1982), p. 433.
197. Elwork, *Jury Instructions*, op. cit., pp. 282-83.
198. Loh, loc. cit.
199. Elwork, *Jury Instructions*, op. cit., p. 283.
200. Ibid., p. 10
201. Davis, op. cit., p. 340.
202. Elwork, *Jury Instructions*, op. cit., p. 284.
203. Ibid., p. 286.
204. Ibid., p. 30.
205. Ibid., p. 31.
206. Loh, op. cit., pp. 539, 543, quoting R.P. Charrow and V. Charrow, "Making Legal Language Understandable," *Columbia Law Review*, Vol. 79 (1979); Laurence J. Severance and Elizabeth F. Loftus, "Improving the Ability of Jurors to Comprehend and Apply Criminal Jury Instructions," *Law and Society* Review, Vol. 17 (1982).
207. Elwork, *Jury Instructions*, op. cit., pp. 292-93.
208. Ibid., p. 293.
209. Ibid., p. 295; Loh, op. cit., p. 539.
210. Ibid., p. 543, quoting Severance and Loftus.
211. Elwork, *The Trial*, op. cit., p. 36; Elwork, *Jury Instructions*, op. cit., p. 290; Hastie, op. cit., p. 169.
212. Second Circuit, op. cit., pp. 88-89.
213. O'Barr, op. cit., p. 27.
214. Elwork, *Jury Instructions*, op. cit., p. 291.
215. Ibid., loc. cit.; Second Circuit, op. cit., pp. 44-48; Peter W. Sperlich, "The Case for Preserving Trial by Jury in Complex Civil Litigation," *Judicature*, Vol. 65, Nos. 8-9 (1982), pp. 418-19.
216. Elwork, *Jury Instructions*, loc. cit.
217. Hastie, op. cit., pp. 98, 168, 232.
218. Ibid., p. 148.
219. See discussion Chapter Four for 90% correct evaluation.
220. *American Jury*, op. cit., p. 429.
221. Hastie, op. cit., p. 231.
222. Interrogatories for juries is nothing new; instances can be found in England in the early 14th century; see Arnold, op. cit., p. xxiii.
223. Munsterman, op. cit., p. 2.

CHAPTER 4

1. 399 U.S. 78 (1970).
2. 406 U.S. 356 (1972).
3. 406 U.S. 404 (1972).
4. 413 U.S. 149 (1973).
5. 435 U.S. 223 (1978).
6. Devitt, op. cit., p. 513, notes that within a year after Colgrove 86 of 95 federal court districts had done so.
7. Padawer-Singer, op. cit., p. 51; Lawrence R. Mills, "Six-Member and Twelve-Member Juries," *University of Michigan Journal of Law Reform*, Vol. 6 (1973), p. 671; in *Williams v. Florida*, op. cit., p. 102, the Supreme Court said the 12-member jury was an "historical accident, unnecessary to effect the purposes of the jury and wholly without significance 'except to mystics'"; for a further discussion of how the 12-person system probably came into existence, see Chapter One above.
8. Padawer-Singer, loc. cit., summarizing *Johnson v. Louisiana*, op. cit.
9. Edward N. Beiser and Rene Varrin, "Six-Member Juries in the Federal Courts," *Judicature*, Vol. 58, No. 9 (1975), p. 426.
10. Mills, op. cit., p. 673.
11. Kessler, op. cit., p. 64.
12. Interview, David S. Shrager.
13. Mills, op. cit., p. 672, quoting Hans Zeisel, "And Then There Were None: The Diminution of the Federal Jury," *University of Chicago Law Review*, Vol. 38 (1971), pp. 713-15.
14. William R. Pabst, Jr., "Statistical Studies of the Costs of Six-Man vs. Twelve-Man Juries," *William and Mary Law Review*, Vol. 14 (1972), p. 328. The actual figures were 21.61 for a six-person and 27.54 for a 12-person panel.
15. Ibid., pp. 326-27.
16. Beiser, op. cit., pp. 428-29.
17. Padawer-Singer, pp. 51 ff. Professor Padawer-Singer was director of the Columbia University Jury Project.
18. Ibid., p. 61.
19. Ibid., p. 51.
20. Ibid.
21. Ibid., p. 53.
22. Ibid.
23. Ibid.
24. Ibid., p. 54.
25. Hastie, op. cit., p. 34.
26. Padawer-Singer, loc. cit.
27. Ibid.
28. Hastie, op. cit., p. 26.
29. Davis, op. cit., p. 343, quoting Kessler (1973).

30. Kessler, op. cit., pp. 84-85, re Zeisel, *And Then There Were None*, op. cit., p. 719.
31. Davis, loc. cit., quoting Diamond and Zeisel (1974).
32. Hastie, op. cit., p. 34; Padawer-Singer, op. cit., p. 52; Kessler, op. cit., p. 72; Mills, op. cit., p. 676.
33. Forer, *Split Verdict*, op. cit., p. 27.
34. Davis, op. cit., p. 349.
35. Ibid.
36. Mills, op. cit., p. 688.
37. Ibid., p. 676.
38. Beiser, op. cit., p. 431.
39. In New Jersey; Hastie, op. cit., p. 33.
40. Roughly; there was considerable skewing by case type; see Mills, op. cit., pp. 688-89.
41. Ibid., p. 674.
42. Hastie, loc. cit. The New Jersey study quoted by Hastie found that when lawyers had a choice on panel size, in 77% of automobile negligence cases which are usually relatively simple and do not take long to try, a six-person jury was selected, but six-person panels were elected in only 15.4% of malpractice suits which tend to be complex and often have much larger sums at stake than automobile cases.
43. Hastie, *Inside the Jury*, op. cit.
44. Ibid., p. 45.
45. Ibid., p. 60.
46. Ibid., pp. 45-46.
47. Lempert, op. cit., p. 50.
48. Hastie, op. cit., pp. 60, 102.
49. This was particularly true with the 10 of 12 juries; ibid., pp. 88-89.
50. Ibid., p. 60.
51. Padawer-Singer, op. cit., p. 57.
52. Lois G. Forer, "One Judge's View of the Split Verdict in Civil Cases," *Pennsylvania Law Journal Reporter*, August 31, 1981, p. 6. (This is an abbreviated version of *The Split Verdict*, op. cit.)
53. Beiser, op. cit., p. 430.
54. Hastie, op. cit., p. 27; Broeder, op. cit., p. 746; *American Jury*, op. cit., pp. 56, 461.
55. Mills, op. cit., p. 683.
56. Saks, op. cit., p. 78; *American Jury*, op. cit., p. 463, quoting Asch *et al*, "Effects of Group Pressure Upon the Modification and Distortion of Judgments," *Readings in Social Psychology* (1952), pp. 398-99.
57. This is exactly what happened on the jury deliberations televised in the *Frontline* documentary, op. cit. The lone holdout made several statements that he still felt the defendant should be convicted but would not stand in the way of the views of the others and cause a hung verdict.
58. Broeder, op. cit., p. 748.
59. Saks, op. cit., p. 97.
60. Hastie, op. cit., p. 60.

61. Ibid., p. 166.

62. Saks, op. cit., p. 97.

63. Padawer-Singer, op. cit., p. 57.

64. Ibid., p. 54.

65. Hastie, op. cit., p. 76.

66. Ibid., p. 79, in terms of perceived thoroughness of the deliberations, seriousness of them, and confidence that a correct verdict had been reached.

67. Ibid., pp. 116-7.

68. Ibid., pp. 42. 59.

69. Dennis Cogan; Moira Dunworth; Donald J. Goldberg.

70. Hastie, op. cit., p. 60.

71. Worksheets supplied by Judge Forer.

72. Hastie, op. cit., p. 87.

73. Ibid., pp. 163-65. A phone survey undertaken by Pound of jurors in Phoenix and Chicago discovered the evidence-driven model was used more than a third of the time, verdict-driven about 10%, and a combination of both in the remainder of the cases. However, the sample was of only 111 jurors, some of whom may have served on the same case.

74. Hastie, op. cit., p. 166.

75. Ibid., p. 165.

76. Strawn, op. cit., p. 446.

77. Hastie, op. cit., p. 28, quoting C.H. Hawkins, *Interaction and Coalition Realignments in Consensus-seeking Groups*, University of Chicago, doctoral thesis (1960).

78. Padawer-Singer, op. cit., p. 54.

79. *American Jury*, op. cit., p. 487.

80. Anapol, op. cit., p. 9.

81. *American Jury*, op cit., pp. 488-89; Broeder, op. cit., p. 747; Zeisel, *American Jury System*, op. cit., p. 80; Elwork, *The Trial*, op. cit., p. 29, citing four studies in addition to Chicago Jury Project.

82. Broeder, op. cit., p. 748.

83. Saks, op. cit., pp. 95-96.

84. Walter-Goldberg, *Note-Taking*, op. cit., p. 13.

85. Anapol, op. cit., p. 11; Kessler, op. cit., p. 82. citing Hawkins, op. cit.

86. Hastie, op. cit., p. 145.

87. Ibid., p. 92.

88. Kessler, op. cit., p. 82, citing Hawkins, op. cit.; Saks, op. cit., pp. 73-74, citing Strodtbeck and Hook, "Social Dimensions of the Twelve-Man Jury Table" (1961).

89. Davis, op. cit., p. 342.

90. Saks, loc. cit.

91. Davis, op. cit., p. 327; Kessler, op. cit., p. 83.

92. Ibid., pp. 83, 91; Erlanger, op. cit., pp. 350-51 citing H. Kalven, Jr., "The Jury, the Law, and the Personal Injury Damage Award," *Ohio State Law Journal*, Vol. 19 (1958), pp. 158-78.

93. Elwork, *The Trial*, op. cit., pp. 23, 29.

94. Erlanger, op. cit., p. 350, citing D.W. Broeder, "Plaintiff's Family Status as Affecting Juror Behavior," *Journal of Public Law*, Vol. 14, No. 1 (1966), pp. 131-141.

95. Walter-Goldberg, *Note-Taking*, op. cit., p. 14.

96. Hastie, op. cit., p. 27; Anapol, op. cit., p. 1; Bermant, op. cit., p. ix.

97. Hastie, op. cit., p. 28.

98. Ibid., pp. 83-85; Saks, op. cit., p. 68.

99. Erlanger, op. cit., p. 347.

100. Anapol, op. cit., p. 11.

101. *American Jury*, op. cit., p. 494.

102. Hastie, op. cit., p. 85.

103. Ibid., p. 28.

104. Ibid., pp. 85, 230.

105. Ibid., p. 230.

106. Peterson, *Cook County*, op. cit., p. 39.

107. Erlanger, op. cit., p. 354, citing R.J. Simon, *The Jury and the Defense of Insanity*, Boston: Little Brown (1967), p. 117.

108. Hastie, op. cit., p. 138, although members of high status occupations did talk the most frequently and made more contributions than low-status members to discussions of the law, and made the most suggestions about organization of the deliberations.

109. Ibid., pp. 141-42.

110. Ibid., p. 142.

111. Saks, op. cit., pp. 63-64.

112. Hastie, op. cit., p. 140.

113. Elwork, *Toward Understandable Jury Instructions*, op. cit., p. 441.

114. Davis, op. cit., p. 334.

115. Hastie, op. cit., p. 143.

116. Elwork, *Toward Understandable Jury Instructions*, op. cit., p. 440, though not using the same age brackets; study shows falloff beginning after age 60.

117. Davis, op. cit., p. 334, citing Simon, op. cit.

118. Hastie, op. cit., p. 139.

119. Ibid.

120. Munsterman, op. cit., p. 12.

121. Hastie, op. cit., p. 140; to a statistically significant degree.

122. Ibid., pp. 143-44; other studies summarized by Hastie reached conflicting results, p. 143.

123. Saks, op. cit., p. 65. The study of 480 mock jurors found this was the best predictor of verdicts. For summaries of other studies of psychological factors, see Davis, op. cit., p. 336; Kessler, op. cit., p. 83.

124. *American Jury*, op. cit., pp. 210-11, found some indications of a "negative sympathy index" by jurors toward black defendants in criminal cases; it must be remembered this study was developed in the 1950s.

125. *First Four Years*, op. cit., p. 20. Chin, *Fairness in Civil Jury Trials*, op. cit., p. 3.
126. *First Four Years*, loc. cit.
127. Chin, *Fairness in Civil Jury Trials*, op. cit., p. 4.
128. Ibid., pp. 8-20.
129. In a Florida tax-evasion trial in 1983, a juror reported anti-Semitic remarks against the defendant as well as the telling of racist jokes offensive to black members of the jury, *Washington Post*, April 19, 1986.
130. Zeisel, *American Jury System*, op. cit., p. 75.
131. Peterson, *Cook County*, op cit., pp. viii, 29-32, 40, 42.
132. Chin, *Fairness in Civil Jury Verdicts*, op. cit., p. vi.
133. Quoted in *Trial Magazine*, Vol. 21, No. 4 (1985), pp. 72-73.
134. Kalven, *The Jury, The Law* . . . , op. cit., pp. 158-59.
135. Mark A. Peterson and Audrey Chin, "Juries Don't Ignore Assets and Identity of Defendant," *National Law Journal*, November 11, 1985, p. 15.
136. John Guinther, *Winning Your Personal Injury Suit*, New York: Doubleday/Anchor Press (1980), pp. 198-99.
137. Peterson, *Juries Don't Ignore* . . . , loc. cit., based on Rand Civil Institute studies.
138. Broeder, op. cit., pp. 756-58.
139. Forer worksheets, loc. cit.
140. Interview, Amiram Elwork.
141. Kalven, *The Jury, The Law* . . . , op. cit., p. 177.
142. Frank, op. cit., p. 142.
143. *First Four Years*, op. cit., p. 21.
144. Kalven, *The Jury, The Law* . . . , op. cit., p. 176; Elwork, interview, op. cit.
145. Ibid.
146. Kalven, *The Jury, The Law* . . . , op. cit., pp. 176-77.
147. Ibid.
148. Department of Health, Education and Welfare, *Report of the Secretary's Commission on Medical Malpractice, Appendix* (1973), pp. 110-12.
149. Frank, op. cit., p. 141; see also discussion, Introduction to Part Two, text infra.
150. *American Jury System*, op. cit., p. 97.
151. Ibid., quoting Judge Albert Stiftel of Delaware.
152. *American Jury*, op. cit., p. 488.
153. Ibid., p. 115.
154. Ibid., pp. 521-3; Forer, worksheets, op. cit.
155. Broeder, op. cit., pp. 751-2.
156. Walter-Goldberg, *Note-Taking*, op. cit., p. 10.
157. Munsterman, op. cit., p. 10.
158. Padawer-Singer, op. cit., p. 55.
159. Ibid., p. 54.
160. Ibid., pp. 54-5.

161. Broeder, op. cit., p. 752.
162. Munsterman, op. cit., p. 13.

PART TWO: INTRODUCTION

1. *American Jury*, op. cit., p. 122; Harry Kalven, Jr., "Dignity of the Civil Jury," *American Trial Lawyers Journal*, Vol. 31, Summer 1971, p. 598; Moore, op. cit., 38: 13-4; Erlanger, op. cit., p. 346.
2. Frank, op. cit., p. 111.
3. Ibid., p. 130.
4. *American Jury*, op. cit., p. 9.
5. Ibid., p. 122; *Duncan v. Louisiana*, op. cit., re Harlan dissent; *Gregg v. Georgia*, 428 U.S. 153 (1976).
6. Donald Alexander, "Civil Juries in Maine," *Maine Law Review*, 34: 63 (1982).
7. *ABA Journal* 65: 1292 (Sept. 1979).
8. Marc Galanter, "Reading the Landscape of Disputes," *UCLA Law Review*, Vol. 31, No. 1 (October 1983), pp. 6 ff., quoting various justice system sources who have used the term.
9. Stephen Daniels, "We're Not a Litigious Society," *Judges' Journal*, Spring 1985.
10. Warren E. Burger, "Our Vicious Legal Spiral," 16 *Judges' Journal* 23.
11. ABA Minor Disputes Resolution Conference, May 22, 1977.
12. 68 *ABA Journal* (1982), pp. 274-77.
13. *U.S. News and World Report*, Dec. 4, 1978, quoting an unnamed judge.
14. Galanter, op. cit., quoting Rosenberg, "Contemporary Litigation in the United States," *Legal Institutions Today* (1977).
15. Daniels, loc. cit.
16. Christopher Manning, 71 *Northwestern Law Review* (1977), p. 767.
17. Galanter, op. cit., p. 6, quoting Fleming, 54 *Judicature* 109 (1970).
18. Ibid., p. 7, quoting McGill, 78 *N.Y. State Journal of Medicine*, (1978), pp. 658 ff., in which the president of Columbia University is quoted as decrying the "adversary morass."
19. *Changing Times*, April 1983.
20. *New York Times*, February 8, 1976.
21. *Newsweek*, January 10, 1977.
22. *U.S. News and World Report*, loc. cit.
23. *New York Times*, July 5, 1981.
24. *Los Angeles Times*, Feb. 12, 1978, quoting Judge J. Anthony Kline.
25. *New York Times*, March 10, 1985.
26. Jerold S. Auerbach, *Justice Without Law*, New York: Oxford University Press (1983), p. 3.

CHAPTER 5

1.   Galanter, op. cit., p. 56.
2.   Ibid.
3.   Ibid., p. 52.
4.   Ibid.
5.   Ibid., p. 59.
6.   Ibid., p. 52.
7.   Ibid., p. 39.
8.   Daniels, op. cit., p. 21.
9.   Ibid., pp. 20-21.
10. Galanter, op. cit., p. 40.
11. Ibid., p. 42.
12. *Business of State Trial Courts*, op. cit., p. 91.
13. Richard Abel in David Kairys, edit., *Politics of Law*, New York: Pantheon Books (1982), p. 186.
14. Sidney Lens, *The Labor Wars*, New York: Doubleday & Co. (1973), p. 5.
15. John Guinther, *Moralists and Managers: Public Interest Movements in America*, New York: Doubleday/Anchor Press (1976), p. 25.
16. Friedman, op. cit., p. 412.
17. Ibid., pp. 262, 410.
18. Stuart M. Speiser, *Lawsuit*, New York: Horizon Press (1980), p. 589.
19. Guinther, *Moralists and Managers*, loc. cit.
20. Speiser, loc. cit.
21. Ibid., p. 122.
22. Friedman, op. cit., p. 277.
23. Speiser, op. cit., p. 140.
24. Ibid., p. 141.
25. Ibid.
26. Friedman, op. cit., p. 262.
27. Speiser, op. cit., p. 127.
28. Friedman, op. cit., p. 411.
29. Speiser, op. cit., p. 126.
30. Friedman, op. cit., pp. 262 ff., pp. 409 ff.
31. Maitland 1, op. cit., p. 54.
32. Cornelius J. Peck, "Judicial Creativity and Tort Law," *Trial Magazine*, Vol. 21, No. 4 (1985), p. 22.
33. Friedman, op. cit., p. 417.
34. Ibid., p. 415.
35. William Prosser, *Handbook on the Law of Torts*, St. Paul: West Publishing Co. (1964), p. 924.
36. Guinther, *Winning Your Personal Injury Suit*, op. cit., p. 198.
37. Friedman, op. cit., p. 416.
38. Ibid., p. 413.
39. Ibid., p. 263.
40. Speiser, op. cit., p. 125.
41. Maitland 2, op. cit., p. 528.

42. Quoted in Speiser, loc. cit.
43. Friedman, op. cit., pp. 417, 489.
44. John Guinther, *Philadelphia*, Tulsa: Continental Heritage Press (1982), pp. 96-97.
45. Ibid., p. 114; International Ladies Garment Workers Union archives.
46. The *New York World*, quoted in Speiser, op. cit., p. 137.
47. Friedman, op. cit., p. 420.
48. Ibid., p. 425, though principally in railroad accident cases.
49. Kairys, *Politics of Law*, op. cit., p. 189.
50. Speiser, op. cit., p. 146.
51. Galanter, op. cit., p. 40.
52. Ibid.
53. *Statistical Abstract 1984*, op. cit., p. 6: U.S. Dept. of Commerce, p. 5.
54. *Business of State Trial Courts*, op. cit., p. 70.
55. *Statistical Abstract of the United States 1976*, Washington, D.C.: U.S. Dept. of Commerce, p. 5.
56. *Statistical Abstract of the United States 1985*, Washington, D.C.: U.S. Department of Commerce, p. 69.
57. *Statistical Abstract 1976*, op. cit., p. 6.
58. *Statistical Abstract 1985*, op. cit., p. xvii.
59. Ibid., p. xxii.
60. Ibid., p. 9.
61. *Business of State Trial Courts*, op. cit., p. 64.
62. *Statistical Abstract 1985*, op. cit., p. 127.
63. *Statistical Abstract 1984*, op. cit., p. 144.
64. Ibid.; the 1983 figure was 18.8%, *Statistical Abstract 1985*, op. cit. p. 134.
65. Ibid., p. 149; *Philadelphia Inquirer*, December 20, 1985.
66. *Statistical Abstract 1984*, op. cit., p. 121.
67. Guinther, *Winning Your Personal Injury Suit*, op. cit., p. 244.
68. *Statistical Abstract 1984*, loc. cit.
69. "Sudden Riches for the Casualty Industry," *Business Week,* May 1, 1978, p. 68.
70. *Statistical Abstract 1985*, op. cit., p. 390.
71. Ibid., p. 426; *Statistical Abstract 1984*, op. cit., p. 443.
72. Ibid.
73. Ibid., p. 422.
74. Ibid., p. 121.
75. Galanter, op. cit., pp. 66-67; Speiser, op. cit., p. 584; Jack Etheridge, *Use of Voluntary Dispute Resolution Techniques*, Washington, D.C.: Roscoe Pound Foundation (1985), p. 5, quoting A.E. Dick Howard, "A Litigation Society," *Wilson Quarterly*, Summer 1981, p. 107; Richard L. Abel, "The Contradictions of Informal Justice," in *Politics of Informal Justice*, Vol. One, New York: Academic Press (1982), p. 275.
76. Galanter, loc. cit.
77. Ibid., p. 11.

78. J. Anthony Kline, "Law Reform and the Courts," 53 *California State Bar Journal* 14 (1978).

79. Galanter, op. cit., p. 66.

80. Abel, op. cit., pp. 272 ff.

81. *Statistical Abstract 1985*, p. 38.

82. Ibid., p. 82.

83. *Statistical Abstract 1984*, op. cit., p. 532.

84. Galanter, op. cit., p. 20, quoting Trubek *et al, Civil Litigation Research Project*, Vol. One, p. 94, for 35%, and J. Ladinsky & C. Susmilch, *Community Factors in the Brokerage of Consumer Problems* 24 (1982), p. 19, for 3%. (On file at *UCLA Law Review*.)

85. *Statistical Abstract 1985*, op. cit., p. 520.

86. Ibid.

87. Interview, Judge Emil F. Goldhaber, U.S. Bankruptcy Court for Eastern District of Pennsylvania, March 5, 1985.

88. Interview, William Trencher, Federal Judicial Center quoting its statistics for 5%, Government Accounting Office for 6%, March 5, 1985.

89. *Statistical Abstract 1984*, op. cit., p. xvii.

90. Galanter, op. cit., p. 12.

91. Alfred E. Hofflander and Blaine F. Nye, *Medical Malpractice Insurance in Pennsylvania*, Menlo Park: Management Analysis Center, Inc. (undated, but study incorporates 1985 figures), p. i.

92. United States Senate Hearing, Dec 3, 1975, Subcommittee on Health of Comm. on Labor and Public Welfare, pp. 154, 220; *Medical Economics*, September 29, 1975; ISO, *All-Industry Medical Malpractice Insurance Committee Report* (1975) quoting Insurance Services Office statistics, p. 20.

93. John Guinther, *The Malpractitioners*, New York: Doubleday/Anchor Press (1978), p. 3.

94. *All-Industry Report*, op. cit., p. 1, in which (in 1975) it is firmly if redundantly stated: "We are living in an increasingly litigious society in which citizens are quick to sue." (p. 6)

95. Insurance Services Office, *Special Malpractice Review: 1974 Closed Claim Survey Preliminary Analysis of Survey Results* (Dec. 1975); Insurance Services Office, *Special Malpractice Review . . . Technical Analysis of Survey Results* (Dec. 1976).

96. *Statistical Abstract 1976*, op. cit., p. 83; *Statistical Abstract 1984*, p. 115.

97. Marion Friedman, M.D., "Iatrogenic Disease," *Postgraduate Medicine*, June 1982, p. 123.

98. Knight Steel, M.D. *et al*, "Iatrogenic Illness on a General Medical Service at a University Hospital," *New England Journal of Medicine*, Vol. 304, No. 11 (1981), p. 638.

99. Friedman, M., *loc. cit.*

100. William B. Schwartz, M.D., "Doctors, Damages and Deterrence," *New England Journal of Medicine*, Vol. 298, 1282, June 8, 1978, quoted in Thomas Goddard, *American Medical Association is*

Wrong—There is No Medical Malpractice Crisis, Washington, D.C.: Association of Trial Lawyers of America (1985), p. 10.

101. Guinther, *Malpractitioners*, op. cit., p. 125. There is no single reputable source for counting malpractice claims, or even any agreement on what constitutes a claim. The 46,000 is a projection based on high-end estimates. Some sources put the mid-1980s frequency either at well under (42,000, according to one) or perhaps double that number (according to another).
102. Galanter, op. cit., p. 13.
103. Hofflander, op. cit., p. iii. The study indicates there may have been a decline in claims during 1983 and 1984.
104. *Statistical Abstract 1984*, op. cit., p. 111.
105. Guinther, *Malpractitioners*, op. cit., pp. 7, 125.
106. HEW Report, op. cit., p. 6; *Hospital Medical Staff Magazine*, May 1975, quoting Carl Weissberg, American Federation of Hospitals. The 3,000 is extrapolated from these sources by working back from the 1966 figures, based on 1-2% increment per annum between 1960 and 1966. No 1960 figures from contemporary sources are available. The 3,000, therefore, is an estimate based on an estimate, and considering that some of the figures on which it is based may be overstated, it errs, if anywhere, on the high side.
107. For example, see Richard Chodoff, M.D., *Doctor for the Prosecution*, New York: G.P. Putnam's Sons (1983).
108. Patricia M. Danzon, *Frequency and Severity of Medical Malpractice Claims*, Santa Monica: Rand Institute for Civil Justice (1982), p. vi; Galanter, op. cit., p. 46.
109. *Citation*, Chicago: American Medical Association, Vol. 30, No. 12 (1974).
110. Ibid., Vol. 31, No. 8 (1975); Vol. 33, No. 12 (1976).
111. Ibid., Vol. 34, Vol. 2 (1976). For a general discussion of the informed consent issue, see Guinther, *Malpractitioners*, op. cit., pp. 87 ff.
112. Maitland 1, op. cit., p. 59.
113. Peck, op. cit., pp. 19-20. The first major enunciation of the privity doctrine apparently occurred in an English case, *Winterbottom v. Wright*, 152 *English Law Reports* 402 (1842).
114. 111 N.E. 1050 (N.Y., 1916); Speiser, op. cit., p. 306.
115. Ibid., p. 308.
116. N.J. 161 A.2d 69 (1960).
117. 59 Cal.2d 57, 377 P.2d 897, *California Law Reporter* (1962); for discussions, see Speiser, op. cit., p. 309; Peck, op. cit., p. 19.
118. Maitland 1, op. cit., p. 55.
119. Friedman, L., op. cit., p. 125 for a discussion of an unusual Ohio case involving the use of dynamite that apparently did not become precedential.
120. *First Four Years*, op. cit., p. 39.
121. Speiser, op. cit., p. 309.
122. *First Four Years*, op. cit., pp. 40-41.
123. Irwin Ross, "A Philadelphia Lawyer's Class-Action Gold Mine," *Fortune Magazine*, September 7, 1981, p. 102.

124. Sir Henry Maine, *The Ancient Law* (1890), quoted in *Trial Magazine*, May/June 1975.

125. *Escola v. Coca-Cola Bottling Co.*, 24 Cal. 453, 462, 158 P.2d 440 (1944).

126. Richard Abel, "Delegalization," in E. Blankenburg *et al*, editors, *Alternative Rechtsformen und Alternativen zum Recht*, Opladen: Westdeutscher Verlag, 1979, pp. 33-34.

127. *NAIC Malpractice Claims*, Milwaukee: National Association of Insurance Commissioners, No. 4 (1976), p. 137.

128. Abel, *Delegalization*, op. cit., p. 30.

129. An exception in California where the judge does the evaluating; see *First Four Years*, op. cit., p. 28.

130. Patricia A. Ebener and Donna R. Betancourt, *Court-Annexed Arbitration*, Santa Monica: Rand Institute for Civil Justice (1985), p. v.

131. Ibid., pp. 9-10.

132. Ibid., pp. 2-4.

133. Jane W. Adler *et al*, *Simple Justice*, Santa Monica: Rand Institute for Civil Justice (1983), p. xiv.

134. Ebener, op. cit., pp. 9-10.

135. Ibid., pp. 62-63.

136. Ibid., p. xiv.

137. *First Four Years*, op. cit., p. 28; Eric D. Green, *The Complete Courthouse*, Washington, D.C.: Roscoe Pound Foundation (1985), p. 18.

138. Ibid.

139. Ibid., pp. 23-4; Ebener, loc. cit.

140. Ibid.

141. Conciliation programs under court control had their origin in Scandinavia during the 19th century; in Norway, no civil case could go to trial that had not first gone through a conciliation attempt. The first American use appears to have been in Cleveland in 1913 where all claims for $35 or less went before a judge who tried to resolve them through appeals to "common sense." Chicago, New York, and Philadelphia followed with their own versions, and by the 1920s, during the heyday of faith in the business community, many commercial cases, frequently of considerable size, were undergoing conciliation or arbitration often under the aegis of chambers of commerce, though with court supervision. In Detroit, in the late 1920s, the judges, facing what they perceived to be a litigation explosion, instituted a mandatory program to attempt settlements of neighborhood disputes without trial, and similar efforts were made in a few other places, but most courts found such programs either unappealing or unnecessary. See esp. Auerbach, op. cit., pp. 72 ff.; Carrie Menkel-Meadow, *For and Against Settlement*, Washington, D.C.: Roscoe Pound Foundation (1985), pp. 6-7.

142. *Problem Solving Through Mediation*, Washington, D.C.: American Bar Association, Dispute Resolution Series No. 3 (1984), p. 15.

143. *Alternative Dispute Resolution*, Washington, D.C.: American Bar Association, Panel Discussion Series—Topic 1 (1982), p. 43.
144. Ibid., p. 44.
145. Ibid., pp. 55-56.
146. Abel, *Contradictions of Informal Justice*, op. cit., pp. 270 ff.
147. Ibid.
148. Ibid., pp. 277-78.
149. Green, op. cit., p. 37.
150. Ibid., pp. 40 ff.
151. Ibid., p. 42.
152. Ibid., p. 44.
153. Ibid., pp. 46, 49.
154. Ibid., p. 46.
155. Lambros, op. cit., pp. 5-6.
156. Ibid., p. 7.
157. Abel, op. cit., p. 289.
158. Harold Kohn, interview.
159. Speiser, op. cit., p. 146.
160. Ibid., p. 144.
161. Ibid., p. 147.
162. Ibid., p. 142.
163. Abel in *Politics of Law*, op. cit., p. 193.
164. Speiser, op. cit., p. 141.
165. Ibid., p. 122.
166. Ibid., p. 116.
167. Ibid., p. 142.
168. ATLA spokesperson.
169. Speiser, op. cit., pp. 196-97.
170. Danzon, op. cit., p. 36.
171. *First Four Years*, op. cit., p. 31.
172. Hofflander, op. cit., p. 98.
173. *Intermountain Medical Malpractice Seminar*, Washington, D.C.: Dep. HEW 76-3150 (1976); interviews by author with medical malpractice specialists for 80%; *HEW Report . . . on Medical Malpractice, Appendix*, op. cit., p. 97.
174. Hofflander, op. cit., pp. 98-100.
175. *ATLA Law Reporter*, Washington, D.C.: Association of Trial Lawyers of America. Reports on such cases are to be found in most issues; see esp. Vol. 26, No. 8 (1983), p. 352.
176. Ibid., Vol. 26, No. 2 (1983), p. 67.
177. Ibid., p. 74.
178. *Youngberg v. Romeo*, 457 U.S. 307 (1982).
179. Sy DuBow, "Employment Discrimination," *Trial Magazine*, Vol. 19, No. 12 (1983), pp. 39 ff.
180. John Guinther, "Only Good Indian," *Philadelphia Magazine*, October 1973.
181. *ATLA Law Reporter*, op. cit., Vol. 27, No. 2 (1984), p. 310; ibid., Vol. 26, No. 10 (1983), p. 459.

182. Ibid., Vol. 26, No. 3 (1983), p. 99.

183. Ibid., Vol. 26, No. 7 (1983), p. 318.

184. Ibid., Vol. 26, No. 8 (1983), p. 358.

185. *Philadelphia Daily News*, June 26, 1985.

186. *ATLA Law Reporter*, op. cit., Vol. 26, No. 3, p. 101; Vol. 26, No. 10, pp. 439 ff.

187. Ibid., Vol. 26, No. 7, p. 290.

188. *New York Times*, June 17, 1978; *Philadelphia Inquirer*, March 26, 1986.

189. Guinther, *Winning Your Personal Injury Suit*, op. cit., p. 262, based on statutes in effect in 1978.

190. *ATLA Products Liability Law Reporter*, Washington, D.C.: Association of Trial Lawyers of America, Vol. 2, No. 7 (1983), p. 108.

191. ATLA Law Reporter, op. cit., Vol. 26, No. 10, pp. 459-60.

192. Ibid., Vol. 27, No. 7, pp. 290-92.

193. Ibid., Vol. 26, No. 5, p. 212.

194. Ibid., Vol. 26, No. 7, p. 325.

195. *ATLA Products Liability Law Reporter*, op. cit., Vol. 3, No. 1 (1984), p. 14.

196. *ATLA Law Reporter*, op. cit., Vol. 27, No. 6 (1984), pp. 252 ff. Five children died in the conflagration. The jury damage award was $8,037,371, the remainder interest payments.

197. Etheridge, op. cit., p. 4, quoting Howard, "A Litigious Society?", *Wilson Quarterly*, Summer 1981, p. 100.

198. Galanter, op. cit., p. 45.

CHAPTER 6

1. William L. Prosser, "The Assault Upon the Citadel," *Yale Law Journal*, Vol. 69, No. 7 (1960), p. 1099.

2. Victor E. Flango and Jeanne A. Ito, "Advance Caseload Report, 1983," *State Court Journal*, Vol. 8, No. 4 (Fall 1984), p. 8. (Hereafter, *1983 Caseload Report*.)

3. *Business of State Trial Courts*, op. cit., p. 15.

4. Ibid., p. 39.

5. *State Court Caseload Statistics: Annual Report, 1980*, Williamsburg: National Center For State Courts (1984), p. 119. (Hereafter, *State Court Statistics, 1980*.) Interview with Victor E. Flango, Senior Staff Assoc., National Center for State Courts.

6. *Business of State Trial Courts*, op. cit., p. 9.

7. *State Court Statistics, 1980*, op. cit., pp. 387 ff., 444 ff., as e.g. re Ohio and Texas.

8. *1983 Caseload Report*, op. cit., p. 12.

9. *Business of State Trial Courts*, op. cit., p. 11.

10. Ibid.

11. Galanter, op. cit., p. 62; Stephen Daniels, "Ladders and Bushes—The Problem of Caseloads and Studying Court Activities Over Time," *American Bar Foundation Research Journal*, 1984, Number 4, pp. 765, 767.
12. *Business of State Trial Courts*, op. cit., p. 2; Flango interview, op. cit.
13. *Federal Court Statistics, 1984*, op. cit., pp. 3, 5.
14. *1983 Caseload Report*, op. cit., p. 9.
15. *Federal Court Statistics, 1984*, op. cit., p. 12.
16. *State Court Statistics, 1980*, op. cit., pp. 159-62.
17. Patent infringement and antitrust cases would be two examples; however, both the state and federal courtloads may be growing increasingly "complex," not in the sense of the difficulty of the underlying legal issues but because of the increasing amount of discovery and other paperwork that seems to surround them. See Molly Selvin and Patricia A. Ebener, *Managing the Unmanageable*, Santa Monica: Rand Institute for Civil Justice (1984), p. viii.
18. *Federal Court Statistics, 1980*, op. cit., p. 126; *Federal Court Statistics, 1984*, op. cit., p. 4.
19. *Philadelphia Inquirer*, December 30, 1985.
20. For a general analysis of predictability problems, see Daniels, *Ladders and Bushes*, op. cit., and esp. pp. 768 ff.
21. *Historical Statistics, Colonial Times to 1970*, Washington, D.C.: U.S. Department of Commerce (1976), pp. 1097-1118; *Statistical Abstract 1985*, op. cit., p. 179.
22. *Philadelphia Inquirer*, loc. cit.
23. *Federal Court Statistics, 1980*, op. cit., p. 125.
24. *Federal Court Statistics, 1984*, op. cit., p. 1.
25. 1970 figures provided by U.S. Courts administrative office; *Federal Court Statistics, 1980*, p. 227; *Federal Court Statistics, 1984*, p. 4.
26. *Federal Court Statistics, 1980*, op. cit., p. 234.
27. *Federal Court Statistics, 1984*, loc. cit.
28. Victor E. Flango and Nora F. Blair, "Relative Impact of Diversity Cases on State Trial Courts," *State Court Journal* (Summer 1978), p. 20.
29. Ibid., p. 21.
30. 1970 figures provided, op. cit.; *Federal Court Statistics, 1984*, op. cit., p. 4.
31. *Federal Court Statistics, 1980*, op. cit., p. 245.
32. *Federal Court Statistics, 1984*, op. cit., Appendix, p. 6.
33. *Federal Court Statistics, 1980*, op. cit., p. 243.
34. Ibid., pp. 231-32; *Federal Court Statistics, 1984*, op. cit., Appendix, p. 7.
35. Ibid.
36. 1970 figures provided, op. cit.; *Federal Court Statistics, 1980*, op. cit., p. 227; *Federal Court Statistics, 1984*, op. cit., p. 4.
37. *Business of State Trial Courts*, op. cit., pp. 5-6.
38. *Federal Court Statistics, 1980*, op. cit., p. 227.
39. *Federal Court Statistics, 1984*, loc. cit.

40. 1970 figures provided, op. cit.; *Federal Court Statistics, 1980*, loc. cit.; *Federal Court Statistics, 1984*, loc. cit.
41. *Federal Court Statistics, 1980*, op. cit., p. 246.
42. *Federal Court Statistics, 1984*, op. cit., Appendix, p. 7.
43. Ibid., p. 6.
44. *Federal Court Statistics, 1980*, op. cit., p. 260.
45. Menkel-Meadow, op. cit., pp. 10-11, quoting M. Rosenberg, *The Pretrial Conference and Effective Justice* (1964), and S. Flanders, *Case Management and Court Management in the United States District Courts* (1977).
46. Ibid.
47. *Federal Court Statistics, 1980*, op. cit., p. 126.
48. *Philadelphia Inquirer*, loc. cit.
49. Robert W. Page, Jr., *et al*, "Can Your Court Afford a Judge?", *State Court Journal*, Summer 1981, p. 20.
50. Flango, *Relative Impact of Diversity Cases*, loc. cit.
51. Ibid., p. 23.
52. Higginbotham, op. cit., p. 55, quoting Devitt, "Federal Jury Trials Should Be Abolished," *ABA Bar Journal*, Vol. 60 (1970), p. 570.
53. *Statistical Abstract 1985*, op. cit., p. 178. Note that figures do not always agree (see, e.g., same source, p. 179) with the difference apparently caused by varying definitions of what constitutes a trial.
54. *Historical Statistics*, op. cit., pp. 1097-1111; *Statistical Abstract, 1984*, op. cit., p.179.
55. *Philadelphia Inquirer*, loc. cit.
56. *Federal Court Statistics, 1980*, op. cit., p. 126.
57. *Philadelphia Inquirer*, loc. cit.
58. *Federal Court Statistics, 1980*, op. cit., pp. 408-09.
59. *Statistical Abstract 1984*, op. cit., pp. 188-89; *Statistical Abstract 1985*, op. cit., p. 179.
60. Ibid.; ibid.
61. *Federal Court Statistics, 1980*, op. cit., p. 299.
62. Galanter, op. cit., pp. 44-45.
63. *Federal Court Statistics 1980*, op. cit., p. 299.
64. Ibid., pp. 407-08.
65. Ibid., pp. 409-10.
66. Ibid., p. 409.
67. Hans Zeisel, Harry Kalven, Jr., and Bernard Buchholtz, *Delay in the Court*, Boston: Little Brown & Co. (1959), p. 52.
68. *Federal Court Statistics, 1980*, op. cit., p. 413.
69. "ABA Discussions Compare British and American Legal Systems," *Legal Intelligencer*, July 23, 1985.
70. *Federal Court Statistics, 1984*, op. cit., p. 60.
71. Ibid.
72. Fuchsberg, loc. cit.; Pressler, op. cit., p. 57.
73. *American Jury*, op. cit., pp. 517-20.
74. Speiser, op. cit., p. 588.

75. *1983 Caseload Report*, op. cit., p. 12.
76. Ibid.; *State Court Load Statistics: Annual Report, 1976*, Williamsburg: National Center For State Courts (1980), pp. 62-67 (hereafter, *State Court Statistics, 1976*); *State Court Statistics, 1980*, op. cit., pp. 58-66.
77. Daniels, *Ladders and Bushes*, op. cit., p. 786.
78. Interview, Flango.
79. Interview, David S. Shrager.
80. Daniels, *Ladders and Bushes*, op. cit., p. 790.
81. *State Court Statistics, 1976*, op. cit., pp. 143-384; *State Court Statistics, 1980*, op. cit., pp. 155-482.
82. Interview, Richard Ross.
83. *Preliminary Examination of Available Civil and Criminal Trend Data in State Trial Courts for 1978, 1981 and 1984*, Williamsburg: National Center for State Courts (1986).
84. Ibid., Summary pp. 1-2; Table 34.
85. *State Court Statistics, 1976*, op. cit., p. 83; *State Court Statistics, 1980*, op. cit., p. 84.
86. Ibid., p. 79; ibid., p. 77.
87. Ebener, op. cit., pp. v-vi, p. 3.
88. *1983 Caseload Report*, op. cit., p. 13.
89. Although there was good news on that front, too, by the mid-1980s. Bureau of Justice Statistics reported a decline in victimization rates between 1973 and 1984 in a number of significant categories: Household burglaries were down 21%; motor vehicle theft, 20%; rapes, robberies and assaults, 5%, suggesting that criminal/civil case management problems, which may have been substantive at the beginning of the 1980s, should have been much less so by mid-decade. See *Bureau of Justice Statistics, Annual Report, Fiscal 1985*, Washington, D.C.: U.S. Department of Justice (1986), p. 6.
90. *Business of State Trial Courts*, op. cit., p. 38.
91. Ibid., pp. 43-44.
92. Ibid., p. 45; Galanter, op. cit., p. 43.
93. *State Court Statistics, 1980*, op. cit., pp. 92-95.
94. *Business of State Trial Courts*, op. cit., p. 50.
95. Ibid., p. 52.
96. Ibid., p. 53; interview, Stephen Daniels, American Bar Foundation, whose research, based on thirty districts across the country, indicates that tort cases are "comfortably a majority and probably more" of all civil jury trials.
97. Ibid., p. 44; Roper, op. cit., pp. 188-89; Flango interview.
98. Padawer-Singer, op. cit., pp. 47-48; *First Four Years*, op. cit., p. 16.
99. Munsterman, op. cit., p. 4. Based on a 1980 population of just under 12 million.
100. Padawer-Singer, loc. cit.
101. *American Jury System*, op. cit., pp. 8-9.

CHAPTER 7

1. Michael Zander, "The Jury in England," *American Jury System*, Washington, D.C.: Roscoe Pound Foundation (1977), pp. 33-34.
2. Zeisel, *Delay in the Court*, op. cit., p. 72.
3. Other terms used are "windfall" and "blockbuster"; for a general discussion, with citations of early use of this term in the 1970s, see Guinther, *Malpractitioners*, op. cit., pp. 250 ff.
4. Kalven, *Dignity of Civil Jury*, op. cit., pp. 597-98.
5. Broeder, op. cit., p. 750.
6. See, for example, Bermant, op. cit., pp. 35-37 in which lawyers gave their reasons for selecting jury or bench trial in complex and protracted cases.
7. Mark A. Peterson, *New Tools for Reducing Civil Litigation Expenses*, Santa Monica: Rand Institute for Civil Justice (1983), p. vii.
8. Audrey Chin and Mark A. Peterson, *Deep Pockets, Empty Pockets*, Santa Monica: Rand Institute for Civil Justice (1985), passim; Peterson, *Cook County*, op. cit., p. 37; Broeder, loc. cit.
9. Peterson, *Cook County*, op. cit., pp. 35-37; *First Four Years*, op. cit., pp. 20-21; Mark A. Peterson and Audrey Chin, "Juries Don't Ignore Assets and Identity of Defendant," loc. cit.; Mark A. Peterson and Michael Shanley, *Unequal Justice*, Santa Monica: Rand Institute for Civil Justice (1985), p. 26. (Draft version, p. numbers and content may differ in published form.)
10. Ibid., pp. vi-viii; Audrey Chin and Mark A. Peterson, *Compensating Plaintiffs*, Santa Monica: Rand Institute for Civil Justice (1986), pp. 5 ff. (Draft version, p. numbers and content may differ in published form.)
11. Peterson, *Unequal Justice*, p. vi, but see discussion throughout on changes in patterns in two cities, San Francisco and Chicago, over time.
12. Peterson, *Juries Don't Ignore*, loc. cit.
13. Peterson, *Cook County*, op. cit., p. ix; *First Four Years*, op. cit., p. 18.
14. *First Four Years*, loc. cit.
15. Peterson, *Cook County*, op. cit., p. 57.
16. Charles Wyzanski, "A Trial Judge's Freedom and Responsibility," *Harvard Law Review* 65, 1281, 1287 (1952), quoted in Scheflin, op. cit., p. 69.
17. Peterson, *Cook County*, op. cit., quoting California Citizens Committee on Tort Reform (1977), p. 1.
18. *NAIC Malpractice Claims*, op. cit., No. 4, p. 101.
19. According to a study by ATLA (1986), this is also true of most large awards, with the average award in million-dollar cases in 1984-85 reduced eventually by 55.2%.
20. Peterson, *Cook County*, op. cit., pp. 46-7.
21. Ibid., pp. ix, 44.
22. *First Four Years*, p. 19.

23. Peterson, *Cook County*, op. cit., p. 57.
24. *New York Times*, March 10, 1985, quoting Jury Verdict Research, Inc.
25. *ATLA Products Liability Law Reporter*, op. cit., Vol. 2, No. 8, p. 124.
26. *ATLA Law Reporter*, op. cit., Vol. 26, No. 2, p. 82.
27. Ibid., Vol. 26, No. 9, pp. 392-97.
28. Ibid., Vol. 26, No. 4, p. 181.
29. Ibid., Vol. 26, No. 10, p. 459.
30. Ibid., p. 460.
31. Ibid., p. 461.
32. Ibid., Vol. 27, No. 1, p. 27.
33. Ibid., Vol. 27, No. 3, p. 130.
34. Ibid., p. 133.
35. Ibid., Vol. 27, No. 7, pp. 290 ff.
36. Ibid., Vol. 27, No. 6, pp. 242 ff.
37. Ibid., p. 286.
38. Ibid., p. 283.
39. Ibid., Vol. 27, No. 7, p. 328.
40. Ibid., pp. 331-32.
41. Ibid., p. 334.
42. Ibid., Vol. 27, No. 5, p. 236.
43. Ibid., Vol. 27, No. 4, pp. 165-66.
44. Ibid., Vol. 27, No. 1, p. 30.
45. Ibid., p. 28.
46. Ibid., p. 35.
47. Ibid., Vol. 26, No. 7, p. 304.
48. Ibid., Vol. 26, No. 10, pp. 450-51.
49. Ibid., Vol. 26, No. 7, p. 306.
50. Ibid., Vol. 26, No. 8, p. 369.
51. Ibid., Vol. 26, No. 9, pp. 401-02.
52. Ibid., Vol. 27, No. 3, p. 129.
53. *Philadelphia Inquirer*, April 18, 1985.
54. *NAIC Malpractice Claims*, No. 4, op. cit., pp. 15, 101.
55. Peterson, *Cook County*, loc. cit.
56. Ibid., p. 18; Chin, *Fairness in Civil Jury Trials*, op. cit., p. 3.
57. Peterson, *Cook County*, op. cit., pp. 19-20.
58. Ibid., pp. 32-33.
59. *Statistical Abstract 1985*, op. cit., p. 466.
60. Ibid., p. 108; *Statistical Abstract 1984*, op. cit., p. 114.
61. *Statistical Abstract 1985*, op. cit., p. 476.
62. Peterson, *Cook County*, op. cit., pp. 50-51.
63. Ibid., p. 9.
64. Goddard, op. cit., p. 6.
65. Peterson, *Unequal Justice*, op. cit., p. 22; Chin, *Compensating Plaintiffs*, op. cit., pp. 10, 70.
66. Ibid.; Mark N. Cooper, *Trends in Liability Awards*, Washington, D.C.: Consumer Federation of America (1986), reaches the same conclusions using different statistical bases (see esp. pp. i-viii).

67. Peterson, *Cook County*, op. cit., quoting F.P. Watkins, "Social Inflation: Our Next Trial," *Insurance*, Vol. 77, No. 10 (1976).
68. *First Four Years*, op. cit., p. 18; Jury Verdict Research, Inc., also reports fewer than 50% victories for plaintiffs in malpractice and product liability cases; corres., Philip J. Hermann, Chairman, Jury Verdict Research, Inc., May 2, 1986.
69. Peterson, *Cook County*, op. cit., p. 38.
70. *Armstrong Industries v. Forer, Respondent's Brief*, Sup. Ct. Penna. 193 (Misc. Docket, 1984).
71. *First Four Years*, op. cit., p. 40.
72. Ibid.
73. *Philadelphia Inquirer*, April 5, 1985.
74. Ibid., August 22, 1985.
75. Ibid., January 1, 1986, re establishment by court of April 1986 deadline for filing of claims.
76. *New York Times*, March 10, 1985.
77. Interview, C. Thomas Bendorf.
78. *New York Times*, loc. cit.
79. *Philadelphia Inquirer*, August 22, 1985, loc. cit.
80. *Philadelphia Inquirer*, January 27, 1985.
81. *Perspective*, Second Quarter 1975, p. 29.
82. *Philadelphia Inquirer*, loc. cit.
83. U.S. Senate Hearing, op. cit., p. 7. Other estimates for defensive medicine in 1975 were as high as $7 million; for a general discussion, see Guinther, *Malpractitioners*, op. cit., pp. 22-24.
84. *Philadelphia Inquirer*, loc. cit.
85. Green, op. cit., p. 24.
86. *Lawyer's Digest*, March 1985; Adam Benjamin, Jr., "Indiana's Medical Malpractice Crisis," *Legislator's Guide to the Medical Malpractice Issue*, Washington, D.C.: Health Policy Center, Georgetown University (1976), p. 38.
87. Guinther, *Malpractitioners*, op. cit., p. 254. During the medical malpractice crisis of the mid-1970s, a number of states passed $500,000 caps on awards even though the average state had less than one such verdict a year. Thus the purpose could hardly have been to prevent the rare, very large awards but rather by setting a maximum on them to force down award sizes on all other verdicts.
88. Goddard, op. cit., p. 9; Stephen Daniels, "Punitive Damages: Storm on the Horizon?", speech at the American Bar Foundation Fellows Seminar, 1986, in which it is noted that even in cases in which punitive damages are awarded, the median total award was less than $50,000. Punitive damage awards are exceedingly rare and when they do occur, the study indicates, they most often are in cases involving personal violence, fraud, false arrest and insurer bad faith, none of which are areas that even the insurers themselves have cited as causing a litigation and resultant insurance crisis.
89. *First Four Years*, op. cit., p. 32, for savings. In Ontario, Canada, where even more stringent reforms were enacted—including elimina-

tion of contingency fees—the result was the raising of insurance premiums by 400%, with many instances of cancellation of coverage and refusal to provide coverage in some fields at any price. See "What Happens to Insurance Rates When 'Tort Reform' is Enacted?", National Insurance Consumer Organization, January 1986.

90. Goddard, op. cit., p. 11.
91. *First Four Years*, op. cit., p. 31.
92. Ibid., pp. 25-26.
93. Proposed Rule 68, Fed. R. Civ. Pro., 98 F.R.D. 337 (1983).
94. *First Four Years*, loc. cit.
95. Exactly what no-fault means, however, varies a great deal from state to state. For a summary of the various laws, see Guinther, *Winning Your Personal Injury Suit*, op. cit., pp. 246-51.
96. Abel, *Delegalization*, op. cit., p. 34.
97. Goddard, op. cit., pp. 10-11.
98. *Philadelphia Inquirer*, November 19, 1985.
99. *Closed Claims Study of Medical Malpractice Insurance, 1975-1982*, Office of the Insurance Commissioner, State of Florida (1983), quoted in Goddard, op. cit., p. 8.
100. Ibid.
101. S. Ferber and B. Sheridan, "Six Cherished Malpractice Myths Put to Rest," 52 *Medical Economics* 150 (1975).
102. Kathleen Gilligan Sibelius, spokesperson for Kansas Trial Lawyers Association; testimony before Special Committee on Medical Malpractice, September 12, 1985.
103. Hofflander, op. cit., p. xx.
104. Ibid., p. xviii.
105. There is nothing new in this. An HEW study in the early 1970s found that nationally 15 hospitals accounted for more than half the claims. See HEW Report, op. cit., p. 9.
106. Abel, *Delegalization*, op. cit., p. 30.
107. Ibid., p. 34.
108. Daniels, *Ladders and Bushes*, op. cit., pp. 756, 794-95.
109. *Business Week*, October 15, 1984; Stanley Wohl, *Medical Industrial Complex*, New York: Harmony Books (1985), p. 182.
110. Graduate Medical Education National Advisory Committee: *Report to the Secretary, Dept. of Health and Human Services*; Washington, D.C.: US Department of Health and Human Services (1980).
111. Paul Starr, *Social Transformation of American Medicine*, New York: Basic Books (1982), p. 437; Jeff Goldsmith, "Death of a Paradigm," *Health Affairs*, Vol. 3, No. 3 (1984), pp. 16-18.
112. Starr, loc. cit.
113. *Medical Economics*, September 9, 1985, pp. 197-211.
114. Wohl, op. cit., pp. 46, 76; Starr, op. cit., p. 441; *Business Week*, loc. cit.
115. Loc. cit.
116. Starr, op. cit., pp. 430-31.

117. "Report of the Fourth Duke University Medical Center Private Sector Conference," *New England Journal of Medicine*, July 19, 1984, p. 205.

118. Starr, op. cit., p. 447.

119. Duke University Report, op. cit., p. 207.

120. Insurance Services Office, *Special Malpractice Review, 1975*, loc. cit.; Insurance Services Office, *Special Malpractice Review, 1976*, loc. cit.

121. For the role of the civil jury in this educational process, see Chapter Nine.

122. Interview, Monte Preiser.

123. Ibid.

124. American Medical Association, *Malpractice in Focus*, prepared by editors of *Prism Magazine*, August 1975, p. 12.

125. *NAIC Report*, No. 4, op. cit., p. 95.

126. *ISO Report* (1975), op. cit., p. 43.

127. A. Russell Localio, "Variations on $962,258," *Law, Medicine and Health Care*, June 1985, pp. 126-27, quoting *Current Award Trends No. 280*, Solon: Jury Verdict Research, Inc.; *Medical Liability Monitor* 9(7):5 (1984). For discussion of average vs. median awards, see ibid. p. 127; Cooper, op. cit., pp. v-viii.

128. Goldberg, "Which Surgeons Are the Biggest Medical Malpractice Targets?", *Medical Economics for Surgeons*, August 1982, p. 40,", quoted in Thomas F. Londrigan, "The Medical Malpractice 'Crisis'," *Trial Magazine*, Vol. 21, No. 5 (1985), p. 25.

129. Tancredi and Barondess, "The Problem of Defensive Medicine," 200 *Science*, 879 (May 1978), quoted in Goddard, op. cit., p. 5; William B. Schwartz, M.D., speech at American Enterprise Institute for Public Policy, December 1976, quoted in Guinther, *Malpractitioners*, op. cit., pp. 263-64.

130. Hofflander, op. cit., p. xxv.

131. Wohl, op. cit., p. 97.

132. Calderone, op. cit., p. 1182, quoting Kronzer, "Jury Tampering—1978 Style," 10 *St. Mary's Law Review* (1979), pp. 399, 400.

133. Or 100,000, according to the Insurance Services Office. Calderone, ibid. The 70,000 is from Insurance Information Institute, "Insurance Facts, 1978."

134. State of New York Insurance Department, *In The Matter of the Medical Malpractice Insurance Association and Insurance Services Office*, Exhibit D, July 1976, pp. 35 ff.

135. Commonwealth of Pennsylvania Insurance Department, *In the Matter of: Request by David S. Masland and the Pennsylvania Medical Society...*, Docket No. R76-6-1.

136. Londrigan, op. cit., p. 24, quoting Dr. Edward Zalta, president of the Los Angeles Medical Society in Carlova, "How Doctors Forced a Malpractice Carrier to Refund $50 Million," *Medical Economics*, July 20, 1981, pp. 171-72.

137. Guinther, *Malpractitioners*, op. cit., pp. 185-88. The actual profit was probably higher, since the study deliberately used statistics that

were most favorable to the insurance industry's contention that it was losing money.

138. Andre Tobias, *Invisible Bankers*, New York: Simon & Schuster (1982), p. 54.
139. Guinther, *Malpractitioners*, op. cit., p. 188; Statement of Association of Trial Lawyers before the Subcommittee on Commerce, U.S. House of Representatives, April 9, 1981, Appendix.
140. *A.M. Best's Casualty Loss Reserve Development*, 1984, quoted in Goddard, op. cit., p. 3.
141. ATLA statement, op. cit., pp. 13-14.
142. Natwar M. Gandhi, Group Director, U.S. General Accounting Office, speech, August 20, 1985.
143. *Philadelphia Inquirer*, January 7, 1986.
144. Ibid.
145. William A.K. Titelman, "'Crisis' of Cost and Lack of Availability of Liability Insurance," *Barrister*, Vol. XVI, No. 4, addendum, p. 1, quoting *Best's Review*.
146. Gandhi, op. cit.
147. Ibid.
148. NICO (National Insurance Consumer Organization) *Newsletter*, Vol. 4, No. 4, pp. 1-2; NICO, January 1986, p. 2.
149. Interview, Mervin Taylor, A.M. Best & Co.; Insurance Information Institute statistics show that industry assets were $22 billion in 1955; $41 billion in 1965; $94 billion in 1975; $197 billion in 1980 and $265 billion in 1984.
150. Ibid.; *Best's Insurance Management Reports*, April 7, 1986.
151. Titelman, op. cit., p. 36, quoting *Best's Casualty Loss Reserve Development* (1985), in which Best's, the insurance industry bible, noted that in 1984 the industry's "own estimate of incurred loss and expense payments increased by the smallest amount since 1977. Yet, at the same time as the rate of growth of losses was declining, premiums increased by the largest margin since 1976, over 13%."
152. NICO, "Insurance Companies on Strike," August 15, 1985, p. 1; statement of Ralph Nader before Subcommittee on Commerce, U.S. House of Representatives, Sept. 19, 1985, p. 2.
153. Titelman, op. cit., p. 5.
154. Guinther, *Malpractitioners*, pp. 190-97; *Forbes Magazine*, April 1976.
155. Titelman, op. cit., p. 36.
156. Taylor interview, Best's, op. cit.

CHAPTER 8

1. *In re U.S. Financial Securities Litigation*, 609 F.2d 411 (1979) (Hereafter USF referring to Ninth Circuit Court opinion overturning lower court decision; see below for cite and future ref. to lower court opinion.)

2.   Ibid., p. 413.

3.   Ibid., pp. 411, 415.

4.   Ibid., p. 415.

5.   Nordenberg, op. cit., p. 422.

6.   USF, op. cit., p. 412.

7.   Ibid., p. 431.

8.   Ibid., p. 413; *In re U.S. Financial Securities Litigation*, 75 F.R.D. 702 (S.D. Cal. 1977), p. 702. (This is lower court decision by J. Turrentine; hereafter referred to as "Turrentine.")

9.   Ibid., p. 709.

10. USF, op. cit., p. 417.

11. Ibid., p. 413.

12. Ibid., p. 417.

13. *In re Japanese Electronic Products Antitrust Litigation*, 478 F.Supp. 889 (1979); also, sometimes known as *Zenith Radio Corporation v. Matsushita Electric Industrial Co., Ltd., et al.* (Hereafter referred to as "Becker" to distinguish it from same titled appeals court decision; see cite and ref. below.)

14. Loh, op. cit., p. 470.

15. Or more. Nordenberg, loc. cit.

16. Loh, loc. cit. Defendants were also worried about anti-Japanese remarks that had allegedly been made by several plaintiff attorneys at earlier stages of the case: They believed that these remarks, if repeated, would prejudice a jury against them. See *In re Japanese Electronic Products Antitrust Litigation*, 631 F.2d 1069 (1980), pp. 1090-91. (This is the Third Circuit Court decision issued by J. Seitz in part confirming and in part reversing Becker; hereafter referred to as "Seitz".)

17. Becker, op. cit., pp. 904 ff.

18. USF, op. cit., p. 413.

19. Ibid., pp. 418-19.

20. Seitz, op. cit., p. 1069.

21. USF, op. cit., p. 422.

22. E.g., see throughout footnotes for representative titles.

23. Interview, J. Becker; Loh, op. cit., p. 466.

24. Richard O. Lempert, "Civil Juries and Complex Cases: Let's Not Rush to Judgment," *Michigan Law Review*, Vol. 80, No. 68, p. 68.

25. Becker interview, op. cit.

26. USF, op. cit., p. 429 fn; Bermant, op. cit., p. 1; Higginbotham, op. cit., p. 47.

27. *Duncan v. Louisiana*, op. cit., pp. 451-52.

28. Becker, op. cit., p. 900.

29. Trubek, op. cit., p. 87. The basis for the estimate is not given, and it is difficult, if not impossible, to reach any verifiable percentage because of the difficulty of defining "complexity"; see discussion below in text this chapter.

30. We are not considering here complex criminal trials; no studies of them have been discovered. However, we know that to the extent

length is any index of complexity, a substantial number of the federal criminal trials run 20 days or more; see *Federal Court Statistics, 1980*, op. cit., pp. 411-12.

31. Bermant, loc. cit.
32. Lay, op. cit., p. 50.
33. Bermant, op. cit., pp. 7-8.
34. Devlin, op. cit., p. 1574.
35. USF, op. cit., pp. 417, 423.
36. Becker, op. cit., p. 907.
37. USF, op. cit., p. 422; Sperlich, op. cit., p. 400; Becker, op. cit., p. 906; Luneberg, op. cit., p. 901; Walker-Dittman, op. cit., pp. 493-94; Loh, op. cit., pp. 464-66.
38. Devlin, op. cit., *passim* presents the historical argument in its most elegant, if not necessarily persuasive, manner.
39. Arnold, op. cit., p. 845.
40. One party, a Dane, objected to the case being tried by a "common jury" in England, but apparently not on the grounds that it would be too complex for them to understand. See Ibid., p. 846.
41. Lempert, op. cit., p. 74.
42. Arnold, op. cit., p. 837.
43. The same apparently was true prior to the Revolution, i.e., cases that were to be preserved for equity jurisdiction rather than common law (where juries were permitted) also varied from colony to colony. See esp. ibid., p. 831.
44. Higginbotham, op. cit., pp. 49-50.
45. Lempert, op. cit., pp. 75-76.
46. *Ross v. Bernhard*, 90 S. Ct. 733 (1970), p. 733; USF, op. cit., p. 422; Becker, op. cit., p. 908.
47. *Ross v. Bernhard*, loc. cit.; Walker-Dittman, op. cit., p. 497.
48. Seitz, op. cit., p. 1083.
49. Becker, op. cit., p. 907.
50. Ibid.
51. Ibid.
52. USF, op. cit., p. 417.
53. Loc. cit.
54. *Ross v. Bernhard*, op. cit., p. 734; Walker-Dittman, op. cit., p. 496.
55. USF, op. cit., p. 424.
56. *Ross v. Bernhard*, op. cit., p. 738.
57. Sperlich, op. cit., pp. 404, 410.
58. Walker-Dittman, op. cit., p. 491.
59. *Ross v. Bernhard*, op. cit., pp. 735, 737-38; USF, loc. cit.; Walker-Dittman, op. cit., p. 492; Kersten, op. cit., p. 106.
60. Becker, op. cit., p. 926; Lempert, op. cit., p. 76.
61. USF, op. cit., p. 425; Walker-Dittman, op. cit., p. 501.
62. Becker, op. cit., pp. 927 ff.; USF, op. cit., p. 426.
63. *Rogers v. Loether*, 467 F.2d 110, 1117-8 (7th Cir., 1972). In Supreme Ct. as *Curtis v. Loether*, 415 U.S. 189 (1974), cited in Walker-Dittman, op. cit., p. 502.

64. USF, op. cit., p. 424.
65. Ibid., p. 425.
66. Becker, op. cit., pp. 929-30; Walker-Dittman, op. cit., pp. 503-4.
67. Maitland 1, op. cit., p. 41.
68. Sperlich, op. cit., p. 410, quoting Huttner, "Unfit for Jury Determination," 20 *Boston College Law Review*, 533.
69. USF, op. cit., p. 417.
70. Seitz, op. cit., p. 1084.
71. Bermant, op. cit., p. 7, speaking for the Federal Judicial Center: ". . . a reasonable proposition seems to be that juries should not be assigned tasks they cannot fairly accomplish."
72. Sperlich, op. cit., p. 411.
73. Preventive detention, in which a person is incarcerated in the expectation he or she will in the future commit an illegal act, is probably the most obvious employment of this device. At various times throughout American history, the injunction has also been misused in this manner.
74. Lempert, op. cit., p. 91.
75. Ibid., p. 95.
76. Luneberg, op. cit., pp. 899 ff.; Clyde Lowell Ball, "Constitutional Law—*In re Japanese Electronics* . . . ," *North Carolina Law Review*, Vol. 59 (1981), pp. 1273-74.
77. Luneberg, op. cit., p. 905, quoting J. Thayer, *A Preliminary Treatise on Evidence at the Common Law* (1898), 96 n. 2.
78. Ibid., pp. 950 ff., 995 ff.; Nordenberg, op. cit., pp. 423-28; Sperlich, op. cit., p. 416; Bermant, op. cit., pp. 65-67.
79. Luneberg, op. cit., p. 908, quoting Justice Murphy's dissent in *Fay v. New York*, 332 U.S. 261 (1947).
80. Nordenberg, op. cit., p. 426.
81. Luneberg, op. cit., pp. 903, 937; *Haas et al v. United Technologies Corp.*, loc. cit.
82. Luneberg, op. cit., pp. 913-15.
83. David U. Strawn and G. Thomas Munsterman, "Helping Juries Handle Complex Cases," *Judicature*, Vol. 65, Nos. 8-9 (1982), p. 445.
84. Luneberg, op. cit., pp. 947-48.
85. Nordenberg, op. cit., p. 426; for rebuttal, see Sperlich, op. cit., generally, esp. p. 409.
86. Kairys, *Jury Representativeness*, op. cit., p. 809 fn.
87. Lempert, op. cit., pp. 118 ff.
88. After the first week. Ibid., p. 118.
89. The majority did in the case of the jurors surveyed in the Pound study.
90. Seitz, op. cit., p. 1087, who presumes judges have the ability to decide complex cases; Ball, op. cit., p. 1270, basing his conclusion on ILC Peripherals case, discussed below in text.
91. Higginbotham, op. cit., p. 53; Lay, loc. cit.; Bermant, op. cit., p. 66; Kersten, op. cit., quoting J. Newman; Becker, op. cit., p. 935.
92. Kalven, *Dignity of the Jury*, op. cit., p. 599.

93. Kersten, loc. cit., quoting J. Newman in "Are Complex Trust Cases Fit for a Jury?", *New York Law Journal*, August 21, 1978. The case over which he presided was *SCM Corp. v. Xerox Corp*, 463 F.Supp. 983 (D. Conn. 1978).
94. Seitz, op. cit., pp. 1092-93. Judge Gibbons' dissent begins on page 1091.
95. USF, op. cit., p. 431.
96. Quoted in Kaufman, op. cit., p. 46. Jefferson also said, "I consider trial by jury as the only anchor ever yet imagined by man by which a government can be held to the principles of the Constitution," quoted in Pressler, op. cit., p. 56.
97. Becker, loc. cit.
98. *Fortune Magazine*, loc. cit.
99. Interview, Harold Kohn; Walker-Dittman, op. cit., p. 507.
100. Higginbotham, op. cit., p. 54.
101. *American Can Co. v. Dart Industries, Inc.*, 205 U.S.P.Q. (BNA) 1006 (N.D. Ill., 1979), p. 1008, quoted in Walker-Dittman, p. 508.
102. Ball, op. cit., p. 1271.
103. Higginbotham, loc. cit.
104. Kohn interview, op. cit.
105. *ILC Peripherals Leasing Corp. v. IBM*, 458 F.Supp. 423, N.D. Calif. (1978).
106. Ibid., p. 448.
107. See esp. Kersten, op. cit., p. 114 fn.
108. ILC Peripherals, op. cit., transcript, p. 19551.
109. Kersten, loc. cit.
110. ILC transcript, op. cit., p. 19532.
111. Ibid., p. 19528. The jury's eventual vote was nine to two for ILC; the judge issued a direct verdict for IBM, see Kersten, loc. cit.; Sperlich, op. cit., p. 405.
112. Bermant, op. cit., p. 1. The quotes are the Federal Judicial Center's summary of Burger's statements.
113. Seitz, op. cit., p. 1086.
114. *Federal Court Statistics, 1980*, op. cit., p. 409.
115. Ibid.
116. Alexander, op. cit, pp. 64 ff.
117. Bermant, loc. cit.
118. Ibid.
119. Ibid., pp. 2-9.
120. Ibid., p. 22.
121. Ibid., pp. 69-75.
122. Ibid., p. 18.
123. Ibid.
124. Kohn interview, op. cit.
125. Bermant, op. cit., p. 26.
126. Ibid., p. 30.
127. Ibid., pp. 30-31.
128. *In re Fine Paper Antitrust Litigation*, 98 FRD 48.

129. Kohn interview, op. cit.
130. Lempert, op. cit., p. 96.
131. Sperlich, op. cit., p. 4l7.
132. Lempert, op. cit., p. ll2.
133. Sperlich, op. cit., p. 4l7, quoting Huttner from 1977 edition.
134. Lempert, op. cit., p. ll3.1135. Ibid., p. ll2; Strawn, op. cit., p. 445.
136. Sperlich, op. cit., p. 4l9.
137. Ibid.
138. Lempert, loc. cit.
139. Ibid., p. l23.
140. Ibid., pp. ll3-l5; USF, op. cit., p. 428.
141. Kersten, op. cit., p. ll7.
142. Lempert, op. cit., p. ll4.
143. Interview, Kohn, op. cit.; Lempert, loc. cit., raises the same question from a slightly different perspective.
144. Ibid., pp. l24-25; Bermant, op. cit., p. 32.
145. Second Circuit Court, op. cit., p. 68; Bermant, op. cit., p. 50; Walter-Goldberg, *Note-Taking*, op. cit., passim.
146. Second Circuit Court, op. cit., p. 58; Strawn, op. cit., p. 447; Lempert, op. cit., pp. l23-24; Sperlich, loc. cit.
147. Ibid.
148. Bermant, op. cit., p. 50.
149. Sperlich, loc. cit.; Strawn, op. cit., p. 446; Second Circuit Court, op. cit., p. 48; Lempert, op. cit., pp. l2l-22.
150. Ibid., p. l22.
151. Bermant, loc. cit.
152. Strawn, loc. cit.
153. Lempert, op. cit., p. l2l; see also discussion of this subject in Chapter Three.
154. Ibid., p. l22.
155. Ibid., p. l07; Strawn, loc cit.
156. Ibid.; Kohn interview, op. cit.
157. Lempert, loc. cit.
158. Ibid., p. l08.
159. Loh, op. cit., p. 473. This was the procedure used by the judge in *SCM Corp. v. Xerox Corp.*, op. cit.
160. Lempert, op. cit., pp. ll0-ll.
161. Forer, *Money and Justice*, op. cit., p. 99.
162. Strawn, loc. cit.
163. Sperlich, loc. cit.
164. Ibid., p. 409.
165. Walker-Dittman, op. cit., p. 505; Ball, op. cit., p. l272.
166. USF, op. cit., p. 432.
167. Seitz (Gibbons dissent), op. cit., p. l093.
168. Sperlich, op. cit., p. 4l2.

CHAPTER 9

1. John H. Wigmore, "A Program for the Trial of Jury Trial," *Journal of American Judicature Society*, 12: 166 (1929), quoted in Frank, op. cit., pp. 127-28.

2. *Sparf and Hansen v. U.S.*, op. cit.; Benton L. Becker, "Jury Nullification," *Trial Magazine*, Vol. 16, No. 10 (1980), pp. 41 ff; Scheflin, op. cit., *passim*.

3. *U.S. v. Moylan*, 417 F.2d 1002; *U.S. v. Dougherty*, 473 F.2d 1113 (1972); *U.S. v. Anderson et al*, USDS NJ Crim. No. 602-71 (1973); *Duncan v. Louisiana*, op. cit., 155-56; it has been argued that death-qualified juries violate the imposition of the conscience of the community since those members who oppose capital punishment are excluded; because this book is generally concerned with attacks on the civil jury, the death-qualified jury issue is beyond its scope; however, for an excellent analysis, see Scheflin, op. cit., pp. 76 ff.

4. *Duncan v. Louisiana*, loc. cit. The Ponting trial in England in 1985 provides a chilling example of the dictatorial power that government in a democracy can unleash and against which the jury may be the only effective weapon. Ponting, an English civil servant, became aware that his superiors in the Ministry of Defense had lied to Parliament about the circumstances surrounding the sinking of the Argentinian cruiser, *General Beltrano*, during the Falkland Islands conflict in 1982. Ponting proceeded to provide information documenting the prevarications to a member of Parliament. The material was politically embarrassing to the administration of Prime Minister Margaret Thatcher but was not, by the government's own admission, classified material. Even so, Ponting was arrested and charged with violation of Section Two of the British Official Secrets Act which makes it a crime, punishable by up to two years in prison, to reveal to anyone any information received during the course of government employment without official approval. At the trial Ponting asserted he had acted in the public interest; the judge dismissed that defense, telling the jury that the interests of the state, i.e., the British people, were identical to the political interests of the government in power, and if officials didn't want to be embarrassed by having their lies revealed, then it was in the public interest that their lies not be revealed. This interpretation left Ponting with no defense; his lawyer told the jurors: "If what he did was a crime in British law, you say so. But if it is, God help us—because no Government will." Despite the judge's instructions, the jury found Ponting not guilty. Were it not for the jury, the authoritarian view would have prevailed. See Clive Ponting, *The Right to Know*, London: Sphere Books, Ltd. (1985).

5. *Local 36 of International Fishermen & Allied Workers of America v. U.S.*, 177 F.2d 320 (9th Circuit, 1949), p. 339, quoted in Scheflin, op. cit., p. 74.

6. California Jury Instructions, Criminal, No. 1, p. 28.

7. Morris, op. cit., p. 78.

8. John Adams, *Works*, Boston: Little, Brown & Co. (1850), Vol. 2, pp. 253-55, quoted in Jon M. Van Dyke, *Jury Selection Procedures*, Cambridge: Ballinger Publishing Co. (1977), p. 228.

9. Ch. 75, 1 Stat 597 (1798), quoted in Scheflin, op. cit., p. 58.

10. Van Dyke, op. cit., p. 230.

11. Ibid., p. 231.

12. *U.S. v. Battiste*, 24 F. Cas. 1042, 1043, C.C.D. Mass., 1835, quoted in Van Dyke, loc. cit.

13. *U.S. v. Morris*, 26 F. Cass., 222-3 C.C.D. Mass., 1851, quoted in Van Dyke, op. cit., p. 232.

14. Ibid.

15. Friedman, op. cit., p. 347.

16. *Sparf and Hansen*, loc. cit.

17. Ibid., quoted in Van Dyke, op. cit., p. 233.

18. *U.S. v. Simpson*, 460 F.2d 515, 9th Circuit.

19. Ibid., p. 519.

20. *U.S. v. Dougherty*, op. cit.

21. Ibid., p. 1139.

22. Ibid., p. 1135.

23. In his dissent, Judge Bazelon pointed out (p. 1141) that the majority's view meant that the justice system has no obligation to be honest in what it tells jurors. For a discussion, see Scheflin, op. cit., pp. 106-7.

24. *U.S. v. Anderson*, op. cit.

25. Interview, David Kairys.

26. *U.S. v. Anderson*, op. cit., transcript p. 8729, quoted in Van Dyke, op. cit., pp. 238-39.

27. The legal issue was alleged government entrapment by overreaching; Kairys, interview, op. cit.

28. Kalven, *Dignity of the Jury*, op. cit., p. 595; *Arschack v. United States*, 321 A.2d 845 (1974), quoted in Scheflin, op. cit., p. 55; Van Dyke, op. cit., p. 242. The judge in the trial filmed by the *Frontline* documentary, op. cit., made the "anarchy" statement in refusing to grant the defense attorney's request for a conscience verdict instruction. The attorney, however, was permitted to develop the thesis in his closing speech, and the jury acquitted on a conscience basis.

29. Kairys, *Politics of Law*, op. cit., p. 1; *American Jury*, op. cit., p. 8; Frank, op. cit., pp. 405 ff. in which he traces the origin of the phrase to Aristotle, and identifies its first appearance in the United States in the Constitution of Massachusetts, primarily authored by John Adams.

30. Ibid., pp. 111-13.

31. Ibid., pp. 114 ff.

32. Ibid., p. 113.

33. Scheflin, op. cit., p. 103.

34. Numerous sources, but Jefferson's quote, *supra*, Chapter Eight, is probably the most famous.

35. *American Jury*, op. cit., p. 495.

36. Numerous sources, but see esp. Van Dyke, op. cit., pp. 225 ff.

37. Scheflin, op. cit., pp. 93-94, quoting Gary J. Simson, "Jury Nullification in the American System," 54 *Texas Law Review*, 488 (1976), p. 514.
38. *American Jury*, op. cit., p. 498.
39. Scheflin, op. cit., pp. 95-96.
40. *American Jury*, op. cit., p. 429.
41. Ibid., p. 433.
42. Van Dyke, op. cit., p. 236.
43. Ibid., quoting Jessica Mitford, *Trial of Dr. Spock.*
44. Ibid., pp. 234-35; Friedman, op. cit., p. 251; Becker, op. cit., p. 44.
45. Quoted in Van Dyke, op. cit., p. 234.
46. Ibid.; Scheflin, op. cit., pp. 82-84; Hans Zeisel, Foreword, *Law and Contemporary Problems*, Vol. 43, No. 4 (1980), p. 3.
47. For a history of, see Friedman, op. cit., pp. 135-36.
48. Scheflin, loc. cit.
49. Ibid., p. 80.
50. Ibid., p. 55.
51. Quoted in Frank, op. cit., p. 128, attribution not given.
52. Friedman, op. cit., p. 423.
53. Frank, op. cit., p. 129; Lempert, op. cit., pp. 81-82, noting that jurors' frequent refusal to apply fellow-servant and assumption-of-risk doctrines eventually caused industries to support workmen's compensation as a way of avoiding paying full compensation in workplace injury cases.
54. Friedman, op. cit., pp. 264, 412-13, 423; Frank, op. cit., p. 120; *Karcesky v. Varia*, 382 Pa. 227, 114 A.2d 150 (1955), quoted in Scheflin, op. cit., p. 70. Even though Pennsylvania, at the time, had a contributory negligence rule, a verdict by a jury which clearly invoked notions of comparative negligence was upheld by the state's Supreme Court, which noted: "The doctrine of comparative negligence . . . is not recognized by the Courts of Pennsylvania but as a practical matter [it is] frequently taken into consideration by a jury . . . Where the evidence of negligence or contributory negligence, or both, is conflicting or not free from doubt, a trial judge has the power to uphold the time-honored right of a jury to render a compromise verdict." Ibid., p. 154.
55. Frank, loc. cit.
56. Peck, op. cit., p. 22.
57. Commentary, *Michigan Law Review*, Vol. 59 (1961), pp. 667ff.
58. Bill 192, Philadelphia City Council, 1984.
59. *New York Times*, February 13, 1987.
60. *Philadelphia Inquirer*, November 20, 1985.
61. *Commonwealth of Pa. v. Neil Ferber*, Ct. of Common Pleas, July term, 1981, Nos. 1048-1053. In this case, the defendant was wrongly convicted of first degree murder apparently principally because of unrebutted perjured testimony. The charges against him were later dismissed.

The Civil Juror:

A Research Project
Sponsored by the
Roscoe Pound Foundation

Bettyruth Walter, PhD
Research Director

Table of Contents

APPENDICES

LIST OF TABLES

ACKNOWLEDGMENTS

This research project could not have been successfully completed without the cooperation of the following judges to whom sincere appreciation is extended:

Hon. Anita B. Brody
Hon. Abraham J. Gafni
Hon. Bernard J. Goodheart
Hon. Richard B. Klein
Hon. William M. Marutani
Hon. Clarence C. Newcomer
Hon. Samuel W. Salus, III

Thanks are also due to the following for their assistance:

Thomas J. Clewley
Donald J. Goldberg, Esq.
Richard W. Goldberg, Esq.
Mary Frances Hoban
Lorrie Nicoletti
Barbara H. O'Neill
Robert Pachinelli
Polly N. Phillippi, Esq.
Judith M. Wohl, Esq.

I. INTRODUCTION

In an effort to determine whether jurors who serve in civil cases understand the system in which they are vital participants, and therefore are able to perform appropriately, the following study was developed. The conceptual underpinnings of the project were based on a view expressed by Konecni and Ebbesen: "In the area of legal decision-making, as well as in many other types of decision-making, the important truths are to be found in the real world rather than in the laboratory . . . we would prefer to base our conjectures about how people make various types of decisions on observations of the actual people making the actual decisions" (1981:487).

The method employed in this study was to question jurors serving in real trials, and to sample as large a population as possible within a reasonable period of time. The population of jurors sampled reached 352, and the data were collected within a one-year time frame. Thirty-eight civil trials were included in the study.

II. METHOD

The research in this study was carried out in three different jurisdictions in the Philadelphia area. The first was the federal court system, represented by the United States District Court for the Eastern District of Pennsylvania. The other two were state courts, one urban, the other suburban: The Court of Common Pleas-Philadelphia, and the Court of Common Pleas-Montgomery County.

The seven judges who participated in this study are listed below. Each of these judges took an interest in the research enterprise and therefore permitted their jurors to answer questions about trials which took place in their courtrooms. Although some judges declined to participate, perhaps in the future others could be encouraged to permit this kind of research which in no way interferes with the legal process. How jurors function in the jury room and how money verdicts are determined is of importance to the court and the population at large.

The number of cases included in this study was limited by two factors. The first was the number of judges who allowed their jurors to be surveyed. The second was the nature of civil law suits. Many of the cases which were to be included in this study were settled just prior to or during the trial. Therefore, what might be considered good for the court system was not helpful for the study, since only cases that went through deliberation could be included. Table 1 (below) indicates which judges participated in which courts, and how many of their trials were included in the study. (See Appendix E for suggestions as to how judges might introduce the project to jurors.)

Note that only one judge participated in federal court, and that court was the only one which required a unanimous decision of its jurors. (See VIII: A, Unanimous and Majority Jurors.) Therefore, any data relative to unanimous juries represents only what transpired in this one judge's courtroom and could be flavored by his judicial habits. Where relevant, this fact is made known.

Table 1. Judge Participation

Judge	Number of trials contributed to study
FEDERAL COURT	
Clarence C. Newcomer	12
COURT OF COMMON PLEAS— PHILADELPHIA	
Abraham J. Gafni	4

Judge	Number of trials contributed to study
Bernard J. Goodheart	1
Richard B. Klein	2
William M. Marutani	3
COURT OF COMMON PLEAS— MONTGOMERY COUNTY	
Anita B. Brody	13
Samuel W. Salus, III	3
Total of trials in study	38

The juror response data was collected by the use of two questionnaires. The first and shorter one (Appendix A) was answered by the jurors in the jury room immediately following the conclusion of the trial, after the verdict was rendered and the jurors excused from their jury service. These completed questionnaires were collected by the deputy clerk who in turn transferred them to the project research director.

The second and longer questionnaire (Appendix B) was completed by the jurors at home and returned to the researcher by mail. Every effort was made to facilitate the return of this questionnaire within two weeks of the conclusion of trial, and without cost and inconvenience to the jurors.

III. SUBJECTS

The subjects in this study were jurors sitting on 38 juries in three different court systems between the dates of January 28, 1985, and January 31, 1986. Persons who are eligible for jury duty in the federal court must be residents of eastern Pennsylvania, which includes Philadelphia. Jurors who are eligible for jury duty in the Court of Common Pleas in Philadelphia must be residents of that city, and those eligible to serve in the Court of Common Pleas of Montgomery County must be residents of that county.

Table 2. Jurors Who Completed at Least One of Two Questionnaires

Jurors in Federal Court	95
Jurors in Common Pleas—Philadelphia	90
Jurors in Common Pleas—Montgomery County	167
Total number of jurors	352

Juror participation was excellent. Even though they had sat through an entire trial and been responsible for determining the verdict in a civil suit, they took the time to voluntarily complete the short questionnaire in the jury room. Only one juror out of 308 did not do so.

The long questionnaire which was to be completed at home was returned by 87% of the jurors. Their only incentive to do so was their interest in the trial process, and a modest $10 remuneration for their time. Although every juror did not answer every question, most questionnaires were nearly or totally completed. (See Appendix D for instructions to jurors for completing the long questionnaire.)

IV. QUESTIONNAIRES

Two questionnaires were used to collect the opinions of jurors concerning their experience of serving on a civil jury. The questions were designed to measure attitudes about issues which critics of the jury system have traditionally used to argue that many jurors do not understand the system of which they are a vital part and, therefore, cannot determine verdicts appropriate to the cases for which they are the decision makers.

Because there were many issues which were to be explored in this study, the questioning of jurors was divided into two parts; hence the two questionnaires. The short questionnaire of 46 questions (hereafter SQ) was designed to be completed in the juryroom within a 10-minute period of time, recognizing that jurors might be exhausted from their jury experience, anxious to return home, and less than enthusiastic about completing a questionnaire.

This also determined the manner in which questions were posed and the use of a simple yes/no format for responses where possible. There were no open-ended questions on this questionnaire. Also, no questions relating to the behavior of the judge or clerk were on the SQ on the assumption that the jurors might be shy about evaluating these persons while sitting in the juryroom.

The long questionnaire (hereafter LQ) was comprised of 78 questions. Jurors took them home where they could complete them at their convenience, but were requested to do so within a 10-day period so that their jury experience would still be fresh in their minds. All questionnaires were filled out anonymously. The jurors returned the LQ along with a pre-stamped envelope upon which they had written a name and address. The $10 remuneration was made out to the name on the envelope, but no records were kept of the names.

Both the short questionnaire and the long questionnaire explored the following issues:

1. The experience of jury service
2. General view of the specific trial
3. Reaction to the plaintiff
4. Reaction to the plaintiff's lawyer
5. Reaction to the defendant
6. Reaction to the defense lawyer(s)
7. Reaction to the judge (LQ only)

8. Deliberations
9. Determination of monetary awards
10. Demographic information

A juror who answered both questionnaires completely would have given information on nearly 124 issues (some questions explored the same issue). However, not every juror answered both questionnaires.

Table 3. Jurors Who Completed Long and Short Questionnaires

	SQ	LQ	% LQ returned
Federal Court	95	90	95%
Common Pleas—Philadelphia	90	68	76
Common Pleas—Montgomery County	122	110	90
Additional jurors from Mont. Co.		45	80
Total number of jurors	307	313	87%

In no jurisdiction did the number of jurors who completed the second and longer questionnaire, the one to be returned by mail, match the number who completed the SQs in the courthouse. However, 268 (87%) of those who completed the SQ did return the LQ.

The pool of LQ respondents from CP Montgomery County was enlarged by the addition of another batch of jurors. One of the participating judges provided the names of 56 jurors who had sat in cases just prior to her participation in this research project. These jurors were contacted by mail, and 45 (80%) of them immediately returned completed questionnaires.

General information was collected for each trial on a Master Sheet (Appendix C). Some of the information on this sheet produced quantifiable data; for example, the difficulty of case as viewed by the judge and juxtaposed with the opinions of the jurors. (See VIII: H.1.)

V. CASES

The types of cases included in this study depended on the chance occurrence of which cases were tried before the participating judges during the time of data collection. For the sake of data evaluation, they were separated into two categories. (The types of cases were identified by the court clerks.)

1. Personal injury:

      Injury from police arrest   2
      Medical malpractice   6
      Motor vehicle accident   6
      Motor vehicle/ Dram shop 1

Other personal injury	9
Personal injury/ Death	1
Product liability	6
	—
	31

2. Nonpersonal injury:

Contract dispute	4
House destroyed	2
Insurance claim	1
	—
	7

Any responses to questions which related to pain and suffering, medical expenses, and seriousness of injury given in nonpersonal injury cases (i.e., jurors responding in error by answering questions which did not relate to their type of trial) were eliminated from the data pool.

VI. DATA ANALYSIS

The two questionnaires completed by jurors produced 620 documents, or 4,978 pages with more than 38,000 responses. These very extensive data were analyzed in several ways.

1. Percentile rankings were determined for each of the three court systems separately, and for the total responses. Where 90% or more of the sample population concurred, those responses were considered to be particularly meaningful.
    For example, for the total population in answer to the question:

    Did you feel free to express how you really felt [during deliberations]? (SQ 26: N = 303)[1]

    Yes: 98%   No: 2%

    The strength of such an overwhelming response should not be ignored.

2. Most of the questions which were asked of the jurors produced nominal (names or categories representing the way people differ) rather than interval or ordinal data (measuring how much of a variable is present.) The alternatives offered the jurors were discrete, nonoverlapping categories and therefore the chi-square statistical test, one which tests for independence, was appropriate. It hypothesizes that there is no relationship between two variables, i.e., a null hypothesis. For example, in answer to SQ 6 which was asked of jurors in each of the three jurisdictions:

    Were you personally satisfied with the decision reached by the jury of which you were a member?

---

[1] This code signifies that the question under discussion is number 26 on the short questionnaire, and that 303 jurors answered the question.

The *null hypothesis* states that there is *no* relationship between the court system in which a juror served and his or her satisfaction with the verdict.

However, if a *significant* p value is achieved during the chi-square test, one may reject the null hypothesis and feel justified in assuming that there *is* a relationship between satisfaction with verdict and the court system within which one served. (Note that although a chi-square test may establish that there is a relationship between variables, it does not assess the strength of that relationship.)

The level of acceptable statistical significance for this study was set at $p < .01$. This means that there is less than one chance in a hundred that the observed pattern of frequencies could have occurred by chance alone. It is common in the discipline of anthropology, as in other social sciences, to accept a level of $p < .05$ as sufficient to reject the null hypothesis. However, in the field of psychology, certain journals are extremely reluctant to accept any research results that do not operate with a .01 level of significance.

Because of the nature of this study, which requires that jurors identify and evaluate their own attitudes and behavior in an unfamiliar environment, i.e., the courtroom and the juryroom, and in some instances to squeal on themselves by providing potentially embarrassing information, the more stringent level of significance at .01 was determined to be more reliable.

3. Unanimous and majority juries were compared to see if correlations could be found. For example, is there a relationship between type of jury, deliberation time, and verdict? That is, do majority juries take longer to reach a verdict? Do they more often find in favor of the plaintiff or the defendant?

4. Eight- (smaller) and 12- (larger) person juries were examined for the same variables.

5. Plaintiff and defense verdicts were examined vis-a-vis such issues as (a) how the jurors felt about the attorneys for each side, (b) how they felt about the plaintiff and the defendant, and (3) their experience as participants in prior law suits.

6. Opinion formation and change of opinion during trial were looked at closely. When and why were decisions made or opinions changed?

7. Did knowledge about insurance benefits available to either plaintiff or defendant have an effect on the determination of the verdict?

8. Demographic effects such as the relationship of age, sex, or education to verdict decisions were examined.

9. Overall statistics such as percentage of plaintiff verdicts in each court system and average size of verdicts were examined.

By using two questionnaires completed anonymously at two different locales, there was some information which was lost. For example, all the demographic information was on the SQ so that no correlations could be made between LQ responses and that information. Also, because of the effort to assure anonymity, no comparisons could be made between the responses of any one juror to the two questionnaires. However, each questionnaire was coded by jury so that all SQ and LQ information on one specific trial could be correlated. Therefore, the data collected by the use of two different sets of questionnaires, although it did preclude some individual juror data, produced extensive information on each jury.

In any controlled experiment, two basic elements must be present. One is a randomly selected population; the other is a control group. In doing research in a naturalistic setting such as a court of law, it is not possible to directly control for either of these elements. However, in the matter of requirement one, the selection of subjects (jurors), "there is no need for the experimenter to arrange for random assignment because random assignment has been part of judicial process itself" (Zeisel 1973:118).

In regard to requirement two, the presence of a control group, this study did lend itself to compliance in some respects. Because jurors in three different court systems were sampled, one could examine for same and different responses to a single issue by three distinct groups who were all serving as jurors in civil trials.

The experimental design most often used in sociolegal research is simulation through the use of mock jurors and/or mock trials, such as in the Hastie, Penrod, and Pennington's study, *Inside the Jury* (1983). "However, simulation is a more serious deviation from the ideal experiment . . . because its impact cannot be readily measured but must instead be assessed intuitively and through circumstantial evidence" (Zeisel 1973:117). "There is always the question as to how far its results can be extrapolated, that is, applied to other places, other times, and other conditions" (ibid., 122).

It would have been desirable to have had a 50/50 sample of control/no control groupings. However, the design of this real-world experimental situation did permit the garnering of information directly from actual jurors, and offered the opportunity to compare three distinct groups performing the same function using a sample population of 352 jurors in 38 real cases.

VII. RESULTS

A. Short Questionnaire   The short questionnaire was completed by 313 jurors in the juryroom after being excused from jury duty. Each of the questions below is followed by the percentage of answers by court system, and by all responders, using the following abbreviations:

FC = Federal Court
CP = Court of Common Pleas-Philadelphia
SUB = Court of Common Pleas-Montgomery County (suburban)
N = Number of jurors who responded to the question

When the responses were subjected to chi-square testing, those results are also reported.

Because the way in which a question is posed can influence the response, the exact choices from which a juror could select are listed as they appear in the questionnaires, which can be located in the Appendix.

Some questions about the TRIAL

1. Did you think this trial was:

	FC	CP	SUB	ALL
	(N = 95)	(N = 88)	(N = 122)	(N = 305)
Extremely interesting	43%	42%	37%	40%
Sometimes interesting	55	51	57	55
Boring	2	7	6	5

Almost all jurors found their trials extremely or sometimes interesting.

2. After both sides had completely presented their case, did you feel that you had a good idea of what really had happened?

	FC	CP	SUB	ALL
	(N = 95)	(N = 90)	(N = 122)	(N = 307)
Yes	54%	48%	48%	49.5%
Fairly good, but I still had questions I wish had been answered	45	50	52	49.5
No	1	2	0	1.0

Almost all jurors in all three court systems reported a good or fairly good understanding of what happened during the trial.

3. During the trial, did any exhibits (such as photographs, charts, medical records) help you make up your mind?

	FC	CP	SUB	ALL
	(N = 94)	(N = 89)	(N = 109)	(N = 292)
Yes	81%	85%	83%	83%
No	19	15	17	17

More than four-fifths of the jurors found exhibits presented during the trial to be helpful.

4. If you did NOT take notes during the trial, would you have liked to?

	FC	CP	SUB	ALL
	(N = 54)	(N = 89)	(N = 121)	(N = 264)
Yes	48%	66%	48%	54%
No	33	21	31	28
I'm not certain	19	13	21	18

Two-thirds of the jurors in the Court of Common Pleas in Philadelphia who did not take notes would have liked to have taken them. About half of all the jurors in the other two courts would have liked to, even in federal court, the only court in which jurors were permitted to take notes.

5. Did you understand the law as the judge explained it to you in the charge?

	FC (N = 95)	CP (N = 90)	SUB (N = 121)	ALL (N = 306)
Yes, most of it	86%	92%	85%	87%
Yes, but only partly	12	8	15	12
No, not very much of it	2	0	0	less than 1

Almost all of the jurors reported that they understood most or part of the explanation of the law by the judge.

6. Just before jury deliberations began, had you already reached a decision, even though that might not have been your final decision? (CHECK ONE)

	FC (N = 89)	CP (N = 84)	SUB (N = 121)	ALL (N = 294)
Yes. Definitely for the PLAINTIFF	15%	19%	12%	15%
Wasn't certain, but was leaning toward the PLAINTIFF	23	51	31	34
Yes. Definitely for the DEFENDANT	25	17	28	24
Wasn't certain, but was leaning toward the DEFENDANT	37	13	29	27

There was a statistically significant correlation found in the responses to this question at $p < .001$. (This indicates that there is less than one chance in a thousand that the observed pattern could have occurred by chance.) There is a significant relationship between the different court systems and the decision which jurors reached just prior to jury deliberation. The jurors in the Court of Common Pleas-Philadelphia tended to be definitely for or leaning toward the plaintiff, and the jurors in federal court and the Court of Common Pleas-Montgomery County tended to be definitely for or leaning toward the defendant.

For all jurors, just prior to deliberations, the decision was split almost in half.

Some questions about the PLAINTIFF

7. If the plaintiff testified, which of the following statements describes your reaction to him or her?

	FC (N = 86)	CP (N = 75)	SUB (N = 108)	ALL (N = 269)
Testimony INCREASED my belief in the plaintiff's case	47%	64%	46%	51%
Testimony DECREASED my belief in the plaintiff's case	53	36	50	47
Little or no change (written in)	0	0	4	2

A chi-square test yielded $p < .05$, which is only somewhat less than a statistically significant finding. The above data seem to indicate that the jurors in CP found that testimony given by the plaintiff increased belief in plaintiff's case more often than it did in the other two courts.

8. What kind of feelings did you have for the plaintiff?

	FC (N = 95)	CP (N = 86)	SUB (N = 114)	ALL (N = 295)
High regard	25%	33%	39%	33%
Low regard	24	8	8	13
No feelings	51	59	53	54

There was a statistically significant correlation found in the responses to this question at $p < .005$. (This indicates that there is less than one chance in 200 that the observed pattern could have occurred by chance.) There is a significant relationship between the different court systems and the feelings which the jurors have for the plaintiff. Although about half of all the jurors claimed to have no feelings for the plaintiff, those who did in FC were evenly divided between high and low regard. But the jurors in CP and SUB tended to have a higher regard for the plaintiff.

Some questions about the PLAINTIFF'S LAWYER

9. Did you think that the PLAINTIFF'S lawyer objected too often?

	FC (N = 94)	CP (N = 88)	SUB (N = 121)	ALL (N = 303)
Yes	11%	9%	11%	10%
No	89	91	89	90

Most of the jurors in all courts did not think that the plaintiff's lawyer objected too often.

10. If yes, did that cause you to think less of the plaintiff's case?

	FC (N = 10)	CP (N = 7)	SUB (N = 11)	ALL (N = 28)
Yes	30%	43%	73%	50%
No	70	57	27	50

For the small number (28 jurors) who replied yes to SQ 9, only in SUB did more than three jurors (eight in SUB) indicate that they thought less of the plaintiff's case because of the objections.

11. Do you think that the lawyer for the PLAINTIFF treated any of the witnesses unfairly?

	FC (N = 94)	CP (N = 88)	SUB (N = 119)	ALL (N = 301)
Yes	5%	10%	8%	8%
No	95	90	92	92

Very few of all the respondents thought that the lawyer for the plaintiff treated the witnesses unfairly.

12. If yes, did that cause you to think less of the plaintiff's case?

	FC (N = 5)	CP (N = 8)	SUB (N = 8)	ALL (N = 21)
Yes	40%	25%	37.5%	33%
No	60	75	62.5	67

Two-thirds or more of those who said yes to SQ 11 reported that it did not cause them to think less of the plaintiff's case. CP gave a response somewhat more favorable to the plaintiff's lawyer.

13. Which statement best describes your feelings about the closing speech of the plaintiff's lawyer?

	FC (N = 89)	CP (N = 82)	SUB (N = 118)	ALL (N = 289)
It caused me to change my opinion about the case	4%	6%	3%	4%
It didn't change my opinion about the case	96	94	97	96

Almost all jurors reported that they did not change their opinions as a result of the closing speech of the plaintiff's lawyer.

Some questions about the DEFENDANT(S)

14. Did you think that the defendant carried insurance?

	FC (N=91)	CP (N=83)	SUB (N=112)	ALL (N=286)
Yes	49%	55%	57%	54%
No	11	4	9	8
I never thought about it	40	41	34	38

More than half of all jurors thought the defendant carried insurance.

15. If you answered "yes," why do you think so? (CHECK ONE)

	FC (N=43)	CP (N=41)	SUB (N=59)	ALL (N=143)
It came out in the testimony.	5%	7%	0%	4%
It was mentioned in the courtroom before the trial began.	0	5	2	2
I know from personal experience that such people or businesses usually carry insurance.	95	88	98	94

Almost all jurors who believed the defendant carried insurance thought so because of their own personal experience.

16. If you believe the defendant had insurance, which covered at least part of the verdict, did that make a difference in your decision?

	FC (N=44)	CP (N=40)	SUB (N=62)	ALL (N=146)
Yes, importantly so	11%	5.0%	3%	6%
Yes, but only in minor way	21	27.5	23	23
I never thought about it	68	67.5	74	71

More than two-thirds, and almost three-quarters in SUB, reported that even if they believed the defendant was insured, it did not make a difference in their decision.

17. If the defendant(s) or a representative from the defendant company testified, which one of the following statements describes your reaction to him or her?

	FC (N=54)	CP (N=75)	SUB (N=100)	ALL (N=229)
Testimony INCREASED my belief in the case for the defense	57%	44%	62%	55%
Testimony DECREASED my belief in the case for the defense	43	56	38	45

Although it appears that CP jurors more often felt that testimony by the defense decreased their belief in the defense case than did jurors in the other two courts, in a chi-square test this difference failed to reach significance. In fact, it appears that defense testimony may go either way; it may increase or decrease belief almost equally.

18. What kind of feelings did you have for the defendant or defendant company?

	FC (N=94)	CP (N=89)	SUB (N=120)	ALL (N=303)
High regard	22%	18%	26%	22%
Low regard	11	9	20	14
No feelings	67	73	54	64

Although a statistically significant correlation was not found in the responses to this question, at $p < .05$ it might be true that with a larger sample significance would be established. The jurors in SUB tended to have low regard almost as often as they had high regard for the defendant or defendant company, but the jurors in FC and CP had high regard for the defendant twice as often as low regard. (See IX.C for further discussion.)

Also notice that more than half of all the jurors, and almost three-quarters in CP, reported that they had no feelings toward the defendant or defendant company. As the defendant was often an insurance company, a corporation, or the city of Philadelphia, rather than a person, this was understandable.

Some questions about the DEFENSE LAWYER(S)

19. Did you think that the DEFENSE lawyer(s) objected too often?

	FC (N=95)	CP (N=85)	SUB (N=121)	ALL (N=301)
Yes	15%	4%	7%	9%
No	85	96	93	91

Most of the jurors in all courts did not think that the defense lawyer(s) objected too often.

20. If yes, did that cause you to think less of the defense case?

	FC (N=12)	CP (N=3)	SUB (N=7)	ALL (N=22)
Yes	8%	0%	57%	23%
No	92	100	43	77

As for the small number (22 jurors) who thought that they did object too often, only in Montgomery County did they indicate to any degree (4 jurors) that they thought less of the defendant's case because of the objections.

21. Do you think that the lawyer(s) for the DEFENSE treated any of the witnesses unfairly?

	FC (N=95)	CP (N=84)	SUB (N=120)	ALL (N=299)
Yes	5%	1%	3%	3% (10 jurors)
No	95	99	97	97

Very few of all the respondents thought that the lawyer(s) for the defense treated the witness unfairly.

22. If yes, did that cause you to think less of the defense case?

	FC (N=4)	CP (N=1)	SUB (N=4)	ALL (N=9)
Yes	—	1 juror	1 juror	22%
No	4 jurors	—	3 jurors	78

Seven of the 10 jurors who responded yes to SQ 21 reported that it did not cause them to think less of the defense case. Only two jurors said that it did.

23. Which statement best describes your feelings about the closing speech(es) of the defense lawyer(s)?

	FC (N=92)	CP (N=84)	SUB (N=121)	ALL (N=297)
It caused me to change my opinion about the case	3%	13%	4%	6%
It didn't change my opinion about the case	97	87	96	94

Almost all jurors reported that they did not change their opinions as a result of the closing speech(es) of the defense lawyer(s).

Some questions about the DELIBERATIONS

24. Which of the following statements describes the jury deliberations?

	FC (N=92)	CP (N=87)	SUB (N=120)	ALL (N=299)
There was a full and open exchange of opinions by just about everyone	98%	93%	98%	97%
Only a few people spoke, and the others mostly just listened	2	7	2	3

Overwhelmingly the jurors reported that there was a full and open exchange by jurors during deliberations.

25. Which one of the following statements best describes how the jury deliberations affected you? (CHECK ONE)

	FC (N=94)	CP (N=83)	SUB (N=120)	ALL (N=297)
The deliberations didn't affect me at all because I had already made up my mind.	17%	17%	28%	21%
The deliberations made me think again about the point of view I already had, but I stuck with my original opinion.	60	60	59	60
I changed my point of view during deliberations.	23	23	13	19

Although it appears that jurors in SUB changed their minds less often than did jurors in the other two courts, in a chi-square test this difference failed to reach significance. Four-fifths (81%) of all jurors reported no change of opinion during deliberations.

26. Did you feel free to express how you really felt?

	FC (N=95)	CP (N=87)	SUB (N=121)	ALL (N=303)
Yes	100%	93%	99%	98%
No	0	7	1	2

Overwhelmingly the jurors reported that during deliberations they felt free to express how they felt.

27. If, during deliberations, some exhibits were in the jury-room with you: (CHECK ONE)

	FC (N=87)	CP (N=67)	SUB (N=112)	ALL (N=266)
At least one of them was important	74%	73%	75%	74%
They really didn't add very much one way or the other	25	19	23	23
Never discussed them at all	1	8	2	3

Three-quarters of all jurors reported that at least one of the exhibits in the juryroom was very important to them. Very few jurors said that exhibits were never discussed.

28. Did the seriousness of the plaintiff's injuries have an effect on your decision in the case?

	FC (N=84)	CP (N=65)	SUB (N=89)	ALL (N=238)
Yes	46.5%	43%	25%	38%
No	46.5	42	68	53
I'm not certain	7.0	15	7	9

There was a statistically significant correlation found in the responses to this question at $p < .005$. There is a significant relationship between the seriousness of the plaintiff's injuries and the effect such injuries had or did not have on juror decisions within different court systems. In FC and CP, the jurors were equally divided as to the effect. But the jurors in SUB tended not to be affected by the seriousness of plaintiff's injuries.

29. Did the extent of the plaintiff's financial losses from the injuries have an effect on your decision in the case?

	FC (N=86)	CP (N=64)	SUB (N=101)	ALL (N=251)
Yes	23%	25%	9%	18%
No	72	67	72	71
I'm not certain	5	8	19	11

Seventy-one percent of all jurors reported that the financial losses of the plaintiff because of injuries had no effect on their decisions. However, for those who reported that their decision was affected, there was a statistically significant correlation found at $p < .005$. In FC and CP, about one-quarter of the jurors said there was an effect, but only 9% of the SUB jurors claimed to be affected by plaintiff's losses.

30. Did you talk about any Blue Cross or Workman's Compensation that the plaintiff might have had?

	FC (N=86)	CP (N=67)	SUB (N=84)	ALL (N=237)
Yes	24%	36%	27%	29%
No	76	64	73	71

About one-quarter of the jurors in FC and SUB talked about compensation that the plaintiff might have had. A slightly larger percentage (one-third) of the jurors in CP did the same.

31. If yes, do you think it made a difference in your decision?

	FC (N=21)	CP (N=22)	SUB (N=21)	ALL (N=64)
Yes, very much so	5%	9%	5%	6%
Yes, but only in minor way	28	55	24	36
No	67	36	71	58

For those jurors who did talk about plaintiff's possible compensation benefits, very few stated that this strongly affected their decisions. About two-thirds of the jurors in FC and SUB indicated that it made no difference, but a few more than half of the CP jurors reported that it did make a difference in a minor way. Although this was not found to be a statistically significant difference, at $p < .05$ it might be true that with a larger sample, significance would be achieved.

32. I think that the deliberations were:

	FC (N=94)	CP (N=74)	SUB (N=117)	ALL (N=285)
Important	98%	99%	97%	98%
Not important	2	1	3	2

Overwhelmingly the jurors reported that they believed the deliberations were important.

If an amount of money was awarded, answer the following questions

33. How did you decide on the amount of the verdict?

	FC (N=64)	CP (N=48)	SUB (N=39)	ALL (N=151)
A figure just sort of grew as a result of our discussion.	44%	15%	21%	29%
We mostly went by the total figure suggested to us by the plaintiff's lawyer.	0	10	15	7
We mostly went by the total figure suggested to us by the plaintiff's lawyer, but we ADDED to it.	3	21	15	12
We mostly went by the total figure suggested to us by the plaintiff's lawyer, but we SUBTRACTED from it.	15	4	21	13
There were several figures suggested by members of the jury, and we took the average.	38	50	28	39

In 82% of FC and 65% of CP cases the amount of award was generated by juror discussion. In SUB, half (51%) of the verdicts were derived from plaintiff's lawyers suggestions, the other half from juror discussion. This difference was statistically significant at $p < .005$.

34. Did you include some money because of the pain and suffering of the plaintiff?

	FC (N = 47)	CP (N = 40)	SUB (N = 22)	ALL (N = 109)
Yes	85%	87.5%	45%	78%
No	15	12.5	55	22

Although many jurors in FC and CP said they awarded some money for pain and suffering, fewer than half the jurors in SUB did so.

Some questions about you

35. When you were first notified to report for jury service, were you:

	FC (N = 91)	CP (N = 78)	SUB (N = 117)	ALL (N = 286)
Looking forward to it	62%	53%	62%	59%
Wanting to get out of it	38	47	38	41

More than half of all jurors were looking forward to jury service.

36. Now that you have served as a juror, do you think the jury is:

	FC (N = 88)	CP (N = 82)	SUB (N = 119)	ALL (N = 289)
A GOOD system	98%	98%	95%	97%
A POOR system	2	2	5	3

After having served as a juror, almost everyone believed the jury system to be a good one. Of the 12 jurors who said it was a poor system, nine of those had come to jury service wanting to get out of it.

37. Are you?

	FC (N = 93)	CP (N = 81)	SUB (N = 121)	ALL (N = 295)
Male	52%	37%	47%	46%
Female	48	63	53	54

Almost two-thirds of CP jurors were female, while in the other two courts males and females were equally represented.

38. What is your age?

	FC	CP	SUB	ALL
Average	41.4 yrs	40.0 yrs	45.7 yrs	42.3 yrs
Average: plaintiff verdict	42.7	38.9	47.2	42.9
Average: defense verdict	40.1	41.1	44.1	41.7

These figures were compared to see if age correlated with verdict or court. No statistically significant correlations were found.

39. What is the HIGHEST LEVEL of education you COM-
    PLETED?

	FC (N=94)	CP (N=80)	SUB (N=120)	ALL (N=294)
Less than high school	3%	9%	4.0%	5%
High school	37	35	28.5	33
Vocational, technical school	7	15	9.0	10
Some college	16	15	23.5	19
College	18	14	19.0	17
Some grad. or professional	10	2	5.0	6
Graduate or professional	9	10	11.0	10

One-third of all jurors had completed high school. More than another third (36%) had completed some or all of college. Only 5% had less than a high school education, with a slightly greater percentage in CP. For all jurors, 16% had received education beyond the college level.

Education was grouped into three levels:

A = Some or all high school, and vocational school
B = Some or all college
C = Some or all graduate or professional school

These three educational levels were then compared against plaintiff or defense verdicts. At $p < .05$, there appears to be a significant relationship between education and verdict. Juries that decided in favor of the plaintiff were comprised of more jurors with vocational, high school, or less than high school education. Juries that decided in favor of the defendant contained more jurors who had completed some or all of college.

Jurors with a graduate or professional school education appeared in equal number on both kinds of juries.

40. What is your occupation?

41. If retired, what WAS your occupation?

See Appendix F for listing of jurors and occupations.

42. Are you?

	FC (N=91)	CP (N=80)	SUB (N=120)	ALL (N=291)
Single	27%	46%	17%	28%
Married	65	43	70	61
Divorced	6	4	11	7
Widowed	2	7	2	4

To a statistically significant degree (p < .001), jurors in the SUB court tended to be married more often than single, and somewhat more often divorced than in FC or CP. Jurors in CP tended to be more often unmarried than they were in FC and SUB.

43. How many children do you have?

	FC	CP	SUB	ALL
Average	1.8	1.5	1.8	1.7

44. Do you live in?

	FC (N = 92)	CP (N = 79)	SUB (N = 119)	ALL (N = 290)
A house	87%	80%	92%	87%
An apartment	10	18	6	10
Other	3	2	2	3

Most jurors reported that they live in houses.

45. What kind of area do you live in?

	FC (N = 94)	CP (N = 81)	SUB (N = 120)	ALL (N = 295)
Residential	76%	83%	76%	78%
Rural	21	1	19	15
Business	0	4	0	1
Part business, part residential	3	12	5	6

Three-quarters or more of all jurors reported that they live in residential areas.

46. If you care to answer, approximately which of the following groups describes your family's yearly income.

	FC	CP	SUB	ALL
A = Less than $10,000	4%	18%	1%	7%
B = At least $10,000 and less than $20,000	18	23	15	18
C = At least $20,000 and less than $40,000	52	40	38	43
D = At least $40,000 and less than $60,000	17	16	30	22
E = $60,000 or more	9	3	16	10

If income groups A and B are combined, and groups D and E are combined, the three court systems yield the following information:

	FC	CP	SUB	ALL
Less than $20,000	22%	41%	16%	25%
$20,000 to <$40,000	52	40	38	43
$40,000 or more	26	19	46	32

In CP, substantially more jurors reported a family yearly income of less than $20,000. In SUB, substantially more jurors reported an income of $40,000 or more. Although this is a statistically significant difference at $p < .001$, because the figures reflect *family* income, the data may be skewed by the higher number of single people in CP, and more married jurors in SUB.

B. Long Questionnaire   The long questionnaire was completed by 313 jurors at home and returned by mail. Each of the questions below is followed by the percentage of answers by court system, and by all responders, using the same abbreviations as were used in the short questionnaire results, with two additions:

PR = Possible responses

This designation is used wherever jurors were invited to select as many options as applied, rather than give one response. For example, when several items are listed from which a juror can select all, several, or none, what becomes meaningful is what percentage of the possible respondent pool selected any one item.

YP = Yes to prior question

The responding pool is only as large as the number of jurors who responded affirmatively to the prior related question.

Here, as for the SQ, when the responses were subjected to chi-square testing, those results are reported.

Some questions about your JURY SERVICE

1. From the time you arrived to begin your jury duty, how long did you have to wait before you were selected for a jury?

	FC (N=90)	CP (N=67)	SUB (N=155)	ALL (N=312)
Less than one day	50%	99%	98%	84%
Two to five days	48	0	2	15
Longer	2	1	0	1

The jurors in FC waited longer to serve. This is a consequence of a different type of juror selection process used in the courthouse. The jurors in the state courts serve for one day or one trial.

2. How would you describe the room in which you waited to be sent to a courtroom? (CHECK AS MANY ANSWERS AS APPLY)

	FC (PR = 90)	CP (PR = 68)	SUB (PR = 155)	ALL (PR = 313)
Comfortable	86%	63%	92%	84%
Crowded	19	53	11	24
Unpleasant	8	9	5	7
Dirty	0	3	1	1

The jurors in FC and SUB most often described their waiting room to be comfortable. But the CP jurors reported that they were crowded almost as often as they said they were comfortable. Very few jurors reported dirty waiting rooms.

3. During the voir dire (or questioning before you were selected as a juror), what opinion did you form about the case?

	FC (N = 89)	CP (N = 68)	SUB (N = 154)	ALL (N = 311)
Somewhat favorable to plantiff	9%	3%	6.0%	6%
Somewhat favorable to defendant	6	0	3.5	4
No opinion	84	91	90.0	88
I don't remember	1	6	0.5	2

Most jurors reported that they formed no opinion during the voir dire.

4. During the course of the trial, how were you treated by the people who work in the courtroom (not counting the judge and the lawyers)? (CHECK AS MANY ANSWERS AS APPLY)

	FC (PR = 90)	CP (PR = 68)	SUB (PR = 155)	ALL (PR = 313)
Politely	98%	90%	95%	95%
Helpfully	59	68	83	73
Rudely	0	0	0	0
They were not very interested in my well-being	0	1	3	2

Overwhelmingly the jurors reported that they were treated politely, especially in FC. They also indicated that they were treated helpfully, especially the jurors in SUB.

5. Was it your impression that your fellow jurors took the duty of jury service seriously?

	FC (N=90)	CP (N=68)	SUB (N=155)	ALL (N=313)
Yes	92%	81%	90.0%	88%
All but a couple of them	8	18	9.5	11
No	0	1	0.5	1

Jurors in all courts reported that their fellow jurors took the duty of jury service seriously. However, those in CP reported a slightly higher percentage of jurors who did not take their duty seriously.

6. Were you personally satisfied with the decision reached by the jury of which you were a member?

	FC (N=90)	CP (N=68)	SUB (N=155)	ALL (N=313)
Yes	93%	84%	88%	89%
No	7	16	12	11

Most jurors reported that they were personally satisfied with the verdict, with the jurors in FC being somewhat more satisfied with the decision reached by the jury of which they were a member. This slightly higher level of satisfaction may be a consequence of FC jurors being required to reach a unanimous decision. (See VIII: A.6 below, Unanimous and Majority Juries.)

Some questions about the TRIAL

7. Did you see any exhibits during the trial that made you doubt the truth of what you heard people testify to?

	FC (N=90)	CP (N=68)	SUB (N=151)	ALL (N=309)
Yes	44%	49%	43%	45%
No	56	51	57	55

These responses split almost in half. In all courts, there were only a few more jurors who did not doubt testimony because of certain exhibits than those who did.

8. Would you have liked to question any of the witnesses yourself, either directly or by having the judge ask the questions for you?

	FC (N=89)	CP (N=67)	SUB (N=125)	ALL (N=281)
Yes	80%	85%	78%	80%
No	20	15	22	20

About four-fifths of all jurors replied yes, that they would have liked to question certain witnesses.

9. Did you hear any testimony about pain and suffering of the plaintiff?

	FC (N=81)	CP (N=56)	SUB (N=120)	ALL (N=257)
Yes	80%	96%	84%	89%
No	20	4	16	11

At least four-fifths, and almost all of CP jurors who answered this question reported hearing testimony about pain and suffering. (Responses given by jurors sitting on nonpersonal injury cases were deleted from the data.)

10. If so, who testified about it? (CHECK AS MANY ANSWERS AS APPLY)

	FC (PR=74)	CP (PR=54)	SUB (PR=101)	ALL (PR=229)
The plaintiff	93%	93%	91%	92%
Member(s) of the plaintiff's family	68	54	90	74
Neighbors, friends or fellow employees	35	0	39	28
Experts (such as doctors or nurses)	69	76	69	71

The jurors who responded yes to the prior question about hearing pain and suffering testimony most often reported that it was the plaintiff who gave such testimony. SUB jurors said members of the plaintiff's family gave like testimony in equal amount. CP jurors reported that no such testimony was given by neighbors, friends, or fellow employees.

11. Was any of the testimony presented to you on a videotape?

	FC (N=89)	CP (N=65)	SUB (N=153)	ALL (N=307)
Yes	48%	85%	43%	53%
No	52	15	57	47

It appears that videotaped testimony was used more frequently in CP.

12. If yes, what was your feeling about it?

	FC (YP=43)	CP (YP=55)	SUB (YP=66)	ALL (YP=164)
I would have preferred to see the witness in person.	23%	67%	62%	53.5%
It made no difference.	49	18	24	28.5

	FC (YP=43)	CP (YP=55)	SUB (YP=66)	ALL (YP=164)
It was easier to concentrate on the videotape because there were no distractions or interruptions as with live testimony.	28	15	14	18.0

Of those who saw testimony presented on videotape, about two-thirds of the CP and SUB jurors would have preferred to see the witness testify in person. However, half of the FC jurors said it made no difference. This was a statistically significant difference between the courts at p< .001.

13. Were any of the exhibits (such as photographs, charts, medical records) used during the trial helpful to you in making up your mind?

	FC (N=89)	CP (N=67)	SUB (N=140)	ALL (N=296)
Yes, in a major way	37%	57%	54%	50%
Yes, but only in a minor way	55	39	35	42
No	8	4	11	8

Ninety-two percent of all jurors reported that exhibits were helpful, and 50% said in a major way. (See IX: A.1 for further discussion.)

14. Did you get the feeling that important information was being kept out of the trial because of lawyers' objections?

	FC (N=89)	CP (N=66)	SUB (N=151)	ALL (N=306)
Yes	18%	24%	25%	23%
No	82	76	75	77

More than three-quarters replied no to this question.

15. If you answered yes, whose objections MOST OFTEN kept out the important information?

	FC (PR=16)	CP (PR=16)	SUB (PR=37)	ALL (PR=69)
Plaintiff's lawyer	63%	44%	51%	50%
Defense lawyer	44	50	57	50

For those jurors who believed that important information was being kept out of the trial as a result of lawyer objections, CP and SUB jurors indicated that it was done almost equally by both sides. However, almost two-thirds of the FC jurors reported that the plaintiff's lawyer did it more often. (Some jurors checked both.)

16. Did you wonder why certain people who were mentioned during the trial didn't testify?

	FC (N=82)	CP (N=65)	SUB (N=149)	ALL (N=296)
Yes	55%	58%	45%	51%
No	45	42	55	49

About half of the jurors did wonder why certain mentioned people did not testify.

17. Did you hold it against the side that didn't call certain people to testify who might have added important information?

	FC (YP=45)	CP (YP=38)	SUB (YP=65)	ALL (YP=148)
Yes	38%	16%	26%	27%
No	62	84	74	73

Of those jurors who did wonder why certain mentioned people did not testify, about three-quarters did not hold it against the side that didn't call them to testify, a few less in FC, a few more in CP.

18. Do you think that too many witnesses testified about the same issue?

	FC (N=90)	CP (N=67)	SUB (N=155)	ALL (N=312)
Yes	18%	12%	24%	20%
No	82	88	76	80

Almost four-fifths said no, with SUB jurors saying yes a little more often, and CP jurors saying no a little more often.

19. Did the plaintiff have medical bills?

	FC (N=75)	CP (N=57)	SUB (N=120)	ALL (N=252)
Yes	83%	79%	75%	78%
No	17	21	25	22

20. Did the defense argue that the bills were wrong?

	FC (N=75)	CP (N=56)	SUB (N=115)	ALL (N=246)
Yes	4%	0%	9%	5%
No	96	100	91	95

The defense rarely argued that the medical bills were wrong.

21. If there was a fight about the medical bills, which side did
    you believe?

	FC (N=9)	CP (N=0)	SUB (N=21)	ALL (N=30)
Plaintiff's side	78%	0%	43%	53%
Defense side	22	0	57	47

This question appears to be ambiguous, as several of the jurors who answered no to the prior question also responded to this one. Therefore, it is not possible to discern what was intended by the above responses.

22. Did the plaintiff claim that he or she would have FUTURE
    medical bills?

	FC (N=82)	CP (N=56)	SUB (N=117)	ALL (N=255)
Yes	48%	52%	41%	45%
No	52	48	59	55

23. If yes, did you believe him or her?

	FC (YP=37)	CP (YP=29)	SUB (YP=45)	ALL (YP=111)
Yes	80%	93%	73%	79%
No	15	7	27	17
Unsure (Written in)	5	0	0	4

Jurors tended to believe the plaintiff's claim that he or she would have future medical bills, with CP jurors most believing of the claim.

24. Did the plaintiff claim that he or she would lose income
    in the future because of the injury?

	FC (N=82)	CP (N=55)	SUB (N=116)	ALL (N=253)
Yes	38%	64%	59%	53%
No	62	36	41	47

25. If yes, did you believe him or her?

	FC (YP=30)	CP (YP=35)	SUB (YP=66)	ALL (YP=131)
Yes	53%	77%	56%	61%
No	47	23	44	39

Jurors tended to believe the plaintiff's claim that he or she would lose income in the future because of the injury. The CP jurors again gave greater credence to plaintiff's claims.

26. At the beginning of the trial, after the lawyers made their opening speeches, do you recall how you felt about the case? (Try to remember your feelings at that time, not what they may have become later.)

	FC (N = 90)	CP (N = 66)	SUB (N = 154)	ALL (N = 310)
I somewhat favored the plaintiff	22%	36%	26%	27%
I somewhat favored the defendant	22	3	12	13
I had no strong feelings one way or the other	56	61	62	60

Although three-fifths of the jurors reported that they had no strong feelings one way or the other after opening speeches, 40% indicated that they somewhat favored either the plaintiff or defendant before hearing one word of testimony.

Furthermore, there was a statistically significant difference between the three courts at $p < .01$. Of those jurors who favored either the plaintiff or the defendant after opening speeches, FC jurors split equally on their preference, and SUB jurors favored the plaintiff twice as often as the defendant. However, CP jurors favored the plaintiff 12 times as often.

27. If the defendant(s) did not take the witness stand, did it:

	FC (N = 44)	CP (N = 30)	SUB (N = 55)	ALL (N = 129)
HELP the defense case	5%	10%	7%	7%
HURT the defense case	25	20	33	27
Make no difference	70	70	60	66

Two-thirds of all jurors said that it made no difference if the defendant(s) did not testify. For the remaining jurors, FC and SUB were five times as likely to say this hurt rather than helped the defense case, but CP said "hurt the case" only twice as often.

28. What was the main claim that the plaintiff made against the defendant(s)?

Most jurors were able to relate the main claim of the plaintiff in a couple of words or a sentence. For example (taken from different trials):

"Pain and suffering due to the accident and future compensation."
"Negligence"
"That a design defect caused an accident which resulted in a man's death."

29. Check all the statements below which describe your feelings about the plaintiff's lawyer.

30. Check all the statements below which describe your feelings about the defense lawyer. (If there was more than
one defense lawyer, check the statements below which describe the one lawyer who remains most clearly in your
mind.)

[Both of these questions were followed by identical statements and jurors
could check as many as they believed applicable. Therefore, there could
have been as many checks as there were jurors who completed questionnaires. The statements are presented here in the order in which they were
most often selected. The percentage is that of the possible number of responses.]

	Plaintiff's Attorney (PR = 313)	Defense Attorney(s) (PR = 313)
Really seemed to believe in his or her case.	82%	68%
Was polite to witnesses.	74	67
Always appeared to know what he or she was doing.	64	58
I usually learned important facts about the case as a result of his or her ques-tioning of witnesses.	58	51
I thought he or she was per-suasive in the speech made to the jury.	47	45
If I ever needed a lawyer, I'd want him or her to help me.	34	40
Asked pointless questions.	27	18
Acted in a superior manner. (*)	24	27
Probably wasn't aggressive enough.	15	28
Was sarcastic.	12	15
Brow-beat some of the wit-nesses.	11	11

(*) There seemed to be some confusion about this statement. From the tenor of
other statements selected, it became clear that some jurors read this to be a com-
pliment to the lawyer, while others read it to be an insult.

The most often selected statements (the first six) for both plaintiff and
defense lawyers were all positive. The negative statements were mentioned
last, and by much smaller percentages of jurors. It seems that the jurors,
by and large, held a good opinion of the lawyers in their trials.

Comparing percentages reveals that jurors held a higher opinion of counsel
for the plaintiff than they did for the defense on all issues except one.
When selecting a lawyer for themselves, more jurors indicated that they
would prefer the defense lawyer to represent them.

31. Did you think that the judge favored one lawyer over the other?

	FC (N=90)	CP (N=68)	SUB (N=154)	ALL (N=312)
Yes	8%	1%	5%	5%
No	92	99	95	95

Overwhelmingly the jurors reported that the judge did not favor one lawyer over the other.

32. If you answered yes, how did this make you feel? (CHECK AS MANY ANSWERS AS APPLY)

[Only 16 jurors responded yes to LQ 31. Therefore, the number of jurors who selected a particular response is given rather than the percentage.]

	Number of Jurors
It didn't make any difference to me at all.	8
The lawyers were doing their job, and so was the judge doing his.	8
I assumed that it was simply a question of the judge not liking one of the lawyers.	4
I didn't think the lawyer knew what s/he was doing, and had it coming to her/him.	4
The judge was unnecessarily harsh toward and critical of the lawyer.	4
It was a battle over who was going to run the courtroom.	2

33. During the course of the trial, which if any of the following impressions did you get of the plaintiff? (CHECK AS MANY ANSWERS AS APPLY)

34. During the course of the trial, which if any of the following impressions did you get of the defendant? If there was more than one defendant, select the impressions below which describe the one defendant who remains most clearly in your mind.
(CHECK AS MANY ANSWERS AS APPLY)

[Both of these questions were followed by identical statements and jurors could check as many as they believed applicable. Therefore, there could have been as many checks as there were jurors who completed question-naires. The statements are presented here in the order in which they were most often selected. The percentage is that of the possible number of re-sponses.]

	Plaintiff (PR = 313)	Defendant (PR = 313)
Generally seemed a likable person.	74%	41%
Appeared to be a person with high moral standards.	51	31
Seemed to be a religious person.	13	4
Even though he or she could have worked, appeared to have made little or no effort to find a job after the accident (or injury).	10	—
Generally seemed an unlikable person.	7	6
Appeared to be a person with low moral standards.	6	8
Appeared to have a drinking problem.	4	4
Had an occupation or way of life of which I don't approve.	3	4
Was divorced.	3	—
Appeared to have a drug problem.	2	0.6 (2 jurors)
Seemed to be a snob, or treated people in a superior way.	2	4
Was living with someone who was not his or her spouse.	1	0.9 (3 jurors)
Probably was a homosexual.	—	0.3 (1 juror)

The more favorable responses were by far the ones most often selected by the jurors, stating with strongest voice that they believed that both plaintiff and defendant were likable persons with high moral standards.

The lower percentiles of defendant responses are not necessarily an in-dication that the jurors had lower regard for defendants. Because the de-fendant was often an insurance company, a corporation, or the City of Philadelphia, jurors would often mark this question as "not applicable" and not respond. Therefore, the actual respondent pool was smaller than the possible pool of 315 jurors.

35. **What was the main defense that was made against the claim of the plaintiff?**

Most jurors were able to relate the main defense that was made against plaintiff's claim in a few words or a sentence. For example (taken from different trials):

> "Corporation claimed plaintiff did not use reasonable caution and common sense to avoid accident."

"That it was the responsibility of the plaintiff's supervisor to do a safety check and report any unsafe conditions."

"The injuries she received didn't occur from the defendant's negligence."

36. Do you recall any particular event in the trial that was most important in making up your mind?

	FC (N=84)	CP (N=61)	SUB (N=146)	ALL (N=291)
Yes	60%	59%	49%	54%
No	40	41	51	46

About half of all the jurors did recall a particular, important event in the trial. However, slightly more FC and CP jurors reported such recall.

37. If yes, what?

Although the question asked for a particular event, the half of the jurors who reported that they did recall such an event sometimes responded with more than one. In all, 170 responses were given by the 158 responding jurors. These answers clustered around four factors:

1. Testimony (including demeanor and missing testimony)   75%
2. Exhibits   18
3. Lawyers   5
4. Judge   2

An overwhelming majority (93%) of the responses related to testimony and exhibits, rather than lawyer or judge effect.

Some questions about the judge

38. Did the judge pay close attention to the case during the trial?

	FC (N=89)	CP (N=67)	SUB (N=153)	ALL (N=309)
Yes	91%	99%	100%	97%
No	9	1	0	3

Overwhelmingly the jurors stated that the judge paid close attention during the trial.

39. Do you think the judge thought this was an important case?

	FC (N=87)	CP (N=67)	SUB (N=150)	ALL (N=304)
Yes	82%	88%	90%	87%
No	18	12	10	13

Almost 90% of all jurors reported that they believed that the judge thought their case was important, a few less in FC.

40.   Did the judge seem to favor one side over the other?

	FC (N=89)	CP (N=68)	SUB (N=155)	ALL (N=312)
Yes, the plaintiff	2%	0%	0%	1%
Yes, the defendant	1	0	2	1
No	97	100	98	98

Overwhelmingly the jurors reported that the judge did not favor one lawyer over the other.

Some questions about the DELIBERATIONS

41.   In making your decision about the case, what was MOST important to you:

	FC (N=76)	CP (N=59)	SUB (N=136)	ALL (N=271)
The law as explained to you by the judge	41%	42%	51%	46%
The facts as told to you by the witnesses	55	53	45	50
The closing speeches given by the lawyers	4	5	4	4

For all jurors, the responses split almost evenly between law and facts. Also, jurors overwhelmingly indicated that closing speeches were not most important to them in making their decision about the case.

42.   How did you decide who would be the foreperson?

	FC (PR=90)	CP (PR=68)	SUB (PR=155)	ALL (PR=313)
Discussed it, and then selected someone	42%	62%	43%	47.0%
One of the jurors volunteered	21	22	25	23.0
Took a vote to name the foreperson	12	15	28	20.0
We agreed that juror number one would be the foreperson	28	15	6	14.0
We didn't; the judge named the foreperson	1	0	0	0.5

The most frequently given method appears to have been discussion followed by selection. A juror volunteering was the second most frequent method of obtaining a foreperson. There were two jurors who reported that the judge had named the foreperson, but as these were both lone choices of jurors on two different juries, they had to be mistaken. Jurors sometimes selected more than one choice, indicating, for example, that there was discussion and then a vote was taken.

43. If anyone took notes, were they used during the jury discussions?

	FC (N=90)	CP (N=60)	SUB (N=127)	ALL (N=277)
Yes	81%	2%	6%	29%
No	19	98	94	71

The jurors in FC were the only ones permitted to take notes, and four-fifths of them reported that juror notes were used during discussions. However, a few jurors in CP and SUB also reported that juror notes were used during deliberations. Since they were not permitted to take notes in the courtroom, these notes must have been made in the juryroom or at home.

44. If yes, what role did the note-taking play?

	FC (YP=73)	CP (YP=1)	SUB (YP=7)	ALL (YP=81)
We referred to them frequently	81%	1 juror	3 jurors	78%
If we disagreed with the notes, we relied on our memories	19	—	4 jurors	22

For those jurors who did take notes, four-fifths reported that they did refer to them frequently.

45. What was your amount of participation in jury discussions?

	FC (N=90)	CP (N=64)	SUB (N=152)	ALL (N=306)
A lot	53%	47%	42%	47%
A moderate amount	46	50	53	50
Very little	1	3	5	3

For nearly all jurors, participation was divided between a lot and moderate.

46. Were you the foreperson?

This question was asked in conjunction with question 45 to determine the self-reported amount of participation of the foreperson. Of the 35 forepersons who responded, 28 (80%) said they participated a lot, six (17%)

said their amount of participation was moderate, and one person did not respond.

47. Did the foreperson dominate the deliberations?

	FC (N=82)	CP (N=67)	SUB (N=154)	ALL (N=303)
Yes	18%	13%	9%	13%
No	82	87	91	87

Very few jurors reported that the foreperson dominated deliberations, even though 80% of the forepersons reported that they had participated a lot.

48. Did your trial require a unanimous decision? (Did ALL the jurors have to agree?)

This question was posed in order to lead into question 49. Nineteen jurors responded incorrectly, which suggests they either did not understand the word "unanimous," in spite of the definition given, or they did not know which kind of decision their jury required.

49. Did you agree with the majority opinion?

	FC **	CP (PR=58)	SUB (PR=141)	ALL (PR=199)
Yes	**	78%	83%	81%
No	**	17	10	12
No response	**	5	7	7

Most jurors reported that they agreed with the majority opinion.
**All jurors in FC sat on unanimous decision juries.

50. If there were just a couple of holdouts over the question of who should win, what was done to convince them to join the others?

	FC (N=76)	CP (N=54)	SUB (N=86)	ALL (N=216)
More general discussion	90%	91%	97%	92%
Small groups were formed to talk with each holdout separately	5	4	0	3
Another way (please specify)	5	5	3	5

"More general discussion" was the method most often selected to convince holdouts to join the others. (There were no hung juries in this study.)

51. Did you change your decision during the deliberation?

	FC (N = 89)	CP (N = 64)	SUB (N = 152)	ALL (N = 305)
Yes	36%	30%	17%	25%
No	64	70	83	75

Twenty-five percent of all jurors reported that they changed their decision during the deliberation. However, there was a statistically significant difference between the three courts at $p < .005$. Jurors in FC and CP tended to change their decision more frequently than did SUB jurors. (See VIII: D below for further discussion.)

52. If yes, why?

	FC (PR = 32)	CP (PR = 19)	SUB (PR = 26)	ALL (PR = 77)
Other jurors brought up points I hadn't THOUGHT ABOUT.	56%	68%	81%	68%
Other jurors brought up points I hadn't RE-MEMBERED.	44	47	15	35
I was the only one who felt a particular way, and I didn't want to cause a problem.	16	0	8	9
I really didn't understand the case so I decided to go along with the other jurors.	0	0	0	0
We had trouble reaching a verdict. When the judge put pressure on us, I decided to go along with the major-ity.	0	0	0	0

The reason most often mentioned by jurors for changing their decision during deliberation was that other jurors brought up points not thought about before. The second most often mentioned reason was that other jurors brought up points not remembered. The last two were mentioned by no one.

53. Was there any discussion about what the jurors believed the judge thought about the case?

	FC (N = 88)	CP (N = 66)	SUB (N = 154)	ALL (N = 308)
Yes	7%	5%	16%	11%
No	93	95	84	89

Very few jurors reported discussion about the views of the judge, with slightly more answering yes in SUB.

54. Did you want to please the judge with your verdict in the case?

	FC (N=88)	CP (N=66)	SUB (N=141)	ALL (N=295)
Yes	11%	9%	9%	9%
No	89	91	91	91

Most of the jurors reported that they did not want to please the judge with their verdict.

55. Did you have an "interrogatory" sheet of paper (which is a list of questions you had to answer in order to reach a verdict?)

	FC (N=89)	CP (N=64)	SUB (N=153)	ALL (N=306)
Yes	84%	84%	60%	72%
No	16	16	40	28

It appears that an "interrogatory" was used less frequently in SUB.

56. If yes, were the questions helpful?

	FC (PR=75)	CP (PR=54)	SUB (PR=92)	ALL (PR=221)
Yes, very helpful	69%	74%	66%	68%
Somewhat helpful	21	22	29	24
Not very helpful	3	2	3	3
They were confusing	12	9	2	7

Jurors often selected more than one of the above options. For example, some jurors responded that the interrogatory was somewhat helpful, but also confusing; or, not very helpful and confusing. However, at least two-thirds (and 74% in CP) of the jurors reported that the interrogatory was very helpful.

57. Did you understand how your answers to these questions would be used?

	FC (N=74)	CP (N=54)	SUB (N=91)	ALL (N=219)
Yes	92%	96%	97%	95%
No	8	4	3	5

Almost all jurors who used an interrogatory sheet said they understood how their answers would be used.

58. Were there any exhibits referred to in the courtroom during the trial that you would have liked to have with you in the juryroom during deliberations?

	FC (N = 86)	CP (N = 63)	SUB (N = 136)	ALL (N = 285)
Yes	28%	57%	32%	36%
No	72	43	68	64

There was a statistically significant difference between the three courts at $p < .001$. Although more than two-thirds of the jurors in FC and SUB said no, almost two-thirds of the CP jurors would have liked to have had exhibits, which were referred to in the courtroom during the trial, in the juryroom.

59. If so, which one(s)?

	FC (PR = 24)	CP (PR = 36)	SUB (PR = 44)	ALL (PR = 104)
Photographs	42%	64%	16%	38%
Charts	29	19	36	29
Medical records	33	25	25	27
Models	8	3	5	5
Other	46	33	25	33

The responses to this question were shaped by two factors. One was the type of case being tried. Models may have been infrequently mentioned because they were not appropriate to the type of complaint.

The other factor which could distort the data is a misunderstanding of the question. From the aggregate of responses for any particular trial, it was clear that jurors were listing exhibits which they did indeed have in the juryroom during deliberations. In other words, "Yes, there were exhibits which I would have liked to have had with me in the juryroom, and these are the ones—and I *did* have them."

The exhibits which were specified under the heading of "Other" fell into two categories. The first was DOCUMENTS, which included:

Depositions
IUD information pamphlet
Police statements
Tax forms
Witnesses' sworn statements from previous trials

The second category was PHYSICAL EVIDENCE, which included such items as:

Chain saw
Gloves
Marked blackboard used in courtroom
Videotaped testimony
X-rays

60. At the BEGINNING of the deliberation of the case, how many of you were in agreement as to which side should win?

	FC (N = 88)	CP (N = 65)	SUB (N = 149)	ALL (N = 302)
All but a couple of us	52%	39%	40%	44%
All of us	26	32	30	29
It was pretty evenly divided	18	20	28	23
I don't remember	4	9	2	4

Seventy-three percent (73%) of all jurors[2] reported that all or all but a couple of the jurors were in agreement at the beginning of deliberations. This implies that 27% of the jurors had to be convinced during deliberations, except on majority juries where one or two dissenting persons could be ignored.

61. If you took votes on the verdict, how was it done?

	FC (N = 86)	CP (N = 63)	SUB (N = 140)	ALL (N = 289)
By secret ballot	0%	0%	9%	4%
By raising hands	88	78	86	85
Sometimes openly and sometimes secretly	12	22	5	11

Jurors most often voted by raising hands.

62. If by secret ballot, was the FIRST ballot taken right at the beginning of the deliberations?

	FC (PR = 10)	CP (PR = 14)	SUB (PR = 19)	ALL (PR = 43)
Yes	2 jurors	1 juror	8 jurors	42%
No	1 juror	7 jurors	7 jurors	58

Because the response rate to this question was low, it implies that some jurors did not remember exactly when the first ballot was taken.

63. Did the way the majority of the jurors voted the FIRST time you took a vote turn out to be the same as the final verdict?

	FC (N = 86)	CP (N = 62)	SUB (N = 151)	ALL (N = 299)
Yes	72%	71%	68%	70%
No	28	29	32	30

Seventy percent of the jurors reported that the initial majority vote held and was indeed the final vote. However, since 30% of the jurors reported that they sat on juries where the original majority did not hold, this implies

---

2   This differs from the percentage of *juries* which were in agreement at beginning of deliberations as discussed on page 342.

that almost a third served on juries where jurors changed their opinions in large enough number to reverse the original majority.

However, this number might also include those who sat on juries where there was no original majority. (See VIII: D below for further discussion.)

64. After the first vote, if there were LATER votes, how were they done?

	FC (N=73)	CP (N=53)	SUB (N=101)	ALL (N=227)
By secret ballot	0%	0%	0%	0%
By raising hands	92	75	97	90
Sometimes openly, and sometimes secretly	8	25	3	10

The method of raising hands for later votes was the one most frequently used but, to a statistically significant degree (p<.001), CP jurors reported that their later votes were sometimes open and sometimes secret.

65. If there was more than one defendant, was the size of the award based on how much insurance you thought each defendant had?

	FC (N=8)	CP (N=25)	SUB (N=16)	ALL (N=49)
Yes	0%	0%	0%	0%
No	100	64	75	73
It was part of the discussion, but it wasn't the main factor in making up my mind	0	36	25	27

No one replied yes and all jurors reported that the amount of defendant insurance was not a factor, or was not the main factor, in determining the size of the award.

66. If your verdict was for the plaintiff, did you consider any of the following matters in reaching your decision? (CHECK AS MANY AS APPLY)

[The number of possible responses to this question was determined according to the number of jurors who sat on juries which decided for the plaintiff, and who also completed and returned the long questionnaire. The percentage given represents the frequency with which a statement was selected by the possible respondents.]

	FC (PR=54)	CP (PR=47)	SUB (PR=71)	ALL (PR=172)
It wasn't a question of whether the defendant was a nice person, or	81%	77%	79%	79%

	FC (PR = 54)	CP (PR = 47)	SUB (PR = 71)	ALL (PR = 172)
if it was a good organization. If the plaintiff was entitled to a verdict, then the defendant should pay him or her fairly.				
How your verdict might prevent other people or companies from doing the same thing as this defendant did.	33	36	23	30
That the defendant should be taught a lesson.	15	21	11	15
If the defendant was a business, that the verdict might force that business to close down, and many people might lose their jobs.	0	4	3	2

That the plaintiff was entitled to the verdict was the issue responding jurors selected more than twice as often as any other one (more than three times as often in SUB). A third of the responders (less than one-quarter in SUB) selected preventing others from doing the same thing. Wanting to "teach a lesson" was selected 26 times out of 172 responses, and the possibility that a business might close as a result of their decision was selected four times.

67. If your verdict was for the defendant(s), which of the following statements express your feelings for the plaintiff: (CHECK AS MANY AS APPLY)

[The number of possible responses to this question was determined according to the number of jurors who sat on juries which decided for the defense, and who also completed and returned the long questionnaire. The percentage given represents the frequency with which a statement was selected by the possible respondents.]

	FC (PR = 36)	CP (PR = 21)	SUB (PR = 85)	ALL (PR = 142)
I felt sorry for the plaintiff, but on the basis of the facts and the law as explained to me by the judge, s/he	78%	95%	76%	80%

	FC (PR = 36)	CP (PR = 21)	SUB (PR = 85)	ALL (PR = 142)
wasn't entitled to any money.				
I might have voted for the plaintiff, but the injuries and losses claimed seemed so exaggerated that it turned me off.	22	14	19	19
I didn't believe the plaintiff from the start.	22	10	14	15
I might have decided in favor of the plaintiff, but I assumed that s/he had insurance coverage anyhow which would cover most of the losses claimed.	8	10	6	7
I was concerned that a verdict for the plaintiff would have been too much of a financial burden on the defendant.	0	5	2	2

The issue most frequently selected by jurors sitting on defense decision juries was that they felt sorry for the plaintiff, but s/he was not entitled to any money. One-fifth of the possible responses noted that the injuries and losses seemed exaggerated, and only 22 responses out of 142 mentioned that the juror didn't believe the plaintiff. Only 10 jurors selected plaintiff insurance, and three indicated that a verdict for the plaintiff would have been too much of a financial burden on the defendant.

If an amount of money was awarded, answer the following questions

68. Did you think that your insurance rates would go up as a result of your verdict?

	FC (N = 44)	CP (N = 36)	SUB (N = 46)	ALL (N = 126)
Yes	0%	11%	7%	6%
No	82	53	76	71
Maybe, but this didn't affect my decision	18	36	17	23

Very few jurors said yes. However, combining "yes" and "maybe" responses and comparing those with "no" responses, it appears that more

CP jurors tended to believe their insurance rates might go up as a result of their verdict than did the other jurors. A chi-square test produced p < .025. Although this is not a statistically significant correlation, it might be true that with a larger sample significance would be achieved.

69. Was the amount of money awarded to the plaintiff lowered because the jurors decided he or she already had some of the losses covered by insurance (such as Blue Cross or Workmen's Compensation)?

	FC (N = 46)	CP (N = 36)	SUB (N = 41)	ALL (N = 123)
Yes	11%	6%	22%	13%
No, it was not discussed	50	25	41	40
It was discussed but it did not have an affect on the size of the award	39	69	37	47

Eighty-seven percent of all jurors (a few less in SUB, more in CP) stated that insurance coverage which plaintiff might have received was either not discussed at all or, if it was, that it did not have an effect on the amount of the award.

70. Was the amount of money awarded to the plaintiff lowered because there were jurors who weren't sure the plaintiff should be paid anything at all?

	FC (N = 54)	CP (N = 36)	SUB (N = 64)	ALL (N = 154)
Yes	54%	33%	45%	45%
No	46	67	55	55

Jurors in FC and SUB were divided almost equally on whether or not the award was lowered because there were jurors who weren't sure the plaintiff should be paid anything at all. But two-thirds of the CP jurors reported that they did not lower the award for this reason.

71. If the defendant was a 'big business', which of the following statements best describes the feelings of your jury:

	FC (N = 28)	CP (N = 10)	SUB (N = 27)	ALL (N = 65)
We thought the business could afford to pay, and that had something to do with deciding for the plaintiff.	7%	0%	7%	6%
We thought the business could afford to pay, but that had nothing to do with deciding for the plaintiff.	43	70	45	48

	FC (N = 28)	CP (N = 10)	SUB (N = 27)	ALL (N = 65)
It was never discussed.	50	30	48	46

Almost all jurors (94%) reported that they never discussed, or that it had no effect on their decisions, that the defendant business could afford to pay. Only 4 jurors said that had something to do with their decision.

72. How do you think the plaintiff is paying his lawyer?

	FC (N = 54)	CP (N = 38)	SUB (N = 75)	ALL (N = 167)
A flat fee	4%	5%	15%	9%
So much per hour	0	0	4	2
A percentage of the total verdict	89	95	76	84
I don't know (written in)	7	0	5	5

Better than four-fifths of the jurors (a few less in SUB, more in CP) believed that the lawyer for the plaintiff would receive a percentage of the verdict.

73. Did you increase the amount of the verdict to cover the lawyer's fee?

	FC (N = 54)	CP (N = 36)	SUB (N = 67)	ALL (N = 157)
Yes	6%	14%	3%	6%
No	94	86	97	94

The award was rarely increased to cover the lawyer's fee. However, the jurors in CP did it more often.

Some questions about you

74. If you have ever been involved in a lawsuit, check the following statements which are true:

I was a plaintiff (27 jurors)
I was a defendant (17 jurors)
I am a plaintiff (Written in by 1 juror)
Case was ended by a settlement (38 jurors)
Case was ended by a trial verdict (4 jurors)
As a result of the case, I gained a favorable impression of how the justice system works (20 jurors)
As a result of the case, I gained an unfavorable impression of how the justice system works (3 jurors)

For further discussion, see VIII: C.2, The Effects on Jurors of Prior Involvement in Law Suits.

75. Was this your first experience as a juror?

	FC (N=89)	CP (N=67)	SUB (N=135)	ALL (N=291)
Yes	76%	78%	76%	77%
No	24	22	24	23

This was the first juror experience for three-quarters of the jurors.

76. How many times have you served as a juror?

77. How long ago were you last a juror?

See Appendix G for complete information on prior juror experience.

78. If you are employed, did your employer pay you while you were a juror?

	FC (N=66)	CP (N=50)	SUB (N=117)	ALL (N=233)
Yes	82%	74%	79%	79%
No	18	26	21	21

Four-fifths of employed jurors were paid by their employers while they served as jurors.

VIII. OTHER RESULTS

A. Unanimous and Majority Juries   Jury verdicts in the civil cases included in this study were either unanimous, where all jurors must concur, or majority. The unanimous condition prevailed in all federal court cases. The majority rule was followed in both Philadelphia and Montgomery County courts.

The majority rule followed in these jurisdictions required that five-sixths of the jurors agree. Therefore, if a jury was comprised of 12 jurors, 10 had to agree in order to reach a verdict. If eight persons sat on a jury, seven persons had to agree. The consequence of a majority decision rule is that a dissenting juror can be ignored and a verdict still reached.

There were 12 unanimous and 26 majority juries in this study. These two types of juries were compared on the following issues to discover similarities and differences:

1. At the beginning of deliberation, how many jurors were in agreement?

Unanimous (12 juries)   All or most: 78%   (All: 26%)
Majority (26 juries)   All or most: 70.5%   (All: 31%)

Both juries reported about the same number of jurors in agreement at the beginning of deliberations.

2. Jurors who said they changed their minds during deliberations:

Unanimous	36%
Majority	23.5%

    More jurors reported that they changed their minds on unanimous juries—as would be necessary to reach unanimity.

3. Did the way the majority voted the first time turn out to be the same as the final vote?

Unanimous	Yes: 72%	No: 28%
Majority	Yes: 69%	No: 31%

    The two types of juries differed very little.

4. The award was determined by averaging the figures suggested by members of the jury:

Unanimous	38%
Majority	39%

    The two types of juries differed hardly at all.

5. Was the amount of money awarded to the plaintiff lowered because there were jurors who weren't sure the plaintiff should be paid anything at all?

Unanimous	Yes: 54%	No: 46%
Majority	Yes: 39%	No: 61%

    Here again, there seemed to be more concessions made by jurors who had to reach unanimity.

6. The jurors were satisfied by the verdict they reached:

Unanimous	93%
Majority	86%

    More jurors on unanimous juries reported that they were satisfied with the verdict. This seems to be a logical finding, for some jurors sitting on majority rule juries may not have agreed with the verdict but a decision could be reached without their approval. However, most jurors indicated that they were satisfied with the verdict.

7. Length of trial in days:

Unanimous	2.7 days
Majority	4.5 days

    The length of the trial was measured by the courtroom deputy clerk from the time that the judge opened the trial until the jurors were excused from their jury service. This included deliberation.

    Notice that all federal cases were surveyed in the courtroom of one judge, and those cases represent all the unanimous verdicts. This may have made a difference to the above result. The fact that unanimous trials averaged a shorter period of time than did majority trials may have been a consequence of the manner in which this judge managed his courtroom, i.e., the data may be skewed because this judge moves trials along very swiftly.

8. Did jurors tend to participate more or less when sitting on one type of jury than the other?

Amount of participation	Unanimous	Majority
Lot	53%	44%
Moderate or little	47	56

Although it appears that jurors on unanimous juries participated more, this difference failed to reach statistical significance in a chi-square test.

9. Length of deliberation in hours:

Unanimous	3.72 hours (3:43)
Majority	2.97 hours (2:58)

The length of deliberation was determined from the time the jurors were sent into the juryroom to begin deliberating until the time that they notified the clerk that they had reached a verdict. As might be expected, unanimous juries in which every juror must agree took longer to reach a verdict.

SUMMARY

Unanimous and majority juries were alike in the following ways:

1. Jurors were in agreement to the same extent at beginning of deliberations.
2. If a majority existed at the time that the first vote was taken, that majority held to the same degree for both types of juries.
3. The award was determined most often by averaging the figures suggested by members of the jury, and to the same degree.

Unanimous and majority juries differed only somewhat on the following issues:

1. Jurors serving on unanimous juries changed their minds somewhat more frequently.
2. Jurors on unanimous juries were somewhat more satisfied with the verdict.
3. Jurors on unanimous juries participated somewhat more.

Unanimous and majority juries clearly differed on the following issues:

1. Lowering the amount of an award because there were jurors who were not certain that the plaintiff should be paid anything at all. Unanimous jurors did it more often.

2. Trials with unanimous decision juries concluded more quickly.[3]
3. Unanimous juries took longer to reach a decision.

B. Small and Large Juries The civil juries in the three jurisdictions which provided the data for this study were both small and large. A small jury, as were all of the juries in federal court and some of those in Common Pleas Courts, can be comprised of six to eight jurors. Eight are selected at the time of voir dire but, if attrition occurs, the trial may continue as long as six of the original eight are present.

A large jury, as were some of those in Common Pleas Courts, can be comprised of nine to 12 jurors. Twelve are selected at the time of voir dire but, if attrition occurs, the trial may continue with as few as nine jurors.

There were 21 small and 17 large juries in this study. These two type of juries were compared on the following issues to discover similarities and differences:

1. Did the way the majority voted the first time turn out to be the same as the final vote?

Small (21 juries)   Yes: 76%   No: 24%
Large (17 juries)   Yes: 65%   No: 35%

Although a statistically significant correlation was not found in the responses to this question (LQ 45), at $p < .05$ it might be true that with a larger sample, significance would be achieved. There appears to be a relationship between size of jury and the agreement of first and final vote. The initial majority vote tended to hold more often in smaller juries, which implies that more jurors tended to change their initial opinions more often in larger juries.

2. Length of case in days:

Small   3.4 days
Large   4.5 days

Both moderately complicated and straightforward cases occurred almost equally for both large and small juries, as well as relatively large or small awards, or none at all. Cases which were tried with more jurors on a jury appear to have taken longer to try, possibly as a consequence of the fact that all federal cases were eight-person juries and were tried in the courtroom of one judge, conditions which did not exist in the other two court systems. When the federal cases are removed from the data and the juries are divided into large and small juries according to *actual number* of sitting jurors, the length of a case in days is only somewhat different:

---

[3] This result may be skewed because all unanimous data was collected in the courtroom of one judge. See VIII: A.7.

> Small Juries—7 to 9 jurors: 4.2 days
> Large Juries—10 to 12 jurors: 4.6 days

3.   Did jurors tend to participate more or less when sitting on one type of jury rather than the other?

Amount of participation	Small	Large
Lot	55%	40%
Moderate or little	45	60

Although a statistically significant correlation was not found in the responses to this question (LQ 45), at $p < .025$ it might be true that with a larger sample, significance would be achieved. There appears to be a relationship between size of jury and amount of participation. Jurors serving on small juries reported that they participated more in deliberations.

4.   Length of deliberation in hours:

Small	3.29 hours (3:17)
Large	3.11 hours (3:07)

Small and large juries deliberated for almost the same period of time.

SUMMARY

Large and small juries were alike in the following ways:

Large and small juries deliberated the same amount of time.

Large and small juries differed on the following issues:

a)   If a majority existed at the time that the first vote was taken, that majority held more often in small juries. It appears that jurors tended to change their initial opinions more often in larger juries.

b)   Trials with more jurors appear to have lasted slightly longer than trials with fewer jurors.

c)   During deliberations, it appears that jurors on small juries participated more than jurors on large juries.

C. Plaintiff and Defense Verdict Juries   Juries which decided for the plaintiff or for the defense were examined for possible differences.

1.   How jurors felt about the plaintiff and the defendant, their testimony and their lawyers:

	Plaintiff Verdict	Defense Verdict
Jurors stated that the testimony of PLAINTIFF:		
INCREASED their belief in the plaintiff's case	78%	0%

Jurors stated that the testimony of PLAINTIFF:	Plaintiff Verdict	Defense Verdict
DECREASED their belief in the plaintiff's case	11	73
Mixed	—	7
No response	11	20

Feelings jurors had for the PLAINTIFF:		
High regard	78.0%	50%
Low regard	11.0	31
Mixed	5.5	6
No response	5.5	13

Feelings jurors had for the PLAINTIFF's attorney:		
Positive	78%	11%
Negative	5	67
Mixed	17	22

Jurors stated that the DEFENSE testimony:		
INCREASED their belief in the defense case	12%	93%
DECREASED their belief in the defense case	53	—
Mixed	—	7
No response	35	—

Feelings jurors had for the DEFENDANT(s):		
High regard	53%	59%
Low regard	20	8
Mixed	20	8
No response	7	25

Feelings jurors had for the DEFENSE attorney:		
Positive	21.5%	79%
Negative	57	—
Mixed	21.5	21

In cases which resulted in a verdict for the plaintiff, at least three-quarters (78%) of the jurors reported that plaintiff's testimony increased their belief in the case, that they had high regard for the plaintiff, and positive feelings for the plaintiff's attorney.

In cases which resulted in verdicts for the defense, 93% of the jurors reported that defense testimony increased their belief in the defense case, 59% had high regard for the defendant(s), and 79% had positive feelings for the defense attorney.

Regardless of the verdict, at least half of all jurors had high regard for both plaintiff and defendant(s).

SUMMARY

Although it appears that jurors may have decided for the litigants and lawyers for whom they held higher opinions, the data may reflect an other-way relationship. That is, jurors may have first formed their own opinions of the case without regard to the personalities of the litigants and lawyers, and then believed and held high opinions of those persons who reinforced their own theory of the case.

2.   Length of deliberations:

The average time of deliberation for the 22 plaintiff verdicts:

3.48 hours (3:29)

The average time of deliberation for the 16 defense verdicts:

2.62 hours (2:37)

It took plaintiff decision juries 52 minutes (about 33%) longer to reach a verdict, which usually included determining a monetary award.

The longest deliberation for a plaintiff verdict was 8 hours [FED: $656,497 award, personal injury—death].

The longest deliberation for a defense verdict was also 8 hours [SUB: motor vehicle].

The shortest deliberation for a plaintiff verdict without determining the amount of award was 5 minutes [CP: insurance claim].

The shortest deliberation for a plaintiff verdict including amount of award was 1 hour [FED: $25,000 award, motor vehicle].

The shortest deliberation for a defense verdict was 10 minutes [FED: injury from police arrest].

3.   The effect on jurors of prior involvement in lawsuits:

Jurors involved in prior lawsuits were asked if, as a result of that experience, they had gained a favorable or unfavorable impression of how the justice system works. This information was considered in light of the verdict of the jury of which they were a part to see if that experience might have affected their behavior as jurors.

	Plaintiff in Prior Lawsuit (N = 24)	Defendant in Prior Lawsuit (N = 17)
Positive view of system	9 jurors (38%)	8 jurors (47%)
Negative view of system	2 jurors (8%)	2 jurors (12%)
No response	13 jurors (54%)	7 jurors (41%)

Although nearly half of the jurors (20) did not respond, most of those who did reported a positive view of the legal system: 82% of those involved as plaintiffs and 80% of those involved as defendants.

Decided for Plaintiff in present study	14 jurors (58%)	10 jurors (59%)
Decided for Defense in present study	10 jurors (42%)	7 jurors (41%)

These figures match almost exactly the averages for the entire study: 58% plaintiff verdicts and 42% defense verdicts.

SUMMARY

Most jurors who had prior involvement in lawsuits held a positive view of the legal system. Their behavior as jurors, regardless of the verdict of the prior lawsuit, was equivalent to that of jurors with no prior lawsuit involvement.

D. Formation and Change of Verdict Decision
1. The following sequence of questions examines at what point in the trial jurors formed an opinion about the case and, if they changed that opinion during the trial, when they did so. The questions are arranged to reflect reported juror opinion in the chronological order of the trial.

LQ 3: During voir dire, what opinion did you form about the case?

	Pro Plaintiff	Pro Defendant	No Opinion
Plaintiff verdict	6%	2%	92%
Defense verdict	6	6	88
All jurors	6	4	90

Very few jurors reported having formed an opinion during voir dire. This was true whether voir dire was conducted by the judge or by the lawyers, both methods being employed in different trials in the study.

LQ 26: After the lawyers made their opening speeches, how did you feel about the case?

	Pro Plaintiff	Pro Defendant	No Strong Feelings
Plaintiff verdict	28%	13%	59%
Defense verdict	26	13	61
All jurors	27	13	60

After opening speeches, some jurors did report formation of opinion. For these jurors, regardless of whether the ultimate verdict was for the plaintiff or the defense, twice as many had positive feelings for the plaintiff as for the defendant. However, three-fifths of all jurors reported no strong feelings at this point in the trial.

SQ 6: Just before jury deliberations began, had you already reached a decision, even though this might not have been your final decision?

	Definitely for or leaning toward plaintiff	Definitely for or leaning toward defendant
Plaintiff verdict	74%	26%
Defense verdict	24	76
All jurors	49	51

Just prior to jury deliberations, half of all jurors were definitely for or leaning toward the plaintiff, the other half for the defense. However, when examined in light of the ultimate verdict, by the time deliberations began three-quarters of both plaintiff and defense verdict jurors were already for or leaning toward the side which finally won the verdict. This implies that a quarter of the jurors changed their opinion during deliberations, allowing for those few serving on majority juries who did not have to be persuaded for the jury to reach a verdict.

SQ 25: How did jury deliberations affect you?

	No effect	Made me think about original point of view —but no change	Changed point of view
Plaintiff verdict	12%	64%	24%
Defense verdict	31	55	14
All jurors	21	60	19

"No effect" and "no change" responses were combined into a no change category, and then change/no change responses were compared. Although a statistically significant correlation was not found, at $p < .05$ it might be true that with a larger sample significance would be achieved. It appears that jurors who sat on plaintiff verdict juries and held an initial pro-defense view, tended to reverse that opinion more often than jurors with an initial pro-plaintiff view reversed theirs. This implies that it is easier for a juror to switch from defense to plaintiff support, than from plaintiff to defense.

Overall, 19% of the jurors reported that they changed their point of view during deliberations.

LQ 51: Did you change your decision during the deliberation?

	YES	NO
Plaintiff verdict	28%	72%
Defense verdict	22	78
All jurors	25	75

Twenty-five percent of the jurors reported that they changed their decision during the deliberation. As in SQ 25 above, a slightly larger number of jurors shifted from defense to plaintiff position, giving plaintiff verdict juries a higher percentage of change.

There was a statistically significant difference at $p < .005$ in how often the jurors in the three court systems changed their decision. Jurors sitting in SUB reported that they changed their decision during deliberations far less frequently than did jurors in the other two systems.

These last two questions, SQ 25 and LQ 51, appear to be addressing the same issue yet producing slightly different results. However, jurors may have perceived the questions differently.

SQ 25 asks the jurors how their deliberations affected them, giving the possible response of "changed my *point of view*." This question was asked immediately following the conclusion of the trial in the juryroom.

LQ 51 asks the jurors if they changed their *decision* during the deliberation. This question was answered within a period of up to two weeks following the conclusion of the trial, away from the courthouse.

Assuming that the questions, because of the difference in wording, may have been construed to be different, and considering that time may have somewhat altered memory, the most accurate reading of these responses is the average of the two percentages, 19 and 25. Therefore, the figure of 22% is the one which best represents the amount of change which occurred during deliberations.

LQ 52: Why did you change your decision during the deliberation?

	Other jurors brought up points I hadn't:		I didn't want to cause a problem
	Thought About	Remembered	
Plaintiff verdict	50%	41%	9%
Defense verdict	82	11	7
All jurors	61	31	8

These were the three reasons most frequently given by those jurors who reported that they did change their decision during deliberations. Note that when jurors changed their decision during deliberation *toward* a defense verdict, it was most often because of new information provided by other jurors.

2. The responses to two questions, LQ 60 and LQ 63, were examined together as complementary information concerning change of opinion during deliberation.

LQ 60: At the beginning of the deliberation of the case, how many of you were in agreement as to which side should win?

All of us
All but a couple of us
It was pretty evenly divided
I don't remember

LQ 63: Did the way the majority of the jurors vote the first time you took a vote turn out to be the same as the final verdict?

Yes or No

Information about how many jurors were in agreement at the beginning of deliberations was juxtaposed with information about whether or not the initial vote held. The related data were examined jury by jury and sometimes provided evidence of formation of opinion or change of vote during deliberation.

a) There were seven juries in which *all* jurors were in agreement at the beginning of deliberations. As expected, there was no change of opinion between initial vote and final verdict.

b) There were 20 juries in which *almost all* of the jurors were in agreement at the beginning of deliberations:

No change between initial majority and final verdict occurred in 10.
Change between initial majority and final verdict in four.
It was not possible to discern the voting pattern of six juries.

c) There were 11 juries for which there was *no majority* at the time the first vote was taken. Therefore, many jurors must have changed or formed their opinions during deliberations in order for the jury to reach either a majority or unanimous verdict. This change of opinion was *clearly* evidenced in only six of the 11 juries.

For the four juries in (b) where there was a change between the initial majority and the final verdict, there had to be a substantial number of jurors who changed their votes in order for the jury to reach a majority in the opposite direction. These four juries out of the 20 represent 20%, which is very near the 22% change rate established in VIII: D.1 above.

SUMMARY

From the evidence provided by jurors in their answers to the above sequence of questions, it is clear that most jurors began the trial with no strong opinions. Opinions were formed over the course of the trial as jurors gravitated toward one litigant or the other.

During deliberations, 22% of the jurors changed their opinions. Of those jurors who did, jurors who began deliberating with a pro-defense view changed it somewhat more often than did those with an original pro-plaintiff opinion.

E. Effect of Knowledge of Insurance on Verdict
1.   Knowledge of plaintiff insurance:

Almost a third of all jurors (29%) talked about compensation that the plaintiff might have had. A slightly larger percentage (36%) of the jurors in CP did the same. (SQ 30)

Fifty-eight percent of the jurors stated that the consideration of plaintiff's possible compensation benefits did not affect their decisions. However, for those who said it did make a difference, only 6% reported "very much so," and 36% said it did, but only in a minor way. (SQ 31)

Only 7% (10 jurors) reported that they might have decided in favor of the plaintiff, but assumed that insurance would cover most of the losses. (LQ 67)

Most of the jurors (87%) stated that the amount of money awarded to the plaintiff was not lowered because of possible plaintiff insurance coverage. (LQ 69)

2. Knowledge of defendant insurance:

> More than half of all jurors (54%) thought the defendant carried insurance. Almost all of those who believed this (94%) did so because of their own personal experience. (SQ 14, 15)
> Almost three-quarters (71%) of the jurors reported that even if they believed the defendant was insured, it did not make a difference in their decision in the case. (SQ 16)
> All jurors reported that if there was more than one defendant in the case, the amount of insurance each defendant had was not a factor, or was not the main factor, in determining the size of the award. (LQ 65)

F. Effect of Seriousness of Plaintiff's Injury on Verdict A statistically significant correlation was found to exist between the seriousness of the plaintiff's injuries and the effect such injuries had or did *not* have on jurors in the three court systems. Although the jurors in FC and CP were equally divided as to effect, the decision of jurors in SUB tended *not* to be affected by the seriousness of plaintiff's injuries. (SQ 28)

G. Effects of Age, Sex or Education on Verdict Decision

1. Age:

> Average age of jurors sitting on: Plaintiff verdict juries 43 years
>
> Defense verdict juries 42 years

> The average age of jurors on both types of juries was almost identical.

2. Sex:

> Male members of: Plaintiff verdict juries 47%
>
> Defense verdict juries 44%

> Female members of: Plaintiff verdict juries 53%
>
> Defense verdict juries 56%

> There was no statistically significant difference between the male/female composition of plaintiff and defense verdict juries.

3. Education:

> There appears to be a relationship between education and verdict. Juries which decided in favor of the plaintiff were comprised of more jurors with vocational, high school, or less than high school education. Juries which decided in favor of the defendant contained more jurors who had completed some or all of college.
> Jurors with a graduate or professional school education appeared in equal number on both plaintiff and defense verdict juries.
> This finding almost reached statistical significance (p < .05), and it was *only* in relation to the verdict that education approached significance. There was no correlation between education and specific court,

or type of case. The explanation for this finding may be attributed to case dependent factors. For example, there may have been differences within the types of cases brought to trial, the lawyers who tried the cases, or the judges who presided. These factors could not be controlled in this study.

What is known from the study is that juries in CP-Philadelphia found for the plaintiff more often (70% plaintiff verdicts) than the jurors in FED (58% plaintiff verdicts) or in SUB (50% plaintiff verdicts).

Looking more closely at these jurors who produced more plaintiff verdicts, we also know from this study that their juries were distinctive in other ways. They contained more persons with less than a high school education and fewer persons who had finished some or all of college (SQ 39). They contained more women (63%) than the juries in the other two courts (SQ 37), the jurors were more often single than married or divorced (SQ 42), and had a lower yearly family income than both SUB and FED jurors (SQ 46). Also, the average award from the CP-Philadelphia jurors was $445,940 (median $460,000) as opposed to the average for all awards in the study of $211,130 (median $37,500). See VIII: H.5.

H. Additional Statistics
1. Degree of difficulty of case

Juxtaposing the judge's evaluation of the difficulty of the cases with the jurors' evaluation of 33 of the same cases produced the following results:

Judge	Jurors	Occurred (33 cases)
Straightforward	Straightforward	60.5% (18 cases)
Straightforward	Complicated	21.0 (8 cases)
Complicated	Complicated	10.5 (4 cases)
Complicated	Straightforward	8.0 (3 cases)

Judges were given three alternatives to describe their evaluation of the difficulty of a case: complex, moderately complicated, or relatively straightforward. Since only one case was described as being complex, this one was added to the 12 cases judged moderately complicated giving a total of 13 cases (34%) termed "Complicated." Twenty-five (66%) were evaluated as straightforward by the judges.

Cases which were deemed straightforward by both judge and jurors occurred with the greatest frequency. Cases which in the opinion of the judge were complicated yet were considered straightforward by the jurors occurred the most infrequently.

When the judge viewed a case as straightforward, the jurors frequently agreed. When a case was viewed to be complicated by the judge, the jurors were divided as to their opinion of complexity. However, the average deliberation time for cases deemed complicated by the judge was 4:38 as compared with 2:28 deliberation time in straightforward cases, indicating that jurors did require more time to reach a verdict in these cases.

2. Time between incident and trial in:

    Federal Court   1 year 4½ months
    Court of Common Pleas—Philadelphia   5 years 9½ months (*)
    Court of Common Pleas—Montgomery   4 years 2¼ months
        County
    Average time between incidence and   3 years 9½ months
        trial

    (*) This includes an asbestos case where 14 years passed between the cessation of employment of the litigant and the beginning of the trial. Excluding this trial, the average for CP is 4 years 9½ months, which is still in excess of the other courts.

3. Questions to the bench

    The number and kinds of questions sent to the bench by the jurors during deliberations were:

	All questions	On law	On exhibits	Other
FC	10	6	3	1
CP	11	4	6	1
SUB	15	0	8	7
TOTAL	36	10	17	9
		(28%)	(47%)	(25%)

    The average number of questions sent back to the bench per trial was less than one. There were more questions about exhibits than about the law or other matters.

4. Request for testimony to be read back:

    There was only one request for testimony to be read back to the jurors during deliberations, and that was in a SUB trial. It was not read back.

5. Amount of Award:

    The largest award was $928,800
    The smallest award was $2,500
    The average award per trial was $211,130 (20 trials)
    The median award per trial was $37,500 (20 trials)

    The *average* award per trial within each court system:

    C.P.—Philadelphia $445,940   [5 Plaintiff money verdicts]
    Federal   214,460   [7 Plaintiff money verdicts]
    C.P.—Montgomery Co.   61,460   [8 Plaintiff money verdicts]

The *median* award per trial within each court system:

C.P.—Philadelphia $460,000
Federal   50,000
C.P.—Montgomery Co.   22,812.50   (plus interest in one case)

There were two other plaintiff verdicts in CP-Philadelphia, but the amount of the awards was not available.

6. Length of deliberation vis-à-vis amount of award:

    Deliberations which lasted from four to 10 hours included all seven verdicts which were in excess of $100,000, plus four other money verdicts of $5,923 to $50,000.
    Deliberations which lasted less than four hours produced nine verdicts of $60,000 or less.
    The average amount of money awarded during the 11 deliberations which lasted four or more hours: $364,949.54.
    The average amount of money awarded during the nine deliberations which lasted less than four hours: $23,128.67.
    It appears that a longer period of deliberation was needed to determine larger awards.

7. Awards in excess of a half-million dollars:

    There were four verdicts which exceeded one-half-million dollars. The natures of these cases were:

    1. Personal injury resulting in death as a consequence of misinformation

    2. Demolition of building containing carpet looms by the City of Philadelphia

    3. Injury on construction site

    4. Medical malpractice

    One case was judged to be complex by the sitting judge, the other three to concern moderately complicated matters.
    Two were federal court cases, the other two were tried in the Court of Common Pleas-Philadelphia.
    Two juries were unanimous decision juries, the other two were majority.
    Three were heard by eight-person juries, one by a 12-person jury.
    Deliberation time extended from four to eight hours, the average time being six hours.
    The trials lasted from four to 10 days, the average being 6½ days.
    All plaintiffs to whom these verdicts were awarded were adult, white males.

IX. CONCLUSIONS

The following are conclusions which have been extracted from the information provided by jurors in the two questionnaires.

A. *Issues upon which jurors agreed:*

1. *The Trial*

Jurors reported that they understood the case for which they served as juror. (99%)

Jurors reported that they understood most or part of the judge's charge. (99%)

Jurors said they found the trial interesting. (95%)

Defense did not argue that medical bills claimed by the plaintiff were wrong. (95%)

Jurors were satisfied with the verdict. (89%)

Opinions were not formed about the case during the voir dire. (88%)

Exhibits used during the trial were helpful to jurors in making up their minds about the case. SQ: (92%) LQ: (83%)

(This question was asked on both questionnaires. Although different percentages of affirmative responses were given, exhibits were clearly helpful during the trial. The difference could be a consequence of the fact that jurors were given two different ways in which to respond to the questions [see SQ 3 and LQ 13], and/or because of elapsed time between the event and the completing of the LQ.)

Jurors remembered hearing testimony about pain and suffering of plaintiff. (89%)

Jurors would have liked to question certain witnesses themselves. (80%)

Jurors did not believe that too many witnesses testified about the same issues. (80%)

The experience of serving as a juror was a positive one for most, with jurors reporting that they had a good understanding of the case, and were satisfied with the verdict.

2. *The Plaintiff*

Juror reaction to the plaintiff was usually favorable. "Generally seemed a likable person" and "appeared to be a person with high moral standards" were the descriptions most often selected.

Juror reaction to the testimony given by the plaintiff was evenly divided, with 51% saying the testimony increased belief in the plaintiff's case and 47% saying it decreased belief.

3. *The Defendant*

Juror reaction to the testimony given by the defense was also evenly divided, with 55% saying the testimony increased belief in the defense case and 45% saying it decreased belief. However, almost two-thirds (64%) reported having no feelings toward the defendant or defendant company. As the defendant was often a business or a municipality, this was understandable.

When jurors did express feelings about the defendant, although they were generally favorable, they were less so than those toward the plaintiff.

4. *Plaintiff's Lawyer*

The closing speech of the plaintiff's lawyer did not change opinion about the case. (96%)

The plaintiff's lawyer did not treat any of the witnesses unfairly. (92%)

The plaintiff's lawyer did not object too often. (90%)

The jurors believed that the plaintiff's lawyer would be paid a percentage of the total verdict. (84%)

5. *Defense Lawyers(s)*

The defense lawyer did not treat witnesses unfairly. (97%)

The closing speech of the defense lawyer did not change opinion about the case. (94%)

The defense lawyer did not object too often. (91%)

The overall opinion of both the plaintiff and the defense lawyers was high.

6. *The Judge*

Did not favor one side over the other. (98%)

Paid close attention to the trial. (97%)

Did not favor one lawyer over the other. (95%)

During deliberations the jurors did not discuss what they believed the judge thought about the case. (89%)

The jurors believed that the judge thought the case was important. (87%)

Jurors consistently held a high opinion of the judge.

7. *Deliberations*

Jurors believed that the deliberation process was important. (98%)

They felt free to express how they really felt during deliberations. (98%)

There was a full and open exchange of opinions during deliberations. (97%)

Law and facts were the most important factors in making decisions about the case. (96%)

They understood how answers to the interrogatory would be used. (95%)

The method of more general discussion was used to persuade hold-outs. (92%)

Votes after the first one were taken by a show of hands. (90%)

Jurors did not wish to please the judge with the verdict. (89%)

The foreperson did not dominate deliberations. (87%)

Votes on the verdict were taken by a show of hands. (85%)

Jurors sitting on majority decision rule juries usually agreed with the verdict. (81%)

The main reason for deciding for the defendant: the plaintiff was not entitled to an award. (80%)

The main reason for deciding for the plaintiff: s/he was entitled to an award. (79%)

8. *Money Awards*

The fact that the defendant was a "big business" had nothing to do with deciding for the plaintiff. (94%)

Jurors did not increase the award to cover the lawyer's fee. (94%)

The amount of money awarded to the plaintiff was not lowered because the jurors decided that he or she already had some losses covered by insurance. (87%)

Some money was included for pain and suffering of the plaintiff. (78%)

9. *Jury System*

After having served, jurors thought the jury system was a good one. (97%)

They were treated politely by people who work in the courtroom (not counting judges and lawyers). (95%)

Jurors believed fellow jurors took their duties seriously. (88%)

Jurors waited less than one day to be selected to serve. (84%)

Jurors described their waiting area as comfortable. (84%)

  B. *Issues upon which there was evenly divided opinion:*
  Testimony by the plaintiff increased and decreased belief in plaintiff's case equally.

If jurors believed plaintiff's attorney objected too often, they may or may not have thought less of plaintiff's case consequently.

Half of the jurors wondered why certain persons mentioned during the trial did not testify.

A few more than half of the jurors recalled a particular event in the trial which was important in making up their minds.

A few less than half of the jurors claimed that certain exhibits made them doubt the truth about the testimony.

A few less than half of the jurors believed plaintiff's claim that he or she would have future medical bills.

A few less than half of the jurors reported that the amount of money awarded to the plaintiff was lowered because there were jurors who weren't sure that the plaintiff should be paid anything at all.

C. *Differences between jurors in the three court systems:*

1. The following is a summary of those issues upon which the BEHAVIOR of jurors in the three court systems differed to a statistically significant degree. The summary also reflects differences which the jurors related in their responses to the questionnaires. All jurors heard different cases with different casts of characters and facts. However, the jurors in federal court differed in one particular respect which might possibly have influenced their behavior: They all served in the courtroom of only one judge.

Federal Court [FC]   Verdicts: Plaintiff 7, Defense 5

a) In regard to seeing testimony presented on videotape, half of the jurors serving in this court said it made no difference. The jurors in the other courts preferred to see the witnesses testify in person. (p < .001)

b) Although more than half of all the jurors reported that they had no feelings for the plaintiff or the defendant, for those jurors who did indicate having feelings for the plaintiff, the jurors in FC tended to have low regard as often as high regard. This was significantly different from the jurors in the other two courts where the jurors had high regard for the plaintiff at least four times as often as low regard. (p < .005)

Summary: In addition to the two statistical findings above, the jurors serving in the federal court differed from those in the other systems in many ways. They were the only jurors who had to reach a unanimous verdict; they were allowed to take notes during the trial; they were all eight-person juries; and they all served as jurors in the courtroom of one judge. They were also the jurors most satisfied with their verdicts (LQ 6) even though, as a result of a different juror selection process, federal jurors waited longer to serve.

They also differed from the other jurors in the following ways. They believed that the plaintiff's lawyer rather than the defense lawyer more often kept out important information by objecting during the trial (LQ 15); they reported hearing less testimony about pain and suffering of the plaintiff than did the other jurors (LQ 9); and they reported hearing less testimony about the plaintiff's loss of future income (LQ 24). Slightly more often than the other jurors, they thought that the judge favored one lawyer over the other (LQ 31), and that the judge didn't think the case was important (LQ 39).

They were more in agreement at the beginning of deliberations (LQ 60), and (bearing in mind that they were required to reach a unanimous verdict) they reported a higher degree of juror participation (LQ 45) and award negotiation (LQ 70) during deliberations. They more often said the reason for changing their minds during deliberations was because they were the only jurors who felt a particular way and didn't want to cause a problem (LQ 52).

In the matter of award determination, federal jurors more often generated the amount of the award from their own discussions rather than accepting the suggestions of the plaintiff's lawyer (SQ 33). If there was more than one defendant, they never based the size of the award on how much insurance they thought each defendant had (LQ 65).

Court of Common Pleas—Philadelphia [CP]
Verdicts: Plaintiff 7, Defense 3

a) The jurors in this court tended to be for or leaning toward the plaintiff just prior to jury deliberations. Jurors in the other two courts tended to be definitely for or leaning toward the defendant. (p < .001)

b) Jurors in this court more often than in the other courts said they would have liked to have certain exhibits which were referred to during the trial in the juryroom during deliberations. (p < .001)

c) These jurors reported that later votes during deliberations (after the first vote) were sometimes open and sometimes secret. Jurors in the other courts used the open method of raising hands more often. (p < .001)

d) After opening speeches, CP jurors favored the plaintiff much more frequently than did the jurors in the other two courts. (p < .01)

(The following issues, although not statistically significant, were so nearly significant that with a larger sample significance might be achieved.)

e) CP jurors tended to believe that their insurance rates might increase as a result of their verdict more often than did jurors in the other courts. (p < .025)

f) Jurors in CP reported that testimony given by the plaintiff increased belief in plaintiff's case more often than it did for jurors in the other two courts. (p < .05)

g) Jurors in this court reported that when they did discuss the fact that plaintiff had Blue Cross or Workman's Compensation it did make a difference to their decision in a minor way. Jurors in the other two courts indicated that it made no difference. (p < .05)

Summary: The jurors in CP seemed more responsive toward the plaintiff, the plaintiff's lawyer and the plaintiff's cause. They were willing to find for the plaintiff even when they expressed concern about their insurance rates increasing as a result of their verdict.

More of them were unmarried and more were women; they had less formal education and lower family incomes than those serving in the other courts. The highest awards came from this court system.

Court of Common Pleas—Montgomery County [SUB]
Verdicts: Plaintiff 8, Defense 8

a) The jurors in SUB tended not to be as affected by the seriousness of plaintiff's injuries in deciding the verdict as were FC and CP jurors. (p < .005)

b) The jurors in SUB tended not to be as affected by the financial losses of plaintiff in deciding the verdict as were FC and CP jurors. (p < .005)

c) Jurors in this court tended to change their opinions less often during deliberations than did jurors in the other two courts. (p < .005)

d) In SUB, the jurors tended to rely on the suggestions of plaintiff's lawyer and juror discussion equally to derive the amount of award. In the other two courts, the amount of award was more often generated by juror discussion alone. (p < .005)

(The following issue, although not statistically significant, was so nearly significant that with a larger sample significance might be achieved.)

e) The jurors in this court, when they expressed feelings for the defendant, tended to have low regard almost equally with high regard for the defendant or defendant company. The jurors in the other courts had high regard for the defendant twice as often as low regard. (p < .05)

Summary: The jurors in SUB were least sympathetic to the case brought by the plaintiff. When they did find for the plaintiff, they reported more often than the other jurors that they considered information presented by the plaintiff's lawyer when determining the amount of the award.

More of them were married and more were divorced, and they had higher family incomes. They seemed to be keeping a tighter grip on the purse strings.

2. The following is a summary of demographic CHARACTERISTICS of jurors in the three court systems which differed to a statistically significant degree.

Federal Court [FC]

The jurors in this court exhibited no characteristics which differed from the other jurors to a statistically significant degree.

Court of Common Pleas—Philadelphia [CP]

a) Fewer jurors in this court were married. (p<.001)
b) More jurors in this court reported a yearly family income of less than $20,000. (p<.001)

Court of Common Pleas—Montgomery County [SUB]

a) More jurors in this court were married than single, and slightly more often divorced than in the other two courts. (p<.001)

b) More jurors in this court reported a yearly family income of $40,000 or more. (p<.001)

D. ***Differences between plaintiff and defense jurors:*** Jurors who sat on plaintiff or defense verdict juries differed to a nearly statistically significant degree (p<.05) on two issues, and these may have reached significance with slightly larger samples.

a) Juries which decided in favor of the defendant contained more jurors who had completed some or all of college. Juries which decided in favor of the plaintiff were comprised of more jurors with less formal education. Jurors with a graduate or professional school education appeared in equal number on both plaintiff and defense verdict juries. (p<.05)
b) Jurors sitting on plaintiff verdict juries tended to change their verdict opinions more often than jurors sitting on defense verdict juries. This indicates that jurors holding an initial pro-defense view more often changed to a plaintiff vote than they changed from an initial pro-plaintiff view to a defense vote. (p<.05)

SUMMARY

All of the above information which was extracted from the responses to the questionnaires presents a distinct picture of the 352 civil jurors included in this research project. Although they heard different cases in the courtrooms of different judges, and differed as individuals do (even taking into consideration that they may have wanted to present the most positive image of themselves), certain facets of their responses remain constant.

One must conclude that, as a group, they understood the trials for which they served as jurors; formed their opinions over the course of the trial primarily on the facts, law, and exhibits; were confident that the verdicts they reached were correct; and terminated their jury service with a good opinion of how the jury system works. This study demonstrated that these civil jurors were civil indeed.

Appendix A: Short Questionnaire

Thank you very much for helping improve our justice system by taking a few minutes to fill out this questionnaire. All answers are confidential. You do not sign your name.

Some questions about the TRIAL

1. Did you think this trial was:

    _____ Extremely interesting
    _____ Sometimes interesting
    _____ Boring

2. After both sides had completely presented their case, did you feel that you had a good idea of what really had happened?

    _____ Yes
    _____ Fairly good, but I still had questions I wish had been answered
    _____ No

3. During the trial, did any exhibits (such as photographs, charts, medical records) help you make up your mind?

    _____ Yes   _____ no

4. If you did NOT take notes during the trial, would you have liked to?

    _____ Yes   _____ No   _____ I'm not certain

5. Did you understand the law as the judge explained it to you in the charge?

    _____ Yes, most of it
    _____ Yes, but only partly
    _____ No, not very much of it

6. Just before jury deliberations began, had you already reached a decision, even though that might not have been your final decision? (CHECK ONE)

    _____ Yes. Definitely for the DEFENDANT
    _____ Yes. Definitely for the PLAINTIFF
    _____ Wasn't certain, but was leaning toward the PLAINTIFF
    _____ Wasn't certain, but was leaning toward the DEFENDANT

Some questions about the PLAINTIFF

7. If the plaintiff testified, which of the following statements describes your reaction to him or her?

    _____ Testimony INCREASED my belief in the plaintiff's case
    _____ Testimony DECREASED my belief in the plaintiff's case

355

8. What kind of feelings did you have for the plaintiff?

    ---- High regard   ---- Low regard   ---- No feelings

    <u>Some questions about the PLAINTIFF'S LAWYER</u>

9. Did you think that the PLAINTIFF'S lawyer objected too often?

    ----- Yes   ----- No

    10. If yes, did that cause you to think less of the plaintiff's case?

        ----- Yes   ----- No

11. Do you think that the lawyer for the PLAINTIFF treated any of the witnesses unfairly?

    ----- Yes   ----- No   (SKIP TO QUESTION 13)

    12. If yes, did that cause you to think less of the plaintiff's case?

        ----- Yes   ----- No

13. Which statement best describes your feelings about the closing speech of the plaintiff's lawyer?

    ----- It caused me to change my opinion about the case.
    ----- It didn't change my opinion about the case.

    <u>Some questions about the DEFENDANT(S)</u>

14. Did you think that the defendant carried insurance?

    ----- Yes   (GO TO NEXT QUESTION)
    ----- No   (SKIP TO QUESTION 17)
    ----- I never thought about it   (SKIP TO QUESTION 17)

    15. If you answered 'yes', why do you think so? (CHECK ONE)

        ----- It came out in the testimony
        ----- It was mentioned in the courtroom before the trial began
        ----- I know from personal experience that such people or businesses usually carry insurance

    16. If you believe the defendant had insurance, which covered at least part of the verdict, did that make a difference in your decision?

        ----- Yes, importantly so
        ----- Yes, but only in a minor way
        ----- I never thought about it

17. If the defendant(s) or a representative from the defendant company testified, which one of the following statements describes your reaction to him or her?

    ----- Testimony INCREASED my belief in the case for the defense
    ----- Testimony DECREASED my belief in the case for the defense

18. What kind of feelings did you have for the defendant or defendant company?

    --- High regard   --- Low regard   --- No feelings

    <u>Some questions about the DEFENSE LAWYER(S)</u>

19. Did you think that the DEFENSE lawyer(s) objected too often?

    ----- Yes   ----- No   (SKIP TO QUESTION 21)

    20. If yes, did that cause you to think less of the defense case?

        ----- Yes   ----- No

21. Do you think that the lawyer(s) for the DEFENSE treated any of the witnesses unfairly?

    ----- Yes   ----- No   (SKIP TO QUESTION 23)

22. If yes, did that cause you to think less of the defense case?

    —— Yes   —— No

23. Which statement best describes your feelings about the closing speech(es) of the defense lawyer(s)?

    —— It caused me to change my opinion about the case.
    —— It didn't change my opinion about the case.

Some questions about the DELIBERATIONS

24. Which of the following statements describes the jury deliberations?

    —— There was a full and open exchange of opinions by just about everyone
    —— Only a few people spoke, and the others mostly just listened

25. Which one of the following statements best describes how the jury deliberations affected you? (CHECK ONE)

    —— The deliberations didn't affect me at all because I had already made up my mind

    —— The deliberations made me think again about the point of view I already had, but I stuck with my original opinion

    —— I changed my point of view during deliberations

26. Did you feel free to express how you really felt?

    —— Yes   —— No

27. If during deliberations, some exhibits were in the juryroom with you: (CHECK ONE. IF THERE WERE NO EXHIBITS IN THE JURYROOM, SKIP TO NEXT QUESTION)

    —— At least one of them was important
    —— They really didn't add very much one way or the other
    —— We never discussed them at all

28. Did the seriousness of the plaintiff's injuries have an effect on your decision in the case?

    —— Yes   —— No   —— I'm not certain

29. Did the extent of the plaintiff's financial losses from the injuries have an effect on your decision in the case?

    —— Yes   —— No   —— I'm not certain

30. Did you talk about any Blue Cross or Workman's Compensation that the plaintiff might have had?

    —— Yes   —— No   (SKIP TO QUESTION 32)

    31. If yes, do you think it made a difference in your decision?

        —— Yes, very much so
        —— Yes, but only in a minor way
        —— No

32. I think that the deliberations were:

    —— Important   —— Not important

    If an amount of money was awarded, answer the following questions
    (IF NO MONEY WAS AWARDED, SKIP TO QUESTION 35)

33. How did you decide on the amount of the verdict?

    —— A figure just sort of grew as a result of our discussion

    —— We mostly went by the total figure suggested to us by the plaintiff's lawyer

——— We mostly went by the total figure suggested to us by the plaintiff's lawyer, but we ADDED to it

——— We mostly went by the total figure suggested to us by the plaintiff's lawyer, but we SUBTRACTED from it

——— There were several figures suggested by members of the jury, and we took the average

34. Did you include some money because of the pain and suffering of the plaintiff?

——— Yes   ——— No

Some questions about you

35. When you were first notified to report for jury service, were you:

——— Looking forward to it
——— Wanting to get out of it

36. Now that you have served as a juror, do you think the jury is:

——— a GOOD system
——— a POOR system

37. Are you ——— male   ——— female?

38. What is your age?   ——— years

39. What is the HIGHEST LEVEL of education you COMPLETED?

— less than high school   — vocational or technical school
— high school   — some graduate or professional school
— some college   — graduate or professional school
— college

40. What is your occupation?

41. If retired, what WAS your occupation?

42. Are you: — single   — married   — divorced   — widowed?

43. How many children do you have?

44. Do you live in   ——— a house
                        ——— an apartment
                        ——— other (please specify)?

45. What kind of area do you live in?

——— Rural   ——— Business
——— Residential   ——— Part business, part residential

46. If you care to answer, approximately which of the following groups describes your family's yearly income.

——— Less than $10,000
——— At least $10,000 and less than $20,000
——— At least $20,000 and less than $40,000
——— At least $40,000 and less than $60,000
——— $60,000 or more

Thank you very much for helping with this part of the study.

Appendix B: Long Questionnaire

Some questions about your JURY SERVICE

1. From the time you arrived to begin your jury duty, how long did you have to wait before you were selected for a jury?

    ----- Less than one day
    ----- Two to five days
    ----- Longer

2. How would you describe the room in which you waited to be sent to a courtroom? (CHECK AS MANY ANSWERS AS APPLY)

    ----- Comfortable
    ----- Crowded
    ----- Dirty
    ----- Unpleasant

3. During the voir dire (or questioning before you were selected as a juror), what opinion did you form about the case?

    ----- Somewhat favorable to the plaintiff
    ----- Somewhat favorable to the defendant
    ----- No opinion
    ----- I don't remember

4. During the course of the trial, how were you treated by the people who work in the courtroom (not counting the judge and the lawyers)?
(CHECK AS MANY ANSWERS AS APPLY)

    ----- Politely
    ----- Helpfully
    ----- Rudely
    ----- They were not very interested in my well-being

5. Was it your impression that your fellow jurors took the duty of jury service seriously?

    ----- Yes
    ----- All but a couple of them
    ----- No

6. Were you personally satisfied with the decision reached by the jury of which you were a member?

    ----- Yes   ----- No

Some questions about the TRIAL

7. Did you see any exhibits during the trial that made you doubt the truth of what you heard people testify to?

    ----- Yes   ----- No

8. Would you have liked to question any of the witnesses yourself, either directly or by having the judge ask the questions for you?

    ----- Yes   ----- No

9. Did you hear any testimony about pain and suffering of the plaintiff?

    ----- Yes   ----- No (SKIP TO QUESTION 11)

    10. If so, who testified about it? (CHECK AS MANY ANSWERS AS APPLY)

        ----- The plaintiff
        ----- Member(s) of the plaintiff's family
        ----- Neighbors, friends or fellow employees
        ----- Experts (such as doctors or nurses)

11. Was any of the testimony presented to you on a videotape?

    ----- Yes   ----- No (SKIP TO QUESTION 13)

    12. If yes, what was your feeling about it?

        ----- I would have preferred to see the witness in person
        ----- It made no difference
        ----- It was easier to concentrate on the videotape because there were no distractions or interruptions as with live testimony

13. Were any of the exhibits (such as photographs, charts, medical records) used during the trial helpful to you in making up your mind?

    ----- Yes, in a major way
    ----- Yes, but only in a minor way
    ----- No

14. Did you get the feeling that important information was being kept out of the trial because of lawyers' objections?

    ----- Yes   ----- No (SKIP TO QUESTION 16)

    15. If you answered yes, whose objections MOST OFTEN kept out the important information?

        ----- The plaintiff's lawyer
        ----- The defense lawyer

16. Did you wonder why certain people who were mentioned during the trial didn't testify?

    ----- Yes   ----- No (SKIP TO QUESTION 18)

    17. Did you hold it against the side that didn't call certain people to testify who might have added important information?

        ----- Yes   ----- No

18. Do you think that too many witnesses testified about the same issue?

    ----- Yes   ----- No

19. Did the plaintiff have medical bills?

    ----- Yes   ----- No

20. Did the defense argue that the bills were wrong?

    ----- Yes   ----- No

21. If there was a fight about the medical bills, which side did you believe?

    ----- Plaintiff's side
    ----- Defense side

22. Did the plaintiff claim that he or she would have FUTURE medical bills?

    ----- Yes   ----- No (SKIP TO QUESTION 24)

23. If yes, did you believe him or her?

_____ Yes   _____ No

24. Did the plaintiff claim that he or she would lose income in the future because of the injury?

_____ Yes   _____ No   (SKIP TO QUESTION 26)

25. If yes, did you believe him or her?

_____ Yes   _____ No

26. At the beginning of the trial, after the lawyers made their opening speeches, do you recall how you felt about the case? (Try to remember your feelings at that time, not what they may have become later.)

_____ I somewhat favored the plaintiff
_____ I somewhat favored the defendant
_____ I had no strong feelings one way or the other

27. If the defendant(s) did not take the witness stand, did it:

_____ HELP the defense case
_____ HURT the defense case
_____ Make no difference

28. What was the main claim that the plaintiff made against the defendant(s)?

_____

_____

29. Check all the statements below which describe your feelings about the plaintiff's lawyer.

_____ Really seemed to believe in his or her case

_____ Always appeared to know what he or she was doing

_____ Asked pointless questions

_____ Was sarcastic

_____ Brow-beat some of the witnesses

_____ Acted in a superior manner

_____ Was polite to witnesses

_____ I thought he or she was persuasive in the speech made to the jury

_____ Probably wasn't aggressive enough.

_____ I usually learned important facts about the case as a result of his or her questioning of witnesses

_____ If I ever needed a lawyer, I'd want him or her to help me

30. Check all the statements below which describe your feelings about the defense lawyer. [If there was more than one defense lawyer, check the statements below which describe the one lawyer who remains most clearly in your mind.]

_____ Really seemed to believe in his or her case

_____ Always appeared to know what he or she was doing

_____ Asked pointless questions

_____ Was sarcastic

_____ Brow-beat some of the witnesses

_____ Acted in a superior manner

————— Was polite to witnesses

————— I thought he or she was persuasive in the speech made to the jury

————— Probably wasn't aggressive enough

————— I usually learned important facts about the case as a result of his or her questioning of witnesses

————— If I ever needed a lawyer, I'd want him or her to help me

31. Did you think that the judge favored one lawyer over the other?

————— Yes   ————— No (SKIP TO QUESTION 33)

32. If you answered yes, how did this make you feel?
    (CHECK AS MANY ANSWERS AS APPLY)

————— I assumed that it was simply a question of the judge not liking one of the lawyers.

————— It didn't make any difference to me at all.

————— The lawyers were doing their job, and so was the judge doing his.

————— It was a battle over who was going to run the courtroom.

————— I didn't think the lawyer knew what s/he was doing, and had it coming to her/him.

————— The judge was unnecessarily harsh toward and critical of the lawyer.

33. During the course of the trial, which if any of the following impressions did you get of the plaintiff? (CHECK AS MANY ANSWERS AS APPLY)

————— Appeared to be a person with high moral standards

————— Appeared to be a person with low moral standards

————— Seemed to be a religious person

————— Appeared to have a drinking problem

————— Was living with someone who was not his or her spouse

————— Probably was a homosexual

————— Appeared to have a drug problem

————— Even though he or she could have worked, appeared to have made little or no effort to find a job after the accident (or injury)

————— Seemed to be a snob, or treated people in a superior way

————— Had an occupation or way of life of which I don't approve

————— Was divorced

————— Generally seemed a likable person

————— Generally seemed an unlikable person

34. What was the main defense that was made against the claim of the plaintiff?

——

——

35. During the course of the trial, which if any of the following impressions did you get of the defendant? [If there was more than one defendant,

select the impressions below which describe the one defendant who remains most clearly in your mind.]
(CHECK AS MANY ANSWERS AS APPLY)

----- Appeared to be a person with high moral standards

----- Appeared to be a person with low moral standards

----- Seemed to be a religious person

----- Appeared to have a drinking problem

----- Was living with someone who was not his or her spouse

----- Probably was a homosexual

----- Appeared to have a drug problem

----- Even though he or she could have worked, appeared to have made little or no effort to find a job after the accident (or injury)

----- Seemed to be a snob, or treated people in a superior way

----- Had an occupation or way of life of which I don't approve

----- Was divorced

----- Generally seemed a likable person

----- Generally seemed an unlikable person

36. Do you recall any particular event in the trial that was most important in making up your mind?

----- Yes   ----- No (SKIP TO QUESTION 38)

37. If yes, what? _____

_____

Some questions about the judge

38. Did the judge pay close attention to the case during the trial?

----- Yes   ----- No

39. Do you think the judge thought this was an important case?

----- Yes   ----- No

40. Did the judge seem to favor one side over the other?

----- Yes, the plaintiff
----- Yes, the defendant
----- No

Some questions about the DELIBERATIONS

41. In making your decision about the case, what was MOST important to you:

----- The law as explained to you by the judge
----- The facts as told to you by the witnesses
----- The closing speeches given by the lawyers

42. How did you decide who would be the foreperson?

----- We didn't; the judge named the foreperson
----- We agreed that juror number one would be the foreperson
----- Discussed it, and then selected someone
----- Took a vote to name the foreperson
----- One of the jurors volunteered

43. If anyone took notes, were they used during the jury discussions?

----- Yes   ----- No (SKIP TO QUESTION 45)

44. If yes, what role did the note-taking play?

   ----- We referred to them frequently
   ----- If we disagreed with the notes, we relied on our memories

45. What was your amount of participation in jury discussions?

   ----- A lot
   ----- A moderate amount
   ----- Very little

46. Were you the foreperson?

   ----- Yes   ----- No

47. Did the foreperson dominate the deliberations?

   ----- Yes   ----- No

48. Did your trial require a unanimous decision? (Did ALL the jurors have to agree?)

   ----- No   ----- Yes (SKIP TO QUESTION 50)

   49. Did you agree with the majority opinion?

      ----- Yes   ----- No

50. If there were just a couple of hold-outs over the question of who should win, what was done to convince them to join the others?

   ----- More general discussion
   ----- Small groups were formed to talk with each hold-out separately
   ----- Another way. (please specify:_____
   _____)

51. Did you change your decision during the deliberation?

   ----- Yes   ----- No (SKIP TO QUESTION 53)

   52. If yes, why?

      ----- Other jurors brought up points I hadn't THOUGHT ABOUT

      ----- Other jurors brought up points I hadn't REMEMBERED

      ----- I was the only one who felt a particular way, and I didn't want to cause a problem

      ----- I really didn't understand the case so I decided to go along with the other jurors

      ----- We had trouble reaching a verdict. When the judge put pressure on us, I decided to go along with the majority

53. Was there any discussion about what the jurors believed the judge thought about the case?

   ----- Yes   ----- No

54. Did you want to please the judge with your verdict in the case?

   ----- Yes   ----- No

55. Did you have an 'interrogatory' sheet of paper (which is a list of questions you had to answer in order to reach a verdict?)

   ----- Yes   ----- No (SKIP TO QUESTION 58)

   56. If yes, were the questions helpful?

      ----- Yes, very helpful
      ----- Somewhat helpful
      ----- Not very helpful
      ----- They were confusing

57. Did you understand how your answers to these questions would be used?

    ----- Yes   ----- No

58. Were there any exhibits referred to in the courtroom during the trial that you would have liked to have with you in the juryroom during deliberations?

    ----- Yes   ----- No (SKIP TO QUESTION 60)

    59. If so, which one(s)?

        ----- Photographs
        ----- Models
        ----- Medical records
        ----- Charts
        ----- Other (please specify:_____)

60. At the BEGINNING of the deliberation of the case, how many of you were in agreement as to which side should win?

    ----- All of us
    ----- All but a couple of us
    ----- It was pretty evenly divided
    ----- I don't remember

61. If you took votes on the verdict, how was it done?

    ----- By secret ballot
    ----- By raising hands (SKIP TO QUESTION 63)
    ----- Sometimes openly and sometimes secretly

    62. If by secret ballot, was the FIRST ballot taken right at the beginning of the deliberations?

        ----- Yes   ----- No

63. Did the way the majority of the jurors voted the FIRST time you took a vote turn out to be the same as the final verdict?

    ----- Yes   ----- No

64. After the first vote, if there were LATER votes, how were they done?

    ----- By secret ballot
    ----- By raising hands
    ----- Sometimes openly and sometimes secretly

65. If there was more than one defendant, was the size of the award based on how much insurance you thought each defendant had?

    ----- Yes
    ----- No
    ----- It was part of the discussion, but it wasn't the main factor in making up my mind

66. If your verdict was for the plaintiff, did you consider any of the following matters in reaching your decision? (CHECK AS MANY AS APPLY) [IF YOUR VERDICT WAS FOR THE DEFENDANT, SKIP TO QUESTION 67]

    ----- How your verdict might prevent other people or companies from doing the same thing as this defendant did

    ----- If the defendant was a business, that the verdict might force that business to close down, and many people might lose their jobs

    ----- That the defendant should be taught a lesson

    ----- It wasn't a question of whether the defendant was a nice person, or if it was a good organization. If the plaintiff was entitled to a verdict, then the defendant should pay him or her fairly

67. If your verdict was for the defendant(s), which of the following statements express your feelings for the plaintiff: (CHECK AS MANY AS APPLY)

_____ I felt sorry for the plaintiff, but on the basis of the facts and the law as explained to me by the judge, s/he wasn't entitled to any money

_____ I didn't believe the plaintiff from the start

_____ I might have decided in favor of the plaintiff, but I assumed that s/he had insurance coverage anyhow which would cover most of the losses claimed

_____ I might have voted for the plaintiff, but the injuries and losses claimed seemed so exaggerated that it turned me off

_____ I was concerned that a verdict for the plaintiff would have been too much of a financial burden on the defendant

If an amount of money was awarded, answer the following questions
(IF NO MONEY WAS AWARDED, SKIP TO QUESTION 74)

68. Did you think that your insurance rates would go up as a result of your verdict?

_____ Yes
_____ No
_____ Maybe, but this didn't affect my decision

69. Was the amount of money awarded to the plaintiff lowered because the jurors decided he or she already had some of the losses covered by insurance (such as Blue Cross or Workmen's Compensation)?

_____ Yes
_____ No, it was not discussed
_____ It was discussed but it did not have an affect on the size of the award

70. Was the amount of money awarded to the plaintiff lowered because there were jurors who weren't sure the plaintiff should be paid anything at all?

_____ Yes   _____ No

71. If the defendant was a 'big business', which of the following statements best describes the feelings of your jury:
(IF THE DEFENDANT WAS NOT A BIG BUSINESS, GO TO NEXT QUESTION)

_____ We thought the business could afford to pay, and that had something to do with deciding for the plaintiff

_____ We thought the business could afford to pay, but that had nothing to do with deciding for the plaintiff

_____ It was never discussed

72. How do you think the plaintiff is paying his lawyer?

_____ A flat fee
_____ So much per hour
_____ A percentage of the total verdict

73. Did you increase the amount of the verdict to cover the lawyer's fee?

_____ Yes   _____ No

Some questions about you

74. If you have ever been involved in a lawsuit, check the following statements which are true: (IF NOT, GO TO NEXT QUESTION)

_____ I was a plaintiff

_____ I was a defendant

_____ Case was ended by a settlement

_____ Case was ended by a trial verdict

––––– As a result of the case, I gained a favorable impression of how the justice system works

––––– As a result of the case, I gained an unfavorable impression of how the justice system works

75. Was this your first experience as a juror?

––––– No   ––––– Yes (SKIP TO QUESTION 78)

76. How many times have you served as a juror? _____

77. How long ago were you last a juror? _____

78. If you are employed, did your employer pay you while you were a juror?

––––– Yes   ––––– No

Appendix C: Master Sheet

Judge: Court:

Plaintiff's attorney: Research Number:

Defense attorney(s):

Date that trial began: Date that trial concluded:

Judge's evaluation of the difficulty of the case:

   a. Complex b. Moderately complicated   c. Relatively straightforward

1.   What was the nature of the case? (for example, motor vehicle accident, medical malpractice, product injury, injury resulting from a fall, injury at work or on construction site, other).

        _____

2.   How many jurors sat for full trial including deliberation?

3.   The number of days that the jurors heard the case: (See note a. below)

4.   Which best describes the duties of the jurors?

      a. Decided only defendant liability
      b. Decided on both defendant liability and the amount of award to plaintiff
      c. Decided on only the amount of award to plaintiff

5.   Check all of the below which describe the person whose injury or death caused the suit to be brought to trial:

      a. Male   e. Black
      b. Female   f. Hispanic
      c. Adult   g. White
      d. Child (under 18)   h. Other (please specify):

6.   How many years passed between the time of the accident and the time of the trial?

7.   Was there more than one defendant?

      a. No   b. Yes. If yes, how many?

8. If there was more than one defendant, how did the jury find?

    a. In favor of all defendants
    b. Against all defendants
    c. In favor of some or one, against other(s)

9. Hours of deliberation:
   (See note b. below)

10. The number and kinds of questions sent back to the bench

   Total number:

      Number of questions having to do with points of law:

      Number of questions having to do with exhibits, photos, records or testimony:

      Other kinds?

11. Did the jury ask for any part of the testimony to be read back?

    a. Yes   b. No

12. Was it read back?

    a. Yes   b. No

13. Verdict:

   For the: plaintiff   defendant   hung jury

      Amount of award:

a.) The number of days a case was heard should be counted from the time the Judge opens the trial, until the time that the jurors are excused from their service. This time can be counted in full or half days. (e.g. 3 1/2 days, 12 days)

b.) The hours of deliberation should be counted from the time the jurors are sent into the juryroom to begin deliberating, until the time that they notify the clerk that they have a verdict. This time can be counted in full or half days (as above) or in hours and/or minutes when appropriate.

Appendix D:
Instructions for Jurors

Bettyruth Walter
Research Director
1830 Rittenhouse Square
Philadelphia, PA 19103

Dear Juror:

Thank you very much for completing the shorter questionnaire in your jury room. Enclosed in this envelope you will find a slightly longer questionnaire, which we ask you to complete at home, when you have a little more time and are more comfortable. There are very few instructions to follow.

First of all, you will find three items in your large, brown, stamped envelope:

1) The first are these instructions.

   Please do read them completely.

2) The second is the questionnaire itself.

   I think you will find it easy to follow.

3) The third is a small, stamped envelope. If you will write your name and address on this small envelope, and enclose it in the large, brown envelope which you will return to us, we will mail it right back to you with a $10 check made out to the name on the envelope. This is our way of thanking you for taking the time to answer the questions on this longer questionnaire.

There are two other matters you should know about. One, we will not attach your name to your questionnaire. You will have complete

371

privacy. *Only the researcher will read the questionnaires. All of the information on both questionnaires will be fed into a computer with no names. The only information we will keep is which questionnaires go with which trials. We will not record your name from your envelope, but will send it right back to you with the check. The judges and clerks will only see the final counts from all the questionnaires in one pool of information, but not the individual ones.*

The other matter which is VERY IMPORTANT is that you must fill out and return the questionnaire as quickly as possible - and certainly within ten (10) days. Your jury service must be fresh in your minds as you answer the questions. Please do not wait. Fill out this questionnaire AT ONCE, and we shall send you your $10 immediately.

Thank you very kindly,

Bettyruth Walter

CHECK LIST

1)   Fill out the questionnaire.

2)   Write your name and address on the small white envelope.

3)   Put the questionnaire and small envelope in the large, brown envelope, and seal.

4)   Mail large, brown envelope.

Appendix E: Suggestions for Judges in Civil Juror Study

At the conclusion of the trial, after the jurors have been excused from their jury service but before they leave the jury box, the judge should introduce the study. For example, you might say something like:

Members of the jury, there is one other thing I would like you to do for the justice system. When you return to the jury room, you will be handed a questionnaire. I would like you to please fill it out. This questionnaire is part of a study being conducted to determine ways in which we can improve the jury system in civil trials, and in particular, to make it easier for future jurors to do their jobs, just as you have done yours. I have looked over the questions, and they seem entirely appropriate.

I think you should know that you are one of many juries who will complete the questionnaire, and that your answers will be completely private. Only the researcher will see the completed questionnaires, and all of the information will be put into a pool of data in a computer. Then the questionnaires will be destroyed. You have complete privacy in answering the questions.

The questionnaires will be handed out by Ms. Bettyruth Walter, the research director [or, my courtroom deputy] and I would appreciate your taking a few extra minutes to complete it. I know you will give Ms. Walter [my deputy] your full cooperation as the court approves this study. There is a second part to the study, but Ms. Walter [my deputy] will tell you about that in the jury room.

This is all that is required from the judge. However, as has been observed in prior jury studies, the enthusiasm with which jurors participate in such studies is directly correlated with the enthusiasm the judge shows towards the research enterprise. It is hoped that you *will* impart enthusiasm to the jurors.

Remember that the questionnaires will be completed anonymously, the responses to the questionnaires fed into a general pool of responses, and then all of the questionnaires will be destroyed. Only the Master Sheets will be retained.

Thank you very much for your assistance in this study.

Bettyruth Walter

24 February 1985

Appendix F:
Jurors by Jury:
Sex, Age, Education, Occupation

Code for Education:

a.	Less than high school	e.	Vocational or technical school
b.	High school	f.	Some graduate or professional school
c.	Some college	g.	Graduate or professional school
d.	College		

[For additional coding information, see last page of this appendix]

SEX	AGE	EDUCATION	OCCUPATION
FEDERAL COURT (FI-N)			4 April 1985 Plaintiff verdict
F	27	f.	Chemical Lab Tech.
F	55	b.	Housewife
F	37	b.	Banking
F	60	b.	Assembler
—	—	b.	—
F	26	g.	Teacher
M	25	e.	S.E.P.T.A.
F	50	b.	Housewife
F2-N			4 April 1985 Plaintiff verdict
M	64	e.	Ret.-U.S. Postal Service
M	68	b.	Ret.-Mechanic
F	24	f.	Customer Service Clerk-DuPont
M	36	e.	Mechanic
M	54	b.	Supervisor

SEX	AGE	EDUCATION	OCCUPATION
M	23	d.	Computer Programmer
M	41	g.	Science Curriculum Supervisor-Pub. Sch.
M	55	f.	Engineer

F3-N 5 April 1985 Plaintiff verdict

SEX	AGE	EDUCATION	OCCUPATION
M	69	a.	Ret.-Truck driver
M	60	b.	Ret.-Socuty [sic] Guard Officer
F	54	b.	Staff Clerk-Secretary
M	31	c.	Over the Road Truck Driver
M	38	b.	Letter Carrier
F	38	b.	Housewife
F	53	d.	Nurse
F	25	g.	Psychiatric social worker

F4-N 8 August 1985 Plaintiff verdict

SEX	AGE	EDUCATION	OCCUPATION
M	34	b.	Millwright
M	37	f.	Aquatic Ecologist/Photographer
M	56	b.	Maintenance-School
M	35	d.	Packaging Engineer
F	28	f.	Student
M	56	b.	Stockman
M	46	e.	Maintenance Mang.
F	57	f.	Residential aid night supervisor for State of Penn. Mental Facility

F5-N 21 August 1985 Defense verdict

SEX	AGE	EDUCATION	OCCUPATION
M	77	a.	Ret.-Printing ink
F	21	c.	Teller
F	51	b.	Secretary
F	27	c.	Administrative Asst.
F	21	c.	Student
M	67	b.	Salesman
M	53	g.	Adm. Asst.

F6-N 30 August 1985 Defense verdict

SEX	AGE	EDUCATION	OCCUPATION
F	53	b.	Housewife
F	22	f.	Pharmacy Intern
M	29	c.	Inventory Analyst
F	23	b.	Secretary
M	60	b.	—
F	44	b.	Ret.-Secretary
F	50	d.	Teacher
F	43	b.	—

F7-N 18 October 1985 Defense verdict

SEX	AGE	EDUCATION	OCCUPATION
M	21	d.	Mechanical Engineer
F	49	b.	Housewife
M	25	c.	Parking Enforsmet [sic] officer
M	47	b.	Towmotor driver

SEX	AGE	EDUCATION	OCCUPATION
F	30	b.	—
F	53	b.	—
F	48	d.	Housewife
—	—		

F8-N	29 October 1985		Plaintiff verdict
F	26	c.	Bartender
F	40	c.	—
F	34	g.	Sales
M	30+	d.	Auditor
M	22	b.	Knitter, Dyer
M	37	g.	Teacher
M	60	d.	—
F	58	c.	Bookkeeper

F9-N	30 December 1985		Defense verdict
M	58	c.	U.S.P. Supvisor [sic]
F	24	b.	Warehouse Clerk
F	27	d.	Recruitment Representative
F	54	b.	Office clerk
M	31	d.	Sales Clerk & Salesman
M	34	e.	Mechanic
M	30	d.	—
M	33	b.	—

F10-N	31 December 1985		Plaintiff verdict
F	25	c.	Data Transcriber
F	21	c.	Medical secretary
M	29	g.	Environmental consulting Engineer
F	47	c.	Homemaker
F	62	g.	Ret.-teacher
M	54	b.	Postal clerk
M	24	d.	Retail Mgmt.
F	37	b.	—

F11-N	31 January 1986		Plaintiff verdict
F	56	c.	Lab technician
F	44	f.	Registered nurse
M	57	b.	Operating Engineer
M	47	d.	Engineer
M	55	b.	Bus driver
M	58	b.	Shipper
M	37	d.	Plant Manager
F	28	e.	—

F12-N	10 February 1986		Defense verdict
M	36	c.	Service Manager
M	57	a.	Ret.-Fireman
M	61	b.	Ret.-Steel worker

SEX	AGE	EDUCATION	OCCUPATION
F	42	f.	Teacher
F	40	d.	Project manager
F	21	d.	Schoolbus driver
M	26	d.	Accountant
M	33	d.	President-Sales Organization

COURT OF COMMON PLEAS—PHILADELPHIA (CP1-M)
5 April 1985   Plaintiff verdict

SEX	AGE	EDUCATION	OCCUPATION
F	63	b.	Ret.-Beautician
M	21	b.	Student
F	53	e.	Home Maker
F	32	e.	Deli Person
M	27	b.	—
F	41	a.	—
M	25	b.	—
M	21	a.	—

CP2-M   26 September 1985   Plaintiff verdict

SEX	AGE	EDUCATION	OCCUPATION
F	31	c.	Adm. Adv. Mgr.
F	49	b.	Ret.-Machine Operator
M	29	b.	Maintainence [sic]
M	37	d.	Caseworker
F	47	c.	A/R Clerk supervisor
F	35–40	e.	Secretary
F	52	b.	Ret.-Housewife
F	40	c.	Secretary
M	28	e.	Ret.-Maint
F	23	c.	Tax examiner
M	30	e.	Railroad Conductor
F	33	b.	—

CP3-G   6 October 1985   Defense verdict

SEX	AGE	EDUCATION	OCCUPATION
F	46	b.	—
F	54	b.	Bookkeeper
M	28	g.	Archaeologist/Anthropologist
F	55	b.	Savings Counselor
F	23	d.	Marketing Research Field Representative
F	53	b.	Secretary
F	38	f.	Medical Secretary
F	46	b.	Billing Supervisor

CP4-M   21 October 1985   Plaintiff verdict

SEX	AGE	EDUCATION	OCCUPATION
F	57	b.	Homemaker
M	70	—	Ret.-Boilermaker
M	37	g.	Design Consultant
M	46	g.	—
F	26	d.	Switch board operator/cashier
M	63	e.	HUAC-Supervisor

SEX	*AGE*	*EDUCATION*	*OCCUPATION*
F	57	c.	Housewife
—	—		

CP5-K	7 November 1985	Defense verdict	
F	67	a.	Housewife
F	24	d.	Production Ass't
M	25	e.	—
M	27	d.	Correctional Food & Svc. Instructor
F	47	b.	Crossing Guard
F	19	b.	Hairdresser
M	31	d.	Auditor
M	37	c.	Sales
—	—		

CP6-G	29 October 1985	Defense verdict	
F	38	g.	Student, Anthropologist
M	29	g.	Audiovisual Producer
F	19	f.	Secretary
F	42	e.	—
F	64	a.	Ret.-City employ
F	68	b.	Ret.-Secretary
F	60	b.	—
F	27	d.	Professional, White-Collar
M	64	d.	City Official
—	—	(3 jurors)	

CP7-G	26 November 1985	Plaintiff verdict	
F	59	b.	Clerical
M	30	c.	Mail courrier [sic]
M	54	b.	Custodial Guard
M	50	a.	Machinist
F	65	b.	Ret.-Health aid
F	56	c.	Nurse (registered)
F	38	d.	Financial accountant
F	35	d.	Personnel Consultant
F	25	d.	Word Processor
F	33	a.	Salesgirl
F	55	g.	Education-Teaching Parent
—	—		

CP8-G	1 December 1985	Plaintiff verdict	
F	25	b.	Exec. Sec./Office Manager
F	27	e.	Administrative Secretary
F	22	c.	Banking
F	53	b.	Energy Conservation Specialist/Dpt. of Energy
M	58	a.	House Inspector (Ret. Policeman)
—	—		

SEX   AGE   EDUCATION   OCCUPATION

CP9-BG   31 January 1986   Plaintiff verdict

Sex	Age	Education	Occupation
M	32	b.	Calibrator of scientific instruments
M	37	c.	Business owner
F	61	b.	Ret.-clerical
F	21	b.	—
M	22	e.	Student
M	33	g.	Computer Programmer/Analyst
M	—	—	—
—	—		

CP10-K   31 January 1986   Plaintiff verdict

Sex	Age	Education	Occupation
F	30	b.	Supervisor
M	21	e.	Auto Mechanic
F	34	b.	General Personnel Clerk
M	51	c.	Prison Officer
F	27	c.	Computer programmer
F	—	e.	Nursing assistant/bookkeeper at supermkt.
M	34	e.	Nursing field

COURT OF COMMON PLEAS—MONTGOMERY COUNTY (S1-B)
13 June 1985   Defense verdict

Sex	Age	Education	Occupation
M	45	b.	—
F	42	b.	Secretary
M	49	e.	Electrician
F	54	d.	Receptionist
F	—	g.	—
M	67	b.	Model Maker
F	28	d.	Parttime service mngr. (dept. store)
M	32	f.	Teaches & administers classes for paramedics & emerg. med. techs.

S2-B   12 July 1985   Plaintiff verdict

Sex	Age	Education	Occupation
M	33	e.	Unemployed
F	41	e.	Administrative Asst.
M	51	e.	Bakery worker
M	26	d.	Investment services
F	54	b.	—
F	64	b.	Beautician
F	54	b.	Housewife
M	30	c.	Ret.-Asst. Mgr. Data Processing

S3-B   21 August 1985   Plaintiff and Defense verdict

Sex	Age	Education	Occupation
M	64	a.	Ret.-Crane oper.
F	22	g.(e.)	Hair stylist
M	56	a.	Ret.-B.F. Goodrich
F	42	b.	Secretary
M	58	c.	Engineer
F	39	g.	Professor/College

SEX	AGE	EDUCATION	OCCUPATION
F	61	b.	Home maker
F	38	b.	Ret.-Secretary
F	34	c.	Executive, at home for few yrs. w/children
M	30	g.	Management consultant
M	67	b.	Ret.-Carpenter
M	42	d.	Computer analyst

S4-B   26 September 1985   Plaintiff verdict

SEX	AGE	EDUCATION	OCCUPATION
F	38	c.	Ass't Nursery School teacher
M	21	b.	Forklift operator
F	26	c.	Watch Comander [sic] Nuclear Security
F	37	b.	Ret.-Sales
M	42	b.	Teleph. Correspondent-Cust. Service
M	49	c.	Ret.-Aviation Electronics Tech.
F	41	b.	Ret.-Assembler
F	40	b.	Clerical-Secretarial
M	52	d.	Secy Trea
M	60	d.	Office Manager
F	67	d.	Housewife
F	44	f.	Research coordinator in pharmaceutical industry

S5-B   14 November 1985   Plaintiff verdict

SEX	AGE	EDUCATION	OCCUPATION
F	57	b.	Homemaker
M	49	c.	Realtor
F	—	c.	—
F	40	e.	Practical Nurse
M	70	a.	Bar
F	52	f.	Nurse, Homemaker, Parttime Sec.
F	51	b.	Housewife
F	57	c.	—
M	64	a.	Ret.-Machinist
M	61	e.	Die Eng.

S6-S   26 November 1985   Defense verdict

SEX	AGE	EDUCATION	OCCUPATION
F	70	a.	—
M	61	b.	Factory Worker
F	44	b.	—
F	46	f.	—
F	51	c.	R.N.
M	56	c.	General Supervisor
F	33	b.	Clerk typist
M	35	d.	Truck Driver
F	67	c.	Housewife
F	62	c.	New account Counselor at a Federal Sav. Bank
F	61	b.	Clerk
F	65	b.	—

SEX   AGE   EDUCATION   OCCUPATION

S7-B	26 November 1985		Defense verdict
F	20	c.	—
F	53	c.	Secretary
F	44	d.	Homemaker
M	22	d.	Accountant
M	31	d.	Accounting Clerk
F	47	c.	Office Worker
F	50+	d.	School teacher earlier-now real estate agt.
F	52	d.	Ret.-Teaching
F	—	b.	—
F	33	c.	Homemaker
F	34	e.	Color consultant
—	—		
S8-S	1 December 1985		Defense verdict
M	64	g.	Biochemist
M	47	b.	Sales
M	25	c.	Assistant Supervisor
F	53	c.	Secretary
M	35	c.	Supervisor
M	49	d.	Auditor-Senior VP
M	51	d.	Teacher
M	27	d.	Bus Driver (School)
F	39	d.	Legal secretary
M	—	e.	Electrician
F	41	d.	Homemaker
F	33	d.	RN: Homemaker
S9-B	6 December 1985		Defense verdict
F	36	g.	Vocational evaluator of the mentally impaired
M	22	c.	Fire fighter
F	28	c.	Phila. Elec. Customer Service Rep.
F	54	c.	Bookkeeper
M	57	f.	Technical Writer/Editor
F	48	b.	Housewife
M	47	g.	Teacher
M	47	g.	School District Business Administrator
M	48	g.	Educator
F	52	b.	Housewife
F	—	c.	Ret.-Secretary
F	30	d.	Teacher
S10-B	10 December 1985		Defense verdict
M	41	c.	Sales
M	32	c.	Self Employed
M	38	g.	Business Management
M	28	b.	Tube Tester

SEX	AGE	EDUCATION	OCCUPATION
F	64	c.	Bookkeeper
M	57	b.	Reciever [sic] Materials Handler
F	47	b.	Salesperson-housewife
F	41	e.	Housewife
M	40	b.	Supervisor
M	39	c.	Training Coordinator
M	34	d.	Accountant
M	22	e.	Plumber

S11-S	31 January 1986		Defense verdict
M	45	d.	Engineer
F	23	d.	Ele. Ed. Teacher
M	66	b.	Ret.-Stockman Inspector (?)
M	30	g.	Teacher
M	41	g.	—
F	52	c.	Housewife
M	33	f.	Civil Engr.
F	60+	c.	Homemaker-sales
F	62	b.	Ret.-Service Rep.
F	39	e.	X Ray technician
M	50	g.	V.P. Sperry Corp
M	42	b.	Shipper

ADDITIONAL CODING INFORMATION:

Each trial is coded according to court, number of case included in study, and the first initial of the last name of the presiding judge. For example, S10-B signifies the tenth trial in Court of Common Pleas—Montgomery County (Suburban); B signifies Judge Anita B. Brody.

Occupation is given exactly as described by the juror. Missing information is indicated by a dash.

Appendix G: Prior Experience as Juror

	How many times have you served as a juror?	*How long ago was your most recent experience?*
Federal Court		
F1-N (*)	3	A few years ago
	2	1 year
	2	8 years
F2-N	2	6 years
F3-N	3	5 years
	2	1½ years
F4-N	2	September 1984
	2	1984
F5-N	2	1941
F6-N	3	2 months
	3	1974
F7-N	—	
F8-N	2	18 years
F9-N	4	20 years
	2	1982
	2	1 year
F10-N	2	Oct.–Nov. 1985
	2	3 years
	2	8 months
F11-N	2	6 months
	4	2 years
F12-N	2	Do not remember

	How many times have you served as a juror?	How long ago was your most recent experience?
Court of Common Pleas-Philadelphia		
CP1-M	2	1 year–1984
CP2-M	2	2 years
	2	About 7 years ago
	2	11 years
	4	1981 or 82 (3 or 4 years ago)
CP3-G	—	
CP4-M	2	12 years
CP5-K	4	2 years
CP6-G	2	2½ years
	2	10 years
CP7-G	3	5 years ago +
	2	2 years
CP8-G	2	23 years
CP9-BG	—	
CP10-K	3	At least 4 to 5 years
Court of Common Pleas-Montgomery County		
S1-B	2	3½ years
S2-B	2	15 years
	2	6 years
S3-B	2	1967
	2	5 years
	2	3 yrs.
	2	3 yrs.
	3	5 or 6 years
S4-B	2	7 months
S5-B	8 ?	3 years
S6-S	2	5 years
S7-B	2	8–10 years
	2	Approximately 1 year
S8-S	2	10 years
S9-B	2	2–3 years
	2	4 years
S10-B	2	8 years
	2	11 years

	How many times have you served as a juror?	*How long ago was your most recent experience?*
S11-S	2	7 years
	2	About 10 years
SX-1-B	3	2 years ago
	3	8 years
SX-2-B	2	13
	2	3 months
SX-3-B	3	Same month, 'April 1985'
	3	2 months
	2	5 days
SX-4-B	3	2 years
	2	15 years
	2	9 years-approximately
	2	4–5 years
SX-5-B	2	1980 (5 years ago)

(*) The cases are coded by court, followed by the number of the case in that court, and finally by the first initial of the last name of the sitting judge. For example, F1-N indicates that this is the first case included in the study which was heard in Federal Court with Judge Clarence C. Newcomer serving as judge.

SX cases are those for which only long questionnaires were completed.

Index

Survey method, of jury research,
  xxvii-xxviii
Swain v. Alabama, 49, 50

Taylor v. Louisiana, 49, 50
Technology, and litigation, 139-
  40
Test-case method, 183
Texaco, Inc., 230
Torts, 42, 111, 112, 113, 114,
  119, 167
Townelet v. Clench, 201
Traffic cases, 144, 145
Travelers Insurance, 194
Traynor, Robert, 127-28, 129
Trials
  by battle, 6-7, 11, 14
  choice between bench and
  jury, 40-41, 199, 206-7
  mini-trial, 133
  numbers of, 39, 155
  by ordeal, 5-6, 9, 11, 14
  See also Jury trial.
Triangle Shirtwaist fire, 116,
  136
Turrentine, Howard B., 198, 201,
  203, 204, 209, 211, 217

Unanimous-verdict requirement,
  12, 97
  removal of, 75-76, 80-84
Uniform Commercial Code, 140
Unionism, growth of, 115-17
University of Chicago Jury
  Project, xvii, xviii, xix,
  xxii, xxvii, 60, 66, 86, 100,
  101, 175, 226
Urbanization, and litigation
  rate, 122
U.S. Financial (USF), 197-98,
  204, 209
U.S. v. Anderson, et al, 223
U.S. v. Dougherty, 223
U.S. v. Haldeman, 49
U.S. v. Simpson, 222

Van Dam, Rip, 28
Vaughan, Sir John, 27, 221
Venire, defined, 49
Verdict
  conscience, 219-27
  correctness, xx, 230
  general and special, 70-73
  juror satisfaction with, 83
  prohibition against
    reexamination, 26-27, 32
  unanimity requirement, 12, 97
    removal of, 75-76, 80-84

See also Awards.
Verdict-driven model, of jury
  deliberation, 85-86
Verdict preference
  age and, 92
  bias in, 93-95
  courtroom exhibits and, 67-68
  credibility factors in, 62-64
  education and, 91
  environmental factors in, 74
  ethnicity and, 92
  evidence and, 64-65
    inadmissible, 66
    order of presentation, 69
  gender and, 91-92
  geographic factors in, 62,
    79, 89-90
  judicial guidance and, 70
  and jury size, 79
  lawyer ability and, 61-62, 64
  likability factors in, 62
  multiple theories for
    recovery and, 95
  objections of lawyer and, 65-
    66
  occupation and, 91
  and opening statement, 60-61
  and plaintiff vulnerability,
    95
  politics and, 92
  predeliberation, 59
  prior contact with justice
    system in, 92-93
  psychological factors in, 93
  religion and, 92
  and summation, 61
  unanimous *v.* non-unanimous
    juries, 83-84
  videotaped testimony and, 66
Videotape
  instructions, 72
  reenactments, xxiii
  testimony, 66
  trial, 67
Voir dire, 49-58, 77
Voter list, jury summons from, 48

Walter-Goldberg, Bettyruth,
  xxviii, 61, 88, 100
Warranty, breach of implied, 127
Wasservogel investigation, 134
Wergeld, 4
White, Byron, xiv, 106, 199, 220-
  21, 227, 231
Whooping cough vaccine, 184-85
Wigmore, John H., 219, 227
William the Conqueror, 6, 7, 8,
  9